INTRODUCTION TO
CANADIAN POLITICS
AND
GOVERNMENT

SEVENTH EDITION

INTRODUCTION TO
CANADIAN POLITICS
AND
GOVERNMENT
SEVENTH EDITION

Walter L. White
Ronald H. Wagenberg
Ralph C. Nelson

HARCOURT
BRACE
CANADA

Harcourt Brace and Company, Canada

Toronto Montreal Fort Worth New York Orlando
Philadelphia San Diego London Sydney Tokyo

Requests for permission to make copies of any part of the work should be mailed to: Permissions, College Division, Harcourt Brace & Company, Canada, 55 Horner Avenue, Toronto, Ontario M8Z 4X6.

Every reasonable effort has been made to acquire permission for copyright material used in this text, and to acknowledge all such indebtedness accurately. Any errors and omissions called to the publisher's attention will be corrected in future printings.

Regarding all government permissions: Her Majesty shall not be responsible for the accuracy of the information in the work and makes no warranty and disclaims all liability to the accuracy of such information.

Canadian Cataloguing in Publication Data
White, W.L. (Walter L.), 1921–1975
    Introduction to Canadian politics and government
7th ed.
Includes bibliographical references and index.
ISBN 0–7747–3589–9
1. Canada - Politics and Government. I. Nelson, R.C.
    (Ralph Carl), 1927-   . II. Wagenberg, R.H., 1939-
    III. Title.
JL75.W5 1998   320.971   C97-930596-8

Acquisitions Editor: Heather McWhinney
Developmental Editor: Megan Mueller
Production Editor: Louisa Schulz
Production Co-ordinator: Carolyn McLarty

Copy Editors: Dallas Harrison and Kathleen Roulston
Interior Design: Dave Peters and Brett Miller
Cover Design: Steve Eby Productions
Typesetting and Assembly: Carolyn Hutchings
Technical Art: Carolyn Hutchings
Printing and Binding: Data Reproductions

Cover Art: *Parliament Hill*, Ron Watts/First Light

This book was printed in the United States of America.

    2 3 4 5   02 01 00 99 98

To   Juel
        Elizabeth
        Louise

Preface

As uncertainty about the future of the Canadian federation continued to weigh on the minds of its citizens after the near miss in the Quebec referendum of 1995, there were perhaps few who believed that a belated recognition of Quebec as a distinct society would somehow dissipate the sovereigntist challenge to Canadian unity. While some pursued legal means to block any unilateral declaration of independence by a Quebec government, the constitutional issue, for the moment, was put aside.

One of the remarkable aspects of Canadian politics in the 1990s has been the widespread agreement, across parties and ideologies, that governments have to face up to the serious problems of public finance, brought on by the long-term accumulation of deficits and the burden of deficit servicing on budgetary decisions. There have been those who deny that the situation is that serious, but those in denial are usually not the actual decision makers. The federal government has been admonished to stay the course in its efforts to control the deficit, and various premiers have addressed the issue by reducing—the buzzword is downsizing—the civil service and cutting medical, educational, and welfare allocations and services. The central issue has become how to achieve a healthy state of public finance without putting at risk the system of social expenditure on health, education, and the alleviation of the plight of the poor and the unemployed. In some instances, there has been an apprehension that politicians who have never been in favour of some public programs and agencies would now take the opportunity to eliminate them altogether. Much debate, for instance, has concerned the future of the Canadian Broadcasting Corporation. The immediate prospect for government services in any case is for reductions and higher costs to citizens, if not in taxes then in higher fees of various kinds.

Continued high rates of unemployment have prompted the awareness that the promises of governments to create jobs (at the same time that they reduce public sector employment) have to be met with a high degree of scepticism, or at least the understanding that the government's role in job creation is at best indirect, public works (infrastructure) projects aside. A generation ago, it was popular to speak of rising expectations; now it is common to speak of diminishing ones.

Reference was made to the radical restructuring of the CBC. Several other important Canadian institutions have recently suffered from scandals and mismanagement. The Somalia affair greatly, and no doubt excessively, damaged the reputation of the Armed Forces, now more than ever involved in peacekeeping missions abroad, in Somalia, Haiti, and Bosnia. The reputation of the RCMP has been tarnished, first by its apparent inability to assure the safety of the prime minister even in his own residence, and second by its conduct in the Airbus investigation.

But these developments are overshadowed by the unsettled nature of that cornerstone of Canadian politics, the party system. The rise of the Reform Party and the Bloc Québécois in the federal election of 1993 went along with the near elimination of the Progressive Conservatives and the considerable reduction in the contingent of the NDP in Parliament. Since neither of the two largely regional parties has been able to act as an effective opposition party, either because they have not offered viable alternatives in matters of public policy or because their interests are too narrow, future federal elections will determine whether they represent electoral aberrations or a fundamental realignment in the political system.

As a result of the federal election on June 2, 1997, the Liberals formed a new government with a reduced majority. The Progressive Conservatives returned from the margin, though theirs is now only the fifth party in terms of its parliamentary delegation. The NDP also increased its share of seats, while the BQ component was reduced, and it is no longer the official opposition, a role now played by the Reform Party. The initial impression after the election was one of fragmentation, with the Liberals overwhelmingly dominant in Ontario, Reform with support only in the west, and the Progressive Conservatives more or less confined to the Atlantic provinces. The BQ, of course, is a purely Quebec party. However, to offset this impression, it is important to note that just about 70% of the popular vote went to the traditionally national parties (Liberal, NDP, and Progressive Conservatives).

Finally, we should note the ongoing debates over physician-assisted suicide, criminal justice, aboriginal self-government, and regional disparities. In addition, relations with the United States, in this era of supposed free trade, have been strained somewhat by trade disputes and the passage of the Helms-Burton Law, whose extraterritorial provisions attempt to impose American laws on citizens and governments of other countries. Given the electoral results in the American federal election in 1996, it is unlikely that these sources of tension will soon subside. A new century will soon begin with Canada facing many of the same old problems.

R.H. Wagenberg
R.C. Nelson
University of Windsor

INSTRUCTIONAL DESIGN

Each chapter in this book contains student-friendly features. Conclusions and Recommended Readings are set at the end of each chapter. The book's endmatter includes a name and a subject index. The appendices include The Constitution Acts of 1867 and 1982. The inside cover features a list of Canadian prime ministers since 1867, and the inside back cover features a list of the governors general since Confederation.

PUBLISHER'S NOTE

Thank you for selecting the seventh edition of *Introduction to Canadian Politics and Government*, by Walter White, Ronald Wagenberg, and Ralph Nelson.

We want to hear what you think about *Introduction to Canadian Politics and Government*. Please take a few minutes to fill out the stamped reply card at the back of the book. Your comments and suggestions will be valuable to us as we prepare new editions and other books.

BRIEF CONTENTS

CONTENTS

PART 1

BACKGROUND

A Brief Outline of the Parliamentary System in Canada

As the new millennium dawns, Canadians are as affected by the processes of government as ever before. Nevertheless, it is likely that even after an intense period of public discussion on constitutional change, including the national referendum of October 1992 and the Quebec referendum of October 1995, many Canadians could not adequately describe the major institutions of their system of government. Thus, we begin with a concise survey of the Canadian system of government and introduce readers to terms that they have probably heard and read but never fully understood.

If asked to describe the governmental system of their country, most Canadians, perhaps grudgingly in the mood of the late 1990s, would likely consider it to be "democratic." If pressed to define more fully what that means, however, they would probably have difficulty in offering anything more than vague concepts of majority rule, freedom, or the preservation of rights. Democracy in the Canadian context operates in the *representative* form and can be best summed up as majority consent to rule by a minority. The consent can be renewed or transferred to another minority by the will of the majority expressed through periodic elections.

Most Canadians would not be entirely satisfied with this definition. They think in terms of rights that are guaranteed by the Charter of Rights and Freedoms, such as those for minorities as well as for the majority, and those major freedoms such as freedom of speech, religion, or assembly that are considered to be an essential part of our political heritage. Thus, although in theory democracy is a means of rule by majority consent, in practice most Canadians view it as much more than that and insist on the rights and freedoms that define a *liberal democracy*.

How close is this theory to reality? In later chapters we will discuss the relationships that actually exist between those few people who operate the political system and the majority who give them the right to do so. It will be seen that many important decision makers are only indirectly subject to the control of the electorate through elected politicians. To say, then, that Canada is a representative liberal democracy is hardly a description that yields a deep understanding of the Canadian political system.

Thus, even though it has in essence a democratic system, there are many instances in which "democratic" is not a very informative adjective to describe governmental and political process in Canada. Canadians share with the citizens of other democratic countries the need not just to accept democratic rhetoric but also to seek out those areas in which the ideal is either ignored or unattained and to offer proposals for democratic reform.

The institutional basis for Canadian democracy is prescribed in the Canadian Constitution, which provides for the *executive, legislative,* and *judicial* branches of government. But the written words of the Constitution do not tell the whole tale. In addition, historically established practices known as constitutional conventions dictate how institutions work and what their relationships are to one another.

The Constitution Act, 1982 did not replace the British North America Act, 1867 (now named the Constitution Act, 1867), which remains the essential document of the Canadian Constitution, but it did add a Charter of Rights and Freedoms as well as a comprehensive amending process omitted by colonial politicians, who wanted government in British North America to be similar in principle to the government in Great Britain. Nonetheless, the different environment of British North America made it necessary to adjust British ideas to a varied population and a vast and still largely unsettled land mass.

Like Great Britain, Japan, Sweden, and many other states, Canada is a *constitutional monarchy*. The powers of the queen as head of state and the embodiment of the executive branch of government are restricted to those granted under the Constitution and the laws of the state. Since Canada shares the queen with Great Britain and other Commonwealth countries, she has a representative in Canada known as the *governor general*.

Like the United States, Switzerland, the Federal Republic of Germany, and other states whose size, ethnic diversity, or historical experience have influenced their choice, Canada adopted a *federal system* of government, in which the constitutional power to make and administer laws is divided between a central authority and a number of constituent political units. A written constitution was necessary to divide legislative authority between the provincial governments and the central (or, as it is usually called, federal) government. That division was considered to be the most appropriate arrangement in 1867; however, as the role of government became more and more complex over time, the relations between Ottawa and the provincial capitals have emerged as the most difficult feature of contemporary Canadian government.

In addition to having a constitutional monarchy and a federal structure, Canada, like Ireland, Israel, and Italy—none of which is either a monarchy or a federation—has a *parliamentary system* of government. In a parliamentary system, the political members of the executive, the prime minister, and the Cabinet are chosen from the elected legislature and are responsible to it. Hence, the term "cabinet government" or "responsible government" is often used in conjunction with parliamentary government.

Thus, Canada's constitutional framework includes three features, each of which is shared with many countries. Canada is one of only a very few states (Australia is another), however, that mixes all three governing principles in its constitution.

FIGURE I.1
THE CANADIAN GOVERNMENT

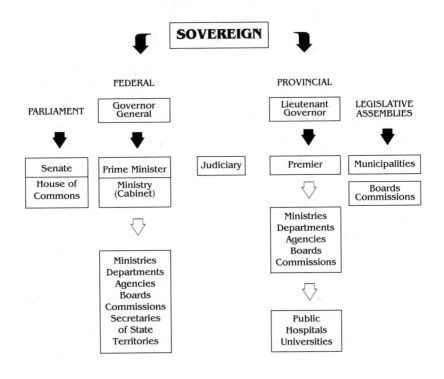

Source: Statistics Canada, *Canada Yearbook 1997*, Catalogue No. 11–402, p. 443. Reproduced by authority of the Minister of Industry, 1997.

THE PRIME MINISTER AND CABINET

The prime minister and Cabinet are the most important examples of the constitutional conventions mentioned above. While the Constitution Act, 1867 talked only of a Privy Council and made no mention of a prime minister, it is the Cabinet, headed by and chosen by the prime minister, that occupies the most important place in Canadian government. This body became part of the Canadian colonial scene before Confederation. All Cabinet members are sworn in as privy councillors, thus acquiring constitutional authority. However, when they cease to be members of the Cabinet, they are divested of authority within the Canadian government even though they may remain privy councillors for life as a purely honorary title.

The Cabinet is drawn from the political party that either has the majority of the members in the House of Commons, or enough members to constitute a majority with the support of another party, and thus is considered to have the confidence of the House. The former situation, not surprisingly, is known as *majority government*, while the latter is known as *minority government*. The leader of the party that either has its own majority or can mobilize support from another party to create a majority becomes prime minister. For instance, in 1979 the Progressive Conservative Party had 137 out of 282 seats in the House of Commons; however, support from the Créditiste Party gave the Progressive Conservative leader, Joe Clark, sufficient backing to retain the office of prime minister in a minority situation until he lost the confidence of the House of Commons (that is, until a majority of members of the House would not vote to support his government and its proposals). Contrasted to this was the situation in 1993, when the Liberals were elected with 177 seats and their leader, Jean Chrétien, became prime minister without the support of any other party.

Prime ministers choose only members of their own party to serve in the Cabinet. Since Cabinet ministers are *collectively responsible* to the House of Commons for the policies of the government, they must present a united front. Ministers will not attempt to formulate and cannot implement a policy without responsible advisors and administrators. In our system these advisors to ministers are usually civil servants in the various departments of government whose activities fall under the direction of the minister, the political head of the department, who is in turn responsible to the House of Commons. While most members of the Cabinet are responsible for a department, there may be others who have responsibilities in policy areas such as federal-provincial relations or women's issues and do not head a department as such. Decisions about the size, composition, and organization of the Cabinet rest with the prime minister.

THE HOUSE OF COMMONS

The House of Commons is composed of 301 members who are elected to represent carefully defined geographic, *single-member constituencies*. Although one generally thinks of the legislature, or House of Commons, as the lawmaker in a parliamentary system, it is also responsible for checking the executive, or Cabinet, publicizing government activities, and educating the public in politics; as John Stuart Mill put it, "it should become a grand committee of grievances for the nation." It may also inquire into individual Cabinet ministers' activities. All money that Cabinet ministers need to carry out their policies in the various departments of government must be approved by the House of Commons. Policies of the government are therefore publicized and critically analyzed, mostly by the opposition parties, in the House and its committees. Members also act as representatives of their constituents, both individually and as a group, to try to resolve problems and provide benefits for which the federal government is responsible. The House may also, on its own initiative, investigate—through a committee—practically any issue that it considers to be of national importance.

It is in the House where the drama and action associated with federal political activity most often takes place. When a Cabinet tends to disregard the traditional rights of the House, the general public may become aroused, although probably less so in the 1990s than in earlier decades. But when an important vote of confidence is taken, the House of Commons becomes the focus of public attention to the issues and personalities involved, as happened in December 1979, when the Clark government fell.

While the traditional theory of parliamentary government places great emphasis on the role of the legislature in making the Cabinet responsible for its actions, in modern times this aim has been difficult, if not impossible, to achieve. Modern political parties with strict internal discipline have allowed a prime minister and Cabinet to dominate the House of Commons through the majority they command. Even during times of minority government, the prime minister and Cabinet are in a strong position, since the system gives them the task of initiating the important business that faces Parliament. Nonetheless, in a minority situation, the opposition parties can combine to remove the government if they choose to withdraw the confidence of the House.

Although the role of lawmaking may be dominated by the Cabinet, it remains the legislature's basic responsibility. Before new laws can be made or old laws amended, they must go through three stages in the House. The introductory stage, called the *first reading*, consists of presenting to the House a draft of the proposed legislation (called a *bill*) prior to its passage into law. The next step, *second reading*, is a general debate on the principles embodied in the bill. If it is acceptable, there follows a clause-by-clause discussion by a *committee* of the House that reports back to the entire House. The *third reading* constitutes the final House ratification, but the bill must then pass a similar procedure in the Senate and receive *royal assent* (the governor general's signature) before it becomes an Act of Parliament.

THE SENATE

The Senate is a second legislative house in Parliament, having 104 members appointed by the prime minister. It was originally intended to fulfil a twofold representative function. First, since Canada was to have a federal system, the representation of regions of the country was considered to be crucial. Thus, initially there were 24 members from each of Ontario, Quebec, and the Maritimes; later, 24 were added for the western provinces, six for Newfoundland, and one for each territory. Second, the Senate was given almost equal powers with the House of Commons, and its members had age and property qualifications so that they might act as a chamber of "sober second thought" to check any radical excesses of the popularly elected Commons. However, its regional representative role was soon usurped by powerful regional representatives in the Cabinet and more recently by provincial premiers, and its role as the representative of the wealthy and conservative sections of the community is no longer accepted as legitimate in a democratic society. In any case, the wealthy have other more effective means of protecting their interests. Thus, the Senate has rarely disagreed with the House of Commons on major proposals, although it may alter the details of some bills. In 1988 the Senate gained unaccustomed notoriety when it refused to pass the Free Trade Bill before an election was held. It is also important to remember that the Cabinet is drawn from the House of Commons (the leader of the government party in the Senate is usually the only exception) and is responsible solely to that body and not to the Senate. So far removed is the Senate from the role for which it was originally constructed that for many years there have been urgings for its reform and even some arguments for its abolition. Westerners, especially Albertans, have seen in Senate reform the potential to address their regional grievances. The most popular prospect has been the *Triple E model*, meaning elected, equal, and effective. A version of that idea was among the clauses of the defeated Charlottetown Accord of 1992.

THE PUBLIC SERVICE

The Cabinet is only the political head of the administration, most of whose members work in the public service. These public servants are the people with whom Canadians do business. As of 1997 they number approximately 200 000, excluding the military, the RCMP, and employees of publicly owned Crown corporations such as Canada Post. Including these brings the number to about 485 000.

The public service is organized into departments, each of which is responsible for administering certain laws. In addition, there are scores of boards, commissions, agencies, and Crown corporations, a few being the Canadian Broadcasting Corporation, the Wheat Board, the Canadian Transportation Agency, the St. Lawrence Seaway Authority, and the National Film Board. New concerns have led to new groups of public servants. For instance, there was no Department of the Environment in 1867. The growth of government is reflected in the fact that since Confederation the population has increased eightfold while the number of employees in the public service has increased more than one hundredfold.

Public servants are usually permanent employees who are recruited from across Canada by competitive examinations (where responsible administrative positions are involved) and who remain in public employment regardless of changes in political leadership. At the head of the permanent employees of the various departments of government are the *deputy ministers*, who are responsible to the ministers for the efficient operation of the department. This responsibility inevitably involves the deputy minister in a policy advisory role to the political head of the department, the minister. These senior public servants have permanent employment, although they may be transferred from department to department, and therefore they may remain in office for a long period, while ministers come and go. It is not surprising that these people, individually and as a group, form a powerful bureaucratic elite whose influence on the policy of any government is widespread.

THE JUDICIARY

The third branch of government is the judiciary. Since the rule of law is so basic to the ideals that Canadians value, some knowledge of this third branch is fundamental to an understanding of Canadian government. The fact that we have a government similar in principle to that of the United Kingdom means that all the rights that have evolved from the Magna Carta down through the centuries of British history, and that were incorporated into *common law*, have been transferred to Canada.

Freedom, both *substantive*, like freedom of speech, and *procedural*, like habeas corpus, is interpreted and maintained by the judiciary. The Charter of Rights and Freedoms has entrenched these traditional freedoms. Citizens have been encouraged to challenge laws whose provisions might negate Charter rights; this has accentuated the role of the judiciary. It has also raised concern that the government-appointed judges might have too much power to overrule democratically elected legislatures.

In addition, since we have a federal system, the courts have a key role in interpreting the respective jurisdictions of the federal and provincial governments. Since the 1880s the courts, therefore, have had a prominent position in the development of the Canadian Constitution. In short, the courts have the responsibility for determining what a law means or even if it is constitutionally acceptable.

There is a single system of courts in Canada. At the national level, the *Supreme Court* and the *Federal Court* each have distinct areas of jurisdiction. Each province has senior courts and district courts whose judges are appointed by the federal government, as well as *provincial courts* whose judges are appointed by the provincial government.

It must be recognized that parliamentary systems similar in structure to that of Canada may operate in different ways in other states. The beliefs and attitudes of the people may lead to vastly different reactions to political circumstances. So while it is important for us to understand the institutions through which our political decisions are made, it is equally important to understand the ways in which political parties, interest groups, and the media make an impact on the system.

This introduction gives only a brief outline of the Canadian political and governmental system; however, it does serve to introduce the reader to the basic institutions of Canadian government. In the following chapters, we will analyze and describe in more detail both the processes and institutions of the Canadian political system.

CHAPTER 1

The Setting for Canadian Politics

The political institutions that are considered appropriate for a country, and the way people operate those institutions and behave in political situations, are influenced by the conditions that face the residents of a territory. Whether it is big or small, tropical or temperate, more powerful than its neighbours or weaker, will all make some difference in the kinds of problems a country's people face and the political solutions they select. Whether they all have a common ethnic background, speak the same language, have the same religion, or differ in these respects will likely have an impact on the way they make political decisions. Thus, to understand the government and politics of Canada, we ought to first learn something about the land and its people.

THE PHYSICAL SETTING

Canada's coat of arms tells us that we stretch from sea to sea, and our national anthem (in English) proclaims us "the true North strong and free." To say, then, that Canada is the world's second largest country in area is to indicate a whole complex of problems that do not plague, for example, The Netherlands. As schoolchildren, Canadians learn of the diversity of the Canadian geographic area—the Canadian Shield, the Appalachian region, and the Cordilleran region covering central, eastern, and western Canada respectively. In addition to these regions, there is the tremendous expanse of the Inuitian region of the Arctic.

Problems of communication and transportation are natural results of Canada's size. These problems are aggravated by physical barriers that have isolated groups of Canadians from each other. The Maritimes are cut off from central Canada by American territory. The Prairies are cut off from eastern Canada by the Laurentian Shield, and British Columbia is cut off from the rest of Canada by the Rockies. These geographical divisions have been translated into regional isolation both physical and mental, and it has been considered a primary task of the Canadian federal political structure to overcome this isolation.

Location as well as size has an influence on Canadian politics. Canada's northern location with its attendant climatic features has obvious implications for Canada's style of life, economic development, and the kind of political problems it faces. The climatic situation has encouraged the bulk of the population to settle along the southern borders, accentuating the impact of its neighbour, the United States—which has been a major factor in Canada's political life. The apprehension that Canadians have about Canada's ability to withstand American territorial expansion and the notion of manifest destiny[1] in the nineteenth century have given way to concern about economic and cultural domination in the twentieth century, as the United States emerged as the world's foremost economic power and leader of the Western military alliance.

RESOURCES

Abundant economic resources have also played a role in Canadian politics. Canada's rich natural resources have provided the basis for one of the highest standards of living in the world. It has been argued that a high degree of economic development is a precondition for democratic government. Thus, Canada's wealth can be considered as one reason for its moderate political culture. To the degree that important radical movements have been part of Canadian life, they have arisen during times of economic stress. Resources are not evenly distributed, so regional economic disparity has been a perennial political problem.

Canada's reliance on staple products and raw materials has been instrumental in determining some of the most important issues of Canadian life. For example, the dominance of wheat farming on the Canadian Prairies has made a large part of the Canadian economy almost totally dependent on world markets. Thus, for any Canadian government, the disposal of wheat becomes a major political issue. The same can be said for Canada's other agricultural, forest, fishery, and mineral products. The concentration of oil in Alberta led to one of the major regional confrontations of the 1970s and 1980s—between western producers and eastern consumers over price—and induced the Trudeau government to develop the controversial National Energy Program. In the 1990s the depletion of the cod stocks off Newfoundland has become a regional, national, and international problem for Canadian policy makers.

The availability of primary resources has attracted massive foreign capital for their development. Canada has been cursed—or blessed, depending on one's point of view—by this infusion of foreign money, which has led to widespread foreign ownership, especially by Americans, of Canada's raw materials and much of the secondary industry of the country. For many Canadians this raises questions about the ability of any Canadian government to exercise real sovereignty in the face of foreign economic domination.

The oil crisis of the 1980s accentuated this dilemma. Canada possesses potential reserves of oil and gas in the Arctic and off Newfoundland, but these are difficult to extract and expensive to transport. The huge amounts of capital, much of it foreign, needed to exploit these resources will have a major impact on the economy and raise serious political issues domestically and with the United States. Provisions of the Canada–US Free Trade Agreement on the sharing of energy resources have generated considerable debate. Resource development caused the government to recognize the need to come to settlements with northern Native peoples over aboriginal rights and land claims. More general environmental concerns have also been raised by such issues. On a more positive note, the food crisis of recent decades has placed Canada in a position of considerable influence, because of its role as a major exporter of agricultural commodities. These issues serve to bring into focus the importance of the nature of Canadian wealth as a determinant of political life.

DEMOGRAPHY

The demography of Canada is another factor that has significant influence on the Canadian political scene. The growing number of Canadians over 65 and the decline in the number of school-age children both have major effects on political issues in the pension, health, welfare, and educational fields. Thus, while the attempt of the Mulroney government in 1985 to limit the inflation protection for old-age pensions was abandoned in the face of the growing political influence of senior citizens, later tax measures were introduced to retrieve money for middle- and upper-income pensioners. By 1997 there was a national debate on what measures were necessary to ensure the viability of the Canada Pension Plan. While it is not the intention here to belabour the relationship between demography and politics, it is interesting to note that at an earlier point in Canadian history the high birthrate of French Canadians was considered by some of them to be a vital factor in their political survival within Canadian federalism. Now, a very low birthrate is a matter of concern for Quebec nationalists. Accordingly, Quebec has been concerned with preserving a majority French-speaking population. The language laws of Quebec are aimed at protecting its French language in the face of its minority status within Canada and North

America. Quebec's interest in sharing control of immigration policy is aimed at integrating newcomers into the francophone community.

The obvious demographic reality that half of Canada's people are women did not create major issues for most of Canadian political history. Except for the struggle for the vote in the early part of the twentieth century, few issues were considered in gender terms. When there were policy matters that could be considered "women's issues," women were the objects of the policy rather than active participants in policy making. The 1921 enfranchisement of women did not lead to the entry of women into political life in anything like representative numbers in the legislative, administrative, or judicial branches of the government. A highly symbolic portrayal of this situation was reflected in the need for the Judicial Committee of the Privy Council to decide in 1929 that the word *persons* in the Constitution included female persons—a notion that apparently was not evident to the Supreme Court.

The situation is dramatically different in the 1990s. A social revolution has fundamentally altered the circumstances of women in Canadian society. Consequently, women have sought legislative and policy solutions to a host of problems that reflect a new reality. Equal rights for women have been a central concern in constitutional discussions in the 1980s and 1990s. Policy questions such as pay equity (in some situations equal pay for work of equal value) and employment equity (equal access to a variety of jobs) have emerged from women's place in the workforce. Questions relating to public policy on abortion, child care, and pornography have been cast as "women's issues." However, questions relating to policy are only part of a new agenda. Participation is an objective that is being sought with equal intensity. Thus, governments have sought in their appointments to represent more fairly the female half of the population. Political parties during the 1990s have begun to make the recruitment and election of women a part of the electoral process. Women's groups themselves have developed to pressure for both government action on an array of women's issues and the wider participation of women in all decision making.

ETHNICITY AND LANGUAGE

Two ethnic groups, French and British (English, Scottish, Welsh, Irish), have historically dominated in Canada, and relations between these groups have been a continuous controversial theme in Canadian politics. These groups and their languages are specially recognized in the Constitution and political traditions of the country. Section 133 of the Constitution Act, 1867 provides for the use of the English and French languages in debates in the Parliament of Canada, the legislature of Quebec, and the courts of Canada. The passage of the Official

Languages Act in 1969 by the federal government, and amendments in 1987, expanded the legal protections to the languages, especially for French outside of Quebec and for employment in the federal public service. But the language laws of Quebec itself have been even more crucial.

After the so-called Quiet Revolution of the 1960s and 1970s, French Canadians, through their government in Quebec, began to use the powers of the state more aggressively to protect their interests and way of life. In 1974 the first Bourassa government brought down Bill 22, a far-reaching law termed the Official Languages Act, which made French the official language of Quebec. As a consequence, French was to be the language used in public administration, in intergovernmental relations, and as a language of labour and business in the province.[2] The most controversial feature of the legislation concerned French as the language of instruction. The bill was greeted with hostility by anglophone Quebeckers and by the rest of Canada, while at the same time it failed to satisfy many Quebec nationalists. In 1977 the newly elected Parti Québécois proposed in Bill 101 a language charter that would not only overcome some of the difficulties of the previous legislation, but would also extend "francisation" beyond the limits accepted by Premier Bourassa. Thus, English was no longer to be used in Quebec's courts and in the Quebec legislature. Camille Laurin, minister of state for cultural development, noted that "the criterion for determining the right of access to instruction in English was one of the most disputed aspects of Bill 22."[3] It was thus proposed to limit access to English education to the children of those who had received such education in the past or those children who were receiving English education at the time the charter was adopted, along with their brothers and sisters.

Although the justifications for the new legislation were cultural, demographic, and economic, the emphasis was sometimes on the socioeconomic consequences of previous practice, sometimes on the preservation of culture at a time of a demographic decline of the francophone population. The most controversial aspects of Bill 101 have been those sections dealing with the language to be used in legal proceedings, those dealing with the Native populations, the language of work, and the language of education.[4] As in the case of Bill 22, Prime Minister Trudeau refused to revive the long unused constitutional power of the federal government to disallow the legislation. However, the opponents of the legislation had recourse to the Supreme Court of Canada to determine whether Bill 101 conflicted with Section 133 of the BNA Act. Ironically, the challenge to Bill 101 was coupled with a challenge to the constitutionality of Manitoba's 1890 legislation against the French. While certain sections of Bill 101 have been ruled as ultra vires—beyond the powers of the provincial national assembly—only a restricted part of Bill 101 has been declared unconstitutional. As to the other contentious parts of the language legislation, it is to be noted that an agreement has been made with the Native population, and the Lévesque government had promised to make other adjustments and accommodations in the administration of Bill 101. One predictable result of this legislation is to deter anglophones from other parts of Canada from emigrating to Quebec, because their children will not have access to English schools and adults will increasingly be obliged to function in French. Two interesting conclusions were drawn from the passage of Bill 101 into law. On the one hand, it was argued that Quebeckers did not need political independence to achieve cultural security;[5] on the other hand, Premier Lévesque argued that independence would provide a solution to the language problem, as if unitary states did not have difficulties with large linguistic minorities.

After the Supreme Court of Canada struck down sections of Bill 101 as unconstitutional in 1988, Premier Bourassa invoked the notwithstanding clause of the Constitution Act, 1982 and then brought in a new language law, Bill 178. This law requires commercial signs to be in French outside, while allowing English to be used in the inside of the establishment. Suffice it to say that this "compromise" did not satisfy anglophone groups like Alliance Quebec, nor did it placate certain Quebec nationalists. Outside of Quebec the law created a degree of hostility that contributed to the failure of the Meech Lake Accord and later to the failure of the Charlottetown Accord. By the summer of 1996, following the close win for the No side in the independence referendum of October 1995, the language situation had heated up again in Montreal, where the two linguistic groups cohabit. Anglophones became more insistent that the limited rights they had in terms of commercial signs be respected, while hard-line nationalist francophones demanded further suppression of English in order to protect the French nature of Quebec.

While French-English relations dominate political debate, Canada is nonetheless a multiethnic state, and few other countries have so many different ethnic groups represented in their citizenry. The concentration on bilingualism since the 1970s has made some of these people, who make up over a quarter of the Canadian population, feel that their contribution to Canadian life has been largely neglected. Especially in western Canada, where there is a relatively small francophone population and the percentage of those with neither an English nor a French background is larger than elsewhere in Canada, the reaction to bilingualism and biculturalism has often been negative. In answer to their claims, however, the argument is put forward that members of these other ethnic groups have normally adopted the lifestyle of English-speaking Canada, even while retaining some of their own cultural heritage. According to this view, the linguistic factor is what divides Canada into two cultural groups made up of English-speaking, Anglo-Celtic, and other ethnic groups on one side, and French-speaking people almost exclusively of French ancestry on the other. In any case, in response to the views of the non-English and non-French groups in Canada, the federal government has encouraged multiculturalism with public funds and appointed a Cabinet minister for multiculturalism. This policy has in turn generated some criticism among Canadians who reject this approach to national integration.

THE ABORIGINAL PEOPLES

To an increasing extent in recent years, the rights and claims of Native peoples have demanded the attention of the Canadian public. This pressure was intensified with the passage of the Constitution Act, 1982, which provided for a constitutional conference whose agenda would include the rights of aboriginal people and in which aboriginal representatives would participate. The clear transition from tutelage to greater self-government for Native peoples presented a challenge for Canadian policy makers that remains unmet in the 1990s. Although some land claims have been settled, most remain unsettled. The Meech Lake Accord did not address Native issues, and Manitoba MLA and Native leader Elijah Harper was able to prevent his province from ratifying the deal. It did not come to a vote. When the Charlottetown Accord was negotiated in 1992, both status and nonstatus Indians as well as Inuit and Métis peoples were part of the process; aboriginal issues were an important part of the agreement. Nevertheless, the referendum of October 26, 1992, resulted in a rejection of the Accord not only among Canadians generally but also by the Native community. With no settlement to date, the accommodation of Native peoples and the cultural, economic, and political relationship that should exist between Native peoples and the Canadian state will continue to be outstanding items on the Canadian political agenda.

THE FOUNDING EUROPEAN PEOPLES

The Canadian populace, while now containing a great variety of ethnic groups, was marked in 1867 by the duality of the two main linguistic elements. Although one could argue that there is a common heritage of Western civilization in the Judeo-Christian sense, it is the differences between the French-speaking and English-speaking traditions in Canada, rather than their similarities, that have been of greatest significance for Canadian politics. Segments of Canadian society have lived according to different lifestyles and have developed different approaches and attitudes to the practice of politics. While the

pressure of modern technology has directed Canadians toward conformity in the last decade of the twentieth century, still some differences
in attitudes to politics of French-speaking and English-speaking
Canadians have not been resolved. Many Canadians may now reject
the idea of founding peoples having significance for contemporary politics, but it is a concept that needs to be understood to interpret
Canadian political development.

The French, who settled along the St. Lawrence and its tributaries,
could and did build a relatively closed rural society. The land was fertile and suited to mixed subsistence farming, and the river was a
means of communication guarding the entrance to the hinterland of
the west. By the time of the English conquest (1759), a pattern of life
had been established through the authority of the ecclesiastical
Roman Catholic hierarchy and the secular seigneurial system.[6] With
the traditional values of the society tied to passive obedience to the
bishops and intendants, the French *fabrique* (the weaving together of
perfectly coordinated values) had developed a strength and homogeneity that no other group could or would accomplish. They were the
original settlers, their leaders the original leaders, their values the original values. Hence, the French displayed the strength and toughness
of a minority that chose partial isolation for nearly two centuries. An
ideology of rural conservatism lasted well into the period when
Quebec had become an urban society. This was based on the belief in
the preservation of the traditional values of the family and of religious
life in a pastoral setting. Within this milieu for much of Canadian history, the authority of the church, embodied in the parish priest, was
unchallengeable. Insofar as there was secular political leadership, it
was in the hands of the so-called notables of the community: lawyers,
doctors, other professionals, and successful businesspeople. The
aggressive, acquisitive Protestant ethic embodied in the Lockean philosophy of English-speaking Canada was largely lacking among French-
speaking Canadians. Thus, even in their homeland, the French
Canadians forfeited control of commercial and industrial life to English
Canadians. While the traditional lifestyle and institutions may no
longer be relevant, the society they nurtured has determined to survive as a "distinct society," in the words of both the Meech Lake
Accord of 1987 and the Charlottetown Accord of 1992. Quebeckers
primarily have looked to their provincial government to secure their
future and their collective rights, and their leaders sought to enshrine
them in those two failed agreements. Other Quebeckers have adopted
the position that only by separation from Canada, to form an independent state, can their language and culture be preserved.

The British who settled in Canada tended to view this vast land as
a commercial entity. Having a sophisticated approach to exploitation,
with some major exceptions,[7] they viewed the new homeland as a
way of breaking out of the rigid class system from which they came.

Land was settled at first for subsistence, but later for entrepreneurial purposes with extended trade links between the commercial agrarian settlements and the British commercial contacts who needed food and raw materials. This presaged the later development of the Prairies and established a contrast to the economic and social activity of the French settlement to the east. The crossroads for the two distinct regions was at the confluence of the Ottawa and St. Lawrence Rivers and the island city of Montreal. Early commercial activity developed naturally at Montreal, with its harbour facilities and commercially enterprising British settlers. With this pattern of settlement and outward-looking commercialism, the basis of Canadian politics assumed a pattern that dominated Canadian history.

English-speaking Canada lives very much in the shadow of the English philosopher John Locke.[8] His concern for the protection of life, liberty, and property has been a keystone of Canadian political ideology since English settlers first came to Canada. Although other more conservative (Tory) doctrines were influential in the early years of English Canadian life, it was the Lockean philosophy that emerged as the dominant one in English-speaking Canada—so much so that, whether they realize it or not, most English-speaking Canadians are more or less devout Lockeans. This tradition embodies the democratic ideals of Canadian life and is reflected in phrases like "government through the consent of the governed." It is also responsible for the widespread belief in the sanctity of private property. This philosophy was well suited to an agrarian frontier society in which property owning was widespread and in which the return to farmers was very much the product of their own work and initiative. The philosophy of possessive individualism (to use Professor Macpherson's phrase)[9] triumphed in Canada.

This philosophy, however, has been tempered by other ideas and conditions in English-speaking Canadian life. There is the Tory tradition, which was powerful in the early years of English Canadian settlement. In the political life of the early government of British North America, this ideology found its expression in the dominance of the Family Compact and Château Clique. This Tory tradition is based on a belief in the organic nature of society and the existence of classes within society, all with different roles to play.[10] A governing class has a responsibility to maintain stability in society by controlling the instruments of government. This of course denies democratic values and instead stresses prescriptive (inherited) rights of governors and the need for natural deference to authority. While these views are unacceptable to most English-speaking Canadians today, they were not without their influence in moulding early Canadian attitudes. It has been fashionable to accord inordinate influence to this Tory tradition. This issue will be examined at greater length in the chapter on ideologies.[11]

POLITICAL EVOLUTION

Tory beliefs were being challenged in all sections of the British North American colonies, as the rebellions in Upper and Lower Canada in 1837–38 demonstrated. Although unsuccessful, they did foster political reform that was embodied in Lord Durham's report. The neighbouring United States and the democratic ideals generated first during the American Revolution and then expanded by the Jacksonian democratic movement of the 1830s—with its emphasis on the rule of the people— affected the political thinking of Canada in the mid-nineteenth century, as did the radical ideas of Jeremy Bentham.[12]

By 1867 all the colonies that joined confederation had achieved responsible government, which meant control over domestic matters by the legislature primarily through the appropriation of money for government use. Whereas in nineteenth-century Great Britain reform revolved around widening of the franchise, in Canada reform centred on curbing preemptory (preferential) rights held by the ruling executives, which had allowed those elites to commit public money to schemes for exploiting the natural resources in Canada without having to account to their legislative assemblies. Since Canada at Confederation was mainly populated by self-sufficient, agrarian people, they expected the same kind of parsimonious attitude in expenditures from government as they themselves practised. Good government meant cheap government; does that sound familiar? Responsibility meant responsibility of the executive, or Cabinet, to the elected representatives who judged their proposals in the legislature. This contrasted with British constitutional principles that made the executive responsible to the Crown—the Crown supposedly embodying the interests of all the people. Parliament had been used in Britain to give the responsibility of government to an executive supported by a gradually enlarged voting public. In essence this was the basis of reform in Britain during the nineteenth century.[13]

Generally, however, in the British North American colonies, the broader franchise was a starting point and Parliament was a vehicle for the electorate to force the government to look toward the people rather than to legitimize its authority by the tradition of a long-standing monarchy embodying the hopes, aspirations, and power of the people. There was, in a sense, an inversion of the British approach in the Canadian parliamentary system. The legislatures in Canada became impatient with executive authority and demanded "people authority." Parliament was adapting to de facto republicanism, whereas the form and structure was de jure a constitutional monarchy.

The modern Canadian political system has developed by adapting the evolutionary British parliamentary system to a different environment. This necessitated a modification of that model to suit the people and the circumstances, a large unexplored land mass that was then under the strong influence of the United States. Canada was an agrarian frontier community, and in this community there was a rough-hewn quality of independence bred on land ownership, yet dependent on co-operation in order to survive the harsh elements of the new country. This of course contrasted strongly with the experience of Great Britain, which had developed over a long time with a small minority of rich landholders generally ruling over a commercial middle class, with gradations down to a large propertyless working class.

The experience of Parliament in the Canadian environment was very different from that in the British. The dictates of the environment created a situation in which the organic concept of hierarchy did not fit as it did in Great Britain. Individualism was tempered by cooperativeness at an early point in Canada, and government was an instrument to develop the country not directly comparable to the United Kingdom. The arguments concerning government in Canada were not so much about who was to participate as about what government was to do for the broad mass of people in the country. At the end of the twentieth century, the debate continues about which aspects of our original British model should be altered or even abandoned to deal with contemporary attitudes.

THE REGIONS

Another major influence over the development of Canadian political institutions and practices is the existence of distinctive geographical and economic regions. It is the degree to which people interpret political realities and adopt their political attitudes as a result of where they live in Canada that makes regionalism a more crucial political factor in Canada than it is in many other countries. Thus, a brief review of the regions will help to identify many of the long-standing issues of Canadian political history, especially relating to the federal system.

Atlantic Canada

The Atlantic provinces continue their struggle to develop into a more economically viable region. Historically, this struggle has been difficult, and streams of people and money have left the region. The Atlantic provinces have suffered from declining coal and steel industries, depleted fisheries, and regional economic inequality. Since the 1950s there have been various attempts in the Atlantic provinces to develop their economic potential. The Atlantic Canada Opportunities Agency, established in 1987, tries to provide planning, attract capital, and encourage capital growth so that the Atlantic provinces can achieve the prosperity of the rest of Canada. Nevertheless, the regional levels of unemployment have consistently been the highest in Canada, and at the end of the 1990s their per capita incomes remain the lowest. Since the inception of large social-welfare programs, particularly after World War II, many Maritimers have felt that they have been forced to become the wards of Ottawa. Some have argued that the government in Ottawa has served central Canada and that it has "milked" the east through high freight rates, tariffs, and other factors militating against the interests of the Atlantic provinces, which were relatively prosperous at the time of Confederation. There developed a general feeling of alienation from the central government in Ottawa because it was viewed as being insensitive to Atlantic interests. An example was the development of the St. Lawrence Seaway, which diverted overseas shipping from Halifax. In the Atlantic provinces, therefore, politics has always been based on a different set of economic conditions than those operating in other parts of Canada.

While the Atlantic provinces are here discussed as a region, one must keep in mind that the individual provinces have their own particular problems and their own political cultures. New Brunswick, for instance, mirrors the Canadian picture as a whole in that its population is composed of English-speaking and a large minority of French-speaking residents. The Acadians of New Brunswick have begun to assert themselves in recent decades. New Brunswick is the only officially bilingual province under the Constitution Act, 1982. Elements of the anglophone population have reacted negatively to this development, and thus language and ethnic issues are important elements of New Brunswick politics.

Newfoundland presents another set of circumstances. It came into Confederation in 1949 after having undergone fifteen years of government by a nonelected commission. The decision to join Canada was based on a very close vote in a plebiscite, which demonstrated that union was not overwhelmingly popular. Confederation for a large percentage of Newfoundlanders revolved mainly around the hope for economic improvement. Economic advantage has not always been readily apparent to the detractors of the federal government. Thus, when the prospect of wealth from offshore oil deposits appeared in the 1980s, the provincial government had public support for its demands to have total jurisdiction over this resource. There has also been pressure for more control over fishing, which is still a federal responsibility despite its crucial place in the Newfoundland economy. The disastrous depletion of cod stocks in the 1990s has served as ample proof. For many Newfoundlanders the federal government has been ineffective in controlling foreign fishing and regulating the fisheries.

Another factor that affected the role of politics in the Atlantic provinces is that they maintained their pro-British, London-oriented viewpoint longer than did most other Canadians. Initially, they did not support the British North American union, and there is still considerable detachment in their attitude toward central Canada. The ethnic composition of their population has not been altered by European immigration as has been the case elsewhere in Canada. Emigration, on the other hand, has been considerable. There is evidence that, although people do leave the Atlantic provinces and go to central Canada, they quite often return to their homes. There seems to be a strong loyalty, based on the depth of feeling they have for the particular pattern of life in the Atlantic region.

The Heartland—Ontario and Quebec

The regional mentality of Canada is aggravated by the uneven distribution of population. Ontario and Quebec form the central core of the country, and approximately 60% of the population lives within their borders. Consequently, they both (but especially Ontario) have enjoyed the lion's share of Canada's commercial and industrial development. This, in combination with the democratic system of Canada, ensures that most governmental decisions must at least be acceptable to the Ontario-Quebec heartland. Moreover, most nongovernmental economic decisions are taken by executives based in the Ontario-Quebec industrial-commercial complex. Small wonder, then, that at the outer reaches—in the Prairies, the Atlantic provinces, and British Columbia—people often feel that their views on how the federal government should react to political problems are ignored. It is easy to understand why these regions feel exploited by the economic and political power of the central region.

But even within the heartland, there is not an even distribution of people and power throughout the region. In the northern areas of Ontario and Quebec, there is a sense of isolation and exploitation similar in some respects to that in the west. The mineral wealth of these regions is controlled in the boardrooms of Toronto and Montreal. The government of these regions is centred in legislatures to the south—in Toronto and Quebec City.

Ontario's people identify themselves first as Canadians to a degree not found in other provinces. Thus, the political importance of regionalism has been less apparent to many of them as they identify their interests with the federal government. Ontario has traditionally been the object of the regional hostility of others rather than the one directing it elsewhere. Although Mitchell Hepburn referred to Ontario as the "Milch Cow of Confederation," for the most part the leaders and the residents of the province have been willing to see some of its wealth redistributed to other provinces through federal equalization payments and other programs. But the energy crisis of the 1970s and 1980s may represent a historic watershed, which saw the Ontario government challenging the policies of Alberta and calling for federal protection. The National Energy Policy (NEP), which outraged westerners, particularly Albertans, responded in part to the concerns of energy consumers in Ontario. The Mulroney government dismantled the NEP, ended the Foreign Investment Review Act (FIRA), and amended the Drug Patent legislation to give firms (mostly foreign-owned and based in Quebec) longer protection from copying by generic drug companies. All of these policies ended legislation that had some support in Ontario. At the same time, the Free Trade Agreement (FTA) with the United States was pushed by the federal government over the objection of the Ontario government. Major job losses were blamed on the FTA by NDP premier Bob Rae, who assumed office in Ontario in 1990 as his government faced massive unemployment and a crippling recession. These kinds of circumstances may move Ontario to be just as aggressive as other regions in pursuing its interests both vis-à-vis the federal government and the other regions. This trend may be borne out by the discussion paper circulated by Premier Harris in the summer of 1996 that called for more provincial power.

Finally, within the heartland itself, in the province of Quebec, there is a feeling that the federal government in Ottawa is basically controlled by English Canadians for the benefit of English Canadians. Hence, instead of considering themselves as powerful agents of the federation, French Canadian legislators have traditionally seen their role as one of preventing the English Canadian masters of Confederation from seriously inhibiting the survival of French Canada. For the first 90 years of Confederation, Quebec was seldom aroused. Quebeckers knew they were different from the rest of Canada, and they did not want that difference tampered with. However, they could not—or would not—let the affluent life that was so visible in Ontario bypass them. They have, therefore, recently demanded two things: a special kind of identity, and modern technology adapted to that identity. Otherwise, they argue, they would be submerged into an anglophone commercial world completely foreign to their tradition, which has grown up since before Confederation. The harshness of the environment has been overcome, and the transition to a technology foreign to the rural French-speaking citizenry has caused an emotional upheaval that reached a climax in the 1980s. Quebeckers have therefore turned to their provincial government to provide social capital and to support and subsidize a particular way of life defined and organized largely on their own terms. One of the important features of the Trudeau governments from 1968 through to the 1980s was that French Canadians achieved Cabinet positions outside of those traditionally reserved for them. For the first time, French Canadian ministers occupied posts that were important for the overall direction of the Canadian government and economy. This development was also seen in the public service, which witnessed an increase in the number of

French Canadians in key posts. These developments have continued under the Mulroney and Chrétien governments. Quebec nationalists, however, remain unimpressed.

The Prairies

Western alienation has been an enduring theme of Canadian political history. This region has felt that its interests have been continually sacrificed for the benefit of central Canada. Prairie Canada began as virtually an economic colony of eastern interests. The effects of the frontier and the harsh climate of western Canada often forced people to adopt approaches that were less common in the east. Usually, this was done by cooperating with other groups to alleviate the harsh everyday existence that the environment forced on them. This was reflected in the development of a hardy type of wheat in order to use the land effectively, as well as in the development of a transportation system, grain elevators, telephone systems, hail insurance, and a cooperative means for the distribution of goods and services. Politically, this gave rise to a spectrum of strategies of organization that would allow westerners to get things done through the existing political institutions. Politics assumed a cooperative nature that gave rise to parties challenging the traditional Liberals and Conservatives of eastern Canada. Often this meant that much of western Canada was not represented in the governing party.

In addition, the ethnic composition of the west has developed differently from that in the east, with only a small percentage of French and large numbers neither British nor French. The concerns of the federal government about the place of the French language in Canada and the demands of the province of Quebec often evoked hostility from western Canadians, who had other demands they wanted addressed. The outrage that was set off in 1987 when a contract to service Armed Forces CF-18s was given to a Montreal firm rather than to a Winnipeg one is symptomatic of the feeling that westerners have that they are denied equal treatment by the federal government.

It is clear that the particular circumstances of the Prairies fostered the growth of an indigenous political culture whose attendant beliefs and values led to approaches to political problems that were different from those adopted in other parts of Canada. With the prosperity and economic power that has emerged in more recent years, the west has become even more insistent on having a greater impact on national decisions and greater control of its own resources. This is especially true of Alberta, whose large share of Canadian oil and natural gas production has given the province a newfound source of strength and confidence. Premier Don Getty's espousal of a so-called Triple E Senate (elected, equal, and effective) reflected the desire to have institutions in which the west would have more influence. The increased economic power of Alberta has a growing impact on political decision making in Canada.

British Columbia

While historically British Columbia has often been combined with the Prairies as the west, its origins as a province, its economy, and its population have combined to give it a distinctive character as a region. The natural resources of land and sea have created the opportunity for wealth that has been exploited not by tens of thousands of independent farmers but by large companies employing unionized labour. This has led to the development of a large metropolitan centre that services the economy and is populated by a cosmopolitan population with a large Asian community. The political culture that has emerged from this environment features a range of political conflict sometimes more extreme than that found elsewhere in Canada. Trade with the United States and the Pacific Rim countries often creates a different set of interests than exists in central Canada. The vast distance from Ottawa itself can contribute to a certain detachment from the problems of other regions. Nonetheless, more than the residents of many provinces, British Columbians have continued to identify themselves as Canadians first. As the 1990s conclude, however, dissatisfaction with federal handling of vital issues, the salmon fishery for instance, has strained relations with Ottawa and may undermine British Columbia's commitment to the federation.

Regional Realities

Despite the various shifts, the centres of power still remain in the metropolitan industrial-commercial complex of Ontario and the city of Montreal. It is in these areas that the interests most often placated by the federal government lie. Western and Atlantic regional bitterness feeds on the feeling that their regional interests will be sacrificed to those of the central metropolises. Government in Canada, therefore, must be a delicate balance between reacting well to the desires of the majority who live in Ontario and Quebec and at the same time paying attention to the problems of the other regions. And while the use of regions may be helpful for understanding historical trends and some political phenomena, such as voting behaviour, it is the individual provinces that have emerged as the more relevant objects of study. For it is these provinces' governments that can pursue the policies giving each of them a distinctive existence.

POLITICAL CULTURE

The interaction of physical environment, composition of the population, and type of political institutions have produced a distinctive

Canadian political culture. A political culture includes the beliefs, norms, and values of a society that are important when political decisions are made. An appreciation of this culture helps to understand why things are done in a certain way in Canada and differently elsewhere. Our discussion thus far has shown that political culture in Canada is not homogeneous; rather, there are marked differences in the beliefs, norms, and values held in different regions of the country.

Characteristically, politicians in Canada have been compromisers and accommodators, not folk heroes who arouse memories of historic national events. While Sir John A. Macdonald or Sir Wilfrid Laurier may be widely respected, Canada has no heroic figures with the stature of Abraham Lincoln, General De Gaulle, or Winston Churchill. Canada's history is lacking in traumatic events that by themselves could produce heroes.[14] Rather than becoming national figures, different people at different times have won the adulation of different sections of the country. Louis Riel was a heroic figure for both the Métis people and Quebeckers, and Lord Simcoe was a hero in early Ontario, but neither was a hero in other areas of Canada. The exploits of early French explorers and missionaries, and later British ones, were not used to develop a national myth for political purposes. English-speaking Canada has lived under the cultural influence of two giants for two centuries (Great Britain in the nineteenth and the United States in the twentieth), encouraging a tendency to adopt their heroes rather than Canadian ones. Even the leaders of incipient revolutions in Upper and Lower Canada, Mackenzie and Papineau, had their particular admirers but never became national folk heroes.

Political life has, therefore, been pragmatic, without the romanticism so evident in the development of other states. Moreover, until the passage of the Charter of Rights and Freedoms in 1982, this pragmatic approach had resulted in the absence of historic documents like the Declaration of Independence, the Magna Carta, the Bill of Rights of 1689, or the French Declaration of the Rights of Man. These symbols in other countries are sanctified, and their symbolism is transmitted to schoolchildren, thereby establishing a lasting emotive appeal and effective political socialization. Canada, on the other hand, whose political development has been evolutionary, has lacked the patriotic stimulus that national symbols evoke. In fact, it was not until the 1960s that the force of events, such as the emergence of the "Quiet Revolution,"[15] spurred a concerted effort to discover a Canadian political identity. It is more difficult to transmit political values to the young in a political culture characterized by stability and pragmatic, nonheroic, nonidealistic norms, than in more flamboyant societies, or even staid ones with a longer history. Canada has neither the advantage of ancient origins nor the knack of national breast-beating to make the inculcation of distinctively Canadian political values in her maturing population a relatively easy and natural process. When one adds the constant bombardment of Canadian minds by American ideas and values through the proximity of their communications media, it becomes even more apparent that it is difficult to socialize Canadians politically in an assertively Canadian way.[16] So great is this factor that some Canadians are actually socialized into the political norms of the United States. Small wonder, then, that the problem of establishing a Canadian identity persists more than 130 years after the birth of the country.

Canadian Identity

This issue deserves further discussion, since it has such an impact on Canadian politics. Comparing the socialization of Canadian youth to that in other countries, one sees the difficulties. A pledge of allegiance to the monarch would be meaningless for many and would arouse hostility in others. Canadian youth are not usually purposefully nurtured in the belief that there is a Canadian way of life that is superior to that of other countries (except in Quebec, where the nationalism that is encouraged is Québécois rather than pan-Canadian). Canadians have never lived through an epic era in which they were convinced that they bore the "white man's burden" and that others were "lesser breeds without the law." Whereas youth in the United States are taught that their first president never told a lie, Canadian students can learn that their forebears believed "better John A. Macdonald drunk than George Brown sober."

A nation has been defined, by an anonymous wit, as a group of people living within defined borders who hate their neighbours with the same intensity and believe the same lies about their forefathers. Canadian political socialization has at times been concerned with fomenting dislike for our neighbours (although rarely has the hatred been particularly or uniformly intense throughout the populace). This dislike, however, has almost never been advanced by the construction of a grandiose mythology about the past and the creation of symbols that would buttress that mythology. There is much to admire in the candour that has characterized Canada, but it must be admitted that honesty has its price.

What has just been discussed provides the background for the concern for cultural sovereignty that was so evident in the debate over the Free Trade Agreement with the United States. Even supporters of the agreement had to go out of their way to reassure Canadians that their cultural efforts would not be swamped by the United States. Opponents, however, manifested their fears of just such an outcome.

Canadian political parties mobilize support for their policies and their leader; if they are successful, they become the government of the day. Whereas in the past an appeal to king and country could arouse a good deal of enthusiasm for a particular political party in different sections of Canada, that appeal today would be relatively ineffective. For instance, John Turner's campaign as Liberal leader in the 1988 federal election was a nationalistic crusade against free trade, but in the end he lost decisively. To be national in scope, Canadian political parties have come to depend less and less on symbolic or emotional appeals (for example, defending the Constitution, upholding the Canadian way of life, or ensuring that the sun never sets on the flag of Canada) than on meeting the practical needs of people in diverse areas and regions.

Attitudes toward Authority

There has never been the extreme kind of crisis regarding authority that one finds in some countries where civil wars or other traumatic national events presaged a drastic change in both politics and, eventually, government. Our government was established to uphold the rule of law and has generally been successful in garnering the support of a law-abiding people. This is true despite the serious crises that developed over policies, such as conscription during the two world wars, and serious economic dislocations, such as the Depression of the 1930s. Events of this nature created conditions that sometimes changed the direction of politics. The October Crisis of 1970, which involved the kidnapping of a diplomat and a provincial government minister and the murder of the latter by the FLQ (Front de la Libération du Québec), occasioned a very strong response by the federal government. While some Canadians felt that the government overreacted and was too quick to invade the civil rights of hundreds of citizens, the overwhelming reaction of both English-speaking and French-speaking Canadians was nonetheless in support of the government. Critics.have sometimes chastised Canadians for being too devoted to public order. Most countries, however, have good cause to envy Canada's combination of democracy and political stability.

LEGITIMACY OF THE CENTRAL GOVERNMENT

In varying degrees the central government is recognized as authoritative in all parts of Canada. The social scientist Max Weber[17] described three kinds of legitimacy: charismatic, traditional, and legal. All three types have been detectable in Canada, but their impact has varied with time, place, and region. As has already been noted, Canadian political life has not been distinguished by heroic characters, and therefore charismatic legitimacy has been less evident in English Canada than perhaps it is elsewhere. However, two prime ministers, Diefenbaker and Trudeau, were able to evoke a charismatic response from some of the Canadian electorate, so it is apparent that this kind of legitimacy is possible in Canada. The appeal to the Quebec electorate of René Levesque in the 1970s and of Lucien Bouchard in the 1990s was highly charismatic. However, legitimacy in Quebec before the 1960s was partly based on custom in that the traditional power of the church—rather than its legal power or the charisma of its priest—was the basis of rural French Canada's acceptance of political authority. Legality, however, is the main basis for legitimacy in Canada. Most Canadians accept political authority because it is embodied in laws that ascribe authoritative roles to certain political offices. Although individuals may enhance the authority of these offices by their own personal qualities (charisma), the basic legitimacy of the office is founded on law.

Just one example may suffice to show both the pragmatic nature of the Canadian political process and the dependence on law for legitimacy. W.L. Mackenzie King, who had Canada's longest tenure as prime minister and head of the Liberal Party, was a colourless, cautious, at times even unpopular political operative. His consummate skills at balancing the interests of the country, however, contributed to victory for his party in successive elections. His authority resided solely in his office, and without the powers of that office he would not have been able to find alternative means to make an impact on Canadian political life.

Legitimacy for national politicians, although based on the rule of law, is also affected by Canadian federalism. One of the most important features of evolutionary, parliamentary government in Canada has been the relationship between the provinces and the central government, based upon a written constitution, the Constitution Act, 1867. As the division of authority became more crucial with the increasing importance of government, the balance of authority rested on interpreting the Constitution. Much of the interpretation was done, particularly in the early stages, by the Judicial Committee of the Privy Council in Great Britain, which was in effect the Supreme Court of the British Empire. Supporters of centralized government have criticized that body for interpretations that gave too much authority to the provinces. Canadian diversity, on the other hand, creates strongly contrasting political attitudes about exactly what the central government and provincial governments should do, and so decentralists could applaud those same decisions. But while the courts have interpreted, the contribution to balancing and stabilizing politics and government after World War II was left to the leaders of the provinces and the Dominion, who met to hammer out workable—if at times ad hoc—arrangements. Politicians and their senior officials in Ottawa and in the provinces attached more importance to maintaining Canadian federalism than to the judicial process itself. Meeting, discussing, and settling by compromise have up to this point made Canada a viable, if a sometimes disturbed, country. But these compromises by a small group of federal and provincial leaders, known as *executive federalism*, have been reached with little input from elected legislatures, let alone other Canadians. This has led to widespread mistrust of remote leadership and secret deals, which have alienated much of the Canadian public and called into question the moral and political positions of leaders, if not their legal powers.

CONCLUSIONS

Canada is not a strongly assimilative society in the melting-pot sense of the United States. The origins of the country were New France. When that colony was conquered by the English, there was no concerted, long-term attempt to end the culture of *les habitants* (French Canadian farmers). Although Lord Durham in his famous report recommended assimilation of the French, this was not the outcome of Canadian history.[18] The result has been that what John Porter has called the French and English charter groups have survived. The logic of this process has meant that there has not been an assertive effort to mould later ethnic groups into a preconceived idea of what a Canadian ought to be. It is true that most adopted the language and lifestyle of English Canadians, but they were also free to retain their ethnic identities. Porter argues that this identification has been lamentable, since it has resulted in an uneven distribution of wealth and influence based on ethnicity, and that the English charter group is in a privileged position at the top of a "vertical mosaic." Porter's statistics have been questioned, and his interpretation of their meaning is open to question, since he does not seem to place enough emphasis on when or where later ethnic groups settled nor on the conscious cultural desires of French Canadians that were a major cause of English Canadian dominance. Studies undertaken by the Royal Commission on Bilingualism and Biculturalism in the 1960s showed that French Canadians continued to be less prosperous even after the rural attitudes—which may have accounted for earlier disparities—had changed dramatically. However, with regard to all ethnic groups, there are no definitive studies available in the late 1990s to show whether their relative position has changed.

Canadian society is wealth oriented. While this was less true at one time of French-speaking Canadians, they are now demanding the same economic standards as other Canadians, even while striving to maintain their cultural heritage. Wealth is very much a function of education, and it is in the educational revolution throughout French- and English-speaking Canada that one sees the instrument for breaking down the advantages that have been transmitted through longer-established generations of British Canadians. British-oriented standards and the symbolism of previous years that gave a greater place to tradition have been supplanted by more materialistic economic standards. Any changes that occur in the relative economic positions of Canadians of different ethnic backgrounds will have their effect on politics. As long as wealth is a standard and access to wealth is not denied to any ethnic group by legal or other means, a tendency toward political power commensurate with the numbers of an ethnic group should be apparent.

The foregoing, however, does not mean that the elimination of economic distress in Quebec will lead to the automatic demise of the Parti Québécois. The nationalist pressures, especially in the area of language, are such that constitutional change of some type will be sought by any Quebec government, regardless of the facts that the sovereignty-association concept of René Lévesque was defeated in the referendum of 1980 and that independence was narrowly rejected in the referendum of 1995.

RECOMMENDED READING

Dyck, Rand. *Provincial Politics in Canada*, 3rd ed. Scarborough: Prentice-Hall, 1996.

Kilgour, David. *Inside Outer Canada*. Edmonton: Lone Pine Publishers, 1990.

McRoberts, K. *Quebec, Social Change and Political Crisis*, 3rd ed. Toronto: McClelland and Stewart, 1993.

Savoie, Donald J. *Regional Economic Development, Canada's Search for Solutions*, 2nd ed. Toronto: University of Toronto Press, 1992.

Whittington, M., and G. Williams, eds. *Canadian Politics in the 1990s*, 4th ed. Toronto: Nelson Canada, 1995.

PART 2

THE CONSTITUTIONAL FRAMEWORK: A RESPONSE TO DIVERSITY

CHAPTER 2

The Constitution

THE WRITTEN DOCUMENTS

The written constitutions of states throughout the world vary considerably. Some are long and detailed; others are short and general. Some are written in beautiful prose, others are businesslike, legalistic documents. The Constitution Act, 1867, like most British-inspired constitutions, is a relatively short, legalistic document, lacking in high-sounding phrasing, that outlines the general rules by which government is to be conducted in Canada. The Constitution of Canada now includes the Constitution Act, 1982 with the Canadian Charter of Rights and Freedoms. If the prose of that document is not likely to inspire Canadians, the freedoms contained within it should.

It is important to recognize immediately, however, that the Constitution Act of 1867 or 1982 does not encompass all of what can be called the Canadian Constitution or constitutional practice. The preamble of the original Act states that Canada is to have "a Constitution similar in principle to that of the United Kingdom." The British Constitution, however, is not embodied in a single document; it is a combination of important laws and practices that have been accumulated through hundreds of years and have thus acquired the sanctity of fundamental law. Consequently, the Magna Carta, the Habeas Corpus Act, and the Bill of Rights of 1689 have all become part of the Canadian Constitution by inheritance (though similar principles are now entrenched in the Charter of Rights and Freedoms), as has the whole tradition of common law in our legal system. In addition, the nature of the relationship between the executive and legislative branches of government has evolved over years of practice, and the concept of responsible government, which is at the core of our constitutional system, is no less valid because it is not explained in detail in the Constitution.

Not all the constitutional practice is inherited from Great Britain. Unwritten and powerful indigenous conventions have been added to our system of government through the evolution of responsible government in Canada within the federal system.[1] In addition, certain written laws have become constitutional in effect and must be regarded as more fundamental than ordinary laws. These are called organic laws, and, while they are passed as ordinary legislation, their subject matter is such that they cannot easily be altered once they are established. The Supreme Court Act of 1875 and the Bill of Rights of 1960 are examples of organic laws. By the Constitution Act, 1982, however, the composition of the Supreme Court is subject to the amendment provisions established under the Act, and the rights embodied in the 1960 Act, which only applied to the federal government, have been entrenched and now apply to both federal and provincial jurisdictions.

The Constitution Act, 1867 originally had 147 sections divided under 11 headings.[2] Some of the provisions, while crucial to the original bargain that created the union, have little or no relevance today, like the intercolonial railway provision and the original subsidies and payments to the provinces. More important are the parts of the Act that provide for the union of the colonies, federal executive power, federal legislative power, provincial constitutions, distribution of legislative powers between the federal and provincial governments, and judicial powers. Three major branches of government are thus established. The executive branch administers (executes) laws, which have been passed (legislated) by the legislative branch (Parliament) and may be interpreted (judged) by the judicial branch.

Canada's Constitution initially reflected its colonial status and did, in fact, facilitate the merging of three colonies into one. The united colonies patterned their constitution on the British model and established ground rules under which independence could evolve. Devising a system that would unite the diverse colonies and cultures, and at the same time would provide a basic framework to maintain their separate identities, was a difficult task for the politicians of British North America.[3] The fundamental political issues in the merging of the colonies were the relationship that had to be established between the French- and English-speaking peoples, and the division of powers between the federal government and the provincial governments. In the 1990s these issues remain crucial, but they now have to share the constitutional debate with concern for aboriginal self-government, maintenance of individual rights and freedoms, and reform of institutions such as the Senate and the Supreme Court.

Prior to Confederation, the one consistent theme that had developed from the time of the English conquest of Quebec in 1759 was the fact that definitive laws had been established for the two groups;[4] however, when the Canadas were joined under the Act of Union of 1840, there were two distinct groups—English and French—subject to one government.[5] Hopeless deadlock ensued, and union with New Brunswick, Nova Scotia, Prince Edward Island, and Newfoundland was sought as a solution to the problem. From the beginning of negotiations, it became apparent that Canada East and Canada West would escape from their political dilemma.

Post-Confederation Problems

Two contradictory constitutional principles had to be embodied in a federal constitution for the British North American colonies. First, the essence of British constitutionalism was its evolutionary and rather imprecise nature. Constitutional change in Great Britain was often the result of social upheavals that challenged rigid but outworn constitutional principles. The Bill of Rights of 1689, the Act of Succession of 1702, and the Reform Act of 1832 were all passed by Parliament to settle pressing political unrest. Parliament was able to do this since it alone was supreme. Second, but in contrast to this evolutionary process, Canada's federal constitution had to be more precise. Politicians realized there had to be two governments affecting the same people: a federal or central government, and a provincial or local government. They sought to establish a united economic and defence unit run by a central government while maintaining a number of diverse social and cultural units run by provincial governments. It was also necessary to include written guarantees beyond those which created provincial governments (including Quebec), to protect both the minority French cultural values (particularly religion and language) and Quebec's English minority.

The Constitution provided for a central government with a range of responsibilities that were considered to be important for the country as a whole, and for provincial governments whose responsibilities were assumed to be strictly local in nature. Each order of government was to be autonomous with regard to the legislative powers that were defined and distributed in the Constitution.[6] Each of these governments was based on the notion of parliamentary supremacy and the responsibility of the Cabinets to the legislature. However, as the relationships between the federal and provincial governments have become ever more widespread and complex, the need for negotiations between the federal and provincial leaders has created greater and greater difficulties for the legislatures to exercise their roles. Thus, contemporary analysts have raised serious questions about the compatibility of the British parliamentary system with Canadian federal practices.

Not only were there compromises made to attract the constituent units federating in Canada, but new relationships between the colonies and the imperial authority also had to be worked out. Responsible government in domestic matters had been granted to all the colonies individually, but now one confederate colony was to represent the interests of all British North America, especially in matters that might affect the British Empire. This was particularly important in Canada because of its proximity to the United States. In the years after 1867, Canadian interests with foreign countries, especially the United States, often differed from those of the British imperial authorities. Over the years Canada became more insistent that attention be paid to Canadian interests, and this ultimately, though gradually, resulted in an international recognition of Canada as a sovereign state.[7]

The 1867 Act left many questions unsettled. A process of amendment was one of these. It was assumed that there would be resort to Great Britain. Federalism was seen as a necessary evil in any case, and some leading Fathers of Confederation hoped it would fade into a centralized form. Hence, a normally important component of a federal plan, the provision for regional expression of interest through a regional upper house, the Senate, was never adequately developed. Over time the provincial governments have become the articulators of regional interests and have, to some extent, intensified the regionalism inherent in the diverse Canadian society. This problem has, of course, been greatly magnified by the tendency of governments at all levels to intervene actively in the lives of Canadians.

DEFINITIVENESS

It is important to contrast precise definition with understood convention in dealing with the Constitution. Some elements of the Constitution resulted from intense negotiation and hence required precise definition; other provisions incorporated certain customs or conventions that were unquestioned, and further clarification was not considered necessary.

A new concept like federalism, since it was foreign to the principles of British constitutionalism, had to be explicitly stated. Those who drafted the Canadian Constitution knew that they had to be definite on what would be the "Canadian" content. They insisted that the legislatures for the new central and provincial governments had to be defined precisely; the need to define jurisdictions was even greater. This had never been a problem in the United Kingdom, which had a unitary system (one level of government with undivided constitutional jurisdiction) and therefore one supreme legislature at Westminster.

Judicial Responsibilities

There was a provision for a judiciary to settle disputes between governments, as well as to dispense justice to individuals, either in their relations with the state or with each other. The central government was therefore permitted, but not required, to establish a supreme court for Canada, as well as to appoint judges to a system of courts within the provinces. However, Quebec civil law was different from the civil law of the other colonies, so only judges from that tradition were to sit on the Quebec Bench. The provinces themselves were to appoint judges to lower provincial courts, which would handle much of the judicial business of Canada. The proposals of the Meech Lake Accord of 1987, repeated in the Charlottetown Accord of 1992, were to entrench the right of Quebec to have three members of its bar on the Supreme Court and to give Quebec and the other provinces the right to submit lists of nominees to the Court from which the federal government would choose new justices. Since these proposals were rejected, the Supreme Court Act still applies. It provides for three Quebec judges on the Supreme Court, but the prime minister retains the power to appoint without provincial input.

Quebec differed not only in civil law but also in language and religion. Consequently, its representatives secured specific sections in the Constitution that protected the right of French-speaking Canadians to use their language in the courts and in the federal Parliament and to have Catholic schools in French-speaking areas.[8] Sections 16 to 22 of the Constitution Act, 1982 entrenched both French and English as the official languages of Canada and the province of New Brunswick. Section 23 ensured minority language educational rights in situations where numbers warranted. Both 1987 and 1992 proposals that Quebec was to be recognized as a distinct society and that its government was to act so as to preserve that distinct society were central but controversial elements in constitutional agreements that failed to be ratified.

Financial/Economic Responsibilities

Another area that required precision concerned the financial relations between the federal and provincial governments. All of Part VIII (24 sections) of the Constitution Act, 1867 concerned revenues, debts, assets, and taxation. It was hoped that when the union became a reality, the written constitution would be particularly clear in relation to the taxing power of each jurisdiction. However, it became evident after Confederation that clarity in jurisdiction was hard to achieve and financial balance between governments even more difficult. The Atlantic premiers began to agitate for so-called better terms. It is understandable that the politicians concerned could not foresee the gradual extension of government and the financial implications that this would have. Prior to the twentieth century, overlap in jurisdiction between the federal and provincial governments did not create serious problems, because governments at all levels were less involved with people's lives.

The laissez-faire idea that a free enterprise competitive economy was self-regulating made it quite reasonable to look upon the nonintervention of the state as essential. Intervention was necessary only to counteract those forces that would hinder the free play of competition, or to provide other forms of protection against dangers—domestic (criminals) or foreign (enemies). The image of the night watchman conveys this idea of state that is outside the economic process, yet related to it by ensuring its unhindered operations. The assumption, therefore, that financial arrangements between the federal and provincial governments could be conclusive was a natural misjudgement at the time. Federalism, particularly in the context of a British parliamentary constitution, was a new experiment. Other federations existed—the United States being the prime example, but it had departed from the parliamentary form in establishing its government.

The Federal System

The Fathers of Confederation were convinced that the colonies could successfully unite only under a federal form of government (although many would have preferred a unitary form). The Constitution had to be definite about this, and it was written to provide for a highly centralized federal system in which the central government had the most important powers. Moreover, the Constitution Act of 1867 departed from classic federal principles by giving the central government the power to intervene in provincial matters through the use of the powers of *reservation* and *disallowance*. These powers, provided for in Section 90 of the Act, allowed the lieutenant governor, a central government appointee, to withhold royal assent for a provincial act pending review of that measure by the government in Ottawa, which could in fact decide to disallow it. These powers ceased to be exercised with any regularity almost a century ago, and now—while they remain in the text of the Constitution—the likelihood of their use is remote. The comments of a newly appointed lieutenant governor of Quebec in 1996, however, did arouse some speculation about whether he would exercise his power to strike down legislation for the secession of Quebec from Canada.

The centralist intentions have been consistently eroded as the provinces have attained competent leadership and political maturity and as the matters over which they have jurisdiction have grown in importance as Canadian society has changed. Whereas the writers of the Constitution assumed that they had created (on paper) a powerful central government and that authority would radiate out from the centre, the political history of Canada since 1867 shows that only during the very early period after Confederation, in wartime, and during the transitional period following World War II has this been true. Yet despite the miscalculation, federalism has proved to be an extremely hardy and flexible arrangement.

The less definitive parts of the Constitution deal with responsible government. Reading the Constitution, it would appear that the governor general (representing the Crown) is the most powerful figure in Canadian government. The position is described and its authority is clearly stated (see Constitution Act, 1867, Part III, Sections 9 to 15). What is not stated, however, is that the governor general may act only on the advice of the government of the day. This follows directly from British practice, where privy councillors advise the Crown. As the representative of the Crown in Canada, the governor general must act on the advice of the Canadian Privy Council, whatever his or her personal opinions might be. However, the position does have a theoretical residue of power (called prerogative power): the governor general may act if at any time the Constitution of the country appears in danger of being undermined. It is conceivable that if any government attempted to seize power unconstitutionally, the governor general could attempt to be a rallying point for those who supported the Constitution.[9]

To understand the system of government in Canada fully, it is clear that more than a knowledge of the written Constitution is necessary. The governor general does not govern Canada but acts on the advice of the privy councillors. For the most part, these are politicians who at one time or another have been elected to the federal Parliament, but at any given time only some of them are in a position to tender advice to the governor general. Only a select group of those elected will become advisors, and of these one is preeminent. This person is the prime minister, whose powers are not described in the Constitution, yet who is the most important governmental official and political personality in Canada. The prime minister is the leader of a political party and is instrumental in getting support for that party during an election. The leader and the party must be successful in winning a majority of seats in the House of Commons (or if not a majority, enough to form a majority with the support of other parties). The governor general, by convention, must then ask this particular political leader to form a government. The prime minister chooses from among the party's Members of Parliament a number of individuals who are to be sworn in as privy councillors. This group of advisors is known as the Cabinet, again a term that does not appear in the Constitution. It should be remembered that political loyalties shift, and a strong and accepted political leader may lose the confidence of the electorate. If this happens, and in an ensuing election a new political leader is endorsed by the people, that person then becomes the prime advisor to the governor general and brings along a new set of advisors. Even though the first set of advisors suffers electoral defeat, they still remain privy councillors for life, but they lose the right to advise the governor general. The Cabinet, then, is in effect that group of privy councillors who are actively engaged in operating the government. None of this is mentioned in the Constitution, but the form had been customary in the colonies prior to Confederation and was assumed thereafter.

TABLE 2.1
DIVISION OF LEGISLATIVE POWER

The Parliament of Canada	The Legislature of the Provinces
PEACE, ORDER, AND GOOD GOVERNMENT: A general power that courts restricted to an emergency power by narrow interpretation.	MATTERS OF A MERELY LOCAL OR PRIVATE NATURE: A general power but indicative of the limited role of the provinces envisioned in 1867.
THE RAISING OF MONEY BY ANY MEANS OF TAXATION: No limits on taxing powers or restrictions on how the revenue is spent.	DIRECT TAXATION FOR PROVINCIAL PURPOSES: Limited to a specific type of tax and only to be used for provincial purposes.
TRADE AND COMMERCE: Not restricted by the phrase "interprovincial." The national government was to foster a national economy.	INCORPORATION OF COMPANIES WITH PROVINCIAL OBJECTS: Responsibility for local economic regulations only.
TRANSPORTATION AND COMMUNICATION: For example, navigation and shipping, postal services, etc.	LOCAL WORKS AND UNDERTAKINGS: Except if Parliament declares otherwise.
REGULATIONS OF THE ECONOMIC AND FINANCIAL STRUCTURE: For example, currency, banking, interest rates, patents, copyrights, weights, and measures.	PROPERTY AND CIVIL RIGHTS: Later interpreted broadly by the courts.
UNEMPLOYMENT INSURANCE (BY A 1940 AMENDMENT): Old age pensions (Section 94A by a 1964 amendment), aboriginal peoples and their lands.	MANAGEMENT OF PUBLIC LANDS IN THE PROVINCE AND OF NATURAL RESOURCES: Section 92A in 1982 added to provincial authority over resources.
THE MILITARY	HEALTH AND WELFARE
CRIMINAL LAW	MUNICIPALITIES
MISCELLANEOUS (to a total of 29 powers in Section 91)	CIVIL LAW AND THE ADMINISTRATION OF JUSTICE
	EDUCATION (Section 93)
	MISCELLANEOUS (to a total of 16 powers in Section 92)

Note: Agriculture and immigration are joint responsibilities (Section 95).

A similar system prevails in each of the provinces. Here the office of *lieutenant governor* mirrors that of governor general; the lieutenant governor is in a sense a head of state for the province. He or she is appointed by the federal government and initially was meant to exercise a restraining influence on the provinces. The growth of the power of the provinces, however, has subverted that purpose, and the position is now largely ceremonial. Thus, the parliamentary system in the provinces, as in Ottawa, is dominated by the premiers and their Cabinets. Contrary to the intentions of the Fathers of Confederation, these provincial leaders now exercise powers that have a tremendous impact on their citizens, perhaps even a larger impact than does the central government itself.

THE DIVISION OF POWERS

The division of powers between the federal and provincial governments is an area that is crucial. Sections 91 and 92 of the Constitution Act, 1867 address this question, though not exclusively. In Section 91, the federal legislature is granted authority to legislate over issues such as postal services, public debt, regulation of trade and commerce, defence, shipping, banking, copyright, and criminal law. These powers were granted to the federal government because it was believed that they were of prime importance in building a new country. In Section 92 most local responsibilities, such as local works, municipal institutions, hospitals, and civil and property rights, are granted to the provinces. Control over education was given to the provinces in Section 93, with the federal government being given powers to intervene on behalf of religious minorities should their rights to separate education be violated. Thus, the federal government was given the authority to create a viable economic unit, while the provinces were given authority over the instruments by which they could protect their local and cultural interests. The federal government, moreover, was given unrestricted taxing powers and was not limited in its authority to spend for any purpose (*the spending power*). Beyond that, it could disallow provincial legislation and declare local works to be of national significance and thus take them over. Clearly, the original Constitution meant to give the central government the last word.

Inevitably, the jurisdictional boundaries between federal and provincial governments were blurred, and there had to be some method to determine the exact boundaries. The Constitution Act, 1867 therefore provided for a system of courts patterned after the British model. This meant the adoption of a unitary system of courts composed of one hierarchy rather than a dual system (state and federal) as in the United States. It also followed the British model closely in that it was based on the common-law tradition of precedent. The term *stare decisis*, which might be translated as "let the decision stand," is therefore vital in the Canadian judicial process. Superior court judges and those of county and district courts were to be appointed by the governor general on the advice of the prime minister, and their salaries set and paid by Parliament. The provinces were to be responsible for the "Constitution, Maintenance and Organization of Provincial Courts" and to administer the justice system in the provinces. Section 101 also permitted, but did not require, the establishment of a General Court of Appeal, or Supreme Court. Such a court was founded in 1875, but until 1949 there could still be appeals on constitutional matters to the highest court in what was then the British Empire: the *Judicial Committee of the Privy Council* of the United Kingdom. Thus, the Supreme Court was supreme in name only, as the Judicial Committee of the Privy Council made most crucial final judgements. The concept of *parliamentary supremacy* contributed to a tradition of a nonactivist Supreme Court, which meant that political settlements, especially on constitutional matters, tended to be dealt with politically at such meetings as federal/provincial conferences and other negotiations, rather than by judicial decisions. However, since 1982 the Charter of Rights and Freedoms has expanded the role of the Supreme Court in matters other than the division of power.

In the last half of the twentieth century, political rapport between governments has depended far more on the ability of the prime minister and his associates to negotiate with the premiers and their advisors in various provinces than on constitutional provisions. Although the original intention was to create a powerful central government, as was implied in the written Constitution, political events—often triggered by linguistic and regional differences—have led to more decentralized government. Despite an attempt to be precise in some clauses of the original Constitution, especially those relating to federal-provincial relations, these provisions have not been nearly as authoritative as intended. Canadian political leaders, as stressed in Chapter 1, tended to adopt a pragmatic approach to politics that stretched the meaning of even the most specific sections of the written Constitution.

GUARANTEES

Up to now, our main concern in examining the Constitution has been to consider the relevance of the various sections to the actualities of politics and government. A somewhat different problem in modern political communities concerns the means by which the rights of minorities and individuals are guarded.

Language and Religious Rights of Communities

By 1867 there was generally high respect for the protection afforded both minority groups and individuals by the British court system. This was certainly the primary reason for omitting any fundamental exposition of individual rights from the Constitution. In Canada the existence of a cohesive and strong French-speaking minority—which in 1871 numbered 1 100 000 out of a total population of approximately 3 500 000—necessitated some concern for minority rights. Although population figures themselves do not reveal the political significance of any particular group, the French minority had a status as the original European settlers. By the 1980s the rights of the aboriginal people had become a major constitutional question as well.

In meeting the demands of the French minority for protection, the Constitution includes a section on education that guaranteed the right of Roman Catholics to be educated in separate schools in Ontario, while the Protestants were given similar rights in Quebec. Section 93 also makes provision for guarantees to other minority religions that could be granted rights by the provinces. If these rights, once granted, are disregarded by the provinces, recourse can be made by appeal to the governor general in Council—that is, to the federal prime minister and his Cabinet. The provision for an appeal has been invoked only once—during the Manitoba schools question of the 1890s. The Laurier government of 1896 ultimately refused to intervene, and it is questionable whether that clause has much contemporary relevance. Obviously, since the vast majority of French-speaking Canadians were Roman Catholics, any guarantee of rights to that religious group was also a guarantee of rights for the ethnic group. In addition, the Constitution provides for the use of French in the federal Parliament and the courts of Canada.

In 1969 the federal government passed the Official Languages Act. Among other things, this Act provides for bilingual districts where the population of a minority French- or English-speaking group is at least 10% and guarantees bilingual services of federal agencies in these districts. It also provides for an official languages commissioner. In December 1979 the Supreme Court ruled that an act passed in Manitoba in 1890 and sections of Quebec Bill 101 violated the linguistic guarantees of Section 133 of the Constitution. These developments contributed to the initiative to include linguistic guarantees in the Charter of Rights and Freedoms of 1982. Furthermore, the Manitoba government in 1983–84 attempted to settle the question within the province in order to preclude a decision by the Supreme Court.

The fact that disputes concerning denominational education were intended ultimately to be settled by the prime minister and his Cabinet (the governor general in Council), all of whom are politicians of the first order, showed that political settlements were to have preeminence over judicial settlements in the Canadian political system. Accordingly, the hypothesis could be advanced that, by leaving the way open for political discussion and settlement of impending constitutional strains, there is more flexibility in constitutional development. Court decisions have a certain finality that could over time alienate certain sections of the community. Political decisions, however, seem more open to compromise that, although perhaps less than fully satisfactory to opposing factions, may cool off the situation and lessen the possibility of complete alienation of any particular group. Unfortunately, the spirit of compromise was not prominent in the controversy over the Quebec sign law in 1988, which was perceived by many as a conflict between individual rights (asserted by anglophone businesses) and collective rights (the defence of Quebec society), in which there was no middle ground.

Although the Constitution Act, 1867 specifically guaranteed certain rights to ethnic and religious groups, it did not contain a bill of rights or entrenched clauses that protected individuals from the actions of government. In fact, there is no mention of civil rights as such, except that in Section 92(13) the provinces were given control over "Property and Civil Rights in the Province." In the context of 1867, this undoubtedly referred to the provinces' "control over private law matters, such as contract, tort, property wills, and mortgages."[10] This interpretation is buttressed by Section 94 of the Act, in which the Parliament of Canada may make provision for the uniformity of all or any of the laws relative to property and civil rights in Ontario, Nova Scotia, and New Brunswick. This is an obvious indication that the legalists who drafted the Constitution undoubtedly equated property and civil rights with private property law, and not with a wider definition of civil rights.

Rather than a highly idealistic proclamation of individual rights, such as existed in the constitutions of the United States and France—both of which had experienced turbulent political crises in the period 1800–67, the politicians in Canada trusted British constitutional practice. However, this traditional basis for protecting rights was considered inadequate by the federal government under Prime Minister Trudeau from 1968 on. Many Canadians who were concerned with civil liberties shared this view and were easily swayed to support a Charter of Rights and Freedoms that would explicitly protect Canadians. Some critics, however, including provincial premiers, recognized that the adoption of an entrenched set of civil rights did indeed have implications for the principle of parliamentary supremacy. It would transfer some degree of power from the elected representatives to the nonelected judiciary.

In the Constitution Act, 1982, a variety of fundamental rights and freedoms were entrenched for Canadians. These include freedom of conscience and religion; freedom of thought, belief, opinion, and expression, including freedom of the press and other media of communication; freedom of peaceful assembly; and freedom of association. In addition, democratic rights, mobility rights, legal rights, equality rights, linguistic and minority education rights (as mentioned above), as well as aboriginal rights and an explicit statement on sexual equality were included. To allay the fears of provincial premiers, a "notwithstanding clause" was inserted allowing legislatures to override guaranteed rights (but only those in Section 2 and Sections 7–15 of the Charter) where they felt that the public interest could be better served by such legislation. Laws passed in this manner, however, would lapse after five years, unless they were passed again. The last years of the twentieth century will bear witness to how the courts will exercise their powers of interpretation and the degree to which parliamentary supremacy will be restricted.

Although Canada's record in respecting individual rights has been relatively good, in some quarters there is deep concern that Canadians are being overgoverned at the expense of the individual for the benefit of the whole. Parliamentary supremacy has worked well in theory, but many constitutional theorists expressed concern that the expansion of government activity results in a huge bureaucracy that can threaten individual rights and constitutional order.[11] A healthy constitutional order should provide enough avenues to question authority so that authority is considerate of the rights of all citizens, and not only the legislative will of the majority and of the bureaucrats representing authority. When this delicate balance is destroyed, order is often sought as an end in itself rather than as a condition for social good, including individual rights.

Not only lawyers but also many other groups of Canadians have become concerned over the shift in rule making from the elected legislature to the Cabinet and senior public servants. At this point one might well question the ability of the Constitution to remain effective at the dawn of the twenty-first century. The emergence of the administrative state stems from popular demands on government to use its collective authority to protect those in society who are, because of conditions beyond their control, unable to protect themselves, and to regulate a complex economy. With the growth in the size of industrial units, continuing poverty in regions of Canada, cyclical, depressed economic conditions, and pollution of air and water, people have turned to the government to intervene on their behalf. Technological change has further complicated both the roles of the individual and of government. Both freedom of information and the right to privacy are modern problems resulting from these changes. Over time more and more Canadians have become concerned with the degree to which governments, federal and provincial, while acting on their behalf might also limit their freedom. The means of control the government adopts should reflect the attitudes and principles of those they govern. These attitudes and principles should find expression in the Constitution that governs the country.

PROTECTING PARLIAMENTARY GOVERNMENT

As the duties of the state toward the citizens increased, many additions were made to governmental machinery. Many decisions that formerly could be made by Parliament were shifted at first to the Cabinet and later, as responsibilities grew, to agencies created by either Cabinet or Parliament. Furthermore, judicial decisions had to be made affecting individuals; as the courts did not have the expertise or personnel to hear such cases, to an increasing extent such decisions have been made by quasi-judicial bodies such as tribunals. Nonetheless, Parliament itself under the Constitution still ultimately wields the power to legislate, and the Cabinet must retain the confidence of the House of Commons to govern. This provides a basic protection against authoritarian government. The recognition that the opposition must play a fundamental role in debating issues in the House is testimony to this function of Parliament. Procedures have been incorporated in the rules of the House of Commons to ensure that the conventional constitutional provision for an opposition is enforced. The effective use of parliamentary procedure to forestall even a majority government was evident on numerous occasions in the 1980s. Another protection contained in the Constitution Act, 1867 (Section 53) requires that all money bills, either to spend or tax, have to be introduced through the House of Commons. Theoretically at least, this constitutes Parliament's ability to check the executive, and in periods of minority government theory can become practice—as Joe Clark learned in 1979.

The nature of our political system, however, as opposed to the constitutional system, is such that the executive exercises more actual power than Parliament. Thus, a situation that bothers many Canadians has developed, in which powerful boards, commissions, and other executive agencies, only nominally responsible to Parliament, have been established in an almost haphazard fashion. A former *auditor general* (the official responsible to Parliament for auditing public expenditures) decried the degree to which many Crown corporations seem to be beyond the reach of Parliament. From the 1960s on, there were various studies to see how effective control by Parliament might be reestablished by reorganizing the executive and streamlining rules in the House.[12] The ability of parliaments to act at both the federal and provincial levels as the guardians of collective and individual rights is crucial to the maintenance of a society that seeks to prevent inordinate power falling into too few hands. The courts may be a supplement to Parliament in this respect, but they cannot be a substitute for it.

Equally as important as protection against the concentration of governmental power is the protection of individual rights from violation by government and other individuals. The principle of parliamentary supremacy historically provided that, within their delegated spheres of jurisdiction, the federal and provincial legislatures could pass such acts as they considered proper—even if those laws contradicted some principles of civil rights that existed by convention. In practice, the courts (before 1982) were limited in their power to prevent injustices to individuals: since specific written legislation overruled convention, the courts were constrained in their ability to maintain traditional civil rights. On some occasions courts could interpret the division of powers to prevent abuses of civil rights. Nevertheless, until 1982 the courts were more likely to uphold any law considered to fall within the jurisdiction of the legislature that passed it, regardless of that law's effect on traditional civil rights embodied in the common-law tradition.

The written Federal Bill of Rights passed by the Diefenbaker government in 1960 did give the courts some leeway to judge the contents of federal laws. While this represented progress in the protection of rights, in the opinion of many it did not go far enough, especially since the Federal Bill of Rights could only be used to challenge federal legislation. Canadians had traditionally relied on political sensitivity, both federally and provincially, to ensure protection of individuals. But while governments can guarantee rights, it is also possible that they may disregard them. There was, therefore, from 1968 onward a growing pressure to have a bill of rights entrenched in a revised Canadian Constitution. In the federal-provincial constitutional conference held in January of 1968, then–prime minister Lester Pearson, on the advice of his minister of justice, Pierre Trudeau, contended that a bill of rights should be entrenched in the Constitution. This would encourage a more activist role for courts and limit parliamentary supremacy in the area of civil rights. The appointment of Chief Justice Bora Laskin in 1973 heralded for some the likelihood of a more activist Supreme Court. One must keep in mind, however, that an activist court runs counter to the doctrine of parliamentary supremacy, which is a key principle of Canadian practice. The practice of judicial restraint that has characterized the Canadian courts is testimony to the respect that Canadian jurists have had for parliamentary supremacy—and may still characterize the Canadian judiciary even with the 1982 Charter of Rights and Freedoms. Section 1 of the Charter states that the rights and freedoms set out in the Charter are guaranteed *subject only to such reasonable limits prescribed by law as can be demonstrably justified in a free and democratic society*. This phrase provides courts with a basis to accept a law even when it does violate a right or freedom.

CONSTITUTIONAL DYNAMICS

Amending the Constitution

A long-standing criticism of the Constitution Act, 1867 was its lack of an amendment procedure. Until 1949 any amendment to the Constitution, except for the provincial constitutions, had to be passed by the British Parliament after an address by both Houses of Parliament in Canada. After 1949 amendments to the Constitution Act, 1867 that affected only certain federal powers could be passed by the federal Parliament itself. For example, Section 99 was amended in 1960, providing for the retirement of Supreme Court judges at the age of 75, and in 1965 Section 29 was amended to retire senators at the age of 75. Amendments by the British Parliament had to be requested by Canada. If any changes to the federal system itself were desired, the federal government could not, it was thought, act unilaterally; consultation with the province or provinces concerned was customary.

The Canadian convention that assumed federal-provincial agreement was necessary before seeking to have Britain amend the British North America Act, 1867 did not prevent some amendments. In 1940, for instance, responsibility for unemployment insurance was given to the federal government. While constitutions are not expected to be changed frequently, the Canadian situation was more rigid than would have been the case if constitutional change had depended simply on a provision established by the Constitution itself.[13] Yet for over 50 years, Canadians attempted to find a written formula for amendment, thus "patriating" the Constitution (bringing it home) and ending an embarrassing carryover from Canada's colonial past. In 1964 what became known as the Fulton-Favreau Formula was almost adopted. That formula tried to balance federal and provincial parliaments by requiring that some amendments would need the consent of all legislatures, others a percentage of the provinces plus the federal parliament, while still others would need only federal parliamentary approval or the approval only of a single affected province. Quebec withheld its consent to the formula.[14]

In February 1971 the prime minister and provincial premiers reached a tentative agreement on an amendment procedure that would allow patriation of the Constitution. At a subsequent federal-provincial conference in June 1971 at Victoria, BC, a Constitutional Charter was worked out; the conference set a time limit of June 28 for approval of all provincial governments. On June 23, despite his earlier agreement in principle, Premier Bourassa of Quebec, upon encountering intense Quebec nationalist pressure, turned down the proposal.

From the 1970s right into the 1990s, constitutional reform remained an almost continuous subject of debate for Canadian political leaders.

The federal government continued to be concerned primarily with an amendment process and patriation; indeed, in 1975 Trudeau threatened unilateral action if the provinces did not come to an agreement. The provinces, however, tended to adopt Quebec's position that substantive changes in their jurisdictions and those of the federal government were what really had to be achieved.

After the sovereignty association proposal was defeated in Quebec in May 1980, the search for a renewed federalism was pursued in a round of federal-provincial negotiations cochaired by Jean Chrétien, federal minister of justice, and Roy Romanow, Saskatchewan's attorney general. These meetings, held successively in Toronto, Vancouver, and Ottawa from June through August 1980, were to prepare the way for a September meeting of first ministers. Twelve issues were up for discussion: 1) a statement of principles to be included in the Constitution; 2) the patriation of the Constitution with an amending formula; 3) a charter of rights; 4) the Supreme Court; 5) a new Upper House to replace the Senate; 6) the principle of equalization; 7) the ownership of offshore resources; 8) control-of-resource policy; 9) powers of the economy to maintain an economic union; 10) family law; 11) fisheries; and 12) communications.[15]

The summer meetings demonstrated that the federal government and the various provinces, which had formed a common front (sometimes called the "gang of eight"), had different ideas about which items were most important and how each item could best be resolved. The federal government was intent on patriating the Constitution along with a means to amend it, enshrining within it a charter of rights, reforming federal institutions, and preserving federal power to affect the economy. Alberta led the provinces over control-of-resource policies; Newfoundland was adamant over its demand for ownership of offshore resources and control of fisheries; Quebec insisted on maintaining all powers necessary to pursue its linguistic and economic policies. Of all the provinces, only Ontario and New Brunswick sided with the federal government.

The failure of the first ministers to reach a unanimous agreement in their week of meetings in September 1980 was hardly surprising, considering the circumstances. The federal government stated that it could only go so far in terms of transferring powers to the provinces, while the provinces were intent on acquiring even greater powers than the decentralizing trends of recent decades had given them.

On the premise that the federal government had an obligation to secure certain objectives for the people of Canada, the Trudeau government resorted to unilateral action. It recalled Parliament and laid before it a resolution. It called for patriation with the amendment formula embodied in the Victoria Charter of 1971, including the proviso that the formula could be altered if the provinces provided an alternative within two years and that alternative was accepted by a referendum. The proposed use of referenda to break constitutional deadlocks especially angered many provinces. The resolution provided as well for a charter of rights, modified somewhat from its original form in light of the objections of some provinces. Finally, it called for the entrenchment of the principle of equalization. A parliamentary committee was commissioned to study the resolution and to report back by December 9, 1980.

The reaction of the provinces was predictably hostile, and many threatened court action to challenge the legality of the federal unilateral initiative. The bill—the Canada Act—was referred to the Supreme Court of Canada for a judgement on its constitutionality. In September 1981, by a seven to two decision, the Supreme Court ruled that the federal government was acting legally in its constitutional resolution aimed at patriating the British North America Act. It added, however, that there was an existing tradition that provincial consent was required to take such an action. In short, the resolution was legal but not conventional.

The decision prompted a final effort by the federal government to establish a substantial consensus with the provinces. In the first phase, a solid phalanx of provincial premiers was aligned against the federal government's position. The key issues concerned were the amending formula and the Charter of Rights. During this phase both Ontario and Quebec renounced their traditional veto over any constitutional change, an act that Premier Lévesque was no doubt to regret at a subsequent stage. In the second and final stage, a substantial consensus was achieved (in November 1981) between nine of the premiers and the prime minister, with only Quebec dissenting. The accord included the so-called Vancouver formula for amending the Constitution and the Charter of Rights.

The provincial concern for a major revision of the distribution of powers was not satisfied by the Constitution Act, 1982; thus, any further amendments would have to be accomplished on the basis of the amendment procedure agreed upon. In the final analysis, that procedure was closer to the wishes of the provinces than to that of the federal government, which accepted it as part of the ultimate compromise. Based on an original proposal by the Alberta government, the procedure calls for the agreement of the Parliament of Canada and the legislative assemblies of at least two-thirds of the provinces, representing 50% of the population. However, provinces that dissent are free to opt out of its provisions—rather a unique provision reflecting the decentralized nature of the Canadian federation. Some provisions still require unanimity for amendment. The Meech Lake Accord proposed to expand the list of clauses that required unanimity in response to Quebec's demand for a veto.

As the Canada Act proceeded through the House, changes were made to strengthen the section on sexual equality in response to demands from women's groups. No change was made in the face of opposition by the Native peoples, although the document included a provision for a constitutional conference to discuss "constitutional matters that directly affect the aboriginal peoples of Canada." (The first meeting occurred in 1983, followed by others in subsequent years, all failing to resolve Native constitutional issues.) Parliament approved the final constitutional resolution in December 1981. In March 1982, the British House of Commons passed the Canada Act, which was proclaimed by the Queen on April 17, 1982.

Whatever rejoicing may have occurred over the Constitution Act, 1982 was surely tempered, or diminished, by the fact that Quebec had not joined the consensus, by the continued opposition of Native peoples, and by the inclusion of the notwithstanding clause in regard to the Charter of Rights. Whether it was outmanoeuvred or was, as has been suggested, the victim of anglophone perfidy, the Quebec government's renunciation of its veto has prompted the commentary that the nature of Canadian federalism has been substantially changed. This situation provided the incentive for renewed negotiations based on a set of five demands by Premier Bourassa. The result was the Meech Lake Accord in 1987, which failed to receive ratification by June 23, 1990 as required. In October 1992, a national referendum rejected the Charlottetown Accord, which again addressed Quebec's concerns and provided for Native self-government and Senate reform.

A few words about Quebec's post-1960 constitutional demands are appropriate at this point. From a variety of Quebec sources have come ideas for change that have ranged from the establishment of two sovereign states, which could then form a common market based on the European model (sovereignty association), to a reinterpretation of the present Constitution that would limit the federal government's ability to interfere in provincial spheres of activity.[16]

A referendum (a proposition presented directly to the voters for their approval or disapproval), initiated by the Parti Québécois and held on May 20, 1980, sought to obtain a mandate from the Quebec electorate to negotiate with the rest of Canada sovereignty association (a combination of political sovereignty with a customs and monetary union). With the defeat of that proposition, Quebec had rejected separation but continued to be governed by a party that has insisted that a renewed federalism is impossible.

The heart of the problem of Quebec in the Canadian federal system is that the role of the provinces as envisioned in 1867 is no longer applicable in the 1990s. The urbanization of Canada and the growth of the social-welfare state gave the provinces, under the original Constitution Act, major responsibilities undreamed of in 1867. This was especially the case in Quebec since the "Quiet Revolution" of the 1960s, when the attitude of Quebeckers toward the role of the provincial government changed dramatically: they demanded a more active involvement of that government in the affairs of Quebec society. With this change, there developed a dissatisfaction with a Constitution that guaranteed linguistic and educational rights but was felt to restrict strong economic and social action by the province. By the 1960s these problems became paramount in Canadian political discussions, especially with regard to Quebec's place in Confederation. Premier Bourassa presented a number of demands at the Meech Lake meeting aimed at bringing about Quebec's full participation in Canada's constitutional development. The clause concerning Quebec as a "distinct society" is significant because previous first ministers' meetings had debated that issue but had not endorsed it. While Premier Bourassa was satisfied that his demands had by then been met, those who favour independence for Quebec—those dominant in the leadership of the Parti Québécois—did not accept this as an answer to their aspirations.

Canadians voted against the Charlottetown Accord for a variety of often conflicting reasons. While those in English-speaking Canada who objected to defining Quebec as a distinct society rejected the accord for that reason, nationalists in Quebec refused to support the amendments because they didn't go far enough, in their opinion. Despite the urging of Ovide Mercredi, the grand chief of the Assembly of First Nations, and other aboriginal leaders who had negotiated the terms of the agreement that related to Native peoples, the accord did not find favour with a majority of them; in fact, on many reserves the referendum was prevented from taking place. Senate reform, which had been a major demand in western Canada, did not prove attractive enough to carry the vote. Groups as diverse as the National Action Committee on the Status of Women and the Reform Party added their negative voices.

In the midst of a serious economic recession, many Canadians voiced frustration that their leaders were spending too much of their time and the taxpayers' money on constitutional questions rather than finding solutions to economic problems. Politicians generally and Prime Minister Mulroney in particular were held in historically low repute, and the referendum provided an opportunity to send a message to them and to the other elites who supported the accord. Canadians, it appears, rejected the proposition that, unless they accepted the settlement of the constitutional wrangling that was offered by the Charlottetown Accord, their country had no future. The election of a Parti Québécois government in Quebec in 1994 under the leadership of Jacques Parizeau set the stage for yet another referendum, held on October 30, 1995. What seemed to be developing as a decisive defeat for the separatist forces turned into a close contest. Lucien Bouchard took over the leadership of the Yes side. Nevertheless, the No side won a very narrow victory. Quebec separatists and pessimists in English-speaking Canada apparently do not subscribe to the old adage that "close only counts in horseshoes and hand grenades," and they began talking immediately about the next referendum, whenever that might be. Bouchard, who ascended to the premiership following the resignation of Parizeau, found that dealing with Quebec's fiscal and economic difficulties, characterized by high unemployment and slow growth, was a more pressing problem than was calling another referendum in the immediate future. Despite the narrow No-side victory, however, Canadians seem to believe that their country does have a future in which to work out its problems.

CONCLUSIONS

Since Confederation there have been cycles of both federal and provincial government ascendancy. While the provinces have become increasingly influential, the central government has retained its ability to make a large impact on provincial policies. As we have seen, the provinces, especially Quebec, are now increasingly concerned about this situation. The question, then, is whether their concern may be eased under the revised Constitution. On behalf of the Constitution, one may argue that its evolution has been an admirable response to diversity.

Since Canada's Constitution is both written and unwritten, much of the response to the diverse demands of governments into the 1990s has taken the form of political arrangements. Certainly, there have been shortcomings in the way in which the Constitution has worked, but those who demand even further constitutional change and a radically new Constitution for Canada are suggesting fundamental changes that might revolutionize the way government operates in Canada. What they fail to realize is that to sweep clean all the positive developments over the last 130 years might create more problems than it would solve. While the idea of a perfectly formulated code that would settle all problems of government for the foreseeable future is appealing, the likelihood of achieving it is questionable. Unless Canadian society changes drastically, any would-be, latter-day Fathers of Confederation would have to accommodate themselves to the reality of a diverse, bilingual country, and the constitution they drafted would have to be a compromise document.

What is most important to remember is that, in considering the most appropriate functioning of our governmental system, changes need not be in the arrangements themselves, but rather in how those arrangements are operated. Fundamental to any discussion of constitutions must be the realization that they have to conform to political circumstances rather than that circumstances conform to constitutions. Constitutions are made for people; people are not made for constitutions.

RECOMMENDED READING

Cairns, Alan C. *Disruptions: Constitutional Struggles, from the Charter to Meech Lake*. Toronto: McClelland and Stewart, 1991.

Cheffins, R.I., and P.A. Johnson. *The Revised Canadian Constitution: Politics as Law*. Toronto: McGraw-Hill Ryerson, 1986.

Greene, Ian. *The Charter of Rights*. Toronto: James Lorimer and Company, 1989.

Hogg, Peter. *Constitutional Law in Canada*, 2nd ed. Toronto: Carswell, 1985.

Morton, F.L. "The Living Constitution," in R.M. Krause, and R.H. Wagenberg, eds., *Introductory Readings in Canadian Government and Politics*, 2nd ed. (41-72). Toronto: Copp Clark, 1995.

Romanow, R.J., J. Whyte, and H. Legson. *Canada Notwithstanding: The Making of the Constitution 1976–1982*. Toronto: Methuen, 1984.

Russell, P.H. *Leading Constitutional Decisions*, 3rd ed. Ottawa: Carleton University Press, 1982.

———. *Constitutional Odyssey*, 2nd. ed. Toronto: University of Toronto Press, 1993.

CHAPTER 3

Federalism

WHY A FEDERAL SYSTEM?

Federalism may be defined as a system of government in which there are two jurisdictions that have the constitutional power to make laws that affect each individual. The one has legislative responsibility for the whole country in a defined group of powers. The other jurisdiction has legislative responsibility for a smaller geographic area (in Canada, known as a province) for a different set of defined legislative powers. Federalism can hardly be overemphasized in any study of politics and government in Canada, for it is no exaggeration to state that Canada could not have been established under any other form of government. If it had been, it certainly could not have survived. It is our purpose in this chapter to investigate why federalism is a basic requirement for a country like Canada and how it has developed.

Why was federalism the only acceptable alternative for the Fathers of Confederation in their quest for the union of the British North American colonies? First, it was a way to create a central government without destroying the identities of Nova Scotia, New Brunswick, Canada West (Ontario), and particularly Canada East (Quebec). Special emphasis is placed on Quebec since it represented not only a traditional political unit like the others but also a cultural unit very different from the others. Second, the geographical size of the proposed united provinces was such that to govern entirely from one central point would have been extremely difficult. Third, a federal system made it easier for other existing colonies (Manitoba, British Columbia, Prince Edward Island, and Newfoundland) to join later and to create new provinces in the great western hinterland. Federalism would allow the provinces to enjoy the benefits of being ruled together in one large unit for some purposes (mainly economic) while retaining a distinguishable local identity. The Canadian system is only one of many federal systems that have been adopted to preserve ethnic identity. Other examples are Switzerland, Belgium, India, and Nigeria. The breakup of federalism in Czechoslovakia and Yugoslavia occurred when ethnic conflict, armed in the latter case, replaced ethnic accommodation.

Despite our assertion that federalism is the only system that could have worked, some astute politicians responsible for the federation—such as Sir John A. Macdonald—would have preferred a *unitary system* in which all sovereign power rested with a central government. Since it was apparent that this was not acceptable, they sought the next best solution, which was to have a federal system in which the powers were stacked in favour of the central government. The Constitution Act, 1867, therefore, did not establish a classic form of federalism where there are two levels of government, each of which is supreme within its own jurisdiction and neither of which can be subservient to the other. Rather, it allowed for a *quasi-federal* approach in which one level of government may interfere with and check the authority of the other.[1] In the Canadian context, the federal government was empowered by the Constitution to interfere with the provinces in several ways. In the first place, the lieutenant governors of the provinces are appointed by and responsible to the federal government. They may refuse to sign the legislation of the provinces, or to withhold approval and refer the legislation to the federal Cabinet, which can disallow the legislation. Moreover, in the delicate area of denominational education, an appeal to the federal Cabinet was guaranteed to any Roman Catholic or Protestant minority that feels it has been deprived of its rights of religious education (separate schools) by a province. More important in the long run, the federal government was given the power to declare works within a province to be for the general advantage of Canada or two or more provinces, and to spend money on matters that did not fall within its own jurisdiction (the *declaratory power* and the *spending power*). These provisions show the strong centralist tendencies of those who drafted the Constitution Act, 1867.

However, the original provisions of the Constitution and the evolution of the federal system are two distinct dimensions. In the first 25 years of Confederation, constitutional practice in Canada reflected the dominance of national politics over the provinces. Since the leaders in federal politics during this first period, especially Sir John A. Macdonald, were responsible for the centralized form of federalism (quasi-federalism) embodied in the Constitution Act, 1867, it was only natural that they adhered to their model. Nation building was foremost in the minds of these politicians, and they used the constitutional powers toward that end. Consequently, the power of appointment of the lieutenant governors of the provinces and the power of disallowance were instrumental in marrying theory to practice.

During the 1880s this early trend began to be restrained by the growing political strength of the provinces, which asserted their rights against the centralist tendencies. This ultimately led to a second period of more classic federalism. The provinces became centres of opposition to the federal government: they realized that cooperatively—through interprovincial conferences—and by legal challenges they could withstand federal pressures and develop their own policies within their jurisdictions. A real turning point came with the election of 1896, when the Liberal Party under Sir Wilfrid Laurier came into national office. This party was pledged to a policy of provincial rights and demonstrated its adherence to this policy almost immediately by refusing, in the Manitoba schools question,[2] to interfere with the educational policies of that province. Since that period the use of constitutional federal powers to overrule provincial policies has diminished to the point where they may be considered inconsequential in the 1990s. Few people, for instance, would have seriously suggested that the federal government disallow the 1988 Quebec legislation barring English in commercial signs, even though the Quebec government had invoked the unpopular notwithstanding clause. The quasi-federal aspects of the written Constitution have been altered so much to accommodate the growing power of the provinces that to describe the workings of the Canadian Constitution as quasi-federal would now be inaccurate.

More important than the powers of the central government to interfere in the jurisdiction of provinces was the fact that the federal government was given jurisdiction over most of what were considered to be the important issues in the realm of government in 1867. In addition, they were given the *residual powers*; that is, all powers not specifically given to the provinces were assumed to be within the federal sphere. The federal government thus acquired responsibility for such things as defence, finance, criminal law, transportation, and the postal service, all considered vital at the time—while the provinces were limited to education, social welfare, municipal institutions, and property and civil rights, which were thought to be of a local nature. Again, in the first 25 years of Confederation, for the same reasons cited earlier, the federal government used both its enumerated and its residual authority aggressively. In doing so it often invaded what the provinces considered to be their jurisdiction. Because of their early political weakness, the provinces could only fight back through the courts; in the latter years of the nineteenth century, the Judicial Committee of the Privy Council in the United Kingdom began to rule in their favour.[3] At the same time, the growing power of the provinces gave them political leverage in addition to the legal victories they were gaining. While some proponents of strong central government in Canada have held the theory that the Judicial Committee was mainly responsible for limiting the powers of the federal government under the Constitution Act, 1867—and no doubt court decisions have hastened the process—nonetheless, the

Canadian political system at both the provincial and federal levels could not have remained as highly centralized as designed in the Constitution Act, 1867. Political accommodation, therefore, had to supplement and eventually replace legal remedies. Today we usually look to federal-provincial conferences and continuing committees (in other words, to political apparatus) to settle the boundaries of federalism rather than turning to the courts.[4] While the Supreme Court did play a crucial role in the constitutional developments of 1981 that led to the Constitution Act, 1982, the amendment process in the Constitution now is rigid. Thus, political settlements based on federal-provincial bargaining will remain crucial.

THE DEVELOPMENT OF FEDERALISM

What were the forces that changed the boundaries of federalism? First and foremost was the growth of the role of government in the lives of people. This affected all levels of government in Canada, but the relative increase in provincial and municipal responsibilities has been most dramatic. During the two world wars, the federal government's defence-related activities were greatly increased, and they completely overshadowed the provincial governments. But the longer-term trends associated with the demands for expanded services in education, health, and social welfare—all related to urbanization—gave the provinces responsibilities that the Fathers of Confederation could not possibly have envisioned.

For instance, while in 1871 fewer than 20% of Canadians lived in centres of over 1 000 population, by 1997 about 80% lived in such centres, and over 25% lived in the three major metropolitan regions of Montreal, Toronto, and Vancouver. The implications of these statistics for municipal government are enormous. Since the provinces are solely responsible for the municipalities under the federal system, it is evident that the role of the provinces has been advanced by the normal shift in population that accompanies the advancing industrialization of any country. The centralist bias of the Constitution Act, 1867 could not prevent a change in the power balance between the federal and provincial governments that followed the population shift.

Municipalities were not mentioned in the Constitution Act, 1867 other than to place responsibility for them firmly in the hands of the provinces. However, as growing centres of power by the 1990s, they have become restive about their inability to take part in decisions affecting urban life. The federal government, through its role in housing, created more contacts with the cities, and under Prime Minister Trudeau the Ministry of State for Urban Affairs was created. That ministry was later abolished, but the federal government retains its involvement in municipal affairs through the Canada Mortgage and Housing Corporation (CMHC). Nonetheless, provinces jealously guard their control over their municipalities and can reorganize them dramatically, as happened with Halifax in 1996 and Toronto in 1997.

Industrialization and urbanization changed our concepts of social welfare. Whereas rural societies could be more self-sufficient (albeit at a low level of service) in caring for the old, indigent, sick, and other unfortunates in their midst, the more impersonal circumstances of urban life demanded state intervention to provide adequate services. Again, the responsibility for these services fell to the provinces.

Spending figures portray this change vividly. Whereas federal expenditures in 1867 totalled $13.7 million, by 1997 they had reached $160 billion. In Ontario the 1867 figure of $1.5 million had grown to over $50 billion by 1990. By the 1990s the total expenditures of provinces and municipalities had long since become larger than those of the federal government, and they had more employees as well—both concrete examples of the shift in relative power.

The growth of provincial responsibilities has created major difficulties for the provinces in finding the money to support their new ventures. The Constitution provides the provinces with powers to raise revenue only by direct taxation, whereas the federal government can use any method available. Direct taxation is normally thought of as tax paid directly by the person taxed, such as income tax. By this definition it would seem that a sales tax is not direct and therefore not available to the provinces. However, legal decisions allowing the provinces to collect sales taxes have been made, so that now most major forms of taxation (except import duties) are available to them. There were particular concerns over the imposition of provincial taxes on natural resources during the 1970s; this led to sharp conflict between Alberta and Saskatchewan on one side and the federal government on the other. A partial resolution of this problem was embodied in an amendment (92A) to the Constitution in 1982, giving provinces more power in that area. Nonetheless, the provinces have been in a weaker position than the federal government in gathering revenue because the federal government started implementing income tax and had the requisite bureaucracy to administer it at an earlier date. Personal and corporate income tax is the largest producer of governmental revenue. There is a limit, however, to how much taxation can be imposed on people, and the provinces have been restrained by the fact that the federal government already occupied the field. The problem of finance has, therefore, placed serious strains on federalism.

The general difficulty provinces have in acquiring the funds needed to discharge their responsibilities is accentuated in some provinces. An unequal level of economic activity has created regional economic disparity. Thus, poorer provinces have less capacity to raise the revenue necessary to provide their people with acceptable standards of education, social welfare, and economic opportunity. This disparity raises questions in the minds of residents of economically depressed provinces about how well Canadian federalism is working to produce economic prosperity.

The continuing tensions in federal-provincial financial relations first assumed serious national proportions in the depression-ridden 1930s. Up to 1930, and particularly in the 1920s, the provinces had been able to keep pace with their growing responsibilities as they conceived them. They were helped by the static nature of federal policies, which allowed federal taxation to be generally reduced and total disbursements by that government to decrease slightly over the 10-year period. This is reflected in the fact that the number of departments and agencies of the federal government remained unchanged at 43 from 1920 to 1930. The onslaught of the Great Depression had no immediate effect on federal policies, since modern Keynesian expansionary economic policies were not understood.[5] The provinces, however, were extremely hard pressed to meet the obligations they had undertaken in education, public works, and social welfare.

Economic distress was a natural fuel for explosive provincial politics, protest movements, and, at times, political demagoguery. Provincial politicians such as Mitchell Hepburn in Ontario, Maurice Duplessis in Quebec, and William Aberhart in Alberta[6] created unprecedented turmoil in federal-provincial politics. New parties came to power: in Alberta the Social Credit Party; in Quebec the Union Nationale Party; and in Saskatchewan the CCF. The CCF gained strength and was ultimately elected in 1944. In addition, it grew into a strong socialist opposition party in several other provinces as well as nationally. These developments have had a major impact on Canadian politics up to the present.

The federal answer to the dislocations of the time was to try to centralize authority to attack these problems. Thus it was in 1935 that Canadians witnessed the strange spectacle of Conservative Prime Minister R.B. Bennett, who was a wealthy corporation lawyer, broadcasting over the CBC a radical "New Deal" for all Canadians. Before Bennett dissolved Parliament and went to the country in the election of December 1935, all legislation to implement the "New Deal" policies had been passed. These policies were never effected, however, because Mackenzie King, leading the Liberals, won the election and immediately referred the legislation to the Judicial Committee of the Privy Council, which promptly ruled it outside the jurisdiction (*ultra vires*) of the federal government. While King's government initiated some legislation[7] that extended the federal government's involvement in the economic life of the country, especially in areas where the crisis was worst, it did not try to replace provincial authority in the way that the Bennett policies might have done. Instead, Canada's most cautious prime minister took the obvious course and appointed a royal commission.

This commission, the Rowell-Sirois Commission, produced what was then the most comprehensive study ever done on federal-provincial financial relations. The recommendations in the report called for a highly centralized structure for both the collection of revenue and the allocation of grants to provinces. Its major recommendation was to provide a national minimum standard of social services for all Canadians. To achieve this, *national adjustment grants* would be paid from the federal treasury to those provinces lacking the economic resources to provide those minimum standards themselves. Inherent in these proposals, however, was a massive shift of authority from the provincial to the federal government. Ontario, British Columbia, and Alberta rejected this approach, but the circumstances of World War II and its aftermath placed the federal government in a strong position to centralize power and to seek to create national welfare policies. One shift in responsibility that did occur was the assumption by the federal government of jurisdiction over unemployment insurance, which was accomplished by a constitutional amendment in 1940. Eventually, the provinces were in a position to reassert their political autonomy within their own jurisdictions. Once that happened it became apparent that the Rowell-Sirois recommendations were not the long-term solutions they were hoped to be. The train of events put in motion by the aggressive provincial leaders and politics of the 1930s was derailed temporarily by World War II and reconstruction, but the fundamental issues raised by those events have still not been finally settled—and in fact are probably permanent features of Canadian federalism.

Contemporary federalism is still grappling with this basic problem of how to finance the responsibilities of the provinces adequately. In the 1940s and 1950s, the federal government fostered the technique of tax rental agreements. Quebec was included initially, but later it disavowed this arrangement. These agreements provided for the federal government to collect all income taxes and to rebate a negotiated percentage of those taxes collected in the respective province. The federal government used its own existing structure to collect the taxes and carried the cost of collection. The agreements were planned to be renegotiated every five years, but this was not always the case for a variety of political and economic reasons. The percentage to be rebated was the major point of contention in the provinces, which continually sought more. Generally speaking, however, the poorer the provinces were, the more they tended to accept the conditions laid down by the federal government, because of their dependency on transfer payments from the federal government to raise their standards of services. On the other hand, the richer provinces had to accept that some of the revenue collected by the federal government within their boundaries would be redistributed to other provinces. Tax rental gave way to tax collection agreements in the 1960s, which provided for tax "abatement" from Ottawa to the provinces in order that the latter could have more revenue without total taxes on citizens going up. However, since then tax-sharing agreements have involved the provinces setting their own rates, and thus the total percentage of tax has risen.

In the 1980s a new aspect of the problem of revenue sharing emerged as a consequence of the energy crisis. Alberta and, to a lesser extent, Saskatchewan (the provinces where the bulk of Canadian petroleum and natural gas reserves were located) were naturally concerned to see these resources yield maximum revenues for the benefit of their governments. The federal government, for its part, wanted to prevent Canadian oil prices from rising to world levels immediately; moreover, it wanted a share of the revenues generated by these resources to help subsidize eastern Canada, which was dependent on imports for its energy. The National Energy Policy of 1980, and the controversy it generated, serve to illustrate the clash between the legitimate concerns of the provinces seeking their own best interests and the federal government, whose responsibilities are nationwide.

From the mid-1970s into the 1990s, the federal government faced yearly deficits as expenditures exceeded tax revenues. The accumulated public debt had reached $600 billion by 1997. The interest payments on this debt had become the largest expenditure of the federal government, and this constrained its ability to spend on other responsibilities. In this atmosphere the federal government sought to reduce its transfers to the provinces just when the latter were desperate for more revenue. These questions of government finance reflect on the fundamental nature of federalism. Undoubtedly, the poorer regions have contributed substantially to the wealth of the richer industrial provinces, because they have been captive markets behind protective tariff barriers. The domestic goods they depended on were often more expensive than imports (especially those from the United States), while at the same time their incomes were lower, reflecting their relative poverty. A vital function of a healthy federal system should be to compensate for any inequities fostered by the system itself. If it does not, the expectations of the poorer regions are continually denied, while those of the richer regions are being fulfilled. The long-run effect of this is permanently to stratify Canada economically and seriously call into question the raison d'être of federalism.

All this is compounded by the fact that the majority of Canadians live in the Ontario-Quebec heartland, as we noted. This majority, which has dominated the federal power structure, has failed to adequately address the grievances of the outlying regions, the Prairies and the Atlantic provinces. Continuing priorities for successive Trudeau governments in the 1970s were to foster regional economic expansion and linguistic equality in Canada. However, these priorities were primarily framed in the context of the central provinces, and one might seriously question whether they would have been the chief priorities if they concerned only the Atlantic provinces or the Prairies.

The sense of western alienation was apparent in the bitter attitude adopted when Alberta and Saskatchewan saw themselves in an advantageous position and noted how quickly the federal government sought to redistribute their wealth to eastern Canada.[8] The French-English question has dominated Canadian federalism to the point where other major problems have remained unresolved. Put another way, regional disparity in Ontario and Quebec, which contain the majority of English-speaking and French-speaking people, is a major concern of the federal government, and the solution of this problem has fallout benefits for other areas. While it is undeniable that the federal government has undertaken many costly programs for regions outside central Canada,[9] they have been piecemeal operations that have not had the sense of urgency associated with the national policies devoted to solving the French-English question.

The federal government, being unable to usurp the functions of the provinces and unwilling to see a number of services go unattended, has developed a compromise approach over the last three decades. This used to be called "co-operative federalism," and its distinguishing feature has been a number of *shared-cost programs.*[10] For these programs the federal government has provided *conditional grants* for a percentage of the total provincial expenditure, on the condition that each province accept certain national standards. They have dealt, for instance, with hospital insurance, welfare, postsecondary education, medicare, and highways. These are in addition to the *unconditional grants* (with no strings attached) that the federal government pays to the provinces. It has been the use of this spending power—the right to conclude agreements to spend money on matters even though they fall under provincial jurisdiction—that has allowed the federal government to pursue national standards of social welfare. Thus, despite the growing influence of the provinces, the federal government has remained in a position of great power.

For their part the provinces are free to opt in or stay out of the shared-cost programs since these programs deal with subjects falling within their jurisdiction. However, federal proposals put pressure on the provinces to accept federal money and the conditions attached to it. The poorer provinces have little choice but to accept. Other provinces may not wish to get involved, but politically speaking they find it practically impossible not to because of the expectations raised among their constituents. What bothers them most about this situation is that the federal government creates circumstances in which provincial authorities find it difficult to set their own priorities. Quebec has been especially adamant about not accepting these programs, because it insists that it should have access to enough money to provide services within its own jurisdiction without federal interference. Although Quebec has received the most criticism for not cooperating with the federal government, it is fair to say that most of the other provinces share that province's misgivings about federal initia-tives. Provision for opting out of programs has been made whereby the province opting out will not suffer financial loss, even if it does not introduce its own program. In practice, however, Quebec—the only province to have opted out—has provided comparable programs in the social-welfare field. An example of this is the Canada Pension Plan, which does not include Quebec; Quebec has integrated its plan into the federal plan and is therefore eligible for federal payments. Thus, the opting-out procedure has allowed Quebec, at least, to exer-cise greater control in the area of social welfare. But the government of Quebec has remained constant in its demand for a larger share of tax revenues in order to determine its own programs. The Meech Lake Accord addressed these concerns by offering a province the right to opt out and receive compensation "if it undertakes its own initiatives or programs compatible with national objectives." The Charlottetown Accord also addressed the question of the federal spending power. While both accords failed, their provisions for shared-cost programs did reflect how conditions had changed since the 1960s.

Having initiated these shared-cost programs, the federal govern-ment by 1976 had become alarmed at the increase in expenditures to which it was committed, especially in the health-care field. Therefore, in 1977 the Established Programs Financing and Fiscal Arrangements Act (EPF) was passed. The growth in federal contribu-tions in the fields of health care and postsecondary education would be constrained. In return provinces received additional tax room. Ultimately, it turned out that the provinces were paying for a greater percentage of increasingly costly programs. Nevertheless, by the early 1990s over 15% of all federal expenditures were in the form of trans-fers of money to the provinces, as either conditional or unconditional grants. Citing the need to reduce its budgetary deficit, in 1995 the federal government announced that a new block grant known as the Canada Health and Social Transfer would be instituted. This grant combined the EPF and Canada Assistance Plan into one and reduced the amount to be transferred.

The federal government remained committed to the idea of national social-service standards, but its fiscal problem, shown by huge budgetary deficits, made it less willing to underwrite the growing costs of these programs. Thus, on one side the period was character-ized by financial policies that limited the growth of federal transfer payments to the provinces, and on the other side measures such as the Canada Health Act of 1984 were introduced to prevent the deteri-oration—as defined by the federal government—of the programs in place. Interest groups that approached governments with their con-cerns often were answered by mutual recriminations on the part of the federal and provincial governments.

Unconditional grants mainly took the form of *equalization payments*. These payments were meant to provide revenue to provinces whose economic health created a poorer tax base than that available to wealthier provinces. The commitment of Canada to see that the citizens of each province were able to receive relatively comparable public services has meant that these provincial revenue shortfalls must be made up by federal transfer payments. Thus, the poorer provinces, especially in the Atlantic area, have substantial proportions of their expenditures funded by equalization grants. The importance of this system led to their successful demand that the principle of equalization be incorporated into the Constitution Act, 1982.

FEDERAL–PROVINCIAL CONFERENCES

The chief instrument that has emerged since World War II to facilitate the operation of Canadian federalism has been the federal-provincial conference. These conferences bring together, from each province and the federal government, a variety of politicians and bureaucrats connected with the subject matter of the conference. The most important matters—those in which decisions cannot be taken by lesser officials—are on the agenda for meetings of the 10 provincial premiers and the federal prime minister. If compromise is to be reached at all in matters of common concern, it will be from the interplay of views that become apparent during these top-level talks. Depending on the urgency of the situation, some agreement may be tentatively arrived at—if only to establish committees to investigate a problem further. At times the federal government may feel impelled to make a take-it-or-leave-it offer if it feels it must make its own policy decisions in the immediate future. This kind of situation is most common in connection with short-term economic problems rather than with longer-term social-welfare problems. The tremendous importance of the relations between the federal and provincial Cabinets and the bureaucrats who serve under them led Professor Donald Smiley to define the current phase as *executive federalism*.[11]

Federal-provincial conferences, therefore, present the Canadian people with a spectrum of political issues that do not fall into the neat constitutional divisions of power made in Sections 91 and 92 of the Constitution. In fact, the federal government has the authority to make decisions that have tremendous implications for certain provinces; at the same time, decisions taken individually by the provinces within their jurisdiction can affect the federal government's policies. For instance, the decision to build or expand an airport is entirely within the federal government's domain, but this decision will affect the highway system, the planned urban development, and a host of other matters that are completely under the aegis of the province. On the other hand, the federal government may decide that economic conditions warrant a balanced budget, and that anti-inflationary policies are needed, and proceed to undertake them only to find that provinces are running budgetary deficits that undermine the policy the federal government is pursuing. Obviously, what this situation suggests is that the federal and provincial governments should attempt to coordinate policies that will be most likely to help the largest number of people. This means avoiding duplication or contradictory policies, but this is easier said than done.

At the political level, the difficulty in achieving a sensible coordination of policy arises from the different concepts of political reality that federal and provincial politicians have of the same problem. Federal political leaders necessarily have to look to the countrywide ramifications of their policies, while provincial political leaders are prone to visualize political reality as contained within their provinces. Quebec leaders especially have been preoccupied with the special situation within their borders, but every other province claims certain distinctive problems as well.

The political perspectives through which federal and provincial leaders see the same problems are related to different sets of political backgrounds. The prospect of an election may be more immediate for some than for others, some may have larger majorities than others, some may have just weathered a serious political storm, and so on. In other words, the electoral variables may be different for federal and provincial leaders, and this variability cannot help but have an effect on their policies. It may therefore be a great temptation for a provincial leader to use the federal government as a scapegoat for the provincial government's inadequacies. In addition, since World War II there has been a tendency in many provinces for one party and one leader to be reelected for several successive terms of office. These leaders have thus developed much greater confidence in their own interpretation of events and, consequently, have tended to oppose the interpretation of the federal government to a much greater extent. In fact, there is now often much stronger opposition to federal policies from the provinces than can be mustered by the opposition in the House of Commons.

Not only do the provincial leaders hold different views of political life in the federation, but also the bureaucracies in the 10 provinces and at the federal level have separate interests in maintaining their own roles. By the 1980s the number of experts employed in the provincial civil services had increased to such an extent that the former supremacy of the federal bureaucracy was challenged. As a result, both levels of government can call upon an army of experts to supply the substantiating "facts" for whatever policy they have decided to pursue. The "facts" produced by the federal bureaucracy may often be countered by "facts" from provincial bureaucracies, which support an alternative provincial policy.[12]

Since all Canadians, except those in the Yukon and the Northwest Territories, live under the jurisdiction of a province as well as the federal government, considerable confusion exists in their minds concerning responsibility for solving the problems that beset them. In some regions there is a stronger tendency than in others to look to provincial governments for redress, since they have felt that their influence was weak in Ottawa. This is especially true of Quebec and the Prairies, although to a certain extent it is also true of the Atlantic provinces. On the other hand, there is some realization, especially in the poorer areas, that only through outside (federal) help can Canadians improve their conditions of life. Ontario, however, is the most populous, richest—though not always in a per capita sense—and most central of the provinces, and its citizens certainly can, understandably, identify with the central government more easily than can the citizens of any other province. The one-third of all Canadian citizens who live in Ontario are less vitally interested in which level of government provides their services, as long as they are provided.

CONCLUSIONS

All of the foregoing discussion illustrates the importance of studying federalism as a dynamic process, rather than as a static constitutional arrangement. With the growth in the demand for government services, it was inevitable that both the federal and provincial governments would overflow the boundaries of their jurisdictions as specified in the Constitution. Moreover, any attempt to interpret federalism in a mechanistic, institutional way would of necessity neglect the effect that ongoing political processes have on any system of government. The existence of provincial or, at best, regional political parties has intensified the inherent tension between the federal and provincial authorities. The building of provincial bureaucratic empires has strengthened the positions of provincial leaders in the face of federal pressures. In short, the entire political process, both federal and provincial, has contrived to make the operation of federalism in Canada a complex and ever-changing challenge.

The greatest challenge to Canadian federalism so far resulted from the first election of the Parti Québécois in November 1976 and its reelection in 1994. Both Ottawa and the other provinces were then faced with a Quebec government convinced that Confederation not only had not worked but also could not be redeemed, and the party had a stake in proving that this was the case. Canadian federalism will obviously be in jeopardy any time the Parti Québécois is the government of Quebec and is in a position to thwart the types of accommodation that have been possible so far in Canadian federalism. The defeat of the referendum proposal of 1980—to discuss sovereignty association—seriously weakened the Parti Québécois position. Nonetheless, it remained the government for several years and after losing office in 1985 returned in 1994, setting the stage for the October 1995 referendum, which narrowly rejected separation. The party appears established enough to continue to play a role in Quebec politics for the immediate future, whether as government or opposition. Thus, Quebeckers will continue to be called upon to review the conditions under which they will take part in the Canadian federal structure. The failure of both Meech Lake and Charlottetown demonstrates the difficulty of resolving that question. The province-oriented view of all provincial political leaders will similarly present challenges to the necessarily more centralist attitudes of federal politicians, of whatever political party. So the federal process in Canada will continue to be marked by a struggle between opposing points of view.

RECOMMENDED READING

Banting, K.G. *The Welfare State and Canadian Federalism*, 2nd ed. Kingston and Montreal: McGill-Queen's University Press, 1987.

Olling, R.D., and M.W. Westmacott, eds. *Perspectives on Canadian Federalism*. Toronto: Prentice-Hall, 1988.

Smiley, D.V. *The Federal Condition in Canada*. Toronto: McGraw-Hill Ryerson, 1987.

Smiley, D.V., and R.L. Watts. *Intra-State Federalism in Canada*. Research Studies Prepared for the Royal Commission on the Economic Union and Development Prospects for Canada, vol. 34. Toronto: University of Toronto Press, 1985.

Stevenson, Garth. *Unfulfilled Union*, 3rd ed. Toronto: Gage, 1989.

PART 3

THE
POLITICAL
PROCESS

CHAPTER 4

Ideologies

The great stress placed on the pragmatic character of Canadian politics throughout this work may lead the reader to conclude that political theories or systems of ideas in terms of which political action is directed are of little importance. This pragmatism, however, operates against the background of an ample ideological consensus, which has been challenged by various spokespeople at the extremes of the political spectrum. We attempt here to set forth those ideologies that have been relevant to Canadian political life, as well as to note at least one that has not been, although it has been believed to be. We refer to the conservative ideology. It should be noted that the ideologies are not coincident with political parties, although in some instances there is a fairly close approximation.[1] All political conflicts are not necessarily ideological. They may, in fact, be disputes between those who share the same political principles. It is clear that Liberalism and liberalism are not identical. Not all liberals are found in the Liberal Party.[2]

But what exactly do we mean by *political ideology*? Here an arbitrary element enters the discussion. The term "ideology" has been used, particularly by followers of Karl Marx, to mean false consciousness, an erroneous picture of social and political life stemming from a class point of view. Others, unwilling to treat the term as an evaluative one, equate ideology with philosophy. We will try to avoid both of these extremes. The term will be used in a purely descriptive way, and it will be considered as operating on a lower level of generality than philosophy. If one wishes to reduce an ideology to first principles concerning human beings, nature, and history, one will be led on a philosophical quest. But one does not have to go that far. In fact, Canadian political ideologies only vaguely suggest underlying philosophical premises.

The era of ideology seems to have begun with the increase of popular participation in government through representative institutions. Ideologies function so as to marshal support in a mass society—either where there is a competitive system, as in liberal democracies, or a one-party monopoly, as in the remaining Communist states, such as China or Cuba.

A political ideology, as we will speak of it here, includes a conception of the social configuration and of political life, a guide to action insofar as it sets down certain aims to be sought, and a statement of the means conducive to achieving those aims. It has a perception of the agencies of political action, the relevant actors, and factors in the political situation. The perception serves as a guide to what can and should be done, and by what means.

The simplest division of political ideologies would be into two groups. On the one hand are those who favour an established order and suspect innovation. On the other hand are those who view the present order as imperfect and hope that change will bring improvement. This would be a division into conservatives and progressives—the forces for stability against the forces for change. However arrayed, this simple dichotomy is not the most useful for the purpose of examining Canadian political ideologies, because it does not correspond to any real set of political forces in combat. Furthermore, the dichotomy is seldom applicable since few political groups are entirely committed to a defence of the status quo. In fact, movements that first appeared under the banner of progress have eventually become defenders of the existing political order. (The most notable case of this was the dominant Communist establishment in Eastern Europe, which was challenged by what has been called the "people's revolution" in Czechoslovakia and East Germany. The so-called people's democracies were in fact party dictatorships.) No political ideology in Canada is committed to an unconditional defence of what exists, and no relevant Canadian political ideology aims at a complete overthrow of Canadian institutions. Canadian political ideologies, even the most radical, are reformist rather than revolutionary.[3]

CONSERVATISM

The year 1867, which marked the beginning of Confederation, also saw the rise to power in England of Benjamin Disraeli with his brand of conservatism, as well as the passage of the great Reform Bill of 1867 that extended the vote to the working classes, the second in the nineteenth-century wave of reform. It is not surprising, therefore, to see a new national state looking to England as it had looked to it in the past for spiritual guidance for its political ideology—whether to the Disraeli vision of one nation or to the liberalism of William Gladstone or John Stuart Mill. Moreover, these influences have been acknowledged and are not simply a matter of conjecture.

We are going to consider the Disraeli model of conservatism because it seems the most relevant to a discussion of the ideological sources of Canadian politics, at least in English-speaking Canada. We have already noted conservative attitudes in the French Canadian context in defence of traditional Roman Catholic and rural values. However, this raises the question of whether this type of conservatism has now or in the past any social importance and social weight, or whether one must conclude that the only really conservative ideology in Canada is in the imaginations of certain philosophers.[4] To this extent, our examination of the conservative ideology will be singular; the other four ideologies examined all have an incontestable relevance.

Conservatism as an ideology in the Anglo-Saxon tradition has been associated with the names of Edmund Burke and Benjamin Disraeli. Significantly, both were parliamentary men, politically active, and, while the one aspired to become prime minister, the other was twice prime minister and closely identified with the notion of "Tory Democracy." Since Disraeli's rise to power coincides with the year of Canadian Confederation, it seems preferable to discuss his notion of conservatism rather than that of Burke.

Conservatism is usually thought to be a defence of political and social arrangements that have been inherited—their very venerability is a strong, no doubt the strongest, point in favour of their retention. Its respect for what is ancient and traditional, and its attempt to postulate the past as normative, raise two questions: first, what previous arrangements are referred to, and second, why should these arrangements be given a normative status? There have been many historical cases that raise serious questions about the justifiability of any conservative theory. For example, it is difficult to explain Cicero recalling the splendour and the virtue of the Roman republic at the moment of its death, Edmund Burke defending English institutions simply because they had existed "time out of mind," or Winston Churchill refusing to preside over the dissolution of a crumbling empire. Its antiquity may be quite irrelevant to its worth if one order is preferable to another. It is for this reason that David Hume's defence of conservatism in terms of its utility is stronger than Edmund Burke's defence in terms of its durability.

Conservatism is based upon a conception of an organic community, clearly delineated class divisions arranged hierarchically and dominated by the landed proprietors, a respect for ancient traditions, and a defence of the establishment, throne, and altar.

The Second Reform Bill, sponsored by Disraeli and the Conservatives, though not originated by them, was based on the confident presupposition that the great body of the English people were conservative. Disraeli rejected the middle-class orientation of liberalism as well as the class-conflict perspective of the socialists. He sought instead to reconcile the classes—the two nations of the rich and the poor—through social legislation.

Disraeli's perception of the political actors is basically in terms of class alignment; his solution can be considered opportunistic or paternalistic. The notion that political predominance belongs to those who have land, leisure, and education became the class basis and social anchor of conservatism. In addition, conservatism in the Disraelian sense supported the close alliance of throne and altar against the strong secularizing tendency of nineteenth-century liberalism. Hence, there is the facetious definition of the Church of England as "the Tory party on its knees."

Disraeli disagreed with liberalism of the utilitarian variety (see Chapter 1), which was avowedly rationalistic and calculative. In fact, he called it "brutalitarian." Disraeli spoke of the importance of the passions in human life, as Burke had spoken of the sentiments. Where liberalism was individualistic, Conservatives spoke of the organic community evolving through time like a plant and not as the result of mechanical—hence manipulative—operation. Furthermore, Conservatives claimed to be the national party whose aim was to overcome the duality of the two nations, while the Liberals were supposedly marked by their narrow class interest.

In retrospect, the appeal to the working man by the Conservatives appeared to be more a tactic aimed at procuring a majority than a kind of alliance they could sustain. In fact, it did not last. Tory democracy hardly survived the demise of Disraeli. It was Peelite conservatism that won out, for the followers of Robert Peel called for a different coalition than had Disraeli. The latter attempted an alliance between the landed interest and the working class against the middle class. Peelite conservatism thrived on the division in the opposing party. Hence, the split over Irish Home Rule in 1880 brought about a Conservative majority based on the assimilation of dissident Liberals, the Liberal Unionists.[5]

Thus, the contrast between liberal doctrine and Disraelian conservatism was sharply drawn. To the liberal reliance on utilitarian reason, Disraeli offered faith, loyalty, and tradition. To individualism, he opposed the organic community and to secularism, the close alliance of church and state. To the workers, he offered an alliance against the party of the middle class, representing the employers and the exploiters. And above all Disraeli claimed that the only true national party was the one he led.

It has been noted often enough that Canada's development has been different from that of its European mother countries. Louis Hartz has written an interesting and provocative book on the development of such fragments as French Canada and English Canada.[6] Because it was not hindered by the task of overcoming a feudal inheritance, English Canada was bound to have a different social perception than that of Disraeli's contemporaries in England. However, according to Hartz, this is only partially true of the country as a whole, since Canada did have a feudal fragment. Although Hartz's theory of the two fragments has been widely accepted, it has been severely criticized.[7] Yet despite some tendencies toward the establishment of a landowning class and home-grown squires, no social institutions analogous to those in England developed. Consequently, neither Disraelian nor Burkean conservatism took root in Canada.

Without a similar alignment of social forces to support it, a Disraelian type of conservatism was bound to wither in Canada. Here there was no successful attempt to create a religious establishment, although again the Quebec situation in the nineteenth century gives cautious pause to generalization. Nor do we find the romantic appeal to the emotions or sentiments at the heart of Canadian conservatism under John A. Macdonald. Disraeli himself would have found it far too utilitarian for his taste.

Of Macdonald it has been said that "he had a partiality for Disraeli over Gladstone" but that "the party under his leadership was not concerned with defending such old-world causes as the monarchy, the established church, and the House of Lords."[8] Macdonald, as a nation builder, found himself in a position where he had to balance one part of the Confederation against another part. "Sir John A. Macdonald envisaged the Senate as a protector of the wealthy few against the many poor, a stabilizer of the social status quo."[9] But one cannot draw the conclusion that he intended the same sort of thing that Disraeli had when the latter defended the power of the House of Lords. After all, nineteenth-century liberalism was as concerned about the despotic tendencies of the democratic masses as were the Conservatives. The Conservatives were distinguished by their attempt to turn these masses against the middle class and consequently for the interests of the landowners.

In conclusion one must note that, although Macdonald adopted certain components of Disraeli's form of conservatism, he did not adopt Disraeli's basic perception. While the social and political perception embodied in an ideology is not the whole of it, it does form an important part of it. Did not Macdonald conceive of Canada in terms of a plurality of interests—economic, social, ethnic, religious, and regional—rather than from a class perspective? And if he did so, is he not then more closely allied, in the final analysis, to the viewpoint of liberalism than to that of Disraeli? Was it not significant that Macdonald belonged to a party called the Liberal Conservatives? The acceptance of such a name seems to suggest much less the defence of conservative values than a conservative liberalism—a liberalism of the right rather than one of the left. The point is very important because conservatism of the past and present shares a common root with liberalism and even with communism. Attempts to create a "new" conservative philosophy, more popular in the United States than in Canada, have foundered because the model used was rooted in semifeudal England, which had managed to maintain its basic institutions while altering the weight given to its parts. Liberal assumptions concerning the inevitability of progress, the virtues of free enterprise, secularism, and social liberty— to use John Stuart Mill's phrase—and the need to conciliate diverse interests were common to both the Conservative and Liberal parties in Canada. Their differences occurred within the context of an ideological consensus.

Some writers imply that differences are superficial if they are not ideological. We have tried to maintain that there are important differences *within* ideologies, even though we aim at sketching out those general features of an ideology that set it apart. The protection versus free-trade dispute in the nineteenth century supposedly took place between two parties with opposing ideologies, but the dispute continued even after the conservative ideology ceased to be an important influence. The dispute has now become a more practical matter and is dealt with more pragmatically. In our society there are no doubt some business interests that benefit from high tariffs and some that do not— tariff arrangements usually look as if someone has been granted a privilege—but the quarrel is between various business interests, not between a landed aristocracy and a rising middle class. It must also be said that those who presently consider themselves free traders are so only "by and large," while protectionists often want to see imported goods competing with the home product if it results in a lowering of prices for products other than their own. The issue of protection versus free trade reveals how difficult it is in an advanced industrial society like Canada to distinguish ideologies on the basis of issues from the perspectives in which the issues are considered—that is, the framework of ideology. The recent quarrels over free trade with the United States are rather different from a conflict of ideas. They are resolutely consequentialist—that is, they reflect not a defence of protection on the one hand and a defence of free trade on the other but concerns about the likely consequences of a far-reaching trading pact. Opponents of the extensive scheme aim at the protection of certain sectors, such as culture. Perhaps only moral issues concerning the criminal justice system, capital punishment, abortion, and pornography produce today the kind of polarization that once divided free traders and protectionists.

LIBERALISM

The fortunes of liberalism in Canada have been closely tied up with the cultural differences between French Canada and English Canada. The animus against liberalism in Quebec in the nineteenth century arose from the identification of political liberalism with religious and political liberalism as they manifested themselves in France. To be liberal in the French sense meant to be anticlerical, a secularist in political life if not an outright atheist. The history of liberalism in England was, however, beset by the problems of an economic system in a developing capitalist setting, the elaboration of social goals, and the role of business in public policy. In France liberalism was also antagonistic to organized religion, which of course meant the Roman Catholic Church, and, in the anticlerical tradition, was determined to crush it as a social force. This kind of liberalism reached its epitome under the government of Emile Combes in 1904, when religious congregations were excluded.

But it is also true that the Roman Catholic hierarchy was antagonistic not only to liberalism as it developed in France but also to it as a political, social, and economic ideology. Economic liberalism was attacked in the Encyclicals of Pope Leo XIII; religious liberalism had been attacked in the famous Syllabus of Errors in the Encyclical *Quanta Cura* of Pope Pius IX (1864). Pius IX was sympathetic to liberalism as a social movement until 1848 and opposed to it thereafter because of the series of revolutionary upheavals in that year. It should also be said that support for liberal democracy from the Roman Catholic hierarchy was rather belated; Pope Leo XIII's qualified approval appeared rather late in the day and perhaps did not receive the general backing of the clergy. There still remained a strong antidemocratic current in Roman Catholic political thought before World War II.

English liberalism might have been opposed to a religious establishment of the kind that Disraeli and his followers approved, but its supporters were by no stretch of the imagination antireligious, as Gladstone is there to witness. How, then, did the confusion of Canadian liberalism with the continental variety become such an important factor in Quebec and, consequently, in Canadian political life? Three explanations seem possible: the ingress of French liberalism in some insidious form in Quebec; the existence of an indigenous movement—the liberal school known as the *Rouges*, founded by Louis-Joseph Papineau—which had discredited the term "liberalism" in the eyes of the clergy; or a misunderstanding, a great *malentendu*, a confusion of ideas, caused by the failure to realize that the term had a number of meanings.

The first explanation seems to have little historical backing. French Canadian culture appeared to be tightly sealed off from the doctrine coming from France in the nineteenth century, except negatively through the imprecations from the pulpit. The second explanation seems to have more validity in view of the phenomenon of the *Rouges*. However, movements such as the *Rouges* are natural reactions to efforts to exert clerical control over the political and social order, and it would be an obvious fallacy to identify all liberals with the *Rouges*. One is led to the third explanation to account for the antiliberalism of the Roman Catholic hierarchy in Quebec. Its attitude was resolutely anti-modernist, against the culture of nineteenth-century liberal society in all its aspects. It had lost the power of discrimination—of sorting the wheat from the chaff—because it retained its loyalty to an outmoded order that had compromised Christianity as much as it had protected it. Resolutely negative in their attitude to these new currents, the clerics were eventually condemned to be without lasting influence. But their influence did endure for a long time.

So it was against this opposition that liberalism as a national ideology had to win its battles. André Siegfried, writing in 1907 from the standpoint of that French liberalism so criticized in French Canada, could still say that the root of social and political differences in Canada remained religious.[10] We may fairly raise the question whether or not this judgement was the result of Siegfried's own predilections. Like the clergy of Quebec, he was perhaps too inclined to see the world through religious spectacles. For Siegfried, Quebec must have represented all that had been happily obliterated in France. Nevertheless, it was true that, for over a quarter of a century, those who spoke for the Liberal Party were on the defensive in Quebec, even after Wilfrid Laurier came to power. In the years after Confederation, "everything waited, therefore, for a French-Canadian leader who would persuade the Québécois that liberalism was not really against their faith, no matter what the bishops said."[11] Of course, without Quebec the Liberals stood little chance, if any, of attaining power. French Canadians voted Conservative because those clergymen in Quebec who adhered to the political ideas of the Vatican had convinced them that to be a liberal was to be irreligious. The clergy, said Laurier, viewed liberalism as "a new form of evil, a heresy carrying with it its own condemnation."[12]

The situation was as follows: neither Edward Blake, George Brown, nor Alexander Mackenzie could have created that synthesis of liberalism and French Canadian support that has been one of the great strengths of the Liberal Party in Canada. They could not do so because they were Protestant and anglophone. On the other hand, a Roman Catholic francophone would have faced the obstacle of English Canada and the need to stand as a nationalist, as did John A. Macdonald. Wilfrid Laurier was admirably suited to bridge the gap between French and English Canada, between Roman Catholics and Protestants, and between Roman Catholics and liberalism.

The task was not a simple one, and the first stage was to establish liberalism as an honourable political allegiance that in no way compromised the religious faith of Roman Catholics. Of course, the inevitable result would not please the Roman Catholic hierarchy in Quebec, since even English liberalism was committed to a distinction between church and state unacceptable to the ultramontane clergy of Quebec. Laurier had small chance of winning over the hierarchy, but he could at least undermine its objections to liberalism. This he did, in season and out of season, through political education as well as through policy decisions that attempted to shift the political dialogue from the plane of theological cleavages and dogmas to that of regional, ethnic, social, and economic differences. This is clear both in the harsh disputes over the Manitoba School Bill and in the matter of the settlement of the Jesuits' Estates.[13]

The liberal idea of secularism does not commit one to the position that religion is unimportant, but to the belief that where possible political decisions should not be made on a religious basis and that religious issues should be circumvented where possible. For instance, instead of basing a judgement concerning the refusal of Jehovah's Witness parents to allow blood transfusions for their child on the worth or lack of worth of that religious belief, the liberal would shift the issue to the more neutral ground of the responsibility of the parents to safeguard the child's health in accordance with the latest medical information. This comes close to saying that religious argumentation is irrelevant in the public forum. For historical reasons, in Canada the pure ideal of liberal secularism cannot be realized, and even in the United States, where a liberal like Thomas Jefferson had immense influence on the American attitude toward church-state relations, the famous "wall of separation" has not been able to provide a complete barrier against government aid to religious institutions, indirect though it may be. Persistent efforts to legislate for religious reasons may be found in calls for Lord's Day Acts or Sunday closings.

Laurier tried to educate the people of Quebec about the real significance of his liberalism and the fact that there was no relationship whatsoever between his liberalism and that of European anticlerical, antireligious liberals. This is illustrated by two speeches he gave before he became prime minister—one in 1877 and the other in 1889. In the first discourse, Laurier was concerned with refuting the claims that his brand of liberalism was the same as what passed for liberalism in France. Although the address was entitled "Political Liberalism," it was more a refutation of French liberalism than a positive expression of his own political convictions. Supporting the idea of responsible government, government of the people by the people—Laurier was also a great admirer of Abraham Lincoln—Laurier examined the proposition that "a Catholic cannot be a liberal." There must be a distinction. The proposition is true if one means by liberal the revolutionary creed in France that had been the enemy of both religious and civil liberty. Laurier echoed Madame Rolland: "The French have had the name of liberty, but they have not yet had liberty itself."[14] But the proposition is false if one means by liberalism that philosophy of liberty that had developed in England under the influence of men like Macaulay, Fox, and O'Connell, names invoked by Laurier. Liberalism is a reformist creed, not a revolutionary one. Laurier then stated his notion of liberal right, the echo of which can be found generally in liberal writings: "The rights of each man, in our state of society, end precisely at the point where they encroach upon the rights of others."[15] Laurier's liberal defence of the individual recalls John Stuart Mill's *On Liberty*, that great utterance of the liberal creed in which he stated that the free expression of opinions, the freedom of association, and the freedom of assembly form part of the fundamental charter of freedom.

This Millian side of Laurier's liberalism comes out in his speech on the Jesuits' Estates in 1889. Laurier declared in a preface to his policy statement on the question of the settlement of the Jesuits' Estates, "I am not and we are not liberals of the French school. . . . I am a liberal of the English school."[16] Laurier evidently thought it necessary to make such a statement to disarm those who would interpret his position as being in some way anticlerical. He proposed that the question be left to provincial jurisdiction—that is, be dealt with in terms of the division of powers between the federal government and the government of Quebec, rather than as a specifically religious problem. This was in line with his general position that implied the refusal "to disallow provincial acts except under extraordinary circumstances,"[17] a theory of federal restraint. But in answer to the question concerning the tolerance of the Jesuits themselves, or the tolerance of groups perceived as intolerant, Laurier stated a view of liberal tolerance that is of the finest that can be found:

> Are we to be told that, because men are inimical to liberty, they should not be given liberty? In our own doctrine and in our own view, liberty shines not only for the friends of liberty, but also for the enemies of liberty.[18]

Enough has been said perhaps about the liberal ideal of individual and social freedom and the spirit of tolerance fostered by Laurier. Liberalism, in the nineteenth-century sense, was identified with the laissez-faire theory of economic development. In domestic politics this meant a policy of "hands off" or "letting alone" by the government, except where interference was required to maintain a competitive economy—anticombines legislation being a typical liberal economic measure. In the matter of foreign trade, the liberals, following the lead of the so-called British radicals Richard Cobden and John Bright, favoured free trade. In Canada the Clear Grits were followers of Cobden and Bright. Brown's aim was to found a business party, a party of the middle class. Mackenzie too was a free trader. However, it has been asserted that this Manchester (England) liberalism, this liberalism of laissez faire and free trade, had little impact on Canada during the important nation-building stage. Certainly, Laurier was more a follower of Macdonald in this matter than he was of his fellow liberals. It is true that we find free-trade sentiments in Laurier's public utterances, but in the matter of national policy he advocated public initiative and not unbridled free enterprise as the solution to the problems of national expansion. Indeed, such a policy was necessitated by the very facts of the case. This can be seen as an example of Laurier's pragmatism, his distaste for fixed theories, and his willingness to accept compromises, sometimes ambiguous middle positions that disturbed some of his followers. If he was an economic liberal, then it was only in a mitigated way. He was in no way a doctrinaire liberal on this point.

While we have discussed the development of liberalism in Canada in terms of Laurier's skill in successfully overcoming the strong objections to liberalism in Quebec, we must not lose sight of the fact that the task before us is the definition of the liberal ideology, not the political ideas of Wilfrid Laurier. He has served this end because he is the archetypal Canadian liberal. The more theoretical question that we face concerns the logical connection between political liberalism and economic liberalism. The socialist critics of liberalism have often maintained that the two are inextricable elements of the same ideology. C.B. Macpherson, for example, would say that the competition between political parties in a liberal society is based on the competitive market economy, with the implication that the elimination of the latter entails the elimination of the former.[19] At any rate, the critics of liberalism on the left maintain that it is compromised as a political ideology by its close connection with capitalism, an association that condemns it morally if not physically.

Such a position is not easy to maintain. It is surely true that demands for representative government in the nineteenth century were coupled with pleas for economic liberalism. However, the history of liberal democracy includes a stage when there was a liberal conception of government, yet not a democratic one; this became increasingly more democratic and at the same time less wedded to an unregulated economy. From the defence of the free economy, liberal societies passed to the stage of "positive freedom," in which government legislation was justified in cases where interference was conducive to the self-development of various disadvantaged groups. From there it moved toward the welfare state and Keynesian economics, if not all the way to socialism in the Marxist sense of the public ownership of the means of production. However, since no liberal democracy has a socialist economy in the sense mentioned, we are dealing with a hypothetical case. We must raise the question of whether there is any contradiction involved in the combination of liberal democracy and public ownership. The question really comes to this: are the differences that manifest themselves in the political forum expressions of or results of basic social differences rooted in the economy (mode of production, relations of property, social stratification), or do they arise from multiple sources that cannot be reduced to the socioeconomic realm? Parties, in the liberal view, perform the function of conciliating interests, but the liberal generally sees interests as broader than simply economic or class differences. Looking at the question from the other side, should we expect political conflicts and a multiparty system to disappear once a regime of public ownership has been implemented?

A provisional reply to these questions might be that liberal societies have shown a certain flexibility in regard to the kind of economic regime they will tolerate; they can adjust to greater planning and collectivization of the economy, provided that noneconomic values, such as political liberty, are not sacrificed in the process. The great fear of liberals such as Alexis de Tocqueville in the nineteenth century was that a society that promoted equality of condition, as opposed to equality of opportunity, would be hostile to political liberty. Put in more modern terms, the liberal fear is that the bureaucracy required in a state committed to achieving a classless society will pose a danger to popular control and political liberty. The liberal has always feared such concentrations of power and has usually tried to build safeguards into the political system to forestall them or to control them where they exist. It is not so much the affection for a capitalist economy that distinguishes a left-leaning liberal from a socialist as it is the distrust of concentrations of power. It is safe to say, concerning the problem of the logical relation between liberal democracy and capitalism, that they have been (and continue to be) joined in fact without going so far as to say that they are joined in principle—that is, that they are necessarily yoked together.

Canadian liberals have usually followed Laurier in rejecting fixed theories concerning the economic system and avoiding either the extreme kind of individualistic economic liberalism voiced in the United States or the thoroughgoing kind of planning espoused by some British socialists (such as Tony Benn, once a prominent spokesman for the left wing of the British Labour Party). Canadian liberalism became converted to Keynesian economics at the end of World War II and has continued to view the problem of government action in the economy in terms of the principles established to combat mass unemployment in advanced industrial societies by stimulating effective demand. It is the rejection of self-adjusting mechanisms held by pre-Keynesian theorists. However, there has been a good deal of criticism of Keynesian economics, not only from those on the right, who had always been opposed to it, but from those who once saw it as the basis of welfare economics and now concluded that one must go beyond Keynes.

As with conservative ideology, liberal ideology is mainly distinguished by its perception of the relevant actors and factors in the social and political environment. The earliest liberal theorists, such as John Locke, were inclined to view society in terms of the relations between atomic individuals joined together because of enlightened self-interest. The political literature of the philosophic radicals in England making their pleas for representative government is couched in the language of individual self-interest, even when they are aware of the importance of aggregates, not the least of which was class membership. Gradually, the crudity of the atomistic approach was replaced by analysis of political conflicts in terms of social, economic, religious, ethnic, and regional diversities. In England the emphasis was on class conflict because of the well-defined class structure there. In other circumstances religious or linguistic differences might be paramount, although seldom in isolation from economic factors. The new liberal perspective came to focus on the voluntary associations that spring up in a society to voice demands in the political sphere; the basic unit of analysis came to be the interest group. We will borrow the words of Theodore Lowi and refer to this new liberal perspective as "interest-group liberalism."[20] Analysis in these terms had the advantage of avoiding the questionable psychological assumptions of the old interest theory, with its concept of calculating human behaviour on the basis of economic factors. The new liberal perspective appeared to be an empirical, and hence realistic, approach to understanding the interactions of a pluralistic society.

The importance of interest-group analysis was first brought to general attention in Arthur Bentley's famous work *The Process of Government* in 1908. Since Bentley's book was based mainly on the American experience, it behooved Canadian political scientists to see whether its analysis was applicable to the Canadian scene. We do have a Canadian counterpart.[21] However, theories such as that of Bentley disclose political realities; they do not create them. It was generally evident that politics in a liberal society had its own special characteristics. Alexander Brady said in a well-known work on constitutional government that "the crucial test of liberal democracy is the facility with which public agreement, resting upon compromises between different interests, can be achieved in common discussion."[22]

The role of the politician and the party is to conciliate—to be an intermediary or broker between interests. This is usually explained by saying that the interest group articulates the demands of its members, and the party has the function of aggregating these groups in order to establish a viable majority. First, compromise achieved in politics works within the party through the process of conciliating what are often incompatible demands; second, it works in the legislative process itself. In such a system, leadership is extremely important for intergroup diplomacy. Sometimes interest groups are distinguished from pressure groups as having the resources to set up a permanent organization to look after their interests. Because such permanent or continuous *lobbying*—as this representational function is known—requires a considerable expenditure that only wealthy organizations can afford, it introduces an undemocratic element into the governmental process. Lobbying in Canada differs considerably from lobbying in the United States, because of party discipline in Canada (see Chapter 7). A system that requires an individual party member to toe the party line is quite different from the lack of party discipline found in the United States, which makes the individual congress member a constant target for lobbyists. Because of the structure of the American civil service, it appears that lobbyists have greater access to it than they do to its Canadian counterpart. Obviously, the lobby is not an accidental characteristic of interest-group liberalism.

Negatively, interest-group liberalism militates against the formulation of clear-cut ideological statements, since the price of coalition is vagueness. There are those who decry the way a brokerage party tries to placate numerous interests at the cost of coherent policy proposals for the public interest. Reformers once proposed the city manager system, in which a professional manager would supposedly take administrative matters out of the political realm. Such an administrator, it was thought, could pursue public interests, free of the obstacles posed by the operation of aggregative politics (building coalitions of interest groups). Ideological, as opposed to interest-group, parties must confront the sober reality that a party wishing to keep its ideology pure risks remaining permanently out of office.

The older liberal view, while conscious of the importance of interest groups and pressure groups in a liberal democracy, looked upon the growing role played by pressure groups with a muted moral disapproval. J.A. Corry, in his work on Canadian government, raises the question of whether lobbying is good or bad.[23]

The reason given for viewing lobbying with alarm is its potential for thwarting the popular will. Here we have an issue that was a central theme in Jean-Jacques Rousseau's political theory. By what means can a policy ensure that the general good (or general will, as Rousseau preferred to say) will not only be sought after but will be achieved in a sound political community? One answer he gave was through the suppression of particular wills. In other words, it can never be conducive to the general will of a society that particular interests prevail. The application of this notion to North American society can be found in the writings of reformers before World War I, who spoke against the dominance of spokesmen for special interests and private trusts in a supposedly democratic society. Proponents of interest-group liberalism answer this type of objection by denying that there is any meaning or substance to phrases like "the general will," "the general good," or "the common good." There are only interests and coalitions of interests.

In contrast to Corry's misgivings about some aspects of interest-group liberalism, Brady[24] is more matter-of-fact about the forms of pressure brought to bear by contending interests and tends to accept their presence and their activities as normal. In this he reflects the dominant trend in North American political science. Liberal thought has really passed through three stages in dealing with the role of pressure groups in a democratic society. First, liberal theory defended the moral ideal of government for the general welfare, even though this ideal was far from realized in practice. Then liberal thought, turning away from a normative political science closely attached to moral philosophy, took up the empirical task of describing and understanding the functioning of a liberal democracy in terms of the actual forces at play in that society, rather than in terms of constitutional law. An underlying assumption was that the legal-normative approach of constitutional law failed to reveal how the society actually worked and confused facts and values, description and prescription. Finally, by limiting itself to a description of the complex interaction of interest groups in the polity, the relation of the parties to the various interest groups, and the process by which group diplomacy culminated in legislative and administrative acts, liberal political scientists gave implicit approval to the system they were describing—that the way the system actually functioned was the normal way for a liberal democracy to function. They had become, no doubt inadvertently, normative theorists because they had elevated efficiency into one of the main values of the political system. Insofar as they did not criticize the failings of the system, some critics would consider them conservative, since after all it was the stability of a liberal society that was at stake. Critics of the supposedly neutral political theory so prevalent in North America, such as Charles Taylor, have tried to uncover the normative premises hidden in these theories. In doing so, they have denied that any political theory can be neutral.

Before terminating this presentation of liberal ideology, it might be of use to discuss two corollaries of interest-group liberalism. One is the role that the cross-cutting of interests plays in achieving a political consensus. Two people have different economic interests, but they may share certain interests because they are both veterans or members of the same ethnic or religious group. There are many such overlapping memberships in a society. This comes down to saying that oppositions are merged with agreements in a great and intricate social network. The second corollary is the notion of party inclusiveness, which is supposed to ensure that various interests — for example, ethnic ones — will be represented among party supporters. As long as parties are regarded as essentially coalition-building devices, we should expect to see this balancing employed.

NEOCONSERVATISM[25]

As there appeared to be a convergence of political parties and programs in the centre of the political spectrum, it became the custom in certain quarters to speak of a decline in ideology. However, the debate sparked by the imposition of controls and the Anti-Inflation Board by the Trudeau government in 1975 revealed burning coals of ideological conflict beneath the grey ashes of consensus. Obviously under the influence of the economic analysis and prescriptions brought forth by John Kenneth Galbraith in his *Economics and the Public Purpose*, Prime Minister Trudeau said that the failures of the modified market system in controlling inflation required the implementation of controls over prices and incomes. The justifications offered for what was called "the new society" led critics to speculate that Trudeau had in mind some form of indicative planning, corporatism, or even socialism. The issue was posed by critics as an opposition between free enterprise, or the free-market economy, and a planned economy; the government, however, maintained that the free enterprise or the economic model of pure competition was surely irrelevant when the problem was how to deal with the weaknesses of a mixed economy. The tenacity with which the neoliberal economic philosophy of the free market is defended is a tribute to the brilliant work of Milton Friedman and other members of the Chicago school in reviving this kind of economic theory. What the controversy over the Trudeau controls highlights is the opposition between the new (positive) liberalism, with its willingness to use economic controls to achieve stability, and the old (negative) liberalism—ironically called neoliberalism—with its call for the government to leave the economy alone. The federal six-and-five program of restrictions on public sector wage increases in the 1970s, as well as similar measures taken by the province of Ontario in the early 1980s, are indications that the main burden of budget restrictions was now being placed on public sector employees. Of course, the federal government hoped that the private sector would follow its lead.

The division within liberalism was confirmed in Great Britain in the period preceding World War I, when the individualist liberalism of Herbert Spencer lost out to the collectivist liberalism of writers such as Leonard Hobhouse and John Hobson.[26] No longer was the state seen as a threat to freedom, but as a positive contributor to it, especially if freedom is defined not just as absence of restraint but as a power to do something. The attempt to combine freedom and social justice as social goals was the hallmark of the "new liberalism." While the new, or collectivist, liberalism could claim victories both in Great Britain and in North America prior to World War I, the postwar period was one of reaction, not only to socialism but also to welfare liberalism. Not until the devastating years of the Great Depression did collectivist liberalism become the mainstream ideology in both Canada and the United States.

However, after more than 40 years of the welfare state under liberal auspices, the possibilities of government's social progress were less visible than its failures to a number of critics. Government bureaucracies had grown immensely, mainly because of the welfare state. Charges of duplication, inefficiency, waste, and corruption could not be ignored. The actions of government were designated by some as the prime cause of the high rate of inflation. It was argued that, far from improving the economic situation, government policies were impeding economic recovery. Rather than trying to eliminate government waste and inefficiency, or trying to make the machine run more smoothly, critics found a certain appeal in proposals to dismantle the government apparatus itself. Thus sounded the neoconservative hour.

From the vantage point of the contemporary welfare state, the proposals for a return to a spontaneous society strike one as utopian. For all its faults, the modern state serves too many interests that would complain if its services were withdrawn. It is precisely the perception of society as a plurality of groups against which neoconservatives react. They do not deny that such groups exist, nor that they have been catered to, or perhaps denied and frustrated. They do not deny pluralism as a fact but as a factor that should be taken into consideration when we examine what the law should be and what government should do. Then they stress that the interest group is to be seen as a threat.[27] The normative neoconservative vision is radically individualistic. The focus is on the interactions of individuals in the marketplace. Apparently, neoconservatives do not want to curb the freedom of association so that individuals cannot combine for economic purposes, although most neoconservatives favour restrictions on labour unions, and logically should also be in favour of anticombines legislation vigorously enforced against business. What neoconservatives cannot abide is that laws made by the legislature should be for the benefit of any particular group. Simply put, the law must apply to everyone or no one, with nothing in between. Let us call this legislative blindness to the existence of particular interests.

For neoconservatives freedom is essentially negative freedom, freedom from restraint and interference. Individuals should not be interfered with in the marketplace. The model for freedom, then, is the freedom of economic entrepreneurs pursuing their purposes by appropriate means. How is this kind of freedom to be made generally accessible? Since very few people are entrepreneurs, neoconservatives appeal to consumers who will have more disposable income if taxes are decreased. Characteristically, economic freedom is more central than political freedom, since with a drastically reduced government political issues lose their importance and political participation loses its attraction.

Unlike conservative paternalism, the liberal notion of sharing, or the socialist ideal of social solidarity, neoconservatism does not concern itself with the social bond. Its radical individualism precludes any instructive views on the nature of the social configuration, except the market model with people united through the cash nexus.

For neoconservative goals to be fulfilled would require a drastic alteration of the kind of society in which we live; practically speaking, this ideology can only be a program for reversing some of the trends in the Canadian polity, not a substitute for what now exists. Thus, the relevant measures appear to be the advocacy of considerable tax cuts, the elimination of a number of government activities, the tightening of requirements for obtaining unemployment insurance benefits (to encourage self-reliance), and the return to voluntarism in the provision of social services.[28] While the short-lived Clark government in 1979 found that its proposal to privatize Petro-Canada was unpopular, the post-1984 Mulroney government had more luck in privatizing Canadair, De Havilland, Teleglobe Canada, and Air Canada. The sale of other public enterprises, including Petro-Canada, became more likely as the 1990s dawned, and even the sale of airports was being discussed. The privatization of governmental activities is an important weapon in the neoconservative arsenal, and its use has even been advocated in regard to the public schools and the monetary system.

The alleged success of "Reaganomics" may have had some impact on Canadian policy making. This kind of supply-side economics aims at improving economic productivity by instituting major tax cuts, controlling the federal budget in the direction of reaching a balanced one, deregulation, and significant changes in monetary policy and federalism. While it has been rather conventional in its use of restrictive fiscal and monetary policies, it claims to be a new departure. What has become apparent is that the three objectives of balancing the federal budget, reducing taxes, and sharply increasing military expenditures are incompatible in theory and in fact. Furthermore, the Reagan tendency was to reduce the welfare state while greatly increasing the capacity for warfare, regardless of the inevitable economic and social consequences of large budget deficits. His successors must now come to terms with the stringencies entailed in servicing the debt. In Canada large deficits at both the federal and provincial levels have placed formidable limits to any new expenditures and have forced cutbacks in existing ones.

Monetarism is the economic theory that has come to be identified with neoconservatism. The assumption is that government action, rather than the demands of labour, business, or foreign cartels, is the principal cause of inflation. The theory finds increased activity of government in regard to the money supply as the cause of inflation in recent times (and the severity of the Great Depression in the 1930s). In its most simplistic formula,[29] monetarism asserts that inflation is a result of the quantity of money; when the rate of increase in the quantity of money exceeds the rate of economic output, inflation occurs. Hence, a reduction in the rate of monetary growth is not just one of several remedies for inflation but the sole cure. As in all economic theories, this proposition—that a decline in the quantity of money will bring about a decline in prices—is based on other factors remaining the same. As far as policy is concerned, monetarism combines prescriptions for tighter credit with fiscal restraint. These measures contrast with the positive liberal proposals for wage and price controls.

What are the social implications of these measures? How do they touch on the oldest political question, cui bono—who benefits? Who benefits from high interest rates, reduced government spending, and lower taxes, and who will bear the burden of them? The consequences of these policies have become apparent after more than a decade of neoconservative influence, and the winners and losers can now be identified.

The sweeping new budget and legislative package brought down by the Bennett government in British Columbia in 1983 was strongly influenced by neoconservative thinking. It consisted in drastically cutting the civil service, by 25%, not by attrition alone, but by massive layoffs as well. It simultaneously eliminated an agency that dealt with the protection of human rights in the province. Such draconian measures effectively abrogate contractual rights and envision nothing less than a radical transformation of the social system. The tendency is clear: the reduction of some government services, which will not be provided by anyone, and the handing over of other functions to the private sector, whose operations in this perspective are always considered beneficial. For instance, the practice of contracting out tasks once performed by government employees was utilized by the Vander Zalm government in British Columbia.

Unlike the other solidly moored ideologies, it is difficult to judge whether neoconservatism is a passing fancy or the sign of a historical reversal of the relation of government to the economy in a liberal democracy. The adoption of the monetarist ideas of Milton Friedman by the British Tory government and by the Republicans in the United States, and the influence of these ideas in Canada, are too recent for us to guess whether or not we are dealing with the gusts of an ephemeral doctrine. Should neoconservative conceptions of governmental activity prevail, that would be a turnabout from the Canadian tradition of public enterprise that has been accepted by the main parties. No one can deny the historical importance of governmental initiatives in the process of nation and province building.

It has been popular recently to describe the increasing emphasis on reducing government deficits as a lurch toward neoconservatism by parties and ideologies formerly exponents of big government. However, when we see leaders of different political parties, and of differing ideological bent, giving high priority to putting the financial house in order, it seems that we are dealing with the recognition of a serious problem calling for attention rather than with a great rush to the political right— that is, toward a major ideological realignment. The main issue is how deficit reduction, now high on the political agenda, will be related to the need to preserve what has come to be known as the social safety net. Unfortunately, certain circles still deny that any critical problem exists in regard to public finance, thus offering a prescription for government business as usual. For the most part, the actual political decision makers have confronted the issue with varying degrees of success.

SOCIALISM

It follows from what has been said up to now that there is no clear confrontation of conservative and liberal ideologies in Canada. The two large parties both view politics as an effort to form a majority by welding together an alliance of different regional interests, linguistic groups, economic interests, and other divergent groups. The differences in the two ideologies stem from the fact that, historically, certain interest groups have looked to the Progressive Conservative Party, or its previous counterparts, for the implementation of their desires, while others have traditionally found a home in the Liberal Party. There are, of course, other interest groups that swing from one to the other. This means that their constituencies, rather than their ideologies, are at variance. Ideologically, the important distinction in Canada is between liberals and socialists. To avoid any ambiguity, socialism will be defined not in a Marxist sense as the public ownership of the means of production but as a political ideology that has a particular perception of the forces in conflict in society, that holds certain values as aims of public policy, and that advocates specific means—nationalization is sometimes one—to realize these values. From this point of view, public ownership of the means of production would be one among other possible means to achieve the socialist view of the good society.

The most celebrated statement of socialist ideology in Canada has been the Regina Manifesto of 1933. This document lays the blame for the social ills of Canadian life upon the capitalist system "with its inherent injustice and inhumanity," in which there is exploitation of one class by another. Had the manifesto gone on to propose a revolutionary solution to this sad condition, it would have differed little from the Communist Manifesto of Marx and Engels. On the contrary, it is a statement of socialist aims that are to be achieved through the seizure of power within the electoral rules of a liberal democracy. Canadian socialism, like socialism generally, is distinguished from liberal ideology by its insistence that class conflict is the central factor in political confrontations. The participants in these political conflicts are classes, broadly divided into the working class versus the capitalist class—the owners and managers of enterprises as well as the whole financial structure of a capitalist society. The working class consists of both farmers and industrial workers. One important mark of Canadian socialism is its origin in agrarian radicalism. (Marx, for example, shared the urban dweller's tendency to look down upon the farmer and what he called "the idiocy of rural life.") The aim of socialist ideology is the establishment of genuine democracy, both political and social. Social democracy means economic equality. Socialists differ in this respect from liberals, who feel that it is sufficient for a just society to have genuine equality of opportunity so that differences of status are not the result of special privileges being given to individuals. The socialist aim is a classless society.

As to the means to achieve this goal of social equality or equality of condition, the socialist is noteworthy for the belief that, since capitalism is the source of social ills, its modification or elimination will provide the remedy for them. But at this point, Canadian socialism shows itself as fairly moderate, although there are some voices for public ownership. The Regina Manifesto foresees a social order "in which economic planning will supersede unregulated private enterprise and competition." It might be argued that liberals too could accept this goal—that, in fact, there is no important political group that wants an unregulated system of private enterprise. As all major parties in Canada have accepted this social goal, at least to some extent, the difference between socialists and liberals lies in the planning used to achieve their goals. Liberal acceptance of this aspect of the Regina Manifesto is an example of the way in which third-party programs are often taken over by the two major parties, thus disarming the socialists and stealing their thunder. The similar plight of the American socialist Norman Thomas leads one to be quite sympathetic with socialist reformers who are bitter about a system that accepts their ideas but rejects their candidates. The Blakeney-Notley Declaration in 1983, aspiring to be a New Regina Manifesto, reviewed the problems of massive unemployment, unacceptable concentrations of wealth and power, and poverty. It called for new policies that would achieve full employment and worker participation in industry. However, its support for an incomes policy would conflict with union opposition to such policies as simply wage controls in disguise.

When members of the NDP try to develop a clear ideological position supporting the goals of economic and social justice—socialism, if you will—they must be careful not to alienate a broader constituency made up of progressives who are not socialists.

The socialist perceives politics as a democratic class struggle that is a method "of expressing and containing the conflict of class interests"[30] or of moderating class interests. This view stands in sharp contrast to the liberal refusal to grant priority to class interests over regional and ethnic interests. Socialist ideology sometimes concentrates on the idea that a greater class consciousness should be brought about and that those who constitute the labourers in society should think in terms of class identity; sometimes it concentrates on the idea that the class struggle has been blurred by the liberal notion of pluralism and the cross-cutting of interests. In other words, in the first case the emphasis is on producing class consciousness, and in the second case the emphasis is on uncovering a latent class consciousness that has been submerged by the propaganda of those who pretend that we live in what is (for all intents and purposes) a classless society, or at least a society with great social mobility that renders class distinctions unimportant.

The most articulate exponents of the socialist ideology in Canada—C.B. Macpherson, Gad Horowitz, and Charles Taylor—have emphasized the need to combat the liberal tendency to denigrate class conflict in favour of analysis in terms of regional and ethnic interests. Charles Taylor in *The Pattern of Politics* offers us a pertinent example of the socialist viewpoint.[31] He opposes to the liberal model of the politics of consensus what he refers to as the politics of polarization, or political alignment on a class basis. He also contrasts the two as the party of principle and the party of compromise. The true bill he brought against liberalism contains the following charges: liberalism advocates the end of ideology; it is elitist and not democratic; it relies on charismatic leadership; it is controlled by, rather than in control of, corporate capitalism; and it has allowed American enterprise to penetrate deeply into the Canadian economy. To the liberal declaration of an end to ideology, Taylor proposes the politics of polarization, in which there will be a confrontation of fundamental opinions, that is, of ideologies. To the elitism and the reliance on charismatic authority (as, for instance, in the case of Pierre Trudeau), Taylor proposes true democracy and political negotiation. To the control by corporate capitalism of the economy, Taylor proposes government control over private investments and pricing policies. And of course the answer to American imperialism is Canadian nationalism, cultural and economic as well as political. The Canadian socialist ideology is strongly nationalistic.[32]

Socialist ideology rests on the assumption that the politics of polarization would be a creative, not a destructive, sort of politics. It would be creative because it would centre on the real problems of Canadian society that are intimately connected with the socioeconomic situation. Socialist ideology insists that the prolongation of the present liberal politics of consensus will ensure that popular discontents and demands for change will be put off, paid off, or simply repressed. The competitive political system, like the competitive economic system, will continue on its way without any regard for the distinction between the interests that should be satisfied and those that should be thwarted. Its neutrality in the current state of affairs prevents it from making such hard decisions. The alternative political system proposed by the socialists is the cooperative commonwealth—that ideal in which functional groups perform socially valuable tasks and are appropriately rewarded.

What we have are two types of political analysis to which correspond two views of the role of political parties and two views of the relation between the economy, the society, and the polity. Liberal analysis sees society in terms of competing interest groups (regional and ethnic, as well as economic), parties as involved in gathering interest groups to constitute a majority, and the government in its role as political broker. Political society is understood in terms of the clash of interests and the means whereby the aims of the competing groups are adjudicated. Interest groups are more extensive than economic groups because regional, ethnic, religious, and cultural interests are not easily reducible to economic interests. The political analysis connected with interest-group liberalism claims to be scientific. Whether this claim is compatible with its tendency to legitimize an interest-group type of political society is questionable. It should be noted that, while democratic socialists may assign a priority to class conflict in theory, democratic socialist governments in practice operate by marshalling the support of interest groups.

The socialist ideology, stemming from Marx but not to be construed as literal Marxism in all respects, gives priority to economic divisions in its analysis and understands groupings, parties, and the political process in terms of basic economic and social cleavages. It is critical of what it considers the consensus politics of interest-group liberalism, which it feels benefits those with wealth and power, to the detriment of the poor, the needy, and the forgotten. It could, although it does not always, criticize this type of liberalism as being undemocratic, because liberalism of this type tends to ensure that the numerical majority will not rule. Like Marx, disciples of this second type of analysis are concerned with uncovering illusions and revealing the true face of the society against the mystifications of the liberals. But its strongest complaint against liberalism is that liberalism is just another form of capitalist ideology—capitalism in its corporate stage.

POPULISM

Populism shares with the socialist ideology a criticism of the powers of finance in a capitalist society; it differs from socialist ideology in that it criticizes certain aspects or institutions of the capitalist system, but not the system in its totality. The populist ideology is not easy to place in the spectrum of ideologies, for while it has its radical side (thus supposedly making it akin to leftism), in the final analysis it has become as reconciled to the capitalist system as have liberal ideology and liberal ideologues.

Although populism is not a term commonly used to designate certain movements such as Social Credit, whose theorist was Major C.H. Douglas and whose main leader was William Aberhart, there are strong reasons for using the term to designate its affinities with populism in North America and with populist movements in Europe. The affiliations of the Canadian variety with other forms of populism precede the discussion of the specific characteristics of the Canadian variety. In other words, Canadian populism will be seen as a species of a particular genus, not as something completely unique. Again, it should be reiterated that what we call populism does not, any more than liberalism, have a one-to-one relation with any political party. Populists have been, of course, particularly evident in the Social Credit movement and in some of its offshoots, but the breed arises in particular circumstances, within a particular social milieu, and from a particular way of thinking about one's situation. Its appeal has been strong among rural communities, but it finds its adherents among urban dwellers as well. Its support depends on the acceptance of its report on the conditions of social and political life—that is, on what we have termed its vision or perception.

If we examine the Social Credit phenomenon in western Canada and the populist movement in the United States in the early years of this century, the resemblances are striking. This coincidence can be explained by the extent of immigration from the United States to Canada at the turn of the century and by the durability of populist attitudes. In both cases we see a radical movement marked by a commitment to democracy and egalitarianism confronting the concentrated power of a financial dictatorship of the bankers. This vision of "the people" arrayed against "the selfish interests" constitutes the primary perception of populist thought. The control the bankers or the financial interests have over the monetary system and credit neutralizes the democratic (numerical) power of the people. In other countries—one thinks of the Narodniks (Populists) in Russia—populism rested on a peasant class. Since no such class existed in North America, the populist appeal must be seen as aimed at the commercial farmers. The historian Richard Hofstadter has described North American populism as "entrepreneurial radicalism," entrepreneurial in the sense that it accepted the basic principles of a capitalistic economic system and radical because of its egalitarian democratic ideals.[33] Let us say, then, that it envisaged a people's capitalism, the attempt to make capitalism work so that the common person could have a share of the profits. When Premier Bill Bennett proposed the privatization of the British Columbia Resources Investment Corporation, and then Prime Minister Clark the privatization of Petro-Canada, one could detect a neoconservative bias; however, when they proposed to distribute shares to the people, by sale or by gift, the tendency was clearly populist. Populist appeals figured prominently in the defence of the old Crow's Nest Pass freight rate, on the premise that the small farmer would be the loser were it to be abrogated.

Populism's perception of social causality led it to see in the monetary system and the manipulation of the monetary system the solution to the problem. This resulted in the attacks on the paper system and the proposals for the free coinage of silver around 1889–90 in the United States, and the expansion of social credit in Canada. We can generalize by saying that populism in North America can be distinguished by its monetary fundamentalism. It has often been remarked that this monetary fundamentalism has been closely associated with religious fundamentalism, as witness the examples of William Jennings Bryan, three times unsuccessful presidential candidate of the Democratic Party in the United States, and William Aberhart, leader of the Social Credit Party in Alberta and premier from 1935 to 1944.

The villains of the piece were, of course, the vested interests of finance, bankers, and monopolists in railroads and industry. The obvious villains were those who controlled credit and those who controlled the cost of transportation, the intermediaries of capitalism. In the populist myth, the independent farmers were looked upon as simple folk preyed upon by selfish interests. This view appealed to a wider section of society, however, for it included small businesspeople and, in fact, all those who were not included in the vested interests. The perception was not of one class against another, as was that of the socialists, but the people against the evil interests.

Populism's monocausal explanation—that is, its identification of one group as responsible for the evils of society—left it vulnerable to the messages of demagogues who could successfully blame economic troubles on a small malevolent group of people, domestic and international bankers, Jews, and communists who were conspiring against the people. While not attempting to define the populist ideology by its pathology or its tendency to paranoia, the anti-Semitism of some of its exponents cannot be ignored. The Keegstra case in Eckville, Alberta, is but one indication that this kind of anti-Semitism is still prevalent.

Socialist attacks upon the capitalist system can see the individual capitalist as much a victim as an exploiter. It is the system that is basically at fault. The populist ideology singles out certain persons supposedly easily identifiable as the cause of social suffering. Hence, there is a danger of populism turning into a witch hunt.

C.B. Macpherson has examined the phenomenon of Social Credit in Alberta and has concluded that the Alberta movement was petit bourgeois, a rejection of the party system, and a trend away from delegate democracy to plebiscitary democracy.[34] He also refers to it as a one-party or a quasi-party system. Without entering into the subtleties of the concept of a quasi-party system, let us examine the question of whether there is any intrinsic relation between one-party monopoly and the populist ideology, or whether the connection is fortuitous and not necessary. Is a one-party system the normal outcome of the successful implementation of a populist ideology or purely a local occurrence without any significance for the essence of populism?

There are various reasons why multiparty systems have not developed in all democratic countries. In the case of the new African states, the founding liberation party claims all adherents, as no one would want to enlist under the banner of a party that was not the "Freedom Party" or the "Liberation Party" or the "Party of the Revolution." Political differences manifest themselves within the heart of the single party. A similar structure and situation can be found in Mexico, which is effectively a one-party state. In some of the Scandinavian countries, one party had such an overwhelming majority as to make the system in reality a one-party state. This is not to ignore the nuances between the Mexican and the Scandinavian cases. So the conditions under which national independence was achieved or the agency by which a revolution was completed or public consent given to the doctrine of social democracy can each give rise to a political process that is, for all intents and purposes, a democracy in which one party has the monopoly of political power.

Now, there are reasons to believe that a populist ideology tends to agglomerate large masses of the population against the exploiting few and, once successful, maintains a people's democracy, although this is in no sense to be confused with the political structures of Eastern Europe. This people's democracy is what is called plebiscitary democracy by Macpherson. However, the success of the Social Credit Party in Alberta and its long monopoly over the internal politics of that province do not offer us a definitive answer to our question as to the relation, if any, between a one-party system and the populist ideology. The evidence is insufficient to venture a categorical judgement. The Social Credit movement, once radical, has now become conservative. The discovery of vast natural resources, not the principles of social credit, has allowed it to satisfy its adherents. Since it affords one of the few instances where disciples of a populist ideology have actually acquired a democratic mandate, it would be fallacious to generalize from this one case.

The social vision of populism is simple, its villains are easily discernible, and its solution to social problems is elementary. Its supporters were and are independent agricultural producers and operators of small businesses. In the populist view, wage earners are also capitalists. Politically, populists are egalitarian democrats. Their principal tactic is a device for the redistribution of wealth in a capitalist society through a change in monetary policy. Although many proposals of the Reform Party, founded in 1987, show an ideological affinity with neo-conservatism, the proposals for grassroots democracy, featuring the referendum, citizen initiatives, and recall, have a decidedly populist flavour to them.

In closing this overview of Canadian ideologies, it might be useful to mention two other ideologies, if only to explain why an extended treatment of them has not been offered. Studies of ideology usually include sections on nationalism and on feminism. There are two salient instances of nationalist ideology in Canada: the nationalism of the left, represented by certain publicists for the New Democratic Party, and Quebec nationalism. Since in the former case it is its socialism that determines its nationalism, rather than the reverse, it constitutes a part of the socialist ideology. Of course, there is the general diffused kind of nationalism that Canadians feel in regard to their gigantic neighbour to the south. But concerning the two salient instances, what could be the common bond between them? There is none. Hence, nationalism as it functions in Canada hardly displays the same coherence as the principal ideological currents. The same may be said of feminism. While no one would question the existence of a movement that in its most popular form articulates an agenda including such aims as pay equity, the legalization of abortion, employment quotas, and publicly financed day-care centres—a less popular form may object to such aims—when an examination is made of various expressions of feminist thought, it becomes clear that feminist ideology is not unified but divided. For instance, a recent study of political ideologies[35] distinguishes between liberal, socialist, and radical feminism. So, like nationalism, feminism generally, and presumably in Canada as well, lacks the kind of coherence we have attributed to the leading Canadian ideologies.

CONCLUSIONS

The four ideologies discussed as relevant to Canadian political life—the liberal, the neoconservative, the socialist, and the populist—would each have its particular critique of the others. The liberal criticizes socialism as divisive, since it fosters class conflict. The liberal also rejects the usual socialist economic recipes as being irrelevant and outmoded in the age of the welfare state. The socialist taxes the liberal with elitism, failure to accept completely a democratic philosophy, and the absence of real community in a society rampant with "possessive individualism." Liberals and socialists no doubt have found it difficult to take neoconservative ideology seriously, rejecting it as a throwback to the nineteenth century. In return, they are seen by the neoconservatives as leading us down the road to serfdom. Both liberals and socialists would criticize populism, with its supposed "funny money" proposals, as simply out of touch with the complications of a modern industrial society. Furthermore, socialists are prone to think of populist movements such as Social Credit and Les Créditistes as manifestations of petit bourgeois discontent, like the *poujadistes* in France between 1954 and 1956. Although equally defenders of capitalism, and superficially similar on other points, neoconservatism and populism tend in opposite directions on monetary matters: the former supports tighter money policies and the latter easier ones.

Each ideology challenges the commitment of the others to the democratic ideal. Each has its particular economic program, whether it be Keynesian, monetarist, Marxist, democratic socialist, or the institution of social credit. They differ in their analysis of the important actors and factors in social life, one emphasizing interest groups, another critical of them, another emphasizing social classes, and another stressing the people and the enemies of the people.

Because each of these ideologies stresses certain aspects of political life while playing down or ignoring others, they all have their analytical inadequacies. This is not to say, by any means, that they are value free.

Their analytical inadequacies are ordinarily the result of their giving priority to some social values over others. A critique of them from the outside, if such is possible, would have to examine their respective worth from the moral and pragmatic viewpoint, as well as from the viewpoint of their analytical adequacy. The moral viewpoint implies a grading of worthwhile objects, while the pragmatic viewpoint concerns the possibility of implementing an ideology.

Political scientists are most keen on the analytic worth of a political theory—its explanatory potential—while the ordinary citizen is no doubt more concerned with the values an ideology defends and the possibility of one's ideological dreams coming true.

Having considered ideologies in a more or less abstract way, in subsequent chapters we will examine the ways in which they are translated by interest groups and political parties into the real world of politics and how they affect the behaviour of elites, masses, and the media that report on them.

TABLE 4.1
THE MAIN IDEOLOGIES IN CANADA

	Main Value(s)	Social Configuration	Policy Orientation
Conservatism	social order	classes*	pragmatic adjustments (e.g., electoral reform)
Liberalism	freedom (and equality)	interest groups (positive)	wage-price control national energy policy
Neoconservatism	freedom	interest groups (negative)	deregulation privatization monetarism
Socialism	equality (and freedom)	classes	redistribution nationalization industrial democracy
Populism	equality (independence)	people versus vested interests	social credit: distributive capitalism

* "The conservative must believe that class distinction can be represented either as a necessary evil or as a social good." Roger Scruton, *The Meaning of Conservatism* (Totowa, NJ: Barnes and Noble Books, 1980), 179.

RECOMMENDED READING

Brooks, Stephen J., ed. *Political Thought in Canada: Contemporary Perspectives.* Toronto: Irwin, 1984.

Christian, William, and Colin Campbell. *Political Parties and Ideologies in Canada*, 3rd ed. Toronto: McGraw-Hill Ryerson, 1990.

Horn, Michiel. *The League for Social Reconstruction: Intellectual Origins of the Democratic Left in Canada 1930–1942.* Toronto: University of Toronto Press, 1980.

Marchak, M. Patricia. *Ideological Perspectives on Canada*, 3rd ed. Toronto: McGraw-Hill Ryerson, 1988.

Qualter, Terence H. *Conflicting Political Ideas in Liberal Democracies.* Toronto: Methuen, 1986.

Taylor, Charles. *Reconciling the Solitudes: Essays on Canadian Federalism and Nationalism.* Montreal: McGill-Queen's University Press, 1993.

CHAPTER 5

Political Parties

THE POLITICAL PROCESS

We often speak of people practising politics at work, at play, or in the home. When we head a section of this book "The Political Process," does it therefore mean that we intend to investigate all those myriad areas of Canadian life in which there are activities with the attributes of politics? Obviously, we would not do that any more than people interested in studying track and field would time every person in Canada running to catch a bus. The definition of politics that we find most useful is this: *Politics is an activity in which people individually and collectively use such power as they may possess to influence decisions about public policy.*[1] Power consists of attributes such as physical force, money, or intelligence; influence is the ability to affect others in such a way that they may do what they might otherwise not do.[2] Public policy encompasses those decisions taken by people acting in the name of that set of social institutions identified as the state. It is the "public policy" part of the definition that restricts our use of the term "politics," for it is obvious that people use such power as they have to influence decisions in almost every phase of their lives.

Politics, in the restricted sense we are using, can be distinguished from activities involving power and influence in areas of life other than those concerned with public policy on other grounds as well. It has an intrinsic value of its own in the realm of public life, whereas similar activities in other areas are much less important than the ultimate aim of the organization. For instance, the preservation of the democratic principle of rule by majority consent in public life is considered essential regardless of the kinds of decisions reached using that technique, whereas in the operation of business concerns, the pursuit of profit is considered more important than any particular method of decision making. It might be noted here that in the past decade there has been strong pressure in many nongovernmental institutions to democratize decision making that would, in effect, politicize these institutions. It can be argued, however, that the concern is more for changing the nature of the decisions taken rather than with politics itself. We will return to this theme later when we discuss participatory democracy.

The political process, therefore, is the dynamic activity within that set of relationships—the political system—that produces public policy. We can liken the political system to a machine that is shut off. All the parts are there ready to go into action. When the machine is working and in production, the operation that is going on is the political process. Put another way, the term "political system" is an abstract description of the relationship between those elements that produce public policy. The political process, however, is something that actually happens.

The political process is so complex—since it can conceivably involve almost everyone who lives in the state—that a comprehensive description would be difficult to follow. We therefore propose to break it down into its various components. The key event within the political process is the actual decision making, which leads directly to a public policy reflected in an administrative action or the passage of a law. This decision making goes on within the legally constituted machinery of the state: the legislature, the executive (including the bureaucracy), and the judiciary, which comprise the formal political system and can be usefully defined as the governmental process. This governmental process could degenerate into meaningless formalism were it not for the variety of informal components of the political process that provide the government with leadership and personnel, as well as with the ideas and issues that form the raison d'être of a decision-making structure. It is useful, therefore, to study separately these two aspects of the political process, although it should be remembered that in practice it is impossible to separate the legal and nonlegal components.

The informal aspects of the political process form the background to the governmental process and permeate it, as well as every other area of public life. The decision to enter into the Free Trade Agreement with the United States provides an example. This decision became embodied in law because it passed through the formal governmental lawmaking process; that is, it was introduced into the House of Commons by a Cabinet minister, went through the formal lawmaking stages in the House and the Senate, and was given royal assent by the governor general. However, the forces that combined to enact this law were much broader than the formal steps described above. First of all, a governing party had to be in office whose leaders believed in free trade and the market-oriented economic philosophy behind it. The prime minister and Cabinet had first to formulate a policy on this vital issue, having regard to a variety of views and pressures both within the party and in society generally. Those Cabinet ministers who were most involved had to chart a course that paid some attention to the views of those Canadians who felt that the provisions of the Free Trade Agreement would threaten vital Canadian interests and values. The decision to negotiate a treaty and then to introduce the legislation created the need to have an advertising campaign to sell the idea. Another election took place in which the governing party had to defend its policy against opposition party attacks. Business interests spent millions of dollars on advertising to support free trade, while labour unions and other interests, such as the cultural community, spent money and effort to prevent the deal by defeating the government. After the Mulroney government was reelected, it passed the legislation but still had to face implications of the policy, such as what support would be provided for those who lost jobs due to free trade. Before free trade emerged, all kinds of political processes came into play, including an election campaign, the involvement of major interest groups, and media coverage of the issue as it unfolded. As this example illustrates, the formal government action that enacts the law is only a small part of the entire train of events necessary for such a law to emerge.

A discussion of the more formal governmental process will be left to later chapters; this section will deal with the more informal or nonlegal elements of the political process. The major hinge between the informal political process and the legal governmental process is the party system, and it is to that system we now turn.

THE POLITICAL PARTY

A political party is an organization devoted to occupying the offices that constitute the institutions of government. These offices in Canada can be found at the municipal, provincial, and federal levels, although it is still uncommon for parties openly to seek municipal office. The only elective offices are in the House of Commons at the federal level and the legislative assemblies at the provincial level. (We will not discuss municipal elective offices.) However, when political parties gain control of elective offices, they are able to place their adherents in other nonelective positions, such as the Senate, the judiciary, and government boards, commissions, and agencies. The most important appointments resulting from a political party's electoral victory are, of course, those of the prime minister and the Cabinet, who occupy the key roles in deciding public policy.

Parties seek control of government in order to carry out their ideas of what public policy should be. The career goals and personal motives of individual party members, however, should not be ignored.

In Canada parties have varied considerably in the degree to which they have adhered to a consistent set of ideas; that is, some have been *ideological*, while others have been *pragmatic*. Those parties that have been ideological have been less successful in gaining electoral support than the pragmatic parties. Since Canada is a pluralistic society, the most successful parties have been those willing to accept a wide enough variety of ideas and their adherents to be able to enjoy widespread support. Thus, Canada's two major parties since Confederation, the Liberals and the Progressive Conservatives (although the latter were reduced to only two seats in 1993), have been notable for their nonideological approach to governing Canada.[3] They have not varied dramatically in their philosophical approach. Rather, their differences have centred on specific issues or sets of issues that change over time (the British connection, tariffs, federal-provincial relations, and, with the rise of neoconservative attitudes in the Progressive Conservative Party, privatization and deregulation), and on personalities—that is, the quality of their leadership. It is interesting to recall that in 1911 the Liberals under Laurier supported free trade and lost to the Conservatives, who used nationalistic arguments against free trade. In 1988 the party positions were reversed, as the Progressive Conservatives under Mulroney fostered free trade and defeated the Liberals under Turner, who tried to muster nationalistic opposition to the idea. Once returned to office in 1993, however, the Liberals negotiated only marginal cosmetic changes to the Free Trade Agreement and continued privatization and government downsizing in response to the trend of public opinion.

On the other hand, periodically parties have arisen that have felt that an entirely new approach is necessary for governing Canada. In the case of the Co-operative Commonwealth Federation (CCF), the new approach was embodied in a philosophy—socialism—that ran counter to the liberal free-enterprise capitalism espoused by the major parties. The successor to the CCF was organized in 1961 as the New Democratic Party. While it retained some of the socialism of the CCF, it was less dogmatic in setting down the policies it pursued, and to some degree it attempted to have a broad appeal like the major parties. The Waffle movement, which was prominent within the NDP during the period 1969–72, urged a return to the basic socialist principles of the Regina Manifesto and added a heavy dose of nationalism. In the end, however, the NDP rejected the movement's demands for ideological purity in favour of a position that would be more attractive to a wider span of voters.[4] Disappointment among NDP supporters surfaced again after the 1988 election. Although the 43 seats won represented their best ever result, none was in Quebec or Atlantic Canada. Most were in western Canada, and the emergence to majority party status did not materialize. In the 1993 election, the NDP gained only 7% of the vote and only nine seats in the House of Commons.

Less philosophical than the CCF but still espousing an approach widely different from the traditional parties was the Social Credit Party, which won office in Alberta in 1935. The major distinguishing characteristic of this party was its theory of monetary management. The party went through a metamorphosis at the federal level, and its main strength was found in Quebec in the 1960s and 1970s before it faded in the 1980s, although it continued as a coalition of conservative forces in British Columbia provincial politics. Other parties have flourished briefly, then waned in response to particular regional, economic, and social conditions. Chief among them was the Progressive Party, which elected 64 members to the House of Commons in 1921. A decade later, however, this party had expired. Western Canada has been the most fertile ground for regional parties, and the Reform Party reflected this tradition beginning in the 1988 election. The Reform Party won 52 seats in 1993. Almost all of these were in Alberta and British Columbia, although it received 20% of the votes in Ontario but only one seat. With no support in Quebec, declining popular support as reflected in polls as the next election drew nearer, and leader Preston Manning unable to create a strong leadership image, it was unclear whether the Reform Party would retain its status as the primary vehicle for right-wing politics at the national level.

In Quebec the Bloc Québécois is the latest manifestation of a nationalist party seeking to influence federal politics. The Bloc won 54 seats in the 1993 election and became the official opposition in the House of Commons. Given its stated intention of pursuing separatist goals in Ottawa, it was hardly taken seriously as the official opposition. It remains to be seen if Quebec voters will give the Bloc a continuing role in federal politics.

At the federal level, Canada can be said to have had a *modified two-party system* for most of its history until 1993. A two-party system is one in which only two parties effectively vie for power, although others may exist. In Canada's case it has been true that only two parties have ever been in a position to form the federal government, but other parties—the CCF/NDP and Social Credit—have maintained a persistent claim on the loyalties of a segment of the national electorate and have been able to form provincial governments. They have thus been in a position to affect the public policy of the country, especially in times of minority government, although even in those times they have been denied representation in the Cabinet. Whether the 1993 election is remembered as a *deviating election* or a *realigning election*, and the beginning of a multiparty system, is a question that will be answered in future elections.[5]

One might well wonder why in a country as diverse as Canada a large majority of the electorate consistently supports the two major parties, whereas in much more ethnically homogeneous countries like France and Italy support is divided among a large number of parties.

Brokerage parties seek to aggregate various interests by exercising a pragmatic flexibility that would be less possible if they adhered to a more rigid ideology—for example, based on *socioeconomic class*. The brokerage approach of the Liberals and Progressive Conservatives is the main reason for the ability to coalesce support for their respective party. A majority of Canadians still rejects the idea of class politics, at least at the federal level, because they look upon themselves as being members of a broad middle class.[6] Moreover, the major parties have catered to and fostered this approach as a means of constructing non-class attitudes and maintaining themselves in power. The success these parties have had by using this approach has thwarted the attempts of minor parties to organize the electorate along more ideological lines. The major parties have seen their role as brokers among various legitimate interests, especially as these interests are reflected in regional and cultural diversity. The fact that the Liberal Party formed the government for 66 of the first 97 years of this century attests to its skill in brokerage politics.[7]

However, from the 1960s through to the 1980s, the Liberal Party had very little electoral success in western Canada, just as the Progressive Conservative Party did very poorly in Quebec until 1984. In that year under Brian Mulroney, a native son of that province, the Progressive Conservative Party made a historic breakthrough, and that result was even surpassed in 1988. The Liberals were reduced to only 12 seats in what had once been the bastion that supported their dominant national role. Even in their 1993 victory, the Liberals got only 19 of 75 Quebec seats as the Bloc Québécois gained from Progressive Conservative losses. Historically, therefore, both major parties have had difficulty in achieving truly national representation. Brokerage among the regions by political parties has become progressively more difficult, and the role of the parties as agents of effective federalism has correspondingly diminished. For instance, during the 1980s a major concern in Ontario, the home of the automobile industry, was the volume of Japanese car imports. Both management and union in that industry agreed that content regulations should be imposed on Japanese car makers. However, those interests in western Canada who exported extensively to Japan, such as the forestry and mining industries, were understandably less anxious to attack the interests of their overseas customers. The Free Trade Agreement with the United States, which took effect on January 1, 1989, initially created similar differences of opinion between a majority of Ontario residents and majorities elsewhere, the former opposing free trade and the latter embracing it.

Major party platforms have usually avoided radical proposals, which tend to polarize interests and thus force the parties to abandon their brokerage function. Party leaders, therefore, have had a difficult stage to perform on because there were often few emotional issues to attract voters. However, since leaders consciously fostered this situation, their middle-of-the-road approach to issues has been of their own making. More recently, the availability of mass media has made it necessary for the politicians themselves to evoke some emotional response based on their personality, even if the political issues do not spark controversy. Thus, the Progressive Conservative leadership contest in 1993 between Kim Campbell, who emerged victorious and became Canada's first female prime minister, and Jean Charest revolved around "winability," not around any major policy differences.

Canadian political history has certainly not lacked colourful political leaders, but they have more often come from provincial politics. Strong characters such as William Aberhart, Maurice Duplessis, Mitchell Hepburn, Joey Smallwood, W.A.C. Bennett, Dave Barrett, René Lévesque, Brian Peckford, and Ralph Klein have enlivened the Canadian political scene. The more restricted area of provincial politics has provided fertile soil for the development of flamboyant politicians. It is at this level that the smaller parties have been able to succeed in gaining victories and putting their leaders in the premier's office. This is especially the case in western Canada, where in the 1970s and 1980s Ed Schreyer and Howard Pawley in Manitoba and Allan Blakeney in Saskatchewan held their provinces for the NDP, and in British Columbia, where first Dave Barrett for the NDP and then Bill Bennett and Bill Vander Zalm for the Social Credit Party controlled the government. In the 1990s Roy Romanow returned the NDP to power in Saskatchewan. Mike Harcourt led the NDP to victory in British Columbia, and Glen Clark retained office in 1996, while Bob Rae, the first NDP premier of Ontario, governed from 1990 to 1995. The victory of the Parti Québécois under René Lévesque in Quebec in 1976 and 1981 and under Jacques Parizeau in 1994 represents a very special case.

At the federal level, Tommy Douglas and Réal Caouette were examples of colourful leaders, but again they appealed to narrower constituencies than have the major leaders. An exception to this generalization, however, was John Diefenbaker. His leadership of the Progressive Conservative Party changed that party's character for almost a decade, and although he did gather a coalition of voters, including Québécois who followed his charismatic leadership for a while, the coalition soon broke up, and under him the Progressive Conservative Party tended to polarize more than coalesce voters. Had his personal appeal been adapted to brokerage politics of the traditional nature, he might well have held power much longer, but he lacked the capacity for welding the various interests of Canada together by compromise. He tried to unite Canadians by a grandiose idealism that would supersede their particular interests; however, when he showed weakness in translating his vision into reality, the voters reverted to the more traditional regional and ethnic responses that he could not adequately serve.

This example brings us back to our argument that the major parties have maintained their hold on power at the federal level by unspectacular, subtle, and low-key pragmatism that offers a little to everyone in all parts of Canada without polarizing the Canadian community. Even though many Canadians (not in the west, however) opted for flamboyance in the leadership of Pierre Elliott Trudeau, there is little indication that they have abandoned their preference for pragmatic, stable policy orientation. The unwillingness of Brian Mulroney to engage in major policy pronouncements in the early months of his leadership of the Progressive Conservative Party showed that he understood the dangers of staking out too clear a position. He did not want to repeat the mistake of a former Progressive Conservative leader, Robert Stanfield, whose wage-and-price-control proposals during the 1974 election put him in the position of defending a policy rather than attacking the government. Mulroney was able to win reelection in 1988 despite his failure to achieve personal popularity. In 1993 Jean Chrétien led the Liberals to victory even though he trailed Kim Campbell in personal popularity for most of the campaign and surpassed her only as voting neared. He capitalized on the unpopularity of the former government by conducting a competent campaign.

On the basis of what has just been argued, it follows that the nature of major and minor parties in Canada has differed sharply. The major parties, which have sought to play a brokerage role, have been mainly organized to get votes; conversely, the minor parties, which have been based on a more cohesive set of ideas, have been more prone to involve their members in study and participation based on their beliefs. Their policies have been less expedient for getting votes, so that the parties have had smaller but much more committed memberships. Their devotion to ideas and causes over long periods of time has enabled at least one minor party—the CCF/NDP—to have some effect on public policy, even though it has not had major electoral success at the federal level. Even in that party, however, there is a constant tension between pragmatism and idealism. For instance, provincial NDP governments in the 1990s, especially the Rae government in Ontario, faced criticism from their own supporters when financial constraints forced them to modify or abandon traditional party goals. Those conflicts were cited as one of the reasons for the NDP's low voter support and disastrous results in the 1993 election.

The Reform Party, under the leadership of Preston Manning, has its major appeal in Alberta and British Columbia but has attracted voters elsewhere. The party has a populist program calling for referendums, constituency rather than party control of MPs, and the threat of recall and parliamentary reform. Equally important, the party has provided a home for disgruntled Conservatives and others who want more deficit reduction, stricter crime control, less immigration, and leaner government. Whether the Reform Party will consolidate its position in future elections is a key question for the future of the party system in Canada.

The Bloc Québécois has given itself a short-term role. That role is to represent the interests of Quebec in the House of Commons until Quebec achieves independence. Bloc hopes to achieve it by 1997 have been forestalled, and this raises the question of how long the party can play a role on the national stage.

Major party organizations have tended to be skeletal between elections, with perhaps two or three events, probably social rather than political, occurring per year. When elections are called, however, many more people work for these parties to mobilize support. This situation is facilitated in part by the fact that the major parties have the opportunity to appoint hundreds of party supporters to be enumerators (who will no longer be needed after the 1997 election, after which there will be a permanent federal voters' list), deputy returning officers, and poll clerks who are paid out of public money, as specified in the Canada Elections Act.[8] This type of patronage has its advantages because, although the amounts of money concerned are minimal, they are enough to encourage public participation in the political process. Members of the minor parties, as we noted previously, have to be more ideologically committed, partly because their parties are less capable of providing them with paid public positions during elections or patronage appointments after elections.

The major parties since the 1960s have tended to create more opportunities than before for policy discussions within the party, in an attempt to give the rank and file an outlet. This trend has not led to grassroots control, and so far the major parties have not had their policy orientation determined by anyone but the leaders of the party. Policy discussions among the rank and file have, therefore, tended more to be occasions for letting off steam and expressing regional and other forms of dissatisfaction than for producing firm party policy. The debate and disagreement within the Liberal Party about the Meech Lake Accord in 1987–88 points out the potential danger of party division on policy. The position of party leader John Turner was undermined by party members who rejected his support of the Accord. The price of democratic party debate on an important policy can be the erosion of public confidence in the party and its leader. Strong leadership from the top in policy formation is still the primary characteristic of the major parties, regardless of their attempts to democratize the policy-making process.

The relationship of the party to its leaders when those leaders also happen to form the government is one that makes party democracy difficult. For although the leaders cannot be indifferent to those who worked for their victory in the previous election, neither can they forget that they are running a government with responsibilities to all Canadians—not just their party supporters. Thus, tensions may develop between the *parliamentary party* (those from the party who have been elected to the House of Commons) and the party organization. Many of this latter group will be more attuned to the problems of their own area than to the national circumstances that must be the first concern of the parliamentary party leaders. For example, while the need for the protection of French-language rights may seem self-evident to a Liberal Cabinet led by Jean Chrétien, it may seem totally irrelevant as far as the local party organizations in Manitoba are concerned.

It is, therefore, always difficult for the major parties based on brokerage politics, which must operate at the top, to reconcile local and national concerns within a framework of party democracy. Sometimes these divisions find their expression in the choice of a new party leader. Regional feeling and ideological commitment, which may or may not have a regional basis, often form a foundation for leadership support. This tendency has been more evident in the Progressive Conservative Party, which, as the opposition party for much of this century, has had more leadership changes than the Liberals. What is perhaps most remarkable about Liberal leadership is the very small number of leaders in this century up to 1997: seven to be exact. The Liberal leadership convention of 1984 to replace Trudeau was the first in that party in 16 years, and its choice of John Turner as leader was a testimonial to that party's commitment to electoral politics rather than ideology. Turner's inability to deliver electoral victory was not the norm for a Liberal leader, and he was succeeded by Jean Chrétien. *Leadership conventions*, therefore, are indisputably the most important events for political parties other than, of course, elections themselves. Returning to the Progressive Conservatives, we would note that the succession of leaders from Diefenbaker to Mulroney reflects the frustration of a party that has tended to blame its defeats on its leaders. Leadership contests during the 1960s, 1970s, and 1980s in that party were hotly and often bitterly fought campaigns that provided some of the most interesting political drama of those decades. Mulroney's resignation in 1993 gave the Progressive Conservative Party a rare opportunity to choose a new leader while governing, rather than after losing an election.

PARTY ORGANIZATION

The organization of the major parties reflects their primary function as vote-getting mechanisms. The demands of federalism necessitate a broad tolerance of intraparty diversity in the parties' operations both during and between elections. The basic and most important unit of the party is at the constituency, or riding, level[9] for both the federal and the provincial branches of the party. There are separate riding associations since federal and provincial riding boundaries are not the same. It is well to keep in mind that the only position contested at both the federal and provincial levels is the office of Member of Parliament or member of the provincial legislature for each constituency.

In each constituency an elected executive is primarily responsible for holding a *nomination meeting* at which its party's candidate is elected. Only a small fraction of Canadians takes an active part in the work of political parties at either the federal or provincial level, and thus the mechanics of representative democracy are in the hands of the few. The executive is elected from party supporters at an annual constituency meeting. While each constituency has a constitution that is supposed to conform to guidelines established by the federal party organization, the informality of local operations is such that they may vary considerably from national norms.

The major function of the party executive is to hold a nomination convention at which the party's candidate for MP can be chosen. However, the executive will go further than this and often try to recruit capable potential candidates to seek nomination. When the party is high in the public's esteem, there may be spirited competition for nominations. If not, it is more difficult to find a willing sacrificial lamb. In this function the local organization acts almost exclusively without interference from outside, although in 1988 there was considerable controversy raised in some Liberal constituency nominations in Quebec, where senior party officials insisted on determining the choice. More typically in the past, when the federal party wanted a person of its choice to seek election in a constituency (for example, where a well-known party figure was seeking a seat), it needed the concurrence of the constituency, as in the candidacy of Brian Mulroney in Central Nova in 1983. If the constituency and federal party disagreed, the federal party usually backed down. The Liberal Party has given its leader some power to name candidates. One reason for this was to prevent nomination of single-issue candidates (e.g., right to life) who might espouse views at variance with those of the party. Another reason was to reserve nomination for star candidates or underrepresented groups (e.g., women). This caused considerable controversy in 1993. Local independence, however, still forms the basis of party organization and normally results in representation by a local person in the House of Commons. When the party is represented by the *incumbent* member, he or she is usually renominated, if the member so wishes.

The role of the local party organization between elections is to keep the constituency informed of the member's activities and, in general, to try to improve his or her chances for reelection. The party may pass on complaints and problems and requests for favours to the elected member, acting as a link between the constituency and its representative. If the party does not have a sitting member, its constituency officials may play an important role in maintaining contacts with elected party colleagues elsewhere. During the election itself, the members of the party executive occupy key positions in planning and executing the campaign and using resources made available to them both locally and nationally. In the past, it has only been during elections that the major parties have promoted participation by a wide segment of the public.

A number of constituencies within a provincial area may combine to form a district association. These are very loosely organized bodies with ill-defined powers. They may act as a coordinating body for arrangements connected with the visits of party dignitaries, and on occasion they may hold conferences related to the common problems of the constituencies represented in the district. Some of them also maintain district offices that act as clearing houses for information and as points of contact with the public. There may also be university or college organizations that take part in party activities.

The next level of organization is the provincial office of the party. This is a coalition of the ridings at the provincial level. The provincial headquarters represents both federal and provincial riding associations within most provinces. The first exception to this was the Liberal Party in Quebec, which initiated separate organizations for its provincial and federal ridings. In 1976 the Liberal Party in Ontario separated its provincial and national organizations, and subsequently the Liberal organizations in several other provinces have followed suit. The purpose of provincial headquarters is to keep ridings informed of the latest developments within the party and to keep records of the members of executives of the riding organizations up to date. This is of key importance, since a knowledge of those who are the power brokers in local areas is vital for mobilizing support for elections and effecting the will of the party leaders. The provincial party is entirely responsible for central direction of provincial elections and is the key organization for federal campaign activities within the province. Parties employ full-time organizers to varying degrees in the different provinces, and these party workers provide support and direction to the part-time volunteers who make up constituency organizations.

The provincial executive is elected by riding delegates to the provincial convention, and this executive directs the work of the party. In addition, there is a full-time professional staff to maintain contact with the riding associations, to do research, and to disseminate information. The operations of provincial party organizations vary from province to province and party to party; thus, all that can be given here is an outline of their major purpose, which is to make sure that each constituency maintains some skeletal organization that can be filled out and set in motion during an election. When a party holds office in a province, the provincial party may have more importance than its federal counterpart. For instance, the Progressive Conservative Party organization of Ontario was dominated by its provincial wing during its long successful period of rule ending in 1985, and this situation reemerged with its return to office in 1995.

The federal level of the party is composed of representatives from the provincial organizations and national women's, youth, and university groups. Its convention chooses a national executive, which directs the work of the party. The national executive is responsible for organizing the annual convention, policy conferences, and, when necessary, leadership conventions to choose a new national leader. There is a full-time staff that conducts research, disseminates information, and coordinates fund-raising activities. The national organization, being centred in Ottawa, maintains close contact with sitting members and, if it is the government party, with the prime minister and Cabinet. Party leaders have paid staff of their own choosing.

As one can see by this sketch of party organization in Canada, the closer one gets to the national level, the more full-time staff and resources are available for deciding policy questions as well as electoral strategy. In addition, at the top level of the party there is closer contact between the party and its parliamentary members. Thus, although major parties have been trying to promote more participation in policy discussions at all party levels, up until now those discussions have been primarily centred in the upper echelons of the party and among intellectuals associated with the party. The constituency organizations have remained primarily election-fighting mechanisms.[10] In the aftermath of the 1988 election, some disgruntled New Democratic Party supporters charged that their party had gone too far in this direction as well and had abandoned party traditions in doing so.

The party system and the ways in which it works have always been the subject of criticism by ordinary Canadians. For one thing, in a supposedly democratic country like Canada, only a small minority plays an active role in party politics, and the rest of the population ranges from some degree of activity to complete detachment.

For most Canadians active political participation in a party is something someone else does.[11] Since government is so involved in people's lives and tends to be the scapegoat for many of the frustrations of modern living, the party system and those who operate it come in for considerable abuse, much of it unwarranted. A reasonable solution to this situation would be for greater numbers of citizens to participate in the processes that contribute to decision making. This increased political activity, called participatory democracy, would involve more people in public policy and might lessen the feeling that it is the work of a small minority. However, participatory democracy in Canadian society at present is more easily wished for than accomplished. The truth is that most people do not have the time; but more important, they lack the inclination to participate in party politics consistently. Thus, a modest expectation of participatory democracy is that political parties will be structured so that all those who wish to participate may do so. Other more direct forms of influencing public policy may be possible through organized interest groups, but it is difficult to envision how people

could have a general continuous impact on federal and provincial policies except through political parties.

The major parties have become more sensitive to this need, and this
development owes much to the example set by the protest parties of
the Prairies in the 1920s and 1930s. In that era disillusionment with
the existing party system led leaders like J.S. Woodsworth, E.A.
Partridge, H.W. Wood, William Aberhart, and M.C. Coldwell to start
movements in which ordinary citizens could study and propose
changes in the structure of government and public policy. The movements generated many reform ideas, which would have taken longer to
emerge from the brokerage parties associated with the status quo.
Protest parties thus provided a catalyst for broader participation. This
atypical development in Canadian party politics, however, was mainly
confined to the Prairies, except for its expression in the CCF/NDP,
which has had a significant national presence for the last 50 years.
Since the 1970s, the tradition of spirited intraparty policy debate has
perhaps been best exemplified in the Parti Québécois, which has represented both a provincial political party and a political movement.

The Progressive Party of the 1920s encouraged a viewpoint that the
Member of Parliament should act as a delegate carrying out the will of
the constituents, rather than as a *representative* (or *trustee*) using personal initiative and presenting his or her record periodically for the
electors to judge. This *delegate* theory was contrary to the concept of
party representation that, it has traditionally been assumed, is crucial
to the working of the parliamentary system. This illustrates a major difficulty in participatory democracy concerning the issues on which a
Member of Parliament should seek out constituents' views. It would be
hard to argue that a Member of Parliament can realistically hope to get
direction from his or her constituents on anything but broad policy (for
example, war or peace) or on very local issues (the need for a new post
office).[12] Most day-to-day government policy involves issues that are
complex and need considerable study and expert advice before rational decisions can be made. Moreover, the requirements of party discipline within the parliamentary system can serve to inhibit the representative role of MPs. John Nunziata, a Liberal MP, was no doubt
representing the views of his constituents in York South-Weston when
he attacked his own party for failing to replace the unpopular Goods
and Services Tax. But by voting against his government's budget in
1996, he violated the basic rule of party discipline and was expelled
from the party caucus.

However, ordinary people can and should have the opportunity to
influence the broad policies that a party adopts. Every citizen can be
considered capable of voicing an opinion about priorities that should
be considered, for example, for more defence or more social welfare.
The refinements (what airplane to build or how to amortize a pension
fund) are not as clear-cut, and it is here that the role of the representa-

tive seems indispensable. Nonetheless, for many people the idea of giving citizens a direct choice by way of using referenda is attractive. During the 1980s, for instance, there were frequent calls for a national vote on capital punishment. In the 1990s the Reform Party espouses these mechanisms of direct democracy.

FIGURE 5.1
PROGRESSIVE CONSERVATIVE PARTY OF CANADA

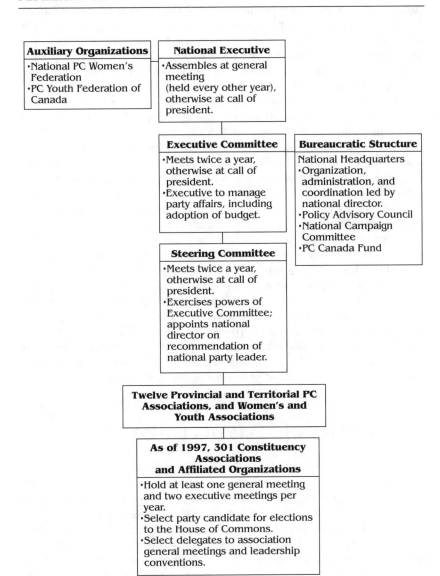

The simple truth is that, so far in our history, people have shown that they participate actively in large numbers only when they feel that a policy is going to affect them personally and directly. Even in those cases, however, the number of people who take direct interest in politics is limited. For the most part, Canadians (and citizens of every other country) have a fatalistic attitude about the amount of influence they can exercise over their government. For some people this attitude might reflect a general satisfaction with the conditions of life in the country. However, when people are deeply concerned about conditions, especially economic conditions, and what the government is doing about them, movements such as the Prairie protest groups that we have discussed find ready acceptance for their pleas that people become involved in order to facilitate change. When the conditions that give impetus to these movements are alleviated and life becomes better, large numbers of marginal participants relapse into their usual non-involvement. Especially in affluent times, people have a number of leisure pursuits that normally take priority over their political activities. More recently, noneconomic issues—such as law and order problems, both sides of the abortion question, pornography, and environmental concerns—have mobilized considerable interest in the community.

It should be noted, however, that most of this activity has taken place outside the confines of party organizations. Major parties with their aggregative and brokerage functions do not find it easy to take definitive stands on issues in which the community is sharply divided or to adopt a policy stance that is perhaps held only by an intensely committed minority. This may lead to charges that, on some of the leading issues of the 1990s, party organizations have abdicated their role in the community to more limited interest groups. It may also be argued that the municipal level of government provides the best opportunity for political involvement. The issues are close at hand and so are those in elected positions. Citizens may be able to influence decisions without having to make as great sacrifices in time and money as may be called for by involvement in federal or provincial politics.

LIMITATIONS TO PARTICIPATION

Lest it be mistakenly thought that we are arguing that everyone in Canada has been in a position to take an active part in political life, let us emphasize here that we make no such claim. Indeed, conditions of extreme poverty, with their attendant lack of adequate health, education, and the other attributes that make political participation possible for other Canadians, effectively deny that opportunity to a scandalously large number of people. If their cause has been taken up at all in the past, it has been represented by people like social workers and other individuals who, though concerned, are nonetheless outsiders. It is only recently that these groups, which include Native peoples, the elderly, the physically disabled, and welfare recipients, among others, have begun to argue their own cause in an assertive manner. As yet, however, these groups have shown little inclination to work within any party and thus remain interest groups outside rather than within party structures.

Another group of Canadians, women, who indeed constitute a majority of eligible Canadian voters, have been traditionally relegated to a minor role in Canadian government. It was not until 1920 that the federal franchise was extended to all women of voting age. (Mothers and wives of military personnel could vote in 1917, and some provinces extended the right before the federal government did.) The long delay in granting even this basic political right revealed the attitude of our male-dominated system toward the role of women in politics. However, this began to change dramatically in the 1970s and 1980s, and more women are now taking part in significant activity within party organizations. More are becoming candidates for election, and more are achieving electoral success. The most striking development in the emergence of women in federal politics was seen in the successful leadership campaign of Kim Campbell, whose victory in the Progressive Conservative race of 1993 made her Brian Mulroney's successor as prime minister. In addition, Audrey McLaughlin in 1989 and Alexa McDonough in 1996 assumed the leadership of the NDP, while in 1990 Sheila Copps was a serious contender for the leadership of the Liberal Party.

The prominent roles played by Monique Bégin and Judy Erola in the Liberal Cabinet of the early 1980s, by Pat Carney, Barbara MacDougall, Flora MacDonald, and Kim Campbell in the Mulroney governments, by Sheila Copps in the Chrétien government and by Deborah Grey in the Reform Party, the election of Iona Campagnolo as president of the Liberal Party and Johanna DenHertog of the NDP, and, above all, the appointment of Jeanne Sauvé, first as speaker of the House and then as governor general, reflected the growing role of women in the elite structure of national politics. The ascent of Kim Campbell to the pinnacle of political success as prime minister did not signal the equality of women in federal politics, but it was certainly a major milestone. At the provincial level, Rita Johnson in British Columbia became the first female premier in 1991, followed by Catherine Callbeck in PEI in 1993. Sharon Carstairs in Manitoba, Linda Haverstock in Saskatchewan, Alexa McDonough in Nova Scotia, Barbara Baird-Filliter in New Brunswick, and Lynn McLeod in Ontario became leaders of their parties. Nonetheless, women continue to be dramatically underrepresented in the ranks of leading party personnel.[13] In 1993 a record 53 women were elected to the House of Commons, but of 22 Cabinet members only 4 were women.

The adoption of the Charter of Rights and Freedoms in 1982 created the opportunity for both Native peoples and women to argue their case for greater recognition in Canadian society. These groups were successful in focusing greater attention on the need to improve their political and legal status. It needs to be pointed out, however, that in both cases their struggles were conducted outside the context of party organizations.

Real participatory democracy is still an ideal to work toward. In the meantime, the party system has to be operated by someone. Those who are unwilling to become involved hardly have a sound basis for criticism of those who do choose to participate actively. They should not be surprised that these active participants seek to mould the party to their own interests, which they usually identify with the public interest. This kind of rationalization is normal, even if we should expect a higher degree of altruism from those who use their leisure time as party activists than from most other groups. If the majority of noninvolved people see a party adopting stances of which they do not approve, this has arisen at least partly by default because they have not been present to fight for alternatives.

This is not to say that parties and their activists are always above reproach. People see that parties are in a position to dispense favours of one kind or another (e.g., senatorial appointments, judgeships, appointments to boards and commissions, and profitable connections, particularly to lawyers). While at times public outrage over some appointments may well be justified, the tendency has been to exaggerate the amount and unseemly nature of this kind of patronage activity. After all, these positions have to be filled somehow, and party organizations serve the function of presenting candidates to the government. The problem arises when reward for party membership is the main criterion and competence is of less concern. While reform in this area would be welcome, the situation has never represented the most serious political problem for Canadians. It may assume serious proportions if the party tends to aim fund-raising activities at recipients of its favours so that the relationship approaches bribery. This point will be discussed in the next chapter, in relation to the raising of campaign funds. However, with politicians at historically low levels of popularity in the 1990s, patronage and the perks of political office have become major irritants to a disgruntled public.

It is evident that average Canadians only actively discuss (let alone participate in) public policy on those occasions when it seems to invade their personal privacy. They would much rather go camping than debate the merits of government's environmental policy, although major questions of lifestyle and even survival are involved. On the other hand, they will be much more concerned about a proposal on taxation that may increase their taxes by $100 a year. Ultimate survival is an abstract concept, while $100 is a very tangible item. In either case, average citizens are unlikely to join a political party in the hope of changing party policy, even on issues of great concern to them. Thus, it is left to those who, for a variety of reasons (including sincere

ideals, crass self-interest, and a general mixture of individual and public motives), involve themselves actively in party politics, whether as a
poll captain or as prime minister.

RECOMMENDED READING

Flanagan, Tom. *Waiting for the Wave: The Reform Party and Preston Manning.*
Toronto: Stoddart, 1995.

Gagnon, A.G., and A.B. Tanguay, eds. *Canadian Parties in Transition*, 2nd ed.
Toronto: Nelson Canada, 1996.

Martin, P., A. Gregg, and G. Perlin. *Contenders: The Tory Quest for Power.*
Scarborough: Prentice-Hall, 1983.

Thorburn, H.G., ed. *Party Politics in Canada*, 7th ed. Scarborough: Prentice-Hall,
1995.

Wearing, J. *The L-Shaped Party: The Liberal Party of Canada 1958–1980.*
Toronto: McGraw-Hill Ryerson, 1981.

Whitehorn, Alan. *Canadian Socialism: Essays on the CCF and the NDP.* Toronto:
Oxford University Press, 1992.

CHAPTER 6

Elections

Elections provide a link between the institutions of government and the wider political process. They constitute an important merging of the legal and extralegal components of the system, which produces public policy. Without elections, we would have to find another way of selecting the legislative representatives who support the Cabinet that provides executive leadership for the country. There seems to be no democratic substitute for this system, which is not to say, however, that there are not alternative electoral systems. The Canadian federal electoral system is based on *single-member constituencies* divided among its provinces according to population determined in the census, but qualified by some constitutional guarantees of minimum representation, including the need to represent the Northwest Territories and the Yukon. The candidate who receives the most votes is elected, whether or not it is a majority of the votes cast. It is often the case that when more than two candidates contest a seat, the eventual winner has only a *plurality* of the votes. This has raised questions about the system, which we will discuss later.

Elections are the democratic means of giving a select group the legitimacy to exercise authority on behalf of the citizens. That is not to say that authority is not exercised by persons other than those elected, but ultimately all authority must be traced back to a mandate given in an election. Thus, an election serves important psychological purposes in a democracy (and even in nondemocratic systems), since it represents a bond between the governors and the governed. If they are not to become shams, elections must be scrupulously carried out, and the system must be based on a logic wholly acceptable to the electorate.

The Charter of Rights and Freedoms stipulates that a House of Commons can sit for no more than five years after the date of the election of its members, except in wartime emergencies. Elections, however, can be and usually are held before the full term of office expires. A government that serves the full term is likely in trouble. The responsibility for calling elections rests entirely with prime ministers, although if they lose what they consider to be a vote of confidence in the House of Commons, they are forced to advise the governor general to dissolve Parliament. *Dissolution* means that that particular Parliament no longer exists; the Members of Parliament are once more private citizens, and an election must be held to fill all those vacant seats. The Cabinet, under its authority as part of the Privy Council, continues to govern until a new House is elected. If the governing party is reelected, its leader, the prime minister, and his or her Cabinet (which he or she will restructure) will retain their positions; however, if the opposition gains a majority, the prime minister and Cabinet will resign and yield power. Historically, most prime ministers have not been forced into elections by defeats in the House of Commons but have been able to exercise their power to call an election at a time they felt was most advantageous to their party. Having an election earlier than Canadians think is appropriate can be a serious mistake. When Prime Minister Chrétien called the 1997 election fewer than four years after his 1993 victory, many Canadians were offended, especially in Manitoba, which was in the midst of a disastrous flood. This had some role to play in the reduced Liberal majority. This system applies in the provinces as well, except that elections in most of them must be within four years of the last one. The premier decides the election date but may err, as David Peterson did in Ontario in 1990.

Once the prime minister decides to call an election and advises the governor general to dissolve Parliament, the governor general orders the *chief electoral officer* to issue *writs of election* to each constituency to hold elections on a specified date. This date (always a Monday) was brought forward from at least 47 days from the time the writ is issued to 36 days by the Canada Elections Act, 1996 and thus shortens future electoral campaigns. In practice, a few more days may be provided, since it takes some time to activate the election machinery. The chief electoral officer is a permanent civil servant appointed by the Cabinet under the authority of the Canada Elections Act and holds the office on good behaviour. This means the person may only be dismissed before retirement age by Parliament. This appointment is, therefore, similar to that of a judge and enables the chief electoral officer to be completely impartial in the administration of elections. In 1997 Jean-Pierre Kingsley, the chief electoral officer, came into unaccustomed prominence because of his power, which he chose not to exercise, to postpone the election in some Manitoba constituencies, which were flood ravaged.

The first duty of the chief electoral officer is to send the writ to each constituency. Section 51 of the Constitution Act, 1867 provides that the number of MPs and how many come from each province be based on population, determined by the decennial census. The Representation Act of 1985 is the latest legislation passed under the authority of Section 51 to achieve the principle of representation by population while at the same time providing guarantees to smaller provinces that they will maintain a minimum number of MPs. The formula was based on the number of MPs as of 1985, which was 282. The Northwest Territories received two seats and the Yukon one, leaving 279 for the 10 provinces. An *electoral quotient* was established by dividing 279 into the population of the 10 provinces. That quotient (87 005) was divided into the population of each province to determine the number of MPs for the province. However, no province would have fewer MPs than the number of senators to which it was entitled, nor would it have fewer MPs than it had in 1976 or during the 33rd Parliament, which passed the 1985 Act. The result of these rules meant that Prince Edward Island and Saskatchewan each had three more seats than entitled to by population. New Brunswick and Manitoba had two more each, and Nova Scotia and Quebec got one more each. The total number of seats became 295. The redistribution based on the 1991 census added four seats for Ontario and two for British Columbia, for a total of 301.

The seat distribution in the House of Commons for the 1997 election, and any others held before the redistribution based on the 2001 census, was as follows: Newfoundland 7, Prince Edward Island 4, New Brunswick 10, Nova Scotia 11, Quebec 75, Ontario 103, Manitoba 14, Saskatchewan 14, Alberta 26, British Columbia 34, Northwest Territories 2, Yukon 1.

Within each province constituency boundaries must be established and readjusted, if necessary, after each decennial census. This is done by *electoral boundaries commissions* in each province, which were originally established by the Electoral Boundaries Act of 1964, since amended several times. As of 1997, it provided for a three-member commission in each province composed of a judge (designated by the chief justice of the province) and two other residents of the province (appointed by the speaker of the House of Commons). Prior to the 1960s, the readjustment of constituency boundaries had been controlled by the House of Commons, and the majority party would do the best it could to draw the boundaries to its own best advantage. This process is known as *gerrymandering*. The new legislation took much partisanship out of the process by establishing the independent commissions.

The chief electoral officer informs the commissions of the number of seats for each province and provides maps giving various alternatives for drawing the boundaries. The number of voters in any constituency should not vary by more than 25% above or below the electoral quotient, except in "extraordinary circumstances." Commissions will attempt to have electoral boundaries conform to those of cities, towns, counties, and so forth, where possible, and to pay attention to historical factors and common interests. Geography, however, will temper the principle of representation by population so that sparsely populated rural and northern constituencies are not inordinately huge. Public hearings are held on each commission's initial proposals, and within a year of beginning the process, the commissions must table a report in the House of Commons. The Standing Committee on Elections and Privileges has 30 days to review the report, and MPs may lodge objections, which the commissions review and either accept or reject.[1]

The results of this process show interesting variations between the provinces. For example, in Manitoba the 1981 census revealed a population of 1 026 241. Manitoba was entitled to 14 seats, and therefore its electoral quota for each constituency was 73 303. Like other provinces, Manitoba's population is characterized by urban and rural differences, as well as by southern and northern variations in density. Nonetheless, the Electoral Boundary Commission of Manitoba was able to construct constituencies that varied from a high of 79 823 in Winnipeg North Centre to a low of 65 254 in Churchill. New Brunswick, on the other hand, with a population of 696 403 and thus an electoral quota of 69 640 for its 10 constituencies, had a much larger discrepancy between Moncton with 85 649 and Restigouche with 54 989. The Ontario Commission decided that northern Ontario should retain the 11 constituencies it had before readjustment, and this resulted in much less populous constituencies—one of which, Temiskaming, had 60 253 people, a full 30.5% below the Ontario electoral quota of 87 122. The most populous constituency was Kitchener, with 98 956 people, 13.6% above the electoral quota.

The revision, which took place for Ontario in 1994, was based on 103 seats and a population of 10 084 885, as reported in the 1991 census. This produced a quotient of 97 912. The population growth was centred in southern, urban Ontario, and this led to a reduction of one seat to 10 in the huge expanse of northern Ontario. Temiskaming was now part of North Bay-Temiskaming, and the constituency of Algoma-James Bay was now the least populous with 76 723 inhabitants, some 21.7% below the quotient. The constituency of Scarborough South now had the highest population, 106 748 or 9.9% above the quotient. Thus, the discrepancy between "one person, one vote" had been reduced, but at the cost of even larger geographical boundaries for the north.[2] By 1997, however, Ontario had a population of 11 million, and the census figures for 1991 were already out of relation with the new realities. Ontario federal boundary divisions took on added importance in 1996 when the Ontario government decided to reduce the size of the Ontario Legislative Assembly from 130 to 103 and to use the same boundaries as the federal Parliament.

As these examples clearly show, the application of criteria other than those based on population has produced significant differences between the number of people represented by each MP. While these differences rightly concern those devoted to the equality of all voters, the demand for minimum representation by provinces in a federal state and the difficulties posed in representing far-flung constituencies require a reasonable compromise between representational principles.

TABLE 6.1
REPRESENTATION BY POPULATION

The map on which the next federal election will be fought, based on the 1991 census.

	Ridings	Average Population per Riding	Largest Riding	Smallest Riding
Newfoundland	7	81 211	101 127	30 379
Nova Scotia	11	81 813	94 160	72 782
New Brunswick	10	72 390	87 613	60 360
Prince Edward Island	4	32 441	34 266	30 058
Quebec	75	91 946	112 409	54 984
Ontario	103	97 912	107 915	76 253
Manitoba	14	77 996	80 872	73 486
Saskatchewan	14	70 638	76 160	56 620
Alberta	26	97 906	117 418	79 837
British Columbia	34	96 531	114 284	74 801
Yukon Territory	1	27 797	—	—
Northwest Territory	2	28 925	36 407	21 242

Source: The Globe and Mail, October 7, 1996. Reproduced with permission of *The Globe and Mail,* Toronto.

In each of the constituencies, *returning officers* are responsible for administering the election. Although officially appointed by the chief electoral officer, their appointments are normally the result of party patronage. However, competent returning officers often survive in office even if the party in power changes. They, in turn, appoint a number of temporary officials whose tenure is limited to the election period itself. These include the *deputy returning officers* who administer the *polls,* which are geographic areas of about 250 voters. The deputy returning officer is assisted by a poll clerk at each poll. All these positions are patronage appointments, formally appointed by the returning officer but chosen from lists supplied by the incumbent party.

An official *voters' list* was compiled for each election until 1997. This was organized by the returning officer, who appointed two *enumerators* in each poll—one from each of the two leading parties in the previous election. The enumeration began after the election was called and was a door-to-door canvass of each poll to find all eligible voters. The Canada Elections Act amendments of 1996[3] provided that the last enumeration would be the basis for a new permanent Register of Electors. Twenty-four days before the election date, voters will receive confirmation that they are on the list, and those who are not will have until the sixth day before the election to get on the list. Revising agents are to be appointed by the returning officer to facilitate this task so that on the fifth day before the election a final official Register of Electors for the constituency will be available. Provisions were made for those who wish, for reasons of privacy, that their names not be on the published list. The list includes almost all Canadian citizens who are 18 years of age and over. The few exceptions include the chief electoral officer, while returning officers vote only in the case of a tie. Judges and people in prisons or mental institutions have had their voting rights restored by Charter-based court decisions. The Royal Commission on Electoral Reform and Party Financing (the Lortie Commission) submitted its report in 1992, and based on some of its recommendations amendments to the Canada Elections Act in 1993 provided for the inclusion of previously disqualified groups and other changes to make it more possible for more Canadians to cast their ballots. In addition, a $1000 limit was placed on partisan advertising by nonparty sources, and the publication of polls was prohibited in the last 72 hours before the election.

The returning officer is also responsible for assigning voting places in each poll. Again, an opportunity for dispensing minor patronage appears, since these voting places, for which a small rental fee is paid, are occasionally in the homes of supporters of the sitting member's party. But more often now, they are in public buildings, such as schools or large apartment buildings whose residents may constitute a poll. Twenty-one days before the election, the returning officer will receive the nomination papers of candidates. Each candidate must be endorsed by at least 100 electors in the constituency and deposit $1000 in order to run. Should a candidate receive at least 15% of the votes cast, the deposit will be refunded. With few exceptions, anyone eligible to vote is eligible to seek office. On the basis of the nominations, the returning officer can then proceed to have the ballots printed. On the ballot appear the names of the candidates in alphabetical order. The Canada Elections Act reforms of 1970 provided that party affiliation be placed on the ballot, but the candidate must belong to an officially registered party for this to be the case. The returning officer must arrange for *advance polls* 10, 9 and 7 days before the election to allow those who must be away from the constituency on polling day to vote. Arrangements are also made for members of the armed forces and diplomatic personnel to vote for candidates in their home constituency. Their ballots are forwarded to the chief electoral officer, and the results of those votes are announced in the home constituency, in conjunction with the results of the advance poll there.

While the returning officer is activating the formal election machinery, the more visible part of the election, campaigning, takes place. The initial requirement for each party is obviously a candidate. Candidates are chosen at *nomination conventions* held in each constituency. These conventions may be attended by dues-paying members. However, loose membership rules have often allowed candidates to sell party memberships to large numbers of supporters (from an ethnic, occupational, or religious group), thus packing the convention with people who are not normally party activists. Another problem has to do with absence of spending limits, which obviously gives an advantage to nominees with large financial backing. The stakes involved in a nomination convention are so high that in a hotly contested race the tactics used may often leave a lot to be desired from a moral point of view. Like any other competitive situation in our society, in politics one should not be surprised that competitors will strain the limits of morality in order to win. Even if candidates are scrupulous, their supporters may be less so. This has led to problems, such as those experienced in Liberal constituency organizations in the Toronto area in 1988 and in 1993, when nomination results were challenged.

Those who seek the candidacy are normally local figures who have some strong connection with the party and have acquired some prominence either by success in their profession, previous political experience, or service to the community. This is not always true; at times parties find themselves facing such hopeless odds in an election that they cannot get anyone of substance to run and are thus forced to search around for an innocent to serve up as a sacrificial lamb. On other occasions a constituency association may be asked to accept a national figure or a promising newcomer from outside the constituency as its candidate. It may be advantageous to the constituency to do this because, if the person is elected, the constituency could then have a potential Cabinet minister as its Member of Parliament and could thus have a more powerful representative in Ottawa. Sometimes, however, constituency organizations reject this "parachuting" of candidates, preferring to support a local person. In either event it is the constituency that normally makes the final decision. The Liberal Party gave its leader the authority to appoint candidates in constituencies where women, ethnic representatives, or star candidates are appropriate. When exercised in 1997, this power proved to be controversial. Nonetheless, all but one of Chrétien's designated candidates was elected. Female candidates are still underrepresented and have often found themselves running in constituencies where their party was not likely to win, but they have become more numerous as parties have adopted policies to ensure that more are nominated. Where a party has the sitting member, only rarely is that person not renominated if he or she seeks the candidacy. Boundary revisions, however, can change or eliminate constituencies, creating contests between sitting members. If the sitting member does seek the candidacy, the nomination is usually uncontested, and the convention serves more as a campaign kickoff.

Once the candidate is selected, the party normally closes ranks behind him or her. Whoever the candidate is must quickly put a campaign committee together. The candidates themselves are the key persons, although their job is to campaign rather than organize campaign strategy. Nonetheless, all aspects of the campaign should be acceptable to them. The most important worker will be the campaign manager, who will work full time on the race. The campaign manager may be a friend or relative of the candidate or someone involved in the riding association. However, if a suitable local person is not available, one will be supplied by the provincial headquarters, especially if the party feels it has a chance to win. The campaign committee is normally broken down into subcommittees, which are responsible for gathering campaign funds, advertising, canvassing, and election-day organization. The finance committee is a separate and extremely important committee, because the amount of money available will dictate the nature and scope of the campaign. The person chairing the finance committee is usually a well-known figure, possessing contacts with potential contributors and an intimate knowledge of people who stand to gain by a victory of the party—both because of its policies and the favours it can dispense. Government is a large enterprise and needs the services of all kinds of private professional and business organizations. Given a choice, all things being equal (and sometimes even if they are not equal), the government is likely to direct its business to those who have supported it.[4] Basically, the two major parties receive the contributions of business because these parties support the free-enterprise system under which business has prospered. Even after its disastrous results in the 1993 election, the Progressive Conservative Party continued to receive major financial support from business, while the Reform Party was more dependent on individual donors. On the other side of the political spectrum, the NDP is the recipient of financial support from organized labour, but the amounts are considerably less than business contributes to opponents of that party.

PARTY FINANCING

At this point we must digress in order to discuss the wider implications of party financing. The danger involved in the financial dependence of the major parties on the business community is that the latter may be able to exert inordinate pressure during elections by denying its financial support. Both major parties were subject to this type of pressure in the 1960s: the Liberals during Walter Gordon's period of influence, and the Conservatives under Diefenbaker. During the free-trade debate leading up to and during the 1988 election, the Liberals encountered difficulty raising money from businesses that supported free trade and entered the election campaign with a $5 million debt. Moreover, the business community spent heavily during the campaign on advertising in favour of free trade. One can hardly criticize businesses for not financially supporting parties whose policies threaten perceived business interests. The fault lies with the parties themselves for not providing a healthier basis for their finances.

The Election Expenses Act of 1974 attempted to reform this shortcoming. To encourage more donors to parties and candidates, it provided for tax deductions for contributors. In 1993 candidates received $42 210 219 in support from 160 944 contributors, 131 245 of them individual donors. It also provided for public money to be made available to reimburse candidates who acquire 15% of the total vote. The original basis for payment was later changed to provide 50% of their reported expenses. In 1993 there were 2153 candidates, of whom 714 qualified for reimbursement, which totalled $14 862 146.[5] In addition to providing money for candidates, the Election Expenses Act limits the amount that may be spent in a constituency. The original amounts (subsequently adjusted for inflation) were as follows: $1 for each of the first 15 000 voters, $.50 for each voter between 15 000 and 25 000, and $.25 for each voter over 25 000. Parties, which must contest at least 50 constituencies to be registered under the Act, were originally limited to spending $.30 (again there has been an adjustment formula added) per voter on the electoral lists of the constituencies in which they had candidates. The 1997 limit for parties that contested all 301 constituencies (the Liberals, the PC Party, and the NDP) was $11 358 749 per party. The Reform Party contested 227 seats, which made its limit $8 503 057, while the Bloc Québécois, contesting only Quebec's 75 seats, could spend $3 019 086. A party receives 22.5% of its declared expenses if it spends at least 10% of its expense limit. In 1993, 15 registered parties received $8 031 497 in public funds, while in 1997 only 10 parties met the criteria to be officially registered by — among other requirements — fielding at least 50 candidates.

Moreover, the use of advertising is prohibited until 29 days before the election, and after that point 6.5 hours of prime-time television must be provided to the registered parties in an agreed-upon allocation. In 1984 the rules were tightened to prevent interest groups or individuals from advertising on behalf of candidates and parties during the election period. This rule was successfully challenged by the National Citizens' Coalition before the courts. The result was considerable nonparty advertising during the 1988 federal election. As mentioned, the Lortie Commission and the 1993 legislation addressed this issue, but only to limit the capacity of groups to engage in partisan support or attacks on particular parties and candidates. They could still spend on advocacy advertising on issues. The limitation was successfully challenged in an Alberta court, again by the National Citizens' Coalition, and was ruled invalid. In 1997 the National Citizens' Coalition launched an advertising campaign intended to help defeat incumbent Liberals who would become eligible for a parliamentary pension if they were reelected. Police associations targeted billboard advertisements at Liberals who supported the "faint hope" clause, which allowed an appeal for parole after 15 years of a life sentence. Nonparty partisan advertising seems to have become an established part of the election process.

Even before the Act, the major parties were making efforts to broaden their financial support base by seeking a larger number of smaller contributors. The Act, as mentioned above, encourages this by granting tax deductions for political contributions. This is, of course, beneficial to the smaller parties—especially the NDP—who are already the recipients of these smaller contributions. The candidates, however, are required to report the source of any contribution in excess of $100. At the national level, the parties are required to register and to report their expenses and the source of their revenue. Thus, the Act seeks to limit the amount of money spent in elections, subsidize serious candidates, and provide for the full disclosure of the sources of campaign funding and the uses to which it is put.[6]

To claim that large campaign contributions guarantee a pliant government if the party that is the recipient of those contributions wins the election is to take an overly simplistic view of the political process in Canada. Governments are subject to many pressures from a multiplicity of interests, and since they want to appeal to enough of those interests to ensure reelection, they must balance their responses to these demands carefully. Thus, campaign contributors can hardly expect to dictate government policy. There is no question that the business community has obtained preferential treatment from government (although business would always advance counterarguments that society in general has been served by such treatment), but it is also unquestionable that governments have pursued policies that were, in their time, directly opposed by business interests. Significant business interests, for instance, were outraged by the National Energy Program of 1980. What must be kept in mind is the difference between the specific benefits gained by particular firms (for example, contracts) and the benefits that accrue to business in general. In the latter case, the general benefits are consistent with the governing party's view of what is good for society, and this is influenced by the presence within the major parties of a majority of elected members who come from the business and professional community. It also reflects the fact that the free-enterprise philosophy espoused by business is still dominant in Canada. As inroads have been made into the philosophy that what is good for business is good for Canada, the business community has often had more difficulty in shaping public opinion, and its influence on government is more often challenged. Nevertheless, the victory of the Free Trade Agreement, the concern over the deficit, the pursuit of privatization, and deregulation—all supported by business—held sway in the 1990s. The party expressing those ideas, the Progressive Conservative Party, was the most successful fund-raiser of the 1980s and early 1990s by a wide margin.

The CCF/NDP has always been critical of the major parties' reliance on fairly large contributions from business. It has claimed, with some justification, that inordinate influence has accrued to the business community as a result. The CCF and its successor, the NDP, have relied mainly on dues-paying members for financial support. Since 1961, when organized labour threw its support behind the NDP, a large proportion of NDP funds has been provided by contributions from union members whose unions have arranged contracts that allow a tickoff for NDP dues. The onus is on workers to instruct the company not to deduct those dues if they do not wish to support the NDP, but peer-group pressures being what they are, many workers would rather allow the small amount to be deducted than face the criticism of fellow workers. (In 1993 in Ontario, dissidents in a few Canadian autoworkers' union locals challenged the relationship with the NDP.) Even though the monthly contribution is small, when it covers hundreds of thousands of workers, it provides the financial basis for the party. Unions can also provide, free of charge, all kinds of facilities that other parties must have donated or pay for themselves. Thus, organized labour has had an influential role in the NDP, and one can argue that the relationship has been even more direct than the influence of business on the major parties. Still, the NDP has traditionally had less money at its disposal than either of the two major parties, although the Election Expenses Act has helped to close the gap considerably. One may make personal qualitative judgements as to whose influence—business or organized labour—is more salutary to good government, but one must remember that the same principle is involved.

THE CAMPAIGN

It is the task of the finance committee to ascertain how much money is available from local sources. The amount will vary from constituency to constituency and, possibly, will be augmented by funds from party headquarters. The national party may be willing to offer substantial financial aid in key constituencies if the contest appears close. Thus, the amount available to a campaign committee may vary from $15 000 to perhaps over $40 000, depending on the money available from the central and provincial headquarters (this will rarely be more than half of the total), local contributions, and the personal wealth of the candidate.

Considering its financial limitations, the campaign committee must then make a number of critical decisions. It will have to decide how much television and radio time, and newspaper space, it can afford, and what type of advertising material yields the highest return for each dollar spent. For instance, a large number of lawn signs may be more effective than expensive billboards in key locations, and bumper stickers may be a better investment than books of matches. The committee will have to decide what points the advertising will stress. Is the candidate going to be associated strongly with the party leader or rely more on local reputation? This will obviously vary with the popularity of the national leader. In 1997, for instance, Jean Charest was the focal point of the Progressive Conservative Party's campaign. What issues are particularly important for the local area, and how will the candidate handle them? While the advice of the national party is available and some training may be provided, these are local issues, and victory in a close race may very well depend on the right decision on these matters. It should be understood that a campaign in a Prince Edward Island constituency will differ greatly from one in Toronto or Montreal, and that the decisions made by campaign committees have to be made in the light of local circumstances.

From the very beginning of the campaign, the candidates' time is carefully apportioned to give them maximum exposure to the electorate. They must campaign primarily in areas of their constituencies where they are neither sure to lose nor sure to win because they would be wasting their time in these areas. Therefore, it is crucial that they know both from the returns of past elections and from the results of polling techniques and *canvassing* conducted continually during the campaign just where supporters live, where opponents live, and where there are uncertain areas. In contemporary elections the door-to-door electioneering by the candidates themselves and by a core of canvassers has been the most important type of campaigning in many urban constituencies. Candidates will also go to factory gates, shopping centres, and other places where large numbers of people congregate. In rural areas, where doors may be kilometres apart and factories and shopping centres less of a factor, the old-style political meeting is still a basic campaign technique.

By the time election day arrives, candidates and their workers have done all they can to attract voters, and all that remains is to ensure that their supporters get to the polls. The election-day organization is set up to promote this end by having car pools to take people, especially the elderly, to the voting booth, providing babysitters, and whatever other services people might request. Parties have *scrutineers* in each poll who have access to the voters' list and can thus report to headquarters who has voted. Workers can then telephone known supporters who have not yet voted and encourage them to get to the polls, offering any assistance that might be necessary.

The polls used to be open from 8:00 A.M. to 7:00 P.M. across Canada. However, in 1996 the legislation changed on the initiative of Anna Terrana, MP for Vancouver East. She voiced the frustration of British Columbians, who often heard that a government was declared elected before BC votes were counted. Thus, the polls are now open for 12 hours, but at different times, 8:30 A.M to 8:30 P.M in Newfoundland and the Atlantic and central time zones, 9:30 A.M. to 4:30 P.M. in the eastern time zone, 9:30 A.M.to 7:30 P.M. in the mountain time zone, and 7:00 A.M. to 7:00 P.M. in the Pacific time zone. When the polls close in the presence of representatives of each candidate, the deputy returning officer counts the votes. The Canada Elections Act specifies precisely the manner in which this is to be done. The major decisions that the deputy returning officer will have to make during the counting concern spoiled ballots. The officer's decisions are final at the time, but objections of candidates' representatives must be registered, and in a recount these decisions may be overturned. Having completed the count, this officer transmits a report to the returning officer of the constituency, who, on a prescribed date (a few days after the election), conducts the official count (although the results are usually known on election night) and declares the victor. The returning officer then makes an official report and returns the *writ of election* to the chief electoral officer.

If the vote is reasonably close, a defeated candidate may request a *recount*. This will take place before a judge. On infrequent occasions a defeated candidate may make charges of serious irregularities. These are dealt with under the Controverted Elections Act and if the charges are substantiated the result will be declared void and a new election will be necessary.

Although voting now takes place at staggered times across the six time zones in Canada, the results from other provinces cannot be publicized in any province whose polls are still open. This precludes voters in the west from being unduly influenced by results already available in the east. Arguments have been advanced that some similar form of restriction should be applied to publishing public opinion polls that may produce the same kind of bandwagon effect in the national electorate. Opponents argue that social scientists, or anyone else, have the right to try to ascertain the mood of the electorate and publish their results. If this has consequences for the parties—for example, by making people feel that they do not have to vote because the election is a foregone conclusion—it is up to the parties to convince their supporters that their vote is still important. The 1993 legislation that proposed a ban on public opinion polls 72 hours before the election is a compromise attempt to deal with their perceived impact. In 1997 media outlets unsuccessfully tried to have the courts invalidate this prohibition. Others wondered how the Internet could be regulated by this provision.

While individual skirmishes go on in constituencies, the major election battle is waged countrywide by the leaders of the national parties and their most prestigious lieutenants. They too must win in individual constituencies, but their national prominence normally ensures their victory in their home riding (Kim Campbell was a major exception in 1993); thus, they are free to campaign across the length and breadth of the land. Since most Canadian voters are more concerned with the parties and leaders than with the individual merits of local candidates, the kind of impact that party leaders make on the electorate is crucial to their party's success at the polls.[7] Along with the leader's appeal, the party's platform and approach to the issues are vital factors. These elements, however, cannot be considered in isolation, although one or another may appear preeminent at times.

If leaders can appear to symbolize the prevailing national mood, then their victory is ensured. This is difficult because it demands from leaders an intangible quality called *charisma*, by which they can touch the emotional depths of people. Diefenbaker in 1957–58 and Trudeau in

FIGURE 6.1
BREAKDOWN OF ELECTION EXPENSES OF CANDIDATES, BY CATEGORY

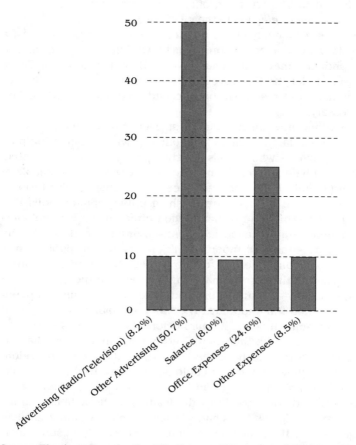

Source: Elections Canada, *Contributions and Expenses of Registered Political Parties and Candidates,* 35th General Election, 1993 (Ottawa: Chief Electoral Officer, 1995), p. xx. Reproduced by authority of the Chief Electoral Officer, 1997.

1968 exhibited this quality and became the central focus of their respective party's successful campaign. In 1993 Kim Campbell, as a fresh new personality and Canada's first female prime minister, raised her party's support dramatically in the early stages of the campaign. However, by the end of the campaign her appeal largely evaporated. In 1997 Jean Chrétien was unsuccessful in maintaining his appeal in English-speaking Canada and suffered from a lack of appeal to franco-phone voters in Quebec. Jean Charest in large measure and Alexa McDonough to a lesser extent generated a personal impact on their respective campaigns. Televised leaders' debates contribute to this phe-nomenon, as does the way in which the mass media cover these cam-paigns.[8] However, when it seems clear that leaders cannot appeal to the voters' emotions, they must appeal to their intellects with carefully pre-pared arguments on important issues. Sometimes the dominant issues may be too important for candidates to appeal to emotions to overcome people's concern with concrete problems. For instance, Diefenbaker's charismatic appeal in 1958 was largely exhausted (except on the Prairies) by 1963, when concern over his handling of government affairs outstripped the emotional appeal of his former years. On the Prairies, however, the emotional bond he had forged with the people of the west had not diminished. Trudeau suffered the same fate starting in the late 1970s, as his policies seemed incapable of overcoming economic dislo-cations, yet he remained the favourite son of Quebec.

A more recent trend has been to concentrate on the weakness of opponents rather than on one's own merits. This has been perfected in *negative advertising*. For instance, in the 1988 election the Progressive Conservatives ran campaign ads that portrayed Liberal leader John Turner as a liar. Similar attacks on Jean Chrétien in 1993 proved unsuccessful. An ad that seemed to highlight physical disfigurement turned into a disaster for the Progressive Conservative Party. The Reform Party ad in 1997 that attacked "Quebec politicians" Jean Chrétien and Jean Charest may have had positive results in British Columbia and Alberta, but it was judged by some analysts to have been counterproductive in Ontario and helpful to the Bloc Québécois in Quebec. Whatever strategies parties adopt, it is clear that television plays a big role in their campaigns.

Notwithstanding the emotional appeal of the leader, there is a rela-tively narrow margin between the winning and the losing parties. The largest percentage of votes ever won by any national party in this century was the 53.6% that the Progressive Conservative Party got in the 1958 Diefenbaker "sweep." Thus, for a variety of reasons, 46.4% of the popula-tion was immune to the "Chief's" charisma. One reason for this stability in voting behaviour is that some people are so partisan that they tradi-tionally support one national party and would not vote for another party even if it was led by a bona fide saint or prophet. While voting studies in the 1980s and 1990s showed that the percentage of strong partisans was declining, they nonetheless remain a large and important group of voters. Second, the very qualities in a leader that evoke a favourable emotional response from some people will have the reverse effect on others. It is not unthinkable that even party supporters who cast their vote for a party do so in spite of a negative emotional response to the party leader, rather than because of the leader's charismatic appeal. Third, the respective merits of the candidates at the local level are a prime consideration for at least some proportion of the electorate, and thus a good candidate—especially a popular incumbent—may offset the effects of a charismatic leader's appeal.

In fact, it is rare in this century for a party to form the government on the basis of an absolute majority (more than 50%) of the vote. Charisma, party platform, or ideology is normally not enough, either singly or in combination, to convince most Canadians that one party deserves overwhelming electoral support. In trying to find reasons for a party's electoral victory, election analysts tend to overrate the effects of single factors and underplay the fact that a wide variety of reasons affects people's choices. Journalists have been prone to dramatize and romanticize the spectacular side of a campaign and thereby ignore the more prosaic but nonetheless vital factors. For instance, in the 1968 federal election, the most frequent explanation for the Liberal victory centred on a phenomenon called "Trudeaumania," which was the media catchword for the charisma generated by Trudeau. In reality, however, research showed that more people voted Liberal because they had always voted Liberal than voted Liberal specifically because of Trudeau's charisma. This was supported by the fact that Trudeau's victory in 1968 yielded 46% of the vote, while Pearson's 1965 campaign gained 40%. Thus, it is easy to see that any realistic assessment of an election must deal with more than the exciting aspects of the race. Voters in the 1990s have shown themselves willing to shift their allegiances for a variety of reasons, and a change of 3 or 4% one way or the other in national results can be decisive in electoral results if they reflect more substantial regional changes. This was evident in 1997 and led to important gains by the Progressive Conservatives and New Democrats in Atlantic Canada, and by the Reform Party in Saskatchewan. The real questions concern how many of this shifting electorate, some of whom are generally uninterested in politics, have been caught up in a leader's charisma, how many have been attracted by party platform promises, and how many have voted for some other reason.[9]

Federal elections tend to attract from 70 to 75% of the electorate (the turnout in 1997 was 67%), which means that in any election many Canadians choose not to vote. Their absence from the polls may have some impact on the result, especially if they are people who have voted for a particular party in the past but withdraw their support by not voting. To some degree this may account for a party doing well in federal elections with higher turnouts but less well in a provincial election, where there are lower turnouts.

FIGURE 6.2
BREAKDOWN OF ELECTION EXPENSES OF POLITICAL PARTIES, BY CATEGORY

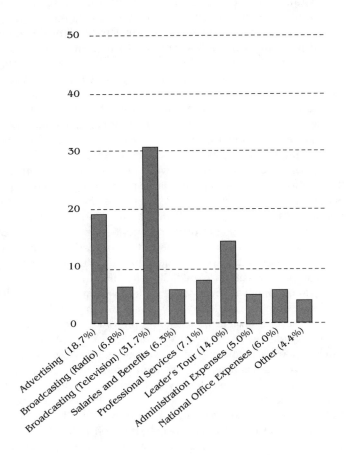

Source: Elections Canada, *Contributions and Expenses of Registered Political Parties and Candidates,* 35th General Election, 1993 (Ottawa: Chief Electoral Officer, 1995), p. xx. Reproduced by authority of the Chief Electoral Officer, 1997.

With these factors in mind, the national campaign committee must plan its strategy. Each campaign presents its own set of circumstances, and of course the government party will have a different campaign strategy than that of the opposition parties. The government party will have a record to defend as well as a program for the future, while the opposition parties will concentrate on the defects of past policy, ignore the accomplishments of the past government, and present their own prescriptions for the future. Every party, therefore, must decide individually what approach or combination of approaches it should adopt. Should the leader be exploited as the chief element in the campaign, or should the party be presented as an efficient team? In 1979 and 1980, for instance, the Liberals concentrated on the leadership of Pierre Trudeau, while the Progressive Conservatives, recognizing the fact that Joe Clark trailed Trudeau in personal public impact, concentrated on the party platform and attempted to debunk Trudeau's leadership capabilities. The 1997 campaign demonstrated that strategies are not necessarily error free, as the Liberal portrayal of Jean Chrétien as the competent leader of a sound government seemed to lose some of its initial appeal as the campaign progressed. During the 1980s and 1990s, generally, there was a trend to negative campaigning. The role of 30-second television advertisements in this process has raised some concern about the trivialization of the whole electoral campaign.

The parties will also have to decide which issues will be the most successful vote getters for them, and in this respect the use of polling techniques is common. Once a decision on the issues themselves has been made, it is up to the parties to establish priorities. The government party will usually have an advantage in ordering priorities, as it can point to its past record and highlight the positive aspects, whereas, in criticizing the party in power, the opposition parties must guard against the tendency to become too negative. This is especially true of minor parties, which, because they know they will form neither the government nor the official opposition, are sometimes in danger of giving the impression that they are merely nay sayers. As well as assigning priorities to different issues, parties must decide how best to use the talent available to them to exploit those issues. Obviously, the important ministers of the party in power will have the advantage in presenting issues and pointing up the fallacies of counterissues presented by the opposition parties. Since the media always concentrate more on established political figures, the public looks to, say, the minister of justice to comment on the Constitution or the minister of the environment to comment on pollution. However, from the 1970s into the 1990s, the media focus on leaders and their tours accelerated the tendency for campaigns to be intensely concentrated on party leaders.[10]

As at the constituency level, national parties at the federal level must acquire campaign funds and make crucial decisions about distributing them for various electoral purposes. Television has assumed great importance but is very expensive. A party will have to decide whether extra minutes of television exposure will yield greater results than the cost of an extra excursion to a particular area by the party leader. Because of considerations such as these, the role of public-relations experts, whose job it is to know how to gauge public moods and how to exploit those moods, has become vital in modern Canadian election campaigns. However, the Canadian electorate is diverse and subject to changing moods, so that even with the most expert advice on what approach to the voters will be best, national campaigns gamble in the hope that they have found a winning combination.

As mentioned previously, a relatively small percentage shift in the electorate can topple a government and elevate another party in its stead. Rarely does a government enjoy office on the basis of the votes of a majority of Canadians. In fact, in 20 of the 23 federal elections from 1921 to 1997 inclusive, elected governments got less than the combined opposition parties. Furthermore, the 1988 Progressive Conservative win was the first time there were consecutive majority government victories for the same party since 1953, and the Liberals only barely duplicated that feat in 1997 by winning 155 seats. Although in most cases the single-member constituency and plurality election system have produced a stable government based on a majority of seats in the House of Commons, it hardly represents the principle of majority rule. Those who feel that it is important to represent more accurately the actual vote of the public have put forward various proposals for proportional representation. In brief, what this system would effect is a situation in which 50% of the votes would yield 50% of the Commons seats, while 20% would give 20% of the seats. In the present circumstances, 50% of the votes may yield 75% of the seats, and 20% would probably yield less than 10% of the seats. For example, in 1997 the Liberals got 155 seats (or 52% with 39% of the vote, while the Progressive Conservatives only got 20 seats with 19% of the popular vote, and the NDP got 21 seats with 11%. Reform came close to having the number of seats, 60, that mirrored its national vote, 19%.

Is good government served by the present system? On the one hand, the Canadian system is modelled on that of the British and has provided Canadians with relatively stable and effective government. On the other hand, large segments of Canadian opinion are denied true representation. This was especially true of Conservatives in Quebec (until 1984) and Liberals in the west. Although these parties might have attracted 15 or 20% of the vote in these regions, they got few, if any, seats. Thus, in the two major parties the views of a major region of the country have been at times largely unrepresented in the parliamentary caucus. Beyond that, minority parties, such as the NDP, do not usually win the number of seats that their vote might yield in a proportional system. However, one cannot have a proportional system without abandoning to some degree the concept of single-member constituencies. This system and the relationship of a single Member of Parliament to his or her electorate have a strong place in the belief system of Canadian voters.

After the 1980 election, some concern was voiced over these regional discrepancies, but over the long run there has never been a strong political reaction to the present system, and the question of proportional representation has remained academic. Like most other aspects of Canadian political life, the electoral system has worked to produce an artificial majority where natural ones rarely exist.[11] While other systems may theoretically be more democratic, one has to ask whether they would have been as successful in keeping together a diverse Canadian body politic. The answer is that probably they would not have, as there is already enough diversity in Canada without encouraging it through the electoral system. The idea, after all, is to encourage regional representation rather than a proliferation of splinter parties.

VOTING BEHAVIOUR

The percentage of votes that parties received in the 1997 election—Liberal 39%, Reform 19%, Progressive Conservative 19%, Bloc Québécois 11%, New Democratic Party 11%, and others 1%—is an aggregate portrayal of millions of voting decisions by Canadians. These percentages tell us nothing about how particular groups of Canadians—distinguished by differences in language, religion, region, social class, family income, union membership, education, sex, or age—behave as voters. It is possible that political parties may attract support within these groups that may be significantly different from the percentage they receive from the total voting public. *Survey research* allows political scientists to get a more complete picture of the way Canadians vote, to probe their reasons for voting for particular parties, and to see how their behaviour changes over time. During the long period of Liberal success in federal elections (from the 1920s until 1984), certain patterns emerged that supported that dominance. The Progressive Conservative landslide of 1984 and its less overwhelming win in 1988, however, reflect changes in the voting behaviour of Canadians that are portrayed in the tables at the end of this chapter. The results of the 1993 and 1997 federal elections reveal changes from 1988, reflecting not only the Liberal resurgence but also the regional successes of the Reform Party and the Bloc Québécois.[12]

Although all Canadian parties hope to attract support from every sector of the Canadian electorate, some parties have been notably more successful with some groups than others. The Canadian electorate in the past could roughly be divided into segments that were prone to favour one party over another. In more recent elections, however, short-term considerations that surround the election campaign have undermined long-term factors such as party loyalty. The most important factors upon which people in the past based their political loyalty were regional and ethnic (in Canada, religion is closely allied with ethnicity). People in certain areas of Canada have traditionally supported one party rather than another, and only in unusual circumstances have they shifted their allegiance. Quebec, for instance, from the days of the

Laurier ministry (1896–1911) until 1984, consistently gave its greatest support to the Liberals, while rural Ontario was a Conservative bastion until 1993. The Prairies and British Columbia were largely PC from 1957 to 1993, but the NDP has had some strength, especially in British Columbia, Saskatchewan, and Manitoba. Newfoundland voted solidly Liberal from 1949 until 1968. Other areas have tended to be less consistent in their support of the two major parties. The Prairies and Quebec have been the areas most hospitable to protest parties, which siphon off the loyalty usually accorded a major party. The results of the 1993 and 1997 elections show this. The largest metropolitan centres of Montreal, Toronto, Vancouver, and Winnipeg voted overwhelmingly Liberal in the 1960s, although the NDP maintained a consistent toehold in some constituencies of the latter three. However, in the elections of the 1970s, the PCs gained strength in the major metropolitan areas, especially those in western Canada. Modern voting patterns for the Liberals and Progressive Conservatives represented shifts from earlier periods. Thus, the voting patterns are not immutable but may be overturned by dramatic events and/or political figures. However, once new regional loyalties emerge, they tend to remain in effect for some time. Diefenbaker, for instance, was instrumental in polarizing much of rural and small-town Canada against the urban centres. Newfoundland remained solidly Liberal as long as Joey Smallwood maintained his political mastery of the island; the Liberal hold was broken only by a combination of dissension in Smallwood's provincial party and the ascendancy of a Maritimer (Stanfield) as PC party chief. Thus, it must be asked if the PC strength established in 1984 and 1988 in Quebec will ever return after the reverse in 1993.

The other major determinant of voting behaviour has been ethnicity. The major ethnic distinction is between those whose ancestors came from the British Isles (English, Scottish, Irish, Welsh) and those of French ancestry. Voting patterns are affected by this distinction to a large extent, although some other ethnic groups have a tendency to favour one party over another. French Canadians have traditionally given heavy support to the Liberals, while British Canadians are more evenly divided in their support for the two major parties. When those of British descent swing to the PCs, it would tend to ensure that party's victory, since they are the largest ethnic group. In fact, however, a much greater percentage of the French vote has traditionally gone Liberal than has the British vote gone Progressive Conservative. This changed dramatically in 1984. Table 6.2 at the end of this chapter shows voting distinguished by language spoken, but while most francophones are ethnically French, the anglophone group includes the 30% of Canadians from neither British nor French ethnic groups. The Bloc Québécois is a party whose appeal is solely to francophones in Quebec, while the Reform Party gets its support from anglophones outside Quebec.

Another reason why the PCs fared poorly until 1984, despite their popularity among British Canadians, was the impact of religion on voting patterns. The Liberal Party attracted greater Roman Catholic support than did the PC Party. The French Canadians are almost entirely a Roman Catholic group, but there is also a large number of Roman Catholic British Canadians. Thus, while the Progressive Conservatives held the advantage over the Liberals among British Canadians on an ethnic basis, this advantage was somewhat mitigated by the religious factor. Third parties, such as the CCF/NDP and Social Credit in the west, claimed more British Protestant support from the PCs than they took French Catholic votes from the Liberals. It is difficult to separate the effects of ethnicity and religion on voting, since these factors are often closely associated in Canada. In 1988 Liberals continued to attract a larger percentage of Roman Catholic voters than of Protestants (see Table 6.3).

TABLE 6.2
LANGUAGE SPOKEN AND VOTE IN THE 1988 FEDERAL ELECTION

	English	French
Total	78.7	21.3
Liberal	30.4	19.5
PC	43.3	62.3
NDP	21.7	11.2
Other	4.7	7.0

TABLE 6.3
RELIGIOUS AFFILIATION AND VOTE IN THE 1988 FEDERAL ELECTION

	None	Roman Catholic	Protestant	Other
Total	10.4	41.9	43.5	4.2
Liberal	18.9	34.2	23.8	33.9
PC	36.4	47.7	50.0	44.9
NDP	41.9	13.9	19.6	18.4
Other	2.8	4.2	6.6	2.8

TABLE 6.4

SUBJECTIVE SOCIAL CLASS AND VOTE IN THE 1988 FEDERAL ELECTION

	Middle Class	Working Class
Total	73.2	26.8
Liberal	27.3	26.1
PC	50.9	39.8
NDP	16.4	29.5
Other	5.3	4.6

TABLE 6.5

FAMILY INCOME AND VOTE IN THE 1988 FEDERAL ELECTION

	Less Than $10 000	$10 000– 25 000	$25 000– 50 000	Over $50 000
Total	7.4	29.8	44.9	17.9
Liberal	32.0	27.6	26.8	26.3
PC	46.7	48.2	45.6	56.3
NDP	15.5	19.6	21.6	14.7
Other	5.8	4.6	6.0	2.7

TABLE 6.6

FAMILY MEMBER IN LABOUR UNION AND VOTE IN THE 1988 FEDERAL ELECTION

	Yes	No
Total	45.6	54.4
Liberal	26.6	29.3
PC	43.7	50.3
NDP	24.9	15.0
Other	4.8	5.5

TABLE 6.7
EDUCATIONAL LEVEL AND VOTE IN THE 1988 FEDERAL ELECTION

	Elementary or Less	Some High School	High School Graduate	Some Post-Secondary	University Graduate
Total	9.7	24.6	22.2	27.0	16.5
Liberal	31.4	29.8	31.4	24.6	24.9
PC	46.3	46.5	44.9	50.2	47.5
NDP	16.0	19.6	18.2	18.7	24.1
Other	6.3	4.1	5.5	6.5	3.5

TABLE 6.8
GENDER AND VOTE IN THE 1988 FEDERAL ELECTION

	Male	Female
Total	49.7	50.3
Liberal	25.1	31.0
PC	51.4	43.2
NDP	18.2	20.6
Other	5.2	5.1

TABLE 6.9
AGE AND VOTE IN THE 1988 FEDERAL ELECTION

	18–29	30–45	46–59	60 and Over
Total	19.3	38.2	24.5	17.9
Liberal	29.1	23.3	28.4	34.9
PC	45.8	50.9	46.2	43.8
NDP	22.0	20.2	19.1	16.4
Other	3.0	5.6	6.3	4.9

Source: The data come from the "Carleton University School of Journalism; 1988 Re-Interview of Respondents to the 1984 National Election Study." Data were provided by Professor Lawrence LeDuc.

TABLE 6.10

PERCENTAGE OF VOTE, NUMBER OF SEATS WON, AND PERCENTAGE OF TURNOUT BY PROVINCE IN THE 1993 AND 1997 FEDERAL ELECTIONS

	Liberal		Reform		PC		BQ		NDP		Other		Turnout	
	1993	1997	1993	1997	1993	1997	1993	1997	1993	1997	1993	1997	1993	1997
NFLD	68 (7)	38 (4)	1 (0)	3 (0)	26 (0)	37 (3)	0	0	42(0)	22 (0)	1 (0)	1 (0)	55	56
PEI	60 (4)	45 (4)	1 (0)	1 (0)	32 (0)	38 (0)	0	0	5 (0)	15 (0)	2 (0)	1 (0)	73	74
NS	52 (11)	28 (0)	13 (0)	10 (0)	23 (0)	31 (5)	0	0	7 (0)	30 (6)	5 (0)	1 (0)	65	70
NB	56 (9)	33 (3)	8 (0)	13 (0)	28 (1)	35 (5)	0	0	5 (0)	18 (2)	3 (0)	1 (0)	70	73
QUE	33 (19)	36 (26)	0 (0)	0 (0)	14 (1)	22 (5)	49 (54)	38 (44)	1 (0)	2 (0)	3 (1)	2 (0)	77	71
ON	53 (98)	49 (101)	20 (1)	19 (0)	18 (0)	19 (1)	0	0	6 (0)	11 (0)	3 (0)	2 (1)	68	66
MB	45 (12)	35 (6)	22 (1)	24 (3)	12 (0)	18 (1)	0	0	17 (1)	23 (4)	4 (0)	0 (0)	69	64
SK	32 (5)	25 (1)	27 (4)	36 (8)	11 (0)	8 (0)	0	0	27 (5)	31 (5)	3 (0)	1 (0)	69	66
AB	25 (4)	24 (2)	52 (22)	55 (24)	15 (0)	14 (0)	0	0	4 (0)	6 (0)	4 (0)	1 (0)	65	59
BC	28 (6)	29 (6)	36 (24)	43 (25)	13 (0)	6 (0)	0	0	16 (2)	18 (3)	7 (0)	4 (0)	68	67
YT and NWT	50 (2)	37 (2)	10 (0)	18 (0)	17 (0)	16 (0)	0	0	21 (1)	27 (1)	3 (1)	2 (0)	67	66
Canada	41 (177)	38 (155)	19 (52)	19 (60)	16 (2)	19 (20)	14 (54)	11 (44)	7 (9)	11 (21)	3 (1)	2 (1)	70	67

TABLE 6.11

NUMBER OF CANDIDATES AND PERCENTAGE OF VALID VOTES RECEIVED, BY
POLITICAL AFFILIATION IN 1993[a]

Political Affiliation	Total Number of Candidates	Percentage of Valid Votes Received	
		0–14.9%	15% or More
Abolitionist Party	80	80	0
Bloc Québécois	75	2	73
Christian Heritage Party	59	59	0
Canada Party	56	56	0
Party for the Commonwealth of Canada	59	59	0
The Green Party	79	79	0
Independent	52[b]	49	3
Liberal Party	295	10	285
Libertarian Party	52	52	0
Marxist-Leninist Party	51	51	0
New Democratic Party	294	246	48
Natural Law Party	231	231	0
National Party	171	171	0
No Affiliation	100	99	1
Progressive Conservative Party	295	149	146
Reform Party	207	49	158
Total	2156	1442	714

[a]In 1997 there were only 10 officially registered parties.

[b]This number includes a candidate who withdrew during the period prescribed by the Canada Elections Act.

Source: Elections Canada, Contributions and Expenses of Registered Political Parties and Candidates, 35th General Election, 1993 (Ottawa: Chief Electoral Officer, 1995), p. xxii. Reproduced by authority of the Chief Electoral Officer, 1997.

In most countries social class is extremely important—often the paramount determinant of voting behaviour. Unlike culturally similar societies, such as the United States, Great Britain, and Australia, social class has had a less pervasive influence on voters in Canada, at least in federal elections. The regional and ethnic considerations in the past and the short-term influences more recently offset the effect of what might be the expected influence of social class on voting behaviour. Social class may be defined either subjectively or objectively, or through a combination of the two—a much more difficult procedure, which we will not attempt here. A subjective approach involves the perceptions that individuals have of their own social standing. Thus, one finds that most Canadians who will answer the question consider themselves to be members of a broad middle class (73.2%), while a smaller, but still significant, number think of themselves as working class (26.8%).[13] Most of those in the working class would not accept the description of themselves as being members of a lower class. The PCs in 1988 outpolled their rivals in both the middle- and working-class groups but had greater success in the middle class. The NDP, which identifies with the working class, did much better with that group than among middle-class voters. The Liberals had a similar level of support in both classes (see Table 6.4).

When one examines objective measures of class based on income and status, one must realize that there is an element of arbitrariness involved. For instance, it is not a simple matter to determine at what level of income a person can be considered as being in the middle class, even though we know that the person is in the middle income range. Cutoff points must be established when using statistics, and it is the cutoff points that introduce the element of arbitrariness; the statistics themselves are objective. At any rate it is safe to say that there are fewer Canadians who consciously identify themselves as upper class than would be recorded as such by objective criteria of class. This is indicative of a situation in which most Canadians conceive of themselves as members of a broad middle class. One would think that this is testimony to the fact that in a democratic society it is considered somewhat unwholesome to designate oneself as upper class. These income groups, however defined, do not behave dramatically differently in casting their votes (see Table 6.5). Where class does seem to have a definite effect on behaviour is in the nonvoter category, where the tendency not to vote increases with a decrease in status and income.

The relationship between voting behaviour and being a member of a family where there is a union member would likely be a strong one if class were a dominant factor in Canadian electoral choice. However, while in 1988 the NDP attracted 24.9% of voters for whom that relationship existed, as opposed to 15% of others, the Progressive Conservatives garnered 43.7% of union-related voters, not that much less than their 50.3% of nonunion voters. This situation is a continuing concern for the NDP, which has a formal relationship with the Canadian Labour Congress (CLC). The CLC, for its part, involved itself more visibly in elections in the 1970s and 1980s to try to change the voting patterns of union members (see Table 6.6).

The level of education that voters have attained usually has some relationship to their income level and class status. Table 6.7, however, does not show that level of education was a significant factor in determining voting behaviour in 1988. The victorious PCs did consistently well among all groups. The Liberals had somewhat less success among the most educated voters than they did with others, while the New Democrats did somewhat better among university graduates than they did with other voters.

There has been a growing interest in the impact of gender on voting behaviour. Studies of the 1963 and 1968 elections showed that, although the Progressive Conservatives got just about even support from men and women, the Liberals consistently got more support from women than men, and the NDP from men than women.[14] The 1974 and 1979 National Election Study results show a continuance of this pattern. In 1988 the PCs were less favoured by women than men, while Liberals continued to get more support from women than men. The NDP was slightly more popular with women than men. The reasons for those results are not readily apparent. The Trudeau appeal in 1968 was supposedly irresistible to women, but the figures show that he attracted 6% more votes from men than did Pearson and 5% more from women. It appears, therefore, that the Liberals have had consistent strength among women. Since there is no inordinate concentration of women in any region, ethnic group, or religion, these factors cannot explain the women's vote. There are more women than men among the over-60 age group, but in this group the Liberals were weakest until 1988; thus, age probably does not explain the women's vote. Neither do education figures give any explanation of female voting behaviour. Any conclusion about why women vote as they do must await more detailed studies, although early polling in the 1993 campaign indicated that the leadership of Kim Campbell was attracting more women to support the Progressive Conservative Party. The present inconclusiveness serves only to point out the difficulty in finding explanations for voting behaviour (see Table 6.8).

The 1988 results (Table 6.9) among age groups (18–29, 30–45, 46–59, 60 and over) reflect different patterns that were evident in the 1960s and 1970s for the PCs and Liberals. Whereas earlier the PCs had their greatest relative success in the oldest age group, in 1988 that was no longer the case. The Liberals, on the other hand, got their best percentage results from the 60 and over group, whereas earlier studies showed them doing less well in that age group. The NDP have had opposite results, with decidedly better support in the younger age groups. Nonvoters were most evident in the youngest age group.

The data that we have presented represent 1988 voting behaviour that is markedly different from trends evident in the 1960s and 1970s, yet one must be cautious in making generalizations based on them. Any decade produces at least some distinctive features that may alter voting patterns. Under the leadership of Brian Mulroney, the Progressive Conservatives made spectacular gains in Quebec as part of a huge national victory in 1984, and this Quebec strength was consolidated in 1988. Whether this was the beginning of a realignment of voter preferences or whether the success of the Bloc Québécois in 1993 and 1997 was a short-term aberration, along with the success of the Reform Party in the west, will be the fundamental question of electoral politics as the new century begins (see Table 6.10). It is, however, safe to say that region and ethnicity (with its closely associated religious implications) have been the dominant influences on voting behaviour in Canada. At the same time, voting behaviour based on social class, which in other countries has assumed preeminent importance, while not insignificant, has not been as relevant in Canada. During the twentieth century, the Liberal Party has held office most often because it has been able to manipulate regional and ethnic interests to its own advantage while at the same time suppressing the class consciousness that could have made Canadian politics more ideological. Under Brian Mulroney the Progressive Conservative Party used the same formula most successfully. As we argued in the first chapter, pragmatism has been the surest instrument for successful electoral strategy.

RECOMMENDED READING

Clark, H.D., et al. *Political Choice in Canada*. Toronto: McGraw-Hill Ryerson, 1980.

————. *Absent Mandate: Canadian Electoral Politics in an Era of Restructuring*, 3rd ed. Toronto: Gage, 1996.

Courtney, John C. "Parliament and Representation: The Unfinished Business of Electoral Redistributions." *Canadian Journal of Political Science* 21.4 (1988): 675–90.

Frizzell, A., J. Pammett, and A. Westell, eds. *The Canadian General Election of 1993*. Ottawa: Carleton University Press, 1994.

LeDuc, Lawrence. "The Canadian Voter," in R. Krause and R.H. Wagenberg, eds. *Introductory Readings in Canadian Government and Politics*, 2nd ed. (369–86). Toronto: Copp Clark, 1995.

Soderlund, W.C., et al. *Media and Elections in Canada*. Toronto: Holt, Rinehart and Winston, 1984.

CHAPTER 7

Society and Polity

Government takes place in a social context that organizes people in a variety of ways. While not organized specifically for political purposes, these social groupings may have significant impacts on government, sometimes purposely and at other times less directly. This chapter will look at the relationship of these societal phenomena to the concerns of Canadians organized for political purposes—that is, the Canadian polity.

INTEREST GROUPS

Not all Canadians who wish to influence public policy have either the time or the inclination to participate in party politics or to seek a career in a government bureaucracy. As we noted in Chapter 5, only a small minority of Canadians plays an active role in party politics. While almost all Canadians are interested in some of the public policy decisions that are made by government, most are not particularly interested in involving themselves in the decision-making process. For the most part, they accept with a greater or lesser degree of passivity most of the decisions made, since Canada is a pluralistic country and public policy decisions that drastically affect some Canadians mean little or nothing to others. The establishment in 1983 of the Tax Court, for example, was of almost no interest to most people outside the legal profession. Most of the government's public policy decisions are of this type and arouse little public reaction outside the groups directly affected. With this in mind, we propose to discuss in this chapter the ways in which people not necessarily connected with political parties attempt to influence the public policy decisions that affect them. For while most Canadians forego party politics, a great many more participate in, or at least belong to, organized groups that seek to influence governments.

These groups are normally called interest or pressure groups. Although there is disagreement on where the line should be drawn between these groups, if one should be drawn at all, a useful distinction can be based on the relative permanence of interest groups as opposed to the more temporary and spontaneous nature of pressure groups. An interest group, therefore, consists of people who recognize that they share certain characteristics and consequently seek goals that will improve their common situation. The situation they have in common may be based on a variety of factors: demographic (age, sex, ethnicity, region), socioeconomic (occupation, income level), and on a number of other interests less easily categorized, such as veterans' interests, human rights, the environment, animal rights, abortion, and pornography.[1] Pressure groups, on the other hand, spring up in response to some current problem or public policy that is considered to have fairly drastic repercussions for those involved. One such group would be the Committee for Fair Taxation, which was organized in response to the federal government's White Paper on Taxation issued in 1970. Another instance might be the formation in 1983 of groups to protest the testing of the Cruise missile in Canada. Groups such as these bring together people of diverse economic interests and social backgrounds in response to a policy they consider to be a threat to their interests. Single-issue groups are perhaps more common at the local level of government. Here we often see the formation of groups such as irate parents who attempt to pressure their local authorities to install a stoplight at a busy intersection, which they think threatens the safety of their children. They may hold up traffic to draw the attention of the local government and public opinion to their cause. Once it has achieved its goal, the group disbands, having no further common interest to hold it together.

Interest groups have a consistent and organized long-term impact on the Canadian political process. The characteristics that unite an interest group have a considerable effect on its organization and success. Generally, demographic interest groups are large and amorphous, and therefore difficult to organize toward agreed-upon ends. For instance, the aged, while developing better representation, are not yet really well organized into an effective and consistent interest group; even less so are the middle aged or the young. Thus, a common approach to the problems of each separate group is rarely articulated by a recognized spokesperson. Governments are, therefore, left to interpret for themselves what the major currents of opinion are. Nonetheless, on the issue of partial deindexing of pensions in 1985, senior citizens reacted strongly to a proposal that attacked their pocketbooks and forced the government to back down. An interesting contemporary phenomenon is the feminist movement, whose various manifestations are organized on the basis of their conception of the common plight of women. The existence of these groups underlines the importance for the members of an interest group to see themselves as primarily members of that group—in this case, disadvantaged women. These groups have a wide agenda of concerns, including pay equity, employment equity, pro- or antichoice stances on abortion, and other legislation to enhance the status of women. The National Action Committee on the Status of Women is an organization that has become a prominent contributor to the policy debate.[2]

In a pluralistic society with large demographic groups, there are a host of counterinterests that make it difficult for a predominant interest based on common demographic factors to emerge. To continue our example of feminism, its development was, and still is, hindered by the reluctance of some women to see their interests only in the context of their sex. In other words, many still conceive of themselves as primarily middle-class, or farmers' wives, or members of a particular religion, or as having a multitude of other interests not based on their sex. In order to establish an effective interest group, the women had to convince a solid core of supporters that the quality of being a woman was their most important shared characteristic and that the most important demands they had to make were based on this factor. For instance, during the Quebec referendum campaign, the Quebec Cabinet minister Lise Payette referred disparagingly to the traditional role of Quebec women by using the term "Yvette," implying that only backward and traditional women would vote against sovereignty association. Her comments had the unexpected result of mobilizing a profederalist movement of women who were proud of their traditional role in Quebec society, the Yvette Movement. Another example was evident in the constitutional debates of 1981, when the National Action Committee, a coalition of women's groups, fought successfully to prevent watering down of the women's equality clause (Clause 28) of the Charter of Rights and Freedoms.

A similar kind of problem exists for creating an effective interest group based on common ethnicity. Canadians of British descent have not banded together to pursue a common interest because most of them view their primary concerns from a perspective other than ethnic affiliation. This is not the case in Quebec, of course, where English-speaking Quebeckers are in the minority and have faced an erosion of their traditional place in Quebec society from the 1970s through the 1990s. Canadians of French descent, however, as well as members of other smaller ethnic groups, are more prone to band together as they perceive the need for common action to preserve their cultural heritage. Thus, we see organizations such as the Société St. Jean Baptiste, Ukrainian national societies, the Canadian Jewish Congress, and many other ethnic associations making concerted efforts to influence the government on issues related to their particular minority interests. The Assembly of First Nations and other organizations that represent aboriginal peoples are a special case given their recognition in the Constitution.

The ethnic interests of the French-speaking people in Quebec are a unique case, because the government of that province is in a position to protect those interests. However, the French-speaking minorities in other provinces are in a dramatically different situation. Hence, the mobilization of Franco-Ontarians and Franco-Manitobans to agitate especially for recognition of linguistic and educational opportunities represents a greater challenge. In the case of the Franco-Manitobans, their pursuit of the reestablishment of historic rights created a hostile reaction from the English-speaking majority of Manitobans. The conflict over the group demands of Franco-Manitobans in 1983–84 represented one of the bitterest episodes in the relations between ethnic and linguistic groups in this century.

As we have illustrated, the pluralistic nature of our society creates many cross-pressures on individuals and makes it difficult for larger interest groups to consolidate their membership for concerted action. A farmer may be a Roman Catholic, a French-speaking Canadian, a resident of Saskatchewan, and have a strong interest in some local service organization. The last affiliation may have very little to do with public policy but may consume so much interest that this individual has little time left to contemplate the effects of public policies on the position of a farmer, a French-speaking Canadian, and a resident of Saskatchewan. Even when the farmer's attention is attracted by a public policy debate, his or her loyalties may be divided. For instance, as a French-speaking Canadian the individual may have natural sympathy with the aspirations of Quebec, but as a western farmer he may be primarily interested in the economic problems of his region. It is therefore easier to aggregate the interests of people whose common characteristics clearly indicate a need for common action.

The economic sphere, because of its crucial effect on people's lives, is the major basis for constructing powerful interest groups in Canada. Within the area of economic activity, several categories of interest groups may be identified. Among these categories are the manufacturing, industrial, financial, commercial, agricultural, and professional societies and the labour unions. Even within some of these, there are subcategories. For example, major industrial corporations lend support to the Canadian Manufacturers' Association, while local chambers of commerce represent the interests of smaller business. The Business Council on National Issues was established in 1976 and has emerged as an influential force for the largest enterprises in the country. The Canadian Federation of Independent Business has developed into a voice for the national small-business community as well. In most instances these three organizations seek common goals because they have similar concepts of what is good and bad for Canadian society. Occasions may arise, however, when public policies are being discussed that could be of benefit to one and detrimental to the others, and in these instances they would obviously be working against each other. Subcategories with sometimes conflicting interests also exist within the trade union, agricultural, and professional categories. On broad public policy issues such as taxation and social welfare, the major economic interests may have some internal consistency, and it is common to see business on one side and labour on the other. But when it comes to more specific public policies, such as setting tariffs on specific imported goods, there may be considerable variation in the attitudes within major groups.

It would be incorrect to assume, however, that all organized pressure directed at government comes solely from economic groups. Religious denominations, for instance, have traditionally acted as agents for pressuring government. Other organizations may be concerned with influencing public policy in the area of censorship, civil rights, penal reform, mental health, or recreation—in fact, in almost every conceivable area where public policy has to be defined. In the 1980s and 1990s, a number of interest groups were active on both sides of the questions of abortion, capital punishment, and gun control. As the century comes to an end, these and other social issues will continue to generate interest-group activity.

Some major interest groups in Canada have established themselves as federations in order to influence the local, provincial, and federal governments within the Canadian federal structure. This has resulted in many of them having head offices in Ottawa and offices in various provincial capitals, all of which are staffed by permanent employees. Other interest groups have their major policy concerns with either the federal government, such as the Canadian Bankers' Association, or with a provincial government, such as the BC Federation of Teachers. It is the responsibility of these officials to establish contacts with those in government who are responsible for the public policies affecting them. These contacts include public servants, Cabinet ministers, and parliamentary committees. Furthermore, they may present briefs to royal commissions or supply information to task forces and parliamentary committees. The more important groups, such as the Canadian Manufacturers' Association or the Canadian Labour Congress, present annual briefs to the Cabinet. Frequently, responsible officials within the interest-group organization are appointed to government boards, commissions, and specialized bodies such as the now-disbanded Economic Council of Canada, the Canada Council, and the Canadian Wheat Board, or as Canadian representatives to the International Labour Organization.

In order to maintain effectiveness, any interest group must make a continuous effort to keep the interest of its members at a high level. This may be achieved by the dissemination of information in the form of a periodic trade journal or newsletter, which may also serve to keep people informed of what is happening in their field. In this way the members may be mobilized quickly to support their leaders' positions.

In these circumstances it is not uncommon for a bureaucracy to speak on behalf of its members, many of whom are passive about the issues exciting their leaders. It may be, however, that only well-established groups can afford the time and effort necessary to take a continuing interest in the affairs of their profession, rather than solely in the practice of it.

In addition to their activities in trying to influence governments directly and in maintaining internal loyalty, interest groups expend considerable effort in trying to convince the public of the legitimacy of their causes. Typically, interest groups try to foster the view that what is good for them is good for the country. The doctors in Saskatchewan, for instance, during their strike in 1964, attempted to convince the public that the interests of the patients were threatened as much as the interests of the doctors; 20 years later the Canadian Medical Association and its provincial components were similarly engaged in an attempt to discredit the Canada Health Act.[3] Interest groups, therefore, are very conscious of their image in the community and devote a great deal of effort to cultivating good public relations. In the 1970s and 1980s, when public concern with pollution heightened and the availability and cost of energy led to controversial policies, many large oil companies shifted their advertising toward portraying themselves as public-spirited corporations attempting to foster the public good. Thus, frustrated in their direct attempts to influence governments, interest groups will arouse public opinion in their support and thereby increase the pressure on governments. Among the ways they do this is by placing advertisements in newspapers and magazines and on TV and radio, drafting form letters for people to send to their Member of Parliament, and even supporting a candidate for the House of Commons from a party whose position is sympathetic to their cause. For instance, when restraint-minded governments in Ontario and British Columbia at different times restricted wage increases and cut back drastically on public services, the public-service unions in those two provinces responded with massive protests and advertising campaigns that reminded the public of the vital services that were at risk.

It is difficult to measure precisely the success of any pressure or interest group, as normally there is little documentary evidence to show a direct link between a particular policy proposed by a group and the acceptance of that policy by governments. Indeed, the goal of an interest group may be to quietly urge the government *not* to do something. When interest groups become involved in the governmental process, their ideas may have to undergo a long and tortuous journey through the bureaucracy and perhaps legislative committees before they reach the focal point of decision making—that is, the Cabinet. It may well be that the government faces little counterpressure, and thus it will be easier to resolve an issue in favour of the interest group. For instance, when the Royal Canadian Legion presses for higher pensions and other benefits for veterans, very few voices will be raised in opposition. There may be financial restraints that the government faces, but no organized group will challenge the moral rightness of the veterans' claims. On the other hand, when changes in labour legislation are being considered, a government will find itself facing pressure from organized labour on the one side and interest groups representing management on the other. In such a situation, the government often compromises, trying to satisfy each side as much as possible within the limits of what it thinks is necessary. Another possibility is that no effective organized interest group will have strong feelings about changes the government considers important. These are likely to be issues that are not economic in nature, and might include parliamentary reform, a reorganization of government, and certain kinds of foreign-policy issues.

These observations reveal that interest groups face a variety of situations to which they must tailor their attempts to influence government. All kinds of variables, such as the personal attitudes and opinions of the prime minister and Cabinet ministers, how close the next election is, the general popularity of the government at the time, and the prevailing social and economic conditions, will have their effect on the ability of an interest group to pressure government.

While there are relatively few published case studies of interest-group campaigns to influence Canadian public policy, one that might serve to show the methods used concerns the drug industry in Canada.[4] Without citing chapter and verse, the events that transpired from 1958 to 1969 may be summarized as an attempt to pressure government not to adopt legislation that would cause lower drug prices. Not only did the Pharmaceutical Manufacturers' Association of Canada (PMAC) pressure the government, but also the Canadian Medical Association—in league with other trade associations—showed concern about the effects of such a policy on their interests. Despite the concerted pressure, the government ultimately passed legislation that the drug lobby tried to prevent. There are many reasons why PMAC failed. For one thing it was very difficult to rally public opinion in favour of higher drug prices, and the government was aware of this. In addition, high-ranking civil servants in the government departments concerned had arrived at the conclusion that lower drug prices were both necessary and possible. PMAC, therefore, was faced not with vulnerable elected officials but with permanent, and therefore secure, bureaucrats. In the end the Cabinet accepted the advice of the bureaucrats, and the efforts of the drug lobby served only to delay the implementation of legislation. This example serves to show that, if the government is not politically insecure on a particular issue, and if it is receiving expert and well-argued advice from the public service, it is difficult for an interest group to deflect the government's purpose.

On the other hand, in 1987 the same interest group was successful in securing lengthier patent protection for its drugs from the makers of generic (therefore cheaper) drugs. This time around PMAC had a friendlier government to deal with, and it was able to win out against other interests that fought against the policy. PMAC had interests that fit into the Mulroney government's agenda, and by 1993 had secured even lengthier patent protection.[5]

It is indisputable that interest groups have been relatively successful in influencing government on a wide range of major and minor issues. In his study of the Senate, Colin Campbell has argued that the members of that body are an effective instrument of the business community. They have altered legislation that the business community finds offensive by introducing amendments that cumulatively blunt the original purpose of the legislation.[6]

Not all organizations can afford to maintain staff to lobby governments. Consequently, individuals and companies have set themselves up in business, mainly in Ottawa, as paid lobbyists. Their major skill or service is a knowledge of how the government works and their personal contacts with decision makers. Many of these lobbyists are former members of the political inner circle, with party and bureaucratic experience. In 1988 the Lobbyists Registration Act was passed to require that they register; by 1993 there were some 2800 registered lobbyists in Ottawa. Public concern about the influence of lobbyists, many with close links to the Mulroney government, led the incoming Chrétien government in 1993 to propose further measures to open lobbyists to closer scrutiny.

The essence of government in Canada is the struggle of competing interests to persuade decision makers to frame public policies acceptable to them.[7] Although there has been abundant criticism of so-called special-interest groups, almost everyone belongs to at least one of them. One should not be surprised at, nor condemn, the legal efforts of anyone to influence the government on his or her own behalf. The area in which criticism is valid is when disadvantaged groups do not have the resources to organize effective pressure on behalf of their own interests. In recent decades these groups have marshalled their resources and are receiving a better hearing, both by government and the public. Unfortunately for them, their proposals for more public spending on social programs clash with a mood of fiscal constraint that has been supported by business and financial interests. It is impossible to dispute that the large business community has access to and influence with decision makers that other Canadians can only envy.

PUBLIC OPINION

While the term "public opinion" is widely used, it is not easy to define precisely. For instance, just what is "the public"? Is it all the people of Canada, those who are eligible to vote, those who do vote, or those who articulate an interest in a particular issue? Actually, the "public" in public opinion differs with every issue, because what interests one group of Canadians may be of no consequence at all to others, and they will likely have no opinion on that issue. Even within a group that may have an interest in some particular public policy, there is a wide variation in the intensity of individual opinions. Similarly, there may be great differences in the amount of information that different individuals within the interest group possess. Although very intense feelings may encourage people to educate themselves about an issue, it is not unusual for people to have strong feelings on an issue about which they have little factual knowledge. Opinions on matters such as abortion, capital punishment, homosexuality, race relations, and other social and moral issues are often generated more by emotional reactions than rational assessments.

Governments, in responding to public opinion, must take into account the emotional climate of opinion in the country because their electoral success depends on it to some extent. Part of good leadership in government is the ability to create within the country an informed and rational public opinion that will in turn allow the government to base its policies on objective standards. Any government that seeks to strengthen its hold on the public by pandering to its baser emotions will ultimately constitute a threat to the country.

At this point we can return to the earlier theme of regionalism, for in Canada there have tended to be pockets of opinion based on regional considerations.[8] Historically, perhaps the best example of this was the widely divergent attitude between Quebec and most of the rest of the country toward conscription during the two world wars.[9] Other issues, such as the marketing of wheat, and policies on fisheries, forestry, and mining, are obviously going to evoke more sharply defined public opinions in the regions where these activities are most important. The questions of bilingualism and multiculturalism in Canada are subject to regional differences in attitude across Canada. Energy policies have generated wide chasms in opinion between producing provinces in the west and consuming provinces in the east. On some issues of national importance, such as the question of war or peace, threats to Canadian sovereignty, and the need to control pollution, there is a likelihood that a national public opinion will develop with varying intensity in different parts of the country. But as we have so often repeated, the issues that face Canadians are usually much more important to one segment of the population than to the whole. Thus, the government of Canada must be attuned to the voice of many different publics speaking on a multitude of issues. This is where interest and pressure groups come in, as they are the chief means of mobilizing public opinions from the nongovernmental side.

PUBLIC-OPINION POLLS

In recent years the conducting and publication of public-opinion polls have been an expanding practice. During elections in the 1980s and 1990s, the reporting of polls became a focal point of campaign coverage, with various polling organizations being commissioned by different media outlets to provide data on voter opinions on a frequent basis. The impact of this phenomenon on the democratic process is by no means certain. Nevertheless, some people have been concerned enough by the possibility that the publication of public-opinion polls might undermine the electoral process that they have suggested that they be banned during election campaigns.

Public-opinion polling, of course, is not conducted solely to discover the political opinions of the population. The technique is widely practised to discover the views of consumers—and as such is a valuable tool for business. The fact that people are willing to make important economic decisions on the basis of polling (survey research) should provide some comfort to those who worry about the validity of poll results. In fact, polling is a scientific exercise, and if a properly constructed random sample is asked a series of carefully developed questions by well-trained people, then a reasonably accurate picture of the population at large can be drawn. The results of such studies cannot be accurate down to the last decimal point, and thus how the data are reported is important. From the point of view of politics, the problem of polling has more to do with how the media use poll results, especially during elections, than with the fact that polls are done.

Governments and political parties use polling to help to define their positions on political questions and the degree of importance that they will attach to various issues. Critics refer to this as an abdication of leadership, while others may ask what is wrong with finding out what the people think in a democratic society. As with most areas of human experience, what is called for is judgement about the degree of importance that should be attached to the information generated by public-opinion polling. What is true in the last decade of this century is that governments find polls to be a useful tool. Political parties find them to be indispensable guides to campaign strategy, the media have adopted them as part of their regular news agenda, and the public seems eager to see the results.[10]

MASS MEDIA

We have spoken of the mobilization of opinions; we will now deal with the communication of these opinions through the mass media—that is, through television, radio, newspapers, magazines, and now the

Internet. As the chief means of disseminating opinions and information throughout Canada, the media perform a vital function in the political process. The way in which they perform this function has been a matter of serious concern for many Canadians. In 1970 a Senate committee spent many months investigating the media and issued a highly critical report.[11] Among the problems the committee discussed were concentration of ownership of newspapers (sometimes in conjunction with control of radio and television stations), the lack of quality in the majority of Canadian newspapers, and the precise definition of the term "freedom of the press." About 10 years later, the Kent Royal Commission on Newspapers was established in order to review the newspaper industry in Canada and to report on the extent to which the concentration of ownership of the industry affects the way in which it fulfils its responsibilities to the public. The main recommendation of the Kent Commission was that the government enact a Canadian newspaper act aimed at guaranteeing the freedom of the press deemed essential in a democratic society. The Commission stressed the need for freedom both from interference by government censorship and from restraints imposed by commercial interests.

The Commission feared that all groups of Canadians may not have equal opportunity to express their views. A relatively small group of owners, and the journalists who work for them, are in a position to determine the kind of information and opinions that will be available to the reading public. While government control of the media is always feared—and rightly so because of its potential power of censorship—it cannot be denied that a form of private censorship may also be practised by a small group. If ownership were more widespread in Canada, the resulting competition would partially reduce that threat. The dimensions of the problem can be seen from the following quotation:

> In 1982, 12 publishing groups produced 88 of Canada's 117 newspapers. . . . The 2 biggest publishers are Thomson with 40 newspapers and Southam with 14. . . . The 6 largest companies, all of them chains or conglomerates, account for 80 percent of the circulation of 5.5 million newspapers. . . . Canada has a higher concentration of ownership in the daily newspaper field than any other developed country. . . . The 2 largest chains, Thomson and Southam, do not compete in any of the 51 newspaper cities where they publish.[12]

This concentrated ownership reflects the difficulty of starting a successful independent newspaper under present economic conditions. Because newspapers are profit-seeking businesses, the economic realities of newspaper publishing are often seen to conflict with the public interest. That concentration of ownership concerned the Kent Commission and eventually led to the proposal of the Canada Newspaper Act of 1983. Subsequently, however, the proposed legislation sank without a trace amid newspaper accusations of unwarranted interference. In the early 1980s, however, the federal government did mandate the Canadian Radio-Television and Telecommunications Commission (CRTC) to prevent all the media in the same locality being owned by the same people. Concern about ownership concentration was expressed again in 1996 when the Hollinger Company, controlled by Conrad Black, gained ownership of newspapers with over half the circulation in Canada.

Television, and to a lesser extent radio, have supplanted newspapers as the main source of information and opinions for Canadians. These electronic media differ from newspapers in the important respect that government owns at least some and regulates all the outlets. It has been accepted that transmission frequencies are public property and can be used by private interests only under government supervision. Unlike the newspapers, radio and television have not been looked upon by government as purely a profit-making enterprise but rather as a service that must be provided to the people of Canada through a nationally owned network. This combination of ownership of part of the electronic media and regulation of the rest again raises the problem of censorship. The CBC is a Crown corporation and therefore not under the direct administration of elected politicians. However, they do control its funding, and this was seriously diminished in the late 1990s, raising questions about how it could pursue its mandate. The CRTC, as the regulating agency, has been concerned with granting licences and setting down the rules regarding Canadian content. By this means it is hoped that radio and television can be made an instrument to help preserve Canadian identity. The spread of cable television and pay television has posed problems for Canadian regulators in regard to this matter of preserving the Canadian interest. It was inevitable that the question of federal versus provincial jurisdiction would become a factor in the problems of regulation, and this was a subject of negotiation in the constitutional debates of 1980–81 and the Charlottetown Accord of 1992.

The whole question of Canadian content arises because of the relative ease with which US media penetrate Canada and thereby threaten to undermine the growth of a Canadian culture. Especially in the publication of magazines, Canadians are particularly vulnerable to competition from US enterprises. There was a long-standing controversy in this regard about the "Canadian" status of the magazines Time and Reader's Digest, both of which were accorded special exemption from regulations that applied to other American publications.[13] In 1976, amid much bitterness, these exceptions were withdrawn, and Time magazine ended its Canadian edition. The problem resurfaced in 1995 when Sports Illustrated produced a split-run edition for Canada. This meant that the American copy was electronically printed in Canada and that Canadian advertisements were added. Canada imposed tax measures to discourage this practice. The Americans then lodged a complaint with the World Trade Organization. This group ruled against Canada in early 1997, causing concern about how Canadian cultural sovereignty might be pre-served. All these questions raise the argument as to whether individual Canadians should themselves determine which magazines they read or which TV and radio programs they watch or listen to, or whether their choice should be limited by government action.[14] From the 1960s into the 1990s, there was a growing tendency to support government regula-tion of foreign influences in the interests of preserving Canadian iden-tity. The Federal Cultural Policy Review Committee of 1981 (Appelbaum-Hebert Committee) was the latest in a long series in the review of Canadian culture, the media, and the role of the government in ensuring that the media help to preserve Canadian culture. During the debate on free trade with the United States in 1988, much attention was placed on the concept of *cultural sovereignty*, which includes, of course, control of the media. Supporters of free trade argued that cultural sovereignty would be unimpaired, while opponents predicted dire results.

It should be obvious from this discussion that the media are not just another form of business enterprise in Canada but also have an impor-tant effect on the political process. Canadians, therefore, have every right to evaluate critically the performance of the media. In doing so they have questioned the reliability of professional journalists to present an accurate picture of the news and opinions that are current in Canada. Too often mediocrity in reporting results from a lack of proper profes-sional training in journalism; nor have media owners been primarily con-cerned with raising the professional standards of the journalists whom they employ. While the national media at times achieve excellence, many local Canadian media—both electronic and print—often present a bland and superficial treatment of the news. One suggestion to rectify this situation is to establish a national press council to provide self-polic-ing for its membership. Journalists in some provinces have already established such councils. If such self-policing and general upgrading of standards do not take place across Canada, there may well be a greater demand that the traditional concept of freedom of the press, which has so far prevented any government regulation of newspapers, give way to more government involvement for the sake of the public interest. No democratic government can risk the development of a society in which there are not adequate means to provide information to the public and ensure that diverse opinions may be open to public debate.

ELITES AND SOCIAL CLASS

So far in this chapter, we have discussed how interests are mobilized to influence governments both directly and through public opinion, the dissemination of which is largely dependent on the mass media. But there are other elements in society that may have a profound influence on the political process, even though they are not primarily political in nature. Among these are the elites, so designated because they occupy prominent positions in various spheres of Canadian society. Of these elites the most important outside the political field are found in the corporate, labour, communications, church, and academic spheres.[15] Relations between these elites and the elected and bureaucratic political elites are suspect, in the view of both some political theorists and ordinary citizens. They fear that there is collusion between small groups of people who wield much more power than is considered healthy in a democratic system. This is especially the case with regard to the corporate elite. The extreme of this position is the Marxist interpretation of society, which argues that those who own and control the productive resources of the country control the whole society, and that political decision makers are merely a front for those in control. No one can deny that the corporate elite wields a great deal of influence in the political process in Canada, but any close investigation of Canadian society shows that there are other sources of influence to which decision makers must respond. Among the elites there will always be disputes about the proper policies for government to follow. The most obvious of these clashes is between the labour and the corporate elites. Because there is a plurality of elites, there is a need for a process of accommodation between them on behalf of the interests— regional, ethnic, economic, and political—that they represent. At least one interpretation of the process of Canadian politics concentrates on the accommodations that have been the hallmark of relations among these elites in Canadian history.

The existence of elites in Canada, as in other societies, depends on the acceptance of the different roles of leaders and followers. In politics, leaders exercise their leadership on the basis of electoral support. However, elected leaders are prone to co-opt advisors, who rapidly become members of the elite because of their close association with the decision makers. If the elected leaders lose office, the advisors lose their influence as well. In the other elites, with the exception of labour, the democratic process has little to do with the achievement of elite status. This implies that either talent or privilege is the main qualification for joining the ranks of the elite. The most cogent criticism can be levelled at those elites that exercise power because of privilege rather than talent. Ideally, everyone should have an equal opportunity to acquire elite status. There are those, however, who argue that equality of condition—not merely equality of opportunity—should be the goal of a rationally organized society. However, although equality of material condition is within the realm of possibility, it does not mean that the concept of leaders and followers would disappear.

In other words, it is likely in any political system that some will have more influence than others, and these may be defined as the elite. Thus, the important question to ask about elites is not about their existence but on what basis those who are influential have gained the opportunity to exercise that influence. It must be kept in mind that in the federal system there will be different elites at the federal, provincial, and municipal levels; although they may overlap, they may also be quite independent in their ability to exert influence in different situations.

There is a danger in assuming that the holding of a particular office, whether in the government or out, or possession of great wealth, both of which are normally indicators of elite status, automatically signifies the exercise of influence. Influence is not restricted to people who have position or money. These provide the opportunity to exercise influence, but they do not necessarily mean that the people concerned will opt to use these instruments to influence public policy.[16] It is not enough simply to identify "big shots" by the position they hold or the money they have and on that basis assume that public policy decisions have been made according to their whims. An adequate study of decision making must be much more comprehensive than a simple account of position and influence. Many Canadians consider that the decisions of governments at various levels are the result of the conniving of small groups of powerful people who give little consideration to the masses. While this interpretation has a comfortable simplicity about it, any thorough study of political developments in Canada would reveal that elected leaders are sensitive to the views expressed by the many publics that comprise the population of Canada.

To identify elites in Canada and describe their backgrounds is a useful exercise in social analysis and reveals many social inequalities, especially the small number of women in their ranks. Although this makes known some of the people who have the greatest opportunities to influence public policy in Canada, it does not necessarily provide the tools for studying how actual influence is exercised. Position is only one component of the ability to influence government. Broadly speaking, it is much better to be in an elite if one expects to wield influence, but this does not guarantee effective influence in a wide range of particular issues.

At least some of the elites in Canada would be considered upper class in terms of objective criteria such as income, occupation, and education, if not by the subjective criteria of self-perceived status. The role of social class is, therefore, another factor that must be considered in the political process of Canada. Many studies have shown that, although the role of social class cannot be ignored in the political process, it plays a lesser role in Canada than in many other countries. There are several reasons for this. Despite the existence of a small select group centred on the colonial governors of early British North America, the broad base of the population consisted of agrarian people facing common frontier conditions. Most people were, therefore, aware of belonging to a broad middle class, and this view of class membership has persisted to the present.

Regionalism and ethnicity are also important features in the failure of class to emerge as a dominant political force in Canada. They have cut across class boundaries, and major Canadian issues have been defined in these terms rather than class. This has been helped by the fact that the leaders of both major parties have sought to discourage class politics. Because of the smaller territory and greater homogeneity of populations in provinces, class-based voting is more evident at that level.[17] The only genuine attempt at national class politics—in the CCF/NDP—has not attracted the support of most Canadians, although it has had a measure of success in western Canada. There is a body of opinion, usually supported by those who would like to see class politics (which they style as "creative politics"[18]), that maintains that, along with the urbanization and resultant homogenization of the Canadian public, class will emerge as a dominant political force. The contemporary salience of the problem of Quebec in Confederation tends to make this view difficult to accept in the near future. It is no accident that some class-oriented theorists in English-speaking Canada would accept the separation of Quebec from Confederation so that the rest of Canada could concentrate on settling what it considers to be the real problems of Canada, which stem from class differentiation.

The dispute over the role of social class in the political process centres on the difference of opinion about the objective to which a political system should aspire. Most Canadians up to now have accepted, as the legitimate role of government, the attempt to achieve consensus among a population characterized by diversity. Proponents of class politics view the polarization of social classes as a more proper political process, resulting in victory for an allegedly downtrodden majority in the working or lower classes. Whatever form of politics emerges in Canada, it is historically true that the constraints of region and ethnicity have combined to thwart the politics of polarization on the basis of class.

POLITICAL SOCIALIZATION

The process that conditions Canadians to accept the political patterns that have evolved in their particular environment is called *political socialization*.[19] People are not born with any innate sense of political values. They must be acquired during the process of intellectual growth. A number of institutions are crucial to this development, and among these the first, and perhaps the most important, is the family. In their formative years, children learn the acceptable responses to various political stimuli mainly through their parents. Most Canadian families do not have highly developed interests in political matters; there is very little direct transmission of political values to the children. What are transmitted, however, are attitudes toward law and order and general feelings toward government and people in authority.

While many people decry this lack of interest in politics, it is a natural consequence of most Canadians' circumstances: their primary concerns are earning a living, raising a family, and filling whatever spare time they have with recreational activities, which do not normally include political involvement. It is therefore not surprising that most political activists come from families where political activity is considered an integral part of life. The nature of the family in which a child is raised has a lot to do with the individual's acquisition of political attitudes. For example, if the head of the family has a better than average education, there is a greater likelihood that the children will be more attuned to political interests. Conversely, where there are various kinds of deprivation in a family (poverty, single parent, extreme authoritarianism by either parent), it is more difficult for a child to become highly politicized. The tragedy of this situation is that those segments of society that most need to use political activity to upgrade their conditions are the groups least likely to acquire a high degree of politicization. They are thus often dependent on the support of sympathetic outsiders to argue their case in the political realm.

Generally, most children in Canada are socialized in an environment that encourages deference to the law and those in authority. By the same token, at an early age they are introduced to the democratic norms that most parents consider the most acceptable for the government of Canada. These two characteristics may, of course, at times be contradictory, and they tend to temper each other in a way that has caused many observers to comment that Canadians are less prone to the democratic excesses sometimes seen in the United States, or to an excess of deference that is considered typical in the United Kingdom. The point is that judgements about deferential attitudes take place in a comparative context, and statements about the deferential character of Canadians ordinarily imply some kind of comparison with the United States. It would be ridiculous to think that Canadians blindly obeyed political or other authorities in the past. Recent commentaries on Canadian public life have argued that Canadians have moved from deference to defiance or, based on survey research, have shown a decline in deference.[20]

The effect of the family has been described as intergenerational, or along a vertical line. Once the formal educational system is entered, a child becomes subject to intragenerational, or horizontal, pressures and is introduced to value systems that may differ from that of the family. By the time adolescence is reached, the tension between these two pressures, if they vary significantly, can be the dominant force in the individual's attitude toward politics and political objectives. While up to the 1960s Canadian school systems emphasized deference to authority, especially in the elementary and secondary levels, there was a noticeable trend away from this deference starting in that decade in all levels of education, particularly in postsecondary school education. In this respect a policy of stimulating individuality, which would be reflected in a wider acceptance of democratic norms, gained currency among progressive educators. This trend, indeed any trend in Canada, has had to face provincial control of education as laid down in the Constitution. Therefore, the political socialization process, as it relates to education, is fragmented into 10 subsystems rather than organized into a centralized national system. This is an important factor in maintaining the regional and, in the case of Quebec, ethnic nature of the socialization process.

Schools in Canada have made little conscious attempt to politicize their students by introducing them to the principles of various kinds of government through formal courses. The attitude of the educational bureaucracy has often been that politics, like sex formerly, should be learned in the streets rather than in the classroom. This lack of opportunity for young Canadians, especially at the elementary level (studies indicate it may be too late at the secondary level), may lead at best to a lifelong uninterest in politics and at worst a perversion in attitude. The generally low level of information about politics that has resulted from this policy has a lot to do with the widespread views that hold politicians and their activities in contempt. It may also lead to an alienation from a system of government whose operation is completely misunderstood. It is well to remember that only a small minority of Canadians goes to university, and of these only a small number study political science. This means that the vast majority of Canadians has had little or no opportunity to study their form of government in an educational institution. The record of educational authorities using the school system as an effective instrument in political socialization has been a sorry one. On the other hand, in the past there was a strong effort on the part of the Roman Catholic Church, which controlled education in Quebec until the 1960s, to instil acceptance of traditional political attitudes. More recently, there has been widespread concern over the incidence of separatist thought among Quebec educators and their efforts to transmit their views to students. This might constitute a larger challenge to Canada's unity than economic dislocation.

A third major factor in political socialization is an individual's work experience. People who work under similar circumstances, such as in the same factory, in the same store, or in the same office, are likely to show common attitudes toward political matters. There is a circular cause-and-effect relationship in operation here, because the patterns of family experience and education will probably have been similar for people who end up working in the same environment. On the other hand, where social mobility has allowed the sons and daughters of manual labourers and farmers, for instance, to enter higher-paying occupations, the new environment will make inroads into the pattern of political socialization developed earlier in life. Depending on the occupation, the workplace brings different instruments of political socialization to bear on a person. For example, since 1961 labour unions in Canada have been powerful advocates of the New Democratic Party, while professional organizations tend to exert more influence in favour of the two traditional major parties. In general, those who work for nonprofit organizations tend to acquire political attitudes that are at variance with the views of those who work in industry and commerce. Although no comprehensive studies have been done in Canada on the effect of the work environment on political socialization, there is a strong impression that similar occupational circumstances tend to be associated with similar attitudes toward political issues.

Once again we must emphasize the importance of the pluralistic nature of society, which creates numerous cross-pressures within the socialization process. Thus, while it is easy to lump people together into various income groups, for instance, and to assume common political attitudes within these groups, it does not always produce an accurate picture. A bank employee may earn considerably less than a person skilled in a trade, but the bank employee's political attitudes are often based on a higher estimation of his or her own status. Therefore, the bank employee may tend to identify with the interests of the more well-to-do. The factors that contribute to the political socialization of individuals can be so diverse that it is difficult to explain just what caused any particular individual to adopt certain political attitudes toward a certain situation. It is only in the larger sense, when one considers large numbers of people, that useful generalizations about the socialization process can be made.[21]

CONCLUSIONS

In this chapter we have examined aspects of the social structure of Canada and their relationship to the political process. While indirectly every social relationship in Canada has some effect on the political process, we have attempted to identify those aspects which have a direct impact on government decision making. As political science has advanced in its methods and techniques, there has been an increasing emphasis on quantitatively measuring the interrelationship between an individual's life in society and his or her role as a citizen. What we have attempted to do is to transmit some of our impressions of the nature of these relationships without the statistical verification one would find in longer, more detailed works.

RECOMMENDED READING

Forcese, D.P. *The Canadian Class Structure*, 3rd ed. Toronto: McGraw-Hill Ryerson, 1986.

Johnson, R. *Public Opinion and Public Policy in Canada*. Toronto: University of Toronto Press, 1985.

Nevitte, Neil. *The Decline of Deference: Canadian Value Change in Cross-National Perspective*. Peterborough: Broadview Press, 1996.

Newman, Peter C. *The Canadian Revolution 1985–1995: From Deference to Defiance*. Toronto: Viking, 1995.

Pammett, J., and M. Wittington. *Foundations of Political Culture: Political Socialization in Canada*. Toronto: Oxford University Press, 1986.

Pross, A. Paul. *Group Politics and Public Policy*, 2nd ed. Toronto: Oxford University Press, 1992.

Romanow, Walter I., and Walter C. Soderlund. *Media Canada: An Introductory Analysis*, 2nd ed. Toronto: Copp Clark Pitman, 1996.

PART **4**

THE
PROCESS OF
GOVERNMENT

CHAPTER 8

The Prime Minister and the Cabinet

The governmental process involves a set of institutions, the operations of which are prescribed by the Constitution and the laws derived from the Constitution. The set of institutions, however, is only the formal machinery through which the process works. It is the people within the institutions whose roles, and the way they play them, determine the vitality, the quality, and—to a certain extent—the uniqueness of the Canadian governmental process. Similar institutions exist in other countries (Great Britain, Australia, and India), but Canadians bring to the operation of their governmental process the values, experiences, and conditioning that have socialized them in the Canadian setting. The governmental institutions are divided into three distinct branches: the executive, the legislature, and the judiciary. Each institution is staffed by people specializing in the needs of that particular branch. The instrument by which the institutions and the people who work within them are linked is the party system. The political parties supply the link not only between the branches of government but also between government and the other forces in society whose combined operation we have called the wider political process.

In this chapter we intend to discuss the executive branch of government. At the head of the executive is the governor general, who represents the Crown in Canada. This role in Canada today is largely symbolic. The real working heads of the executive are the prime minister and the Cabinet, who are drawn from the elected House of Commons (with a few exceptions) and can be termed the political executive. They are responsible for a bureaucracy of full-time public servants who are, in the main, insulated from the pressures of partisan politics and constitute a body of experts both in the formulation and execution of public policy. The study of public administration is concerned with the bureaucracy and merits a separate chapter, which will follow. We will therefore devote the rest of this chapter to the study of the symbolic role of the governor general and, more important, the operational role of the prime minister and the Cabinet.

THE GOVERNOR GENERAL

In Chapter 4 we noted that the Constitution was not definitive about the actual practice of executive authority in Canada, although it says a great deal about the powers of the governor general. Indeed, it states, if one reads it literally, that the governor general has supreme authority in the executive. This is not the case in practice, since constitutional convention has dictated that the governor general follow the advice of the prime minister and the Cabinet. Thus, although the Canadian government is formally referred to as "His or Her Government" and theoretically is responsible to "Him" or "Her," its real responsibility, recognized by it and all other Canadians, is to the elected House of Commons. While the governor general appoints the prime minister and theoretically has some say in the matter, the actual decision is made by the electorate when they give one party a majority of seats in the House of Commons. When no party receives a majority of seats, it is conceivable that the governor general might have to use some discretion, but even here the designation of the prime minister will be determined by party processes. The governor general also has the power to grant clemency, but again he or she acts only on the advice of the Cabinet. Whereas in the nineteenth century strong governors general might have had some influence on policy matters, today the governor general's rights to give advice and be advised on matters of public policy count for little. Whatever importance the office now has rests on the esteem in which the incumbent is held. Governor General Schreyer, for example, is reputed to have exercised influence during the constitutional developments of 1981. It is possible to imagine a situation in which the governor general might attempt to disregard the advice of the Cabinet if that advice seems to subvert the Constitution. However, if a government decided to pursue an unconstitutional course and assumed, for instance, dictatorial powers, the governor general's refusal to accept advice, as noble a gesture as it might be, would not likely alter the course of events.[1]

It should be apparent that the most important role of the governor general's office is ceremonial. As head of state, the governor general accepts the credentials of foreign ambassadors, entertains foreign dignitaries at state dinners, bestows honours, generally embodies the majesty of the Canadian state that is above mundane politics, and may, therefore, act as a cohesive force with which all Canadians may identify. We should hasten to add, however, that this role, while admirable in its intent, has fallen far short of providing a national focus. This calls into question the major tenet on which a constitutional monarchy is based. While in the United Kingdom the monarchy still provides a symbol of national unity, in Canada, although a particular governor general may enjoy wide popular appeal (for example, General Georges Vanier), the institution itself has never received the unqualified support of all Canadians. Nowadays, there are mixed feelings about the Crown, ranging from fierce loyalty (especially in the older generation) to downright hostility. The majority of people between these extremes exhibit monumental uninterest. This might lead one to conclude that the monarchy in Canada may slowly atrophy. It is unlikely that a Canadian government would seriously consider abolishing the monarchy in the near future, because the emotionally charged political consequences of that action could hardly be justified in terms of its supposed benefits.[2] The consent of Parliament and of 10 provincial legislatures to the constitutional amendments that this would necessitate would not be worth the turmoil. Even proposals to enhance the position of the governor general have been greeted with anger by people who resent any attempt to downgrade the monarchy.

In addition to the governor general, the Constitution makes frequent reference to the Privy Council. This term is the formal designation of the body of advisors to the governor general. From the wording of the Constitution, one would assume that the governor general has wide powers to appoint or replace privy councillors; however, as we have noted before, it simply provides for the appointment of those politicians who have, by party support, received the confidence of the House of Commons by popular mandate. The term "Cabinet" does not appear in the Constitution, but by constitutional convention it has assumed the key role in the executive of the government of Canada. It is this term that we will use henceforth in referring to the working political executive. Since the term has no legal standing, when Cabinet ministers are designated by the prime minister, they are sworn in as privy councillors so that their activities may be vested with constitutional executive authority. Once sworn in as privy councillors, they remain so for life, but by convention again they exercise executive authority only when they are members of the Cabinet of the day. Other people may also be accorded the honour of being made privy councillors (e.g., premiers of provinces and leaders of opposition parties) without having any authority to render advice to the governor general.

THE PRIME MINISTER

The office of prime minister is not mentioned in the original Constitution (although it is referred to in Section 37 of the Constitution Act, 1982); it is, nonetheless, the most important political office in Canada. The prime minister is at the head of the Cabinet and has sole responsibility for choosing and dismissing its members. In some matters this individual alone advises the governor general. Because the prime minister has broad discretionary powers in exercising the authority of the office, he or she may choose to dominate the Cabinet very forcefully or act as the captain of a team.[5] In election campaigns the public focuses a great deal of attention on which party leader would make the best prime minister.

Previously, we have stressed the importance of political leadership. There is a paradox here between that fact and the equally relevant fact that Canada has had relatively few political folk heroes. The resolution of this paradox lies in the fact that Canadian voters are willing to support astute political operatives while also refusing to hold them in awe or reverence. Put more colloquially, Canadian voters seem traditionally to have said to their prime ministers, "What have you done for me lately?" No amount of goodwill can save a prime minister who does not have an adequate answer to that question. If the purpose of a political system is to satisfy the interests of a large number of the people who have at least some power to affect the system, then one can say that the traditional political attitude of Canadians is a healthy one, for it has made leadership responsive. Thus, there is a link between the prime minister and the entire country, even though this individual is elected from one particular constituency.

The symbolic role of the prime minister as leader has filled a vacuum that was left because the Crown in Canada, represented by the governor general, has not been able to lend cohesion to the body politic. If grandiose concepts are necessary for national policy, only the prime minister can galvanize support from all regions of the country. This is what distinguishes the appeal of Macdonald, Laurier, Diefenbaker (in 1958), and Trudeau (in 1968) from that of others. Yet in times of either national crisis or national complacency, a leader with little symbolic appeal can maintain office merely by showing ability as a political operative. Nonetheless, the really great prime ministers have been no less pragmatic than the others; in fact, they have been even more pragmatic than most, but they have been able to invest their pragmatism with an aura of idealism. Sir John A. Macdonald cloaked his politics in the garb of building a nation from sea to sea. Sir Wilfrid Laurier expounded the theme that the twentieth century belonged to Canada. John Diefenbaker's vision of Canada made at least a short-run impact on the Canadian electorate, as did Pierre Trudeau's idea of the just society in 1968.

Political party leaders are scrutinized by the public as potential prime ministers. Public-opinion polls regularly ask respondents to name whom they think might make the best prime minister. However, many other factors help to determine who becomes prime minister. In 1988 Brian Mulroney was reelected as head of a Progressive Conservative government, while Ed Broadbent—despite higher personal popularity—could provide only a somewhat better than usual third-place finish for his New Democratic Party. The lack of personal appeal by John Turner in both 1984 and 1988, however, cannot be disregarded in assessing the outcome of those elections, the first of which he entered as prime minister. When Jean Chrétien succeeded Turner as Liberal leader, he was dismissed by some as "yesterday's man," but he eventually gained a degree of popularity by not being Brian Mulroney. Chrétien's popularity grew during the 1993–96 period, but ironically not in Quebec, where he did not benefit from being a native son. When he made a disastrous television appearance in December 1996, his popularity began to decline, and this made his party strategists concerned about how that would affect the next election.

There are many decision-making powers that the prime minister alone, as head of the government, may exercise. These include the authority to advise the dissolution of the House of Commons to set the date for the next election, to appoint the members of the Cabinet, and to appoint lieutenant governors, senators, judges, and many other important public officials. Of course, in the exercise of these responsibilities, the prime minister seeks the advice of colleagues, and, although the leader's word is final, members of the Cabinet and other advisors to the prime minister are by no means without influence. Any prime minister who tries to act unilaterally too often may lay the foundation for trouble, because such action will alienate powerful forces both within and outside the governing party. In this respect it is always important to keep in mind that no Canadian prime minister has ever received more than 53.6% of the vote of the electorate.[4]

Not surprisingly, the office of prime minister varies with each incumbent. Some are jealous of their prerogatives, while others tend to defer to the judgements of strong Cabinet colleagues. A key element in the strength of any prime minister lies in an ability to coordinate the various policies of the different departments headed by Cabinet colleagues. The leader must harmonize these policies in order to create a government that appears to be following a specific course of action based on well-planned priorities. The strength or weakness of the prime minister's administration depends on how well the incumbent can impose some order on public policy. It is his or her ability to appear to be in charge of the administration and to be giving purpose to it that inspires confidence among the voters. For instance, the Mulroney administration of 1984 to 1988 was fortunate to preside over a period of economic growth, which usually leads to voter contentment. Nonetheless, a variety of scandals that plagued his government, coupled with his own inability to become personally popular with the electorate during those years, contributed to an erosion of support for his party and its policies, including free trade. Had the Liberals been able, as the election approached, to portray themselves and their leader John Turner as a unified party of good managers, the 1988 election result might well have been different. It is the prime minister who gives the tone to both politics and government.

The prime minister's strength as principal coordinator and decision maker is based on the position of party leader. The office is dependent on the party's getting a majority of seats in the House of Commons or, failing that, enough to form the government. Often the party's victory depends substantially upon the prime minister's performance as leader. If this is the case, the prime minister will be able to exact considerable loyalty from a party that owes its success to its leader.

Obviously, the circumstances in which a leader comes to power vary with each election, but once prime minister—regardless of the margin of victory—the incumbent is in a position to help friends, grant favours, and use the *power of appointment* to strengthen his or her own position. The political careers of the members of the party depend on the choices that the prime minister makes. The most important of these choices are those of Cabinet appointments. Theoretically, the prime minister can appoint anyone to the Cabinet; in practice, the incumbent is somewhat restrained by the need to satisfy regional expectations of Cabinet representation, to repay political debts, and to ensure that major interest groups have a spokesperson in the Cabinet. For instance, in 1984 Mulroney had to treat Joe Clark, former prime minister and party leader, with respect by giving him the prestigious post of secretary of state for external affairs. Nevertheless, it is the prime minister alone who decides who in the Cabinet will be the most influential and who will occupy the most important portfolios. In addition, the prime minister has to make a number of other appointments, such as *parliamentary secretaries* (who are members of the House of Commons assisting Cabinet ministers, and who are usually thought of as being potential Cabinet ministers),[5] senators, members of boards and commissions, and some party officials. The fact that the prime minister is in a position to further or impede the political careers of the members of the party gives the incumbent tremendous leverage over them.

Having assumed office, a prime minister has almost complete authority to organize a staff to operate in the manner that suits the incumbent personally. During the Trudeau years (1968–84), this led to an expansion of the *Prime Minister's Office* (PMO), which was further expanded under Prime Minister Mulroney. He introduced the key position of *chief of staff*, who, along with the principal secretary, is the major figure in organizing and running the PMO.[6] In addition, the press secretary and senior communications advisor, as well as a special media coordinator, testified to the importance placed on relations with the media and the public. A variety of other assistants provided for caucus liaison, support, and advice in a variety of policy areas. Under Mulroney, the position of *deputy prime minister* was given a prominence not known previously, and this Cabinet minister and his two parliamentary secretaries, as well as the prime minister's own parliamentary secretary, were also included within the PMO. These senior officials were supported by staff numbering over 100. While Chrétien's PMO is somewhat smaller, the same functions are more or less provided for. This office provides the prime minister with personal services, such as organizing the schedule, receiving and answering the mail, bringing matters to his or her personal attention, advising on the large number of appointments to be made, as well as supplying policy and political advice. There are those who interpret this trend as a move toward the presidential system, since it seems to concentrate power in the Prime Minister's Office at the expense of the Cabinet and House of Commons. Notwithstanding the obviously dominant position of the prime minister, such an interpretation is somewhat superficial because, rather than increasing the potential power of the prime minister, it organizes the way in which the prime minister exercises power more than ever before. There are no statutory requirements that specifically state a rigid formula for the Prime Minister's Office, so future prime ministers are free to accept or reject the 1990s approach. The essence of the American presidential system is that the president's office is independent of the legislature; this system cannot be introduced in Canada merely by reorganizing the Prime Minister's Office.[7]

The prime minister has no departmental portfolio, but he or she does have an equivalent administrative organization to facilitate a coordinating role. This is called the *Privy Council Office* (PCO). The duties of the PCO, including the Cabinet secretariat, are to do the groundwork for Cabinet decision making by organizing the information necessary for decisions to be made. This office is responsible for making sure that information flows from various Cabinet committees to the full Cabinet and that the mechanism of Cabinet government runs smoothly through the circulation of the agenda and the keeping of minutes. After Cabinet decisions are taken, it is the function of the PCO to transmit those decisions to the various organs of government responsible for their execution. In this regard they are responsible for the preparation of *orders-in-council*, which are formal embodiments of Cabinet decisions. Although people working within the PCO are permanent public servants, their mode of operation depends primarily on the direction of the prime minister, rendering this office another instrument of his or her personal powers.

The prime minister's organization of the Cabinet reflects the incumbent's approach to coordinating policy and provides another means of retaining the kind of control desired.

THE CABINET

The Cabinet, headed by the prime minister, is the most important organ of government. As mentioned earlier, in exercising the responsibility to form a Cabinet, a prime minister follows a number of political conventions whenever possible. These include the practice of having at least one member from every province in which the party has elected members, adequate representation from Quebec, representatives from metropolitan centres and other regions within the larger provinces, a growing number of women, and a mixture of representatives of ethnic, business, and labour interests. In addition, a prime minister must appoint members who represent the various attitudes and tendencies within the party. To have achieved the leadership of the party, the prime minister must have acquired some political debts that can be repaid by appointment to the high office represented by a Cabinet post. All these considerations underline the fact that the Cabinet is the apex of the party and government systems. There is no established size for the Cabinet, but its representational nature, plus the need to provide a political head for each of the 21 departments (this figure can change with each government reorganization), make it a large body that the prime minister must mould into an efficient decision-making executive. In 1984 it reached its highest figure ever, with 39 ministers plus the prime minister. The Cabinet appointed by Prime Minister Kim Campbell in June 1993, on the other hand, had only 25 members, and Jean Chrétien continued this trend with a Cabinet of 23, including himself.

A minister may have no departmental responsibility—for example, the government leader in the Senate is usually in the Cabinet or may have multiple responsibilities. Within each Cabinet, there invariably emerges a smaller "in group" of senior ministers whose advice on policy is important beyond their own departments. The members of this inner group are usually assigned to the key departments, such as finance, external affairs, justice, and the Treasury Board, and to whatever other departments that are responsible for the policy questions most important for the government. In the Trudeau era, this group became formalized as the *Priorities and Planning Committee*, and under Mulroney this Cabinet committee was recognized as the inner Cabinet, with authority to make final decisions on some matters. In 1989 there were 19 members on the Priorities and Planning Committee, chaired by Mulroney and including the chairpersons of other Cabinet committees plus others of his choice. However, Chrétien, with his smaller Cabinet, eliminated the Priorities and Planning Committee and reduced the number of committees to four. One was the Treasury Board, which is required by law. Others were the Economic Policy Committee, the Social Policy Committee, and the Special Committee of Council. Chrétien also created a new category of secretaries of state, with status below that of Cabinet minister, and appointed eight of his newly elected MPs to fulfil some of the goals of representation discussed above. They and the regional, ethnic, gender, or other interests they represented were no doubt disappointed by this lesser status. Downsizing may have its advantages from an operational standpoint and as a way of showing the public that the government is frugal, but it has its price in limiting the representational aspects of the Cabinet. The importance of any particular portfolio may vary over time, and the power of a particular minister depends on the prime minister's assessment of his or her skills. A strong prime minister controls the influence of the ministers; however, under a weak or poorly organized prime minister, Cabinet ministers may be able to extend their power and influence to the point where the prime minister's coordinating role becomes jeopardized as conflict between ministers develops.

Cabinet ministers are responsible both individually and collectively to the House of Commons. Their individual responsibility for heading a department of government merges with their collective responsibility for general policy. For example, the minister of defence is responsible for the administration of the Department of National Defence and its policies, but although he or she is a key figure in the determination of those policies, they are not the minister's policies alone but those of the whole Cabinet. Thus, while the Somalia Inquiry of the 1990s required reaction from that minister, every other minister had to defend it in public and in the House of Commons. Any Cabinet minister may have doubts about a government policy; in fact, it is natural to expect strong differences of opinion among a group of powerful political figures. However, once policy is decided, a minister whose views have been overruled must support the policy or resign. The House of Commons, for its part, holds the Cabinet responsible for any policy, and any attack is more often directed at the whole government than at an individual minister. A *motion of lack of confidence* in the House of Commons is the procedure by which the opposition in the House attempts to indict the government as a whole; if the motion gets a majority of the votes cast, the government must resign. It must be remembered, however, that when the government party has the majority of seats in the House, it is unlikely to be defeated.

Not only is the Cabinet responsible to the House of Commons for its exercise of executive authority in administering existing laws, but it also occupies the key role in presenting legislative proposals. In doing this, it has to organize the discussion of those proposals according to the procedures of the House. The Cabinet is the most important organ of the government, both in conducting the daily business of government and in planning for the future. As a consequence of its increasing authority, allied with the fact that it usually has majority support in the House of Commons, people have questioned whether one can realistically say that the Cabinet is in fact responsible to the House. At times in Canadian political history, the House has appeared to act as a mere rubber stamp for Cabinet proposals. This was the case in the last years of the long tenure in office of the Liberals under King and St. Laurent from 1935 to 1957. After so many years in power, some Cabinet ministers treated the House as an inconvenience rather than as the highest representative body of the people. Their ultimate downfall is testimony to the fact that the people in a democratic system will not abide the arrogance of power forever. The ability of the opposition to use the House of Commons as an instrument to challenge the Cabinet will, of course, have an impact on the ability of the Cabinet to have its own way.

A major factor contributing to the Cabinet's power is the latitude it has in administering the laws of Canada. Many, if not most, of these laws provide that either the whole Cabinet or an individual minister may exercise discretion in executing the law and may develop operational rules to administer legislation. The Cabinet issues *regulations* that give specific effect to the general provisions of acts. The House of Commons has delegated part of its legislative power so that those who execute the law may adopt methods to apply the legislation to concrete situations. The regulations made on this basis are known as *delegated* or *subordinate legislation*. When the legislature approves a law, it cannot hope to cover all possible situations that will arise in the context covered by the law; it must therefore give at least some discretionary powers to those who apply the law. Although discretionary authority is provided for by the act and therefore has legal validity, the wider the area of discretion, the more it appears that those who apply the law are acting on their own authority rather than on the authority granted in the original act. Wide delegation of power to the executives is exemplified in the extreme by the War Measures Act, which was applied during the two world wars and the Quebec crisis of 1970. In effect, by passing the Act, the legislature gave blanket approval for the executive to pursue any policies it felt necessary without seeking legislation. These measures transformed the Canadian political system into a quasi-dictatorship of the executive, and such powers are granted only in emergencies. Under normal circumstances, delegated legislation is seen in operation when an immigration officer exercises discretion at the border, when an employment officer at an employment centre observes a certain procedure in interviewing applicants for a job, or when the minister of fisheries declares a ban on commercial fishing in polluted waters. These individuals are all acting on the basis of laws passed by Parliament, but none of those laws could hope to specify precisely in all possible situations the way in which public servants should apply them.

Each Cabinet minister is responsible for the administration of all existing laws that come under that department's jurisdiction. Furthermore, a minister may be responsible for acting as the spokesperson to the House of Commons for a group of semi-independent agencies, boards, commissions, and Crown corporations—even though rarely intervening in their day-to-day administration. For instance, a large department such as the Department of Transport must administer more than 50 acts, such as the Canada Shipping Act, the Aeronautics Act, the Government Railways Act, and the Navigable Waters Protection Act. In addition, the transport minister reports to Parliament for Via Rail Canada Incorporated, the Canadian Transport

Commission, the National Harbours Board, and the St. Lawrence Seaway Authority. Under these acts the minister must take responsibility for the administration of the department as it carries out its day-to-day activities. In practice, Cabinet ministers intervene very little in routine departmental operations that are performed by public servants headed by a deputy minister; they are responsible for changes in present procedures and the launching of new areas of jurisdiction that will necessitate the passing of legislation.

It is normally only when things go wrong that a minister intervenes in the routine operation of the department. Such intervention may result from a request from a Member of Parliament to look into a problem in the member's constituency, or it may result from a question in the House that intimates inefficiency or malpractice within the department. More seriously, a crisis that may have political ramifications will demand the minister's immediate intervention. A major airline disaster or a ship sinking in the St. Lawrence Seaway is a crisis in which the transport minister might be expected to take a personal hand in carrying out a thorough investigation and reporting to the House. During the 1990s a series of incidents involving members of the Canadian Armed Forces serving in peacekeeping operations brought embarrassment to the Department of National Defence. This continued to be a subject of questions in the House of Commons and resulted in widespread media coverage. As a result the minister David Collenette felt obliged to initiate an investigation and was required to defend his department publicly. His successor, Doug Young, continued to be preoccupied with the fallout of these problems, and the minister of defence became unusually prominent in a peacetime Cabinet in Canada. If the political consequences of an issue are significant enough, the whole Cabinet may become involved, even though the situation falls within the jurisdiction of a particular minister. For instance, when Minister of Justice Allan Rock had to apologize for a leaked letter that implicated former Prime Minister Brian Mulroney in the so-called AirBus affair, the political consequences fell upon the whole Cabinet. While some critics called for Rock's resignation, political opponents were quick to attempt to tie the prime minister to the problem and hence further undermine the credibility of the government.

This example underlines the collective responsibility of the Cabinet. While each minister is responsible for a particular area of jurisdiction, the Cabinet collectively is responsible to the House of Commons for the activities of each minister. Thus, even though the minister of finance has the job of directing the day-to-day financial affairs of the country, the policies will be based on Cabinet priorities and defended publicly by all ministers. The most important constitutional convention that demands collective responsibility is that, when a prime minister resigns after losing a vote of confidence in the House of Commons, the whole Cabinet must resign as well.

Many of the most important decisions that the Cabinet must make concern policies based upon general legislation passed perhaps decades before. For instance, important decisions such as the revaluation of the dollar, recognition of the People's Republic of China, withdrawal of troops from the North Atlantic Treaty Organization, and the testing of Cruise missiles in Canada were all made by the Cabinet under its executive authority without the need for new legislation. The role of the legislature in these matters is often limited to questions during the daily House of Commons question period. Decisions in many of these vital areas must be made with dispatch in order to keep abreast of rapidly changing circumstances, and thus the need for legislation in every new situation would prevent the executive from dealing adequately with contemporary affairs.

As well as exercising executive authority, the Cabinet plays the leading role in planning the legislative program for the House of Commons. Its preeminent position in both the executive and legislative life of the governmental process is crucial to our system of responsible government. Its legislative role has a constitutional foundation in Section 54 of the Constitution, which stipulates that only ministers of the Crown may introduce legislation for the raising or expenditure of money. Since most legislation of any consequence requires some expenditure, the Cabinet is required carefully to formulate and introduce into the House of Commons a legislative program that it considers necessary in the national interest. Basically, the program includes two kinds of legislation. First and most common are amendments to existing laws, usually sponsored by individual ministers. These changes normally originate from within a department and are based on the advice of public servants whose experience in administering the law suggests to them ways in which it can be improved. Such things as reorganization of the national parks, changes in food-and-drug acts, various acts regulating the marketing of agricultural products, export and import permits—in fact, most changes in existing legislation—originate in suggestions from those people directly responsible for administering the acts. These changes might be administrative and have little political implication. However, to the extent that proposed changes have political consequences, the Cabinet must consider them on grounds other than that of administrative efficiency. Because of the subject matter treated, some changes in existing laws would affect large numbers of people and therefore fall into the second category of Cabinet legislative proposals, which are major changes in policy. The introduction of the Goods and Services Tax (GST) was not a simple decision based on the advice of public servants that it was better than the Manufacturers' Sales Tax and would raise more money. Cabinet ministers who are sensitive to the political realities of Canada know that very few things arouse the passions of Canadians as much as a new tax. Before legislative changes are proposed, the Cabinet weighs every possible alternative. Included in the second category of what might be called grand policy are legislative proposals that deal with new responsibilities or government response to social changes. Examples are social-welfare measures like medicare, environmental legislation, and criminal law reform. The introduction of the Free Trade Agreement and later the North American Free Trade Agreement required legislation brought forward with much controversy.

Cabinets arrive at their decisions by combining the expert advice of their bureaucracy with their own sense of political necessity. At times, however, they are unwilling to be totally dependent on bureaucratic advice for their decisions, and in these instances they appoint *royal commissions* or other investigatory bodies such as *task forces* that may include public servants and people outside the government.

Royal commissions have legal powers and are far more formal instruments for gathering information than task forces. Major royal commissions in the last three decades have investigated and made recommendations on the organization of the federal government, health care, taxation, bilingualism and biculturalism, and the financial management and accountability of the federal government. The MacDonald Commission recommended the negotiation of the Free Trade Agreement with the United States. These commissions normally travel from coast to coast, call witnesses, and hear submissions from all interested parties. Upon receipt of a commission's report, the Cabinet accepts those suggestions that it considers both apt and politically acceptable. Sometimes, because of the drawn-out period of investigation, a royal commission may be appointed by the government in order to avoid immediate action.

Task forces are less formal information-gathering groups whose objectives are usually more limited, thus enabling them to report more quickly. The fact that they are sometimes headed by ministers or are directly responsible to a minister or the Cabinet suggests that they will not be as politically neutral as a royal commission. No matter how the government acquires information, it does not necessarily frame legislation immediately. What it may do is issue a *white paper* that outlines as specifically as possible the government's policy orientation. After a period of debate on the basis of the white paper, the government will introduce legislation translating policy ideas into law.

Aside from these formal information-producing bodies, the Cabinet is the focal point for public pressure from a variety of interests. Chief among these is the political party of which the prime minister is leader and the Cabinet ministers are the regional lieutenants. Most actions of the Cabinet, therefore, have at least some degree of partisan motivation. Since the Cabinet usually seeks to broaden the basis of support for its actions, it cannot ignore the pressures exerted on it by interest groups representing major sectors of Canadian society. Obviously, the policies that the Cabinet adopts cannot satisfy all these groups equally, but the Cabinet would hope to steer a course that avoids alienating any of them completely. Again this is brokerage politics at the highest level. It is not always possible to avoid alienating a powerful interest, but a Cabinet will only do so if it considers that it will get strong support elsewhere. One is much more likely to find unpopular but necessary policies that may tend to upset powerful interests in society undertaken just after an election victory—or at least in midterm—rather than when an election is imminent. In the former case, the long-term benefits will have a chance to mature before the government's term expires, and therefore any bitterness will tend to be eroded. On the other hand, if an election is in the offing, the government will reap the harvest of discontent at the polls.[8]

From all this discussion, it becomes evident that there is a wide range of policies to be set by the Cabinet and a variety of contributing factors that affect the decisions ultimately taken. President Truman's remark about his position in American government, that "the buck stops here," can be applied equally well to the Cabinet in the Canadian system. Whereas many Canadians may express opinions as to how the political affairs of the country should be conducted, it is the small group that comprises the Cabinet, dominated by the prime minister, that decides the way things will be. To aid the Cabinet in making decisions, there exists a number of institutions, the most important of which are the committees of Cabinet and the *central administrative agencies* that serve them.

In 1997 there were four standing committees of Cabinet. The Treasury Board, responsible for spending control, was chaired by the president of the Treasury Board, with the minister of finance as vice-chair and four other members. The Economic Development Policy Committee had 14 members whose departments dealt with economic questions, while the Social Policy Committee had 12 members whose departments were oriented to social questions. The Special Committee of Council had six members who dealt with routine procedural matters for Cabinet.

Cabinet's role is to set broad policy and to give adequate attention to the various demands of society that the programs of diverse departments of government are intended to serve. In addition to medium- and long-range planning, this body must concern itself with the crucial question of the allocation of resources. What should be done, how quickly, and how much can Canada afford are all questions that must be answered. The Privy Council Office has developed as a key agency in helping to organize the information and policy alternatives necessary for the Cabinet and its various committees.

Despite reorganization of the Cabinet, the *Treasury Board* remains a pivotal Cabinet committee. Unlike other committees, its authority is founded in law, in the Financial Administration Act, rather than on administrative choice. Its membership, noted above, as with all

Cabinet committees, is appointed by the prime minister. The decisions that the Treasury Board makes are issued in the form of Treasury Board minutes. In carrying out its work, the Treasury Board is assisted by a bureaucratic organization called the *Treasury Board Secretariat.* This highly specialized group works with departments and agencies of government to ensure that their requests for money are justified by the programs that the government envisions. This process is known as the *estimates,* and the results of this are presented annually to Parliament in the statement of the government's proposed spending. In addition, personnel management policy, human resources utilization, compensation, pensions and insurance, and staff relations are covered by the Secretariat. Moreover, it negotiates the terms of collective agreements with various bargaining agents. To sum up, the Treasury Board, through its bureaucracy, is concerned with the development of effective managerial practices and efficient administration throughout the government.

In 1978 the *Office of Comptroller General of Canada* was created to serve the Treasury Board as well. Its role is to foster sound management practices. The establishment of this office was a reflection of growing concern for control of the huge government bureaucracy and for making it both efficient and accountable.

The *budget,* which deals with the revenue raising and borrowing of government, usually represents the most important legislative proposal of the Cabinet. The minister of finance is responsible for recommending tax proposals that will yield the revenue needed to carry out the government's spending policies and to influence the economy of the country in the desired direction. This is called *fiscal policy.* A major function of the Department of Finance is to make projections on the revenue yields of certain kinds of taxes and to balance these with other fiscal measures, such as borrowing. In this area there are basically three decisions a government can make: it can balance expenditure with revenue (a *balanced budget*), it can have an excess of revenue (a *surplus budget*), or it can have an excess of expenditure (a *deficit budget*). Starting in the 1940s, these decisions began to be based on Keynesian economics, which, very simply stated, prescribes that, when private spending and investment are inadequate to maintain full employment, the government must take up the slack (*prime the pump*); inversely, when there is inflation or overexpenditure in the private sector, the government attempts to cool off the economy by withdrawing money from the private sector. Unfortunately for government economists and the Cabinet they advise, economic conditions are so complex that textbook solutions do not always apply, and traditional Keynesian economics has come under considerable fire. Through much of the 1970s and 1980s, the two problems of inflation and unemployment appeared at the same time—a condition that was labelled "stagflation" (stagnation with inflation). In this period the government was hard put to find any adequate answer to Canada's economic problems. In the late 1980s and 1990s, the size of the federal government's annual deficit and accumulated public debt became a central topic of political debate. In this climate deficit reduction became the major theme of the budgets of Paul Martin, minister of finance under Chrétien. This meant reductions in the number of federal government employees, smaller transfer payments to provinces for health and social programs, and cuts to agencies such as the CBC. Just as earlier budgets expanded the role of government, more recent ones have downsized the federal government.

In conjunction with its fiscal policy, the Cabinet, especially the minister of finance, is responsible for *monetary policy*. Monetary policy is the management of the interest rate, the supply of money and credit, and the day-to-day financing of government by short- and long-term borrowing. The minister of finance depends not only on the Department of Finance but on a semi-independent body, the *Bank of Canada*, for advice. Although the Bank of Canada was founded as an independent body, it is now an established convention that the activities of the Bank of Canada cannot run counter to the policies of the government.[9] The importance of this financial function of government has been stressed by the *monetarist school*, under the influence of Milton Friedman, and resulted in the 1970s and 1980s in policies that led to extremely high interest rates.

The foregoing discussion of estimates and fiscal and monetary policy delineates the key role of the Cabinet in decisions affecting economic life in Canada. A free-market economy is still the predominant economic system in Canada; nonetheless, the federal government, even after downsizing, remains the largest single enterprise in the economy. Its decisions on when and how to borrow and what services the government will supply all have a pronounced effect on Canada. Not only do the government's decisions affect its own operations, but they also affect the economy as a whole.

Everything in this chapter shows the preeminence of the prime minister and the Cabinet in the governmental process. The Cabinet is ultimately responsible for the tens of thousands of decisions on public policy that are made by bureaucrats in their administration of the laws of the country. The most important policy decisions that directly affect a large number of the population and attempt to redirect society will be made not just under the authorization of Cabinet but by the ministers themselves. Cabinet authority accompanies every executive decision, but the Cabinet itself has time for only the most important public-policy changes. This situation has grave implications, because the size of the bureaucracy that administers the laws is so great that all its actions cannot be supervised. The Cabinet's critical position as the link between the wider political process and the bureaucratic element of government cannot always ensure that the interests of the people take precedence over the vested interests of large bureaucratic organizations. There is always a danger when large administrative structures are created, because in their quest for administrative efficiency, they tend to forget that their ultimate purpose is to serve the public. The existence of powerful public-service unions introduces another element of difficulty, in that their goal is to enhance the position of their membership as employees, and this may not always mesh with the public's traditional expectations about public servants. It is a constant struggle for the Cabinet and individual ministers to see that larger goals prevail over those engendered by the bureaucratic process itself.

The Cabinet is at the centre of the maelstrom of pressures from various interests, domestic and international factions, personality conflicts, career expectations, technological and social changes, and the myriad forces that form the background for decision making. It is vital that the Cabinet has an understanding of all these forces and is able to assess their relative strengths. This is the essence of its political position and explains why it has such an important role in the Canadian parliamentary system. No other group is in a comparable position to translate policies into governmental administration. This puts awesome power into the hands of a small group of people, and later chapters on the legislature and judiciary will describe the safeguards that exist to keep this power within reasonable bounds.

RECOMMENDED READING

Aucoin, P. The "Prime Minister and Cabinet," in R.M. Krause and R.H. Wagenberg, eds. *Introductory Readings in Canadian Government and Politics*, 2nd ed. (167-92). Toronto: Copp Clark, 1995.

Bakvis, Herman. *Regional Ministers: Power and Influence in the Canadian Cabinet*. Toronto: University of Toronto Press, 1991.

Donaldson, G. *Eighteen Men: Canada's Prime Ministers*. Toronto: Doubleday, 1985.

Hockin, T., ed. *Apex of Power: The Prime Minister and Political Leadership in Canada*. Scarborough: Prentice-Hall, 1977.

Mancuso, M., R. Price, and R.H. Wagenberg. *Leaders and Leadership in Canadian Politics*. Toronto: Oxford University Press, 1994.

Pal, Leslie A., and David Taras. *Prime Ministers and Premiers: Political Leadership and Public Policy in Canada*. Scarborough: Prentice-Hall, 1988.

CHAPTER 9

The Bureaucracy

The bureaucracy is the only part of government that most Canadians deal with on a direct personal basis. Contacts with Cabinet ministers are rare; dealings with Members of Parliament can be more frequent but are still uncommon for the average Canadian; and business in courts before judicial officials, while widespread, is hardly a daily event for the average citizen. But many people deal with an employment counsellor, encounter a member of the RCMP, correspond with and sometimes meet personally with income-tax officials, and come face to face with customs and immigration officials when crossing the border. Thus, when people speak of dealing with the government, they are normally talking of some contact they have had with a public servant, or bureaucrat. These officials are usually at the bottom of a towering and complex bureaucratic pyramid. While authority comes from the top, the actual services are performed by the people at the bottom. Many Canadians are frustrated by the seeming inflexibility and complexity of what they feel should be simple procedures. This so-called red tape is a result of the fact that every activity of public servants is directed toward carrying out some specific law of the land. Thus, they assume a different kind of responsibility from most people offering services in society. Store clerks, farmers, labourers, or professionals are in a position to use their discretion within the limits of their own or their company's policy without the personal hazard of having to violate a law in order to meet their customer's needs. Public servants may wish to apply their own personal discretion where the law seems inappropriate to the situation, but they must always remember that it is they who will suffer the consequences of stretching the rules. The people at the bottom of the pyramid are burdened by the weight of a monumental set of rules and regulations that they must apply but have hardly any role in formulating.

This situation is the price that we must expect to pay if we are going to deny arbitrary power to public servants. While most Canadians grumble at the red tape, on reflection most would admit that to a large extent it is necessary and unavoidable if we want to see laws equally applied to all citizens. The public expects revenue, for instance, to be handled in the most scrupulous manner and becomes incensed if it sees any dishonesty where tax dollars are concerned. This results in the need to fill out, often in triplicate, complex forms so that a close scrutiny may be kept on the spending of the public's money. While complexity may at times tax the patience of the public, the alternative is to have a system in which it is relatively easy for officials to dip their hands in the public till or to give preferential treatment to their friends and relatives.

We have referred above to the employees of the bureaucracy who are visible to the public and who condition most people's attitudes toward public servants. People seldom encounter the senior public servants who direct the work of bureaucrats in the field across Canada. This group includes top public servants who are in frequent contact with political leaders. In this chapter we will discuss not only the organization of the rank and file of the bureaucracy but also the policy-making function of its higher officials. Part of the discussion must therefore cover the rationale for organization and the structure of governmental executive bodies. We will also consider the recruitment and conditions of employment of public servants and the government's role as an employer. We may then assess the quality and character of the Canadian public service.

The size, structure, and operations of any governmental bureaucracy depend on the role that society gives to the state. It is therefore no surprise that Canada has a very different bureaucracy today from that in 1867. At that time Canadians expected very little interference in their daily lives from the government, and the role of the state has been described as that of a night watchman.[1] There was no personal or corporate income tax, family allowance, Canada Pension Plan, unemployment insurance, medicare, radio, television, satellites, airlines, atomic energy, and all the other attributes of a modern technological society. There were only a rudimentary militia, postal service, customs and immigration service, system of courts, public works, and in general those services necessary to maintain a semblance of order in a rural society. Public servants of the day had little need of any other expertise than the ability to read and write and keep accounts. While a few professional people were needed at the headquarters of departments of government, most positions could be filled by *patronage appointments* from among supporters of the party in power.[2] This situation gradually changed with the advent of the new and more purposeful role of government that has been described as *collectivism*. This term denotes a number of activities, mainly regulatory, by means of which the state took a greater part in the lives of citizens in order to mitigate the excesses of the free-enterprise system. Railways were regulated, labour legislation came into effect, marketing and pure food-and-drug standards were set and enforced, and policies were adopted to protect citizens from the sharp practices of powerful interests in the community. People began acting collectively through government for their own protection. A new breed of civil servant to operate a more complex administration was now necessary. Consequently, pressures were exerted on government for civil service reform because the patronage system could not provide the experts needed.

The collectivist period ended by the outbreak of World War I, which demanded of government the machinery to mobilize the entire economy. A number of new taxes—the most important and enduring of which was the income tax—heavy domestic borrowing in the form of Victory Bonds, and the raising and equipping of a large military force raised government activity to a new plane. It was in this period that the organization of the civil service and its recruitment policies assumed their modern form. The demands of war weighed so heavily on the machinery of the state that the use of the federal bureaucracy for partisan political advantage was no longer acceptable to either the public or the politicians. Thus, the *merit principle* was introduced and gradually expanded through competitive examinations administered by the Civil Service Commission. The provinces were slower in reducing patronage. Finally, the Depression of the 1930s, World War II, and the reconstruction of the late 1940s made the public service the backbone of the social-welfare state as it continued to develop in the 1950s and 1960s. It was in this latter period that the state assumed responsibility for maintaining full employment with economic stability and the provision of basic welfare measures to all Canadians. The government also realized that it could regulate the economy by fiscal and monetary policies and, by its own leadership, affect the demands that people made on the state. Examples of this are unemployment insurance, family allowance, old-age pensions, the Canada Assistance Act, employment retraining, medicare, and a host of other legislation. To administer programs of this type, the public service needed to expand its staff to include doctors, lawyers, economists, actuaries, scientists, and professionally skilled administrators. While increased social services provided the impetus for the growth of the bureaucracy, the government's key role in technological advance placed an added burden on the administration. The development of broadcasting, air transportation, and atomic energy comprises only three examples of the areas where government assumed a major responsibility.

Figure 9.1 shows public service employment levels as documented in the *Public Service Commission Annual Report 1992*, with December 1995 levels added in brackets. The new numbers reflect downsizing, and there has been pressure to reduce them. By 1996, including the military, about 498 000 people—some only part time and others on contract—worked for the federal government. The number has declined as some government-owned enterprises have

been privatized, as the military has shrunk to 68 000 full-time personnel and 28 800 reserves, and as other public servants have taken
early retirement or been laid off.

FIGURE 9.1

FEDERAL GOVERNMENT EMPLOYMENT, DECEMBER 1992

Viewed by Statistics Canada, the Treasury Board, and the Public Service
Commission

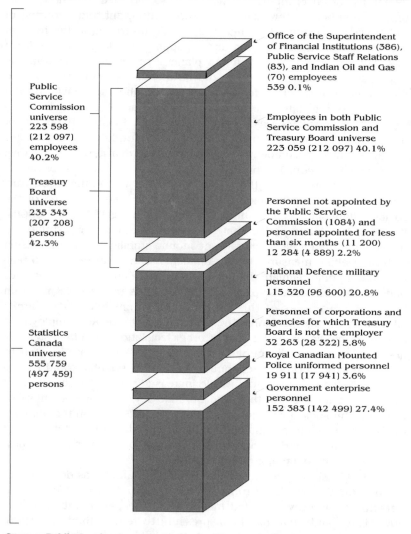

Public
Service
Commission
universe
223 598
(212 097)
employees
40.2%

Treasury
Board
universe
235 343
(207 208)
persons
42.3%

Statistics
Canada
universe
555 759
(497 459)
persons

Office of the Superintendent
of Financial Institutions (386),
Public Service Staff Relations
(83), and Indian Oil and Gas
(70) employees
539 0.1%

Employees in both Public
Service Commission and
Treasury Board universe
223 059 (212 097) 40.1%

Personnel not appointed by
the Public Service
Commission (1084) and
personnel appointed for less
than six months (11 200)
12 284 (4 889) 2.2%

National Defence military
personnel
115 320 (96 600) 20.8%

Personnel of corporations and
agencies for which Treasury
Board is not the employer
32 263 (28 322) 5.8%

Royal Canadian Mounted
Police uniformed personnel
19 911 (17 941) 3.6%

Government enterprise
personnel
152 383 (142 499) 27.4%

Source: Public Service Commission Annual Report, 1992. The numbers in brackets are as of December 1995, from Statistics Canada,*Public Sector Employment,
Wages, and Salaries Bulletin* 72-209xPB. Reproduced with permission.

Public servants are organized in departments, departmental corporations, agency corporations, proprietary corporations, and other agencies. Those who are the direct responsibility of the Treasury Board number approximately 207 000. The others are employees of a variety of agencies that are the responsibility of the federal government in one way or another. This complex organizational structure is described in the Financial Administration Act[3] and varies depending on how much direct ministerial control is called for by law. For instance, in 1997 there were 21 departments of government, such as Foreign Affairs and International Trade, Finance, Human Resources Development, Industry, Justice, National Defence, and Transport. *Departmental corporations*, such as the Agricultural Stabilization Board, or the Atomic Energy Control Board, perform services of an administrative, regulatory, or supervisory type. The *agency corporations*, such as Atomic Energy of Canada Ltd. and the Royal Canadian Mint, are involved in trading or service operations as well as in management, procurement, construction, or disposal functions for the government. The third group, *proprietary corporations*, are in effect businesses owned by the government. Some 140 000 Canadians work for organizations such as the Canadian Broadcasting Corporation, Via Rail, and Canada Post. A final group includes *unclassified Crown corporations*: the Bank of Canada, the Canada Council, and the Canadian Wheat Board. In addition, there are scores of boards, commissions, and councils with both full-time employees and part-time members. Together in their various forms, the people who are dependent on the federal government for their payment constitute a considerable sector of the community. However, provincial and municipal government employees have been a growing component of the labour force, and they now outnumber federal employees. Total government employment in 1996 was approximately 1 200 000 and thus represents about 12% of the entire Canadian workforce. While this number seems large, it should be remembered that it represents a response to a growing number of government services for a growing population. Critics may delight in bashing the bureaucracy, but people must understand that a modern welfare state—which cares for the people, the economy, and the environment of a huge country such as Canada—cannot operate without an adequate number of employees (see Table 9.1).

DEPARTMENTAL ORGANIZATION

What is the basis for organizing federal employees? There are several alternatives, each of which has some merit. Departments may be organized according to the *purpose* they are expected to fulfil. In fact, most federal departments are organized this way and change to suit their

TABLE 9.1
THE 13 FREQUENTLY USED SERVICES AUDITED

Department	Major Services	Service Outputs	
Citizenship and Immigration Canada	Applying for Canadian citizenship	Citizenship granted	220 000
Foreign Affairs and International Trade Canada	Applying for Canadian passport	Passports issued	1 398 000
Foreign Affairs and International Trade Canada	Obtaining consular services at a Canadian mission overseas	Canadians assisted	1.5 to 2 million
Public Works and Government Services Canada — Reference Canada	Calling the 1-800 numbers (in the Blue Pages) and asking how to contact specific government units	Enquiries answered	747 976
Revenue Canada — Customs	Going through customs inspections at an airport or a border crossing	Travellers processed: Airports Land crossing	13.4 million 87.9 million
Environment Canada	Getting weather information through telephone and other means	Public forecasts produced Enquiries answered (automated)	500 000 50 million
Canadian Heritage	Visiting Canadian national parks	Visitors to parks	4.9 million
Revenue Canada — Taxation	Enquiring about taxation matters at a counter or by telephone	Enquiries answered: Counter Telephone	2.4 million 8.2 million
Human Resources Development Canada	Applying for Employment Insurance benefits	Applications processed Payments made	3 million 27.2 million
Human Resources Development Canada	Applying for Old Age Security or Canada Pension Plan benefits in Income Security Program	Applications processed Payments made	2.5 million Over 100 million
Royal Canadian Mounted Police	Obtaining police assistance in towns and villages served by the RCMP	Population served Number of calls for service	6.4 million 1.5 million
Industry Canada and Partners	Obtaining information from a Canada Business Service Centre	Enquiries answered	686 536
Statistics Canada	Obtaining statistical information at the local Reference Centres of Statistics Canada	Enquiries answered: Telephone Walk-in	460 000 28 000

Source: Report of the Auditor General of Canada, September 1996, p. 14–10. Reproduced with the permission of the Minister of Public Works and Government Services Canada, 1997.

immediate purpose. For instance, the Department of Foreign Affairs and International Trade was the result of a reorganization meant not only to carry out the foreign policy of Canada but also to support international trade. Therefore, the staff with the skills thought necessary to perform these duties was consolidated in this department. Organization on the basis of *common skills* led to the consolidation in the 1970s of most information services of separate departments into one department housing specialists in the dissemination of information. But by 1976 the result, Information Canada, had been disbanded. An entirely different basis for organization would be based on the kind of people to whom the service would be directed. Veterans, fishers, farmers, and Native peoples are examples of sections of the *population served* by departments that were established to deal with their particular needs. Finally, departments may be organized on a *geographical basis* (e.g., the Department of Indian Affairs and Northern Development), in which case a number of different services may be rendered by the same department in a particular area. Within each department a number of these principles may be in operation; that is, a department based on a particular function may have units based on a section of the population or geographic considerations, or one unit, such as a legal division, may service the whole department.

The principles on which a department is created may not continue to be applicable as society and public policy change. As northerners, for instance, successfully agitate against control from Ottawa, the geographical basis for the Department of Indian Affairs and Northern Development might be phased out as, in all likelihood, the Northwest Territories and Yukon would become provinces. The government white paper of 1969 on Indian Affairs in effect proposed an end to the ethnic basis for administering the government's policy for Native peoples and recommended that they be served by the same departments that serve other Canadians. Nearly 30 years later, however, the department still existed; there was a continuing constitutional debate on how best to deliver services to Native peoples and, more broadly, the degree of self-government that they might exercise.

Periodically, governments initiate studies to analyze the structure of departments and other agencies with a view to increasing their efficiency. Two examples are the royal commission appointed in 1960, popularly known as the Glassco Commission, and the Lambert Commission, which reported in 1979.

The Glassco Commission's most important observation was that the organization of the public service was rather inefficient and concerned more with administrative convenience than with political responsibility. The Commission proposed a number of improvements that would apply the principle of responsibility more strictly, not only in the departments of government headed by ministers, but also in the boards, commissions, and Crown corporations whose operations span the whole country. These latter institutions were especially prone to be insulated from political pressure because their day-to-day operations were not subject to direct ministerial control. On the other hand, some of these semi-independent structures cannot avoid public pressure.

FIGURE 9.2
CHANGE IN THE ORGANIZATIONAL STRUCTURE OF REVENUE CANADA

1992 — BEFORE ADMINISTRATIVE CONSOLIDATION

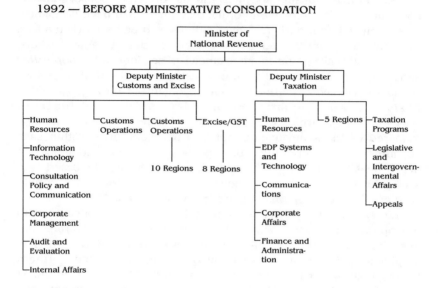

1996 — AFTER ADMINISTRATIVE CONSOLIDATION

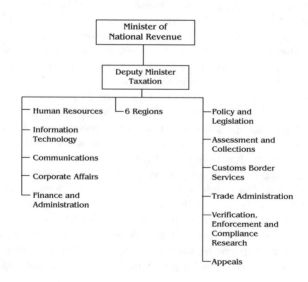

This is particularly true in the broadcasting field, in which the Canadian Radio-Television and Telecommunications Commission is charged with the responsibility for regulating broadcasting; at the same time, however, partisan politicians have strong views about public policy in this area. For instance, the granting of a licence for an all-news cable TV channel was supposedly a CRTC decision in 1988. Nonetheless, pressure from back-bench Progressive Conservative MPs on behalf of an Edmonton-based company forced the minister of communications and the Cabinet to review the CRTC decision to give the licence to the CBC. No matter what the minister did, she was going to bear the brunt of the political backwash. This illustration shows that it is one thing to say that an independent body, free from political interference, should regulate broadcasting, and quite another thing for the public to accept that the politicians should have no control. There is really no organizational theory that offers a blueprint for the handling of such problems. What attitude the electorate will adopt on such problems will obviously be a function of the general political climate that prevails at any period.

The Glassco Commission offered some specific recommendations as to how the public service could better achieve the twin goals of public responsibility and efficiency. It recommended "that departments and agencies be given the necessary authority and be held responsible for the management of money and staff, with greater powers to contract, to authorize payments, and especially to select, classify, train, promote and discipline their personnel."[4] While the government did not accept all of the Commission's recommendations, it went a long way in vesting more powers in the individual departments. Just as important as the recommendations themselves was the intellectual ferment that the Commission stimulated among senior public servants. The people at the top of the public service began to reassess their roles and responsibilities instead of slavishly adhering to their former practices. In this ferment questions were raised about how the central-control agencies of the public service should work.

The most direct manifestation of change brought about by the Glassco Commission recommendations was the reorganization of both the Treasury Board and the former Civil Service Commission. The Treasury Board, which had been an agency within the Department of Finance, was elevated to the status of a department under its own minister, the president of the Treasury Board. While the departments were given more independence in financial and personnel matters, the Treasury Board's role as a management agency for the bureaucracy was more sharply defined. Rather than having to check closely the day-to-day operations of departments, it is now established as the body chiefly responsible for developing management policies to regulate the operations of all departments. For example, the introduction of sophisticated computer operations for various departments could be undertaken with guidelines established by the Treasury Board. Long-range planning became one of the functions of the Treasury Board, and with the emergence of the *Policy and Expenditure Management System* (PEMS) and its *expenditure envelope* concept, the Treasury Board had a new instrument for developing expenditure policy.

In 1978 the Office of Comptroller General was added, and it is responsible to the Treasury Board to advise on program evaluation and administration policy. Moreover, the Treasury Board assumed the role of management in the collective-bargaining process that was introduced in 1967. This was an entirely new function because prior to this date government employees had not bargained with their employer, as had organized workers in the private sector.

As a result of the reorganization of the Treasury Board, the Civil Service Commission became the *Public Service Commission* with the passing of the Public Service Employment Act of 1967. This Act broadened the Public Service Commission's staffing function to enable it to recruit potential employees for the various departments. It recruits through competitive examinations and interviews in which merit is the deciding factor. The Public Service Commission was also relieved of responsibilities in personnel management formerly executed by the Civil Service Commission. These responsibilities are now under the jurisdiction of the Treasury Board.[5]

In addition to these central agencies, a number of departments have performed functions for other departments so that they can in turn serve the public better. A major reorganization in 1993 combined the former Department of Public Works, the Department of Supply and Services, the translation service in the Secretary of State's Office, and the Government Telecommunications Agency to create the Department of Public Works and Government Services. This new department carries out central administrative functions such as the provision of office space, acquisition of goods and services, information management and communication, translation, and many other tasks for all the other departments.

Much of the growth in government in Canada has taken place in the area of *Crown corporations*. Insofar as they are to some extent removed from direct ministerial influence, questions have been raised concerning their accountability to public officials. The *auditor general* of Canada argued in the 1980s that Crown corporations were out of control. Since the auditor general's role is to present an annual accounting of public expenditure, he was understandably concerned that such a large portion of public enterprise was not within his reporting power. More generally, some Canadians—especially those who fear the growth in government—object to governmental involvement in previously private businesses. The public generally is critical when some of these ventures, such as Canadair in 1983, suffer huge financial losses. At issue here are both the ideological question of the appropriate role of government and the administrative question of how government enterprise can be both efficient and accountable. In 1984 the election of a Progressive Conservative government signalled an era of *privatization*—a process by which Crown corporations are sold to private investors. The process continued after the Liberal government took office in 1993.

We have outlined in the last few pages the complex organization of the huge federal bureaucracy. Our comments have only opened discussion in the field of public administration, which is a distinct subfield of political science. However, the purpose we hope to accomplish in this introductory text would not be served by probing in depth the multiplicity of organizational theories that might shed light on the subject.[6] Instead, we intend to turn now to a brief investigation of the working conditions of members of the public service.

FEDERAL EMPLOYMENT

Working for the federal government is not like working for Eaton's, London Life, Imperial Oil, or General Motors. First of all, for a job with any challenge to it in the public service, you have to do more than submit a résumé to a potential employer, followed by a short interview with the personnel department. Instead, you are required to write an examination for which thousands of others are eligible, because public service jobs must be made equally accessible to all Canadians. To prevent personal connections influencing the examiners, the candidate's identity is reduced to that of a number at the top of an examination paper. If you pass the examination and rank high enough, you may then, after waiting several months, be invited for an interview in which your numerical profile is filled in with flesh and blood. If your performance in this interview is satisfactory, within a few weeks you may be offered a position. The need to be scrupulous and fair makes recruiting for the public service, at least in areas that require some degree of training and skill, a much more cumbersome procedure than hiring someone in private industry. Even for less skilled jobs, it may take four weeks or longer to qualify.

Once a person has qualified for a position and is working in the public service, promotion is hedged by many rules that aim to create equal opportunities for similarly qualified people. In private industry, if a person attains the rank of an assistant superintendent and the superintendent retires or leaves, the assistant is normally in line for the promotion. In the public service, however, though usually having an advantage, the assistant has to go through a competition open to a large number of aspirants, some of whom may be in other departments or in other cities. While this introduces lateral movement in the public service, it makes upward mobility somewhat less certain and far more cumbersome than it is in private industry. This is even truer in the higher ranks of the public service, in which 21 departments, many of which are comparable to large corporations, must advertise the availability of senior positions throughout the service. The very top position in each department, that of the deputy minister, is appointed by the prime minister. The public service is often an instrument to achieve public goals through its employment policies. Thus, greater stress was placed on bilingualism from the 1960s on; later pay equity and employment equity standards for women and other disadvantaged groups in the workforce were pursued. The pressure is great on government to reform standards for its own workforce as a model for the private sector.

In the performance of their jobs, public servants in the lower ranks of the various departments have very little opportunity to exercise initiative and imagination. While this may not be very different from comparable situations in private industry, this limitation in the public service has been created and maintained by explicit laws and regulations to prevent arbitrary decision making by those who deal with the public. At the higher levels, there are greater opportunities for imaginative expression. Decisions must be made about cases that do not fit neatly into the law. Moreover, these public servants sometimes originate suggestions for changes that will facilitate better administration of the law, and political leaders often turn to these public servants for an evaluation of the probable effects of new policies. We will return to this shortly when we analyze the policy-making role of the public service.

The differentiation between the creative and noncreative jobs in any department is often based on whether a person is in a so-called *line* position or has a *staff* assignment. A line position is one in which a person is directly responsible for carrying out the purposes of the department; for example, actually delivering the mail is a line function. A staff function is one aimed at facilitating the line operation. People who study how to implement automation within the post office are performing a staff function. Those working in staff as opposed to line organizations are much more likely to assume a policy advisory role. People near the top of the line organization, by virtue of the importance of their office, are likely to perform staff duties as well.

Finally, in assessing the occupational circumstances of public servants, we must look at two areas in which their rights as Canadian citizens vary considerably from people in private industry. The first has to do with the right to organize for collective bargaining as employees. Until 1967, at the federal level, this right was denied to public servants, although organizations lacking the legal status of labour unions but still representing their interests had a long history. It was assumed by the government that these organizations were strictly advisory and had no authority to bargain for wages and fringe benefits. The Civil Service Commission was responsible for recommending pay scales and classification, and the Treasury Board had the authority to grant what the Commission recommended. This obviously denied to public servants a basic right possessed by other Canadians. The 1967 legislation changed this, and public service unions were recognized as bargaining agents for those they represented. Depending on the nature of the employment of their members, public service unions were given the option of compulsory arbitration of disputes or the right to strike. This abandoned the theory that the state was sovereign and thus that its servants could not strike against it. The use of the strike weapon by public servants has been controversial because its effect on the Canadian community is generally more widespread than strikes in the private sector. Many Canadians have not yet accepted the view that public servants should have the right to strike. Governments, for their part, have legislated strikers back to work and, in other instances, suspended normal collective bargaining. Such has been the case in Ontario, British Columbia, and Quebec, as well as with the federal government. Public service unions have become some of the largest and most militant in Canada, and the question of collective bargaining and the right to strike of public servants emerged as a major political issue in the 1970s and 1980s. This question becomes especially difficult when governments apply wage restraints to their employees as part of government economic policy, and is evident in attempts to reduce budget deficits in the 1990s. When large-scale reductions in the workforce are undertaken, the most important goal of unions, job security, is at issue, and no one should be surprised by the growing militancy of public sector unions.

Another activity that was traditionally restricted for public servants, especially at the senior level, was the right to participate actively in partisan politics. The public service, based on the merit system, demands neutrality from those who carry out the policies of their political masters. While Cabinets come and go and the political parties in power alternate, the public servants' responsibility is to ensure that government services continue, and they must serve with equal loyalty whomever the Canadian people decide should form the government. This is easier said than done, especially at the higher levels where policy advice is given. It is even more difficult when one government remains in office for an extended period of time and public servants develop a personal relationship with politicians from one party. While it is impossible to prevent senior public servants from developing a preference for one party over another, it is possible to limit their right to take part publicly in partisan politics. Thus, they are denied the right to run for office while remaining public servants—even the right to campaign publicly for a candidate. The prohibition is less stringent on lower-level employees; these individuals, it is thought, are less likely to offer themselves as candidates, which is allowed, than to campaign actively, which is forbidden. Senior civil servants, however, have both the background and knowledge to be prime candidates for political office. It could be said that the attempt to neutralize the public service politically has gone beyond reasonable bounds. Can it really be argued that by actively campaigning for a federal political party a person becomes less effective as a translator, clerk, or agricultural inspector? It is only when people have a role in the making of public policy that their involvement in partisan politics may influence their work for a minister from an opposing party. Thus, public servants have had to give up the exercise of certain rights that other Canadians enjoy in order to remain employees of the federal government.[7]

POLICY ROLE

Our discussion of political neutrality indicated that public servants in the top ranks within departments and central organizations are called upon to take part in the policy-making process. Let us now turn to a discussion of the policy role of those senior public servants.

At the top of the hierarchy in each department are the deputy ministers.[8] They are normally individuals who have been public servants for many years, although it is not unusual for people to be recruited to high levels in the public service and to achieve deputy minister status rather quickly. Because of their position at the head of a large organization and their experience in government administration, it is natural that deputy ministers should be called upon by their ministers to offer advice on the development of new policies and to manage the department. Assistant deputy ministers and heads of divisions, who also have high office and experience, are often called upon to take part in the framing of policy. It should be kept in mind that this policy-making role is not undertaken to the exclusion of efficient day-to-day management of the department. Let us use the Department of Human Resources Development, created in 1993, as an example of the policy-making role of bureaucratic officials. The department includes the former Department of Labour and is thus responsible for a number of laws regarding labour relations in Canada. Among its functions is the provision of conciliation and arbitration services in industrial disputes. Therefore, if the minister of labour (there continued to be a separate minister even though the department was consolidated) considered that there should be new policies adopted in this area, he or she would consult the deputy minister, who in turn would seek the advice of the assistant deputy minister for labour relations. Under this latter official, there are grouped branches that deal with conciliation and arbitration, labour-management consultation, employee representation, and fair-employment practices. Certainly, the director and leading officials in the department would be consulted to ascertain how the changes would affect the operation of the department and what adjustments would have to be made to administer the new policy. Once all this information was gathered, it would be transmitted by the deputy minister to the minister. It would then be up to the minister to evaluate the department's recommendations, along with those received from labour unions, management, and any other interested group, and then to recommend a policy to the Cabinet. In some instances this may mean the drafting of legislation either to amend existing laws or to create new ones.

Perhaps the new policy represents a change that would affect other departments as well. Ministers of those departments would want their senior officials to study the new policy and make their recommendations known. This might result in an interdepartmental committee of senior officials from all the departments involved. A policy recommendation from such a group would undoubtedly carry great weight when Cabinet formulates its own proposal. The central agencies, such as the Privy Council Office and the Treasury Board Secretariat, become important at this level in finding a place for the policy recommendation on the Cabinet agenda and in evaluating the financial implications of the proposal.

Since public servants are involved with the day-to-day administration of laws, they naturally develop ideas about how those laws could be improved. Moreover, most departments have research branches that are constantly investigating the particular sector of the community that their department services, so that, rather than merely advising the minister on new ideas, ministry officials often generate new policy proposals of their own for the minister's consideration. Senior public servants especially would like their operations to be as efficient as possible, and sometimes they see the need to extend the scope of their services.

There may be some danger in all this. What may appear as advantageous from an administrative point of view may be a disadvantage from the point of view of service to the public. Large bureaucracies often have a tendency to lose sight of their ultimate purpose in striving for internal efficiency. For example, the use of only the English language in administrative operations has obvious advantages in terms of efficiency but hardly renders adequate service to those in the public who are French speaking. Yet in some cases, that was the situation in Canada until the 1960s.

For a variety of reasons, then, a department supposedly responsible to the minister, and through him or her to Parliament, can invert the relationship. Since departments are reservoirs of information and expertise, they may have the upper hand in their relationship with the ministers who are usually amateurs in the particular area for which the department is responsible. For instance, the minister of fisheries and oceans is rarely an expert in either field. The minister with strong ideas and the ability to carry them out will bend that department to his or her will. On the other hand, a weaker minister who owes the position more to political factors—such as regional representation—than to policy skill will be used by the senior officials of the department as a mouthpiece for their ideas. When this happens one may hardly describe the system as one of responsible government. The tail is wagging the dog. This situation is most likely to develop when one party is so dominant in the House of Commons and has such wide support in the country that it has little fear of defeat in the next election. Such parties are therefore less politically responsive and tend to govern administratively rather than politically. In this situation the permanent administrators—that is, the public servants—are bound to be accorded more latitude in the exercise of power. This was especially evident when there was a need for strong administration in the central government in the period just prior to, during, and after World War II.

During the last few decades, attempts have been made to counterbalance this. There has been a two-pronged approach to checking bureaucratic power. First, since the early 1960s there has been rising interest in and much research on the creation of the office of *ombudsman*, or parliamentary commissioner. This office would be patterned after the Scandinavian example, which has operated in Sweden for over 200 years. Basically, the supreme procurator or, as the office later became, the ombudsman is to investigate whether laws and regulations have been fairly and justly administered in cases where adversely affected individuals or groups have appealed. Furthermore, each year the ombudsman reports to the Swedish Parliament those agencies that have, in the view of that office, misused the authority granted to them. Since 1956 there has been pressure to create such an office in Canada. While the provinces have established ombudsmen,[9] the federal government has not yet done so. The federal government, however, has established a Human Rights Commission, a commissioner of official languages, an Information Commission, and a prison ombudsman to fulfil some of these functions. Second, there has been established a Joint Committee of the House of Commons and the Senate on Regulations and Other Statutory Instruments to review all delegation of authority by the Cabinet and to study the power of boards and commissions responsible for various activities—such as, for example, unemployment insurance and old-age pensions, which affect thousands of Canadians.

In addition, a more enlightened public has resulted in a greater array of organized interest groups. Recipients of social assistance, who were at one time expected to accept the paternalistic guidance of administrators in the various departments dealing with them, are now demanding that their voice be heard in determining the policies that directly affect them. Native peoples no longer passively accept the edicts issued by the Department of Indian Affairs and Northern Development. Even the lone consumer who was overpowered by huge corporations now has a more effective voice through a variety of pressure groups. In addition, decision makers tend to take a wider perspective before forming policy. The prime minister's personal staff has grown, as mentioned earlier, and central organs of government such as the Treasury Board and the Privy Council Office are in a position to limit empire-building aspirations within departments of governments.

The growth of the social-welfare state has led to the development of a huge bureaucracy to serve the public. There are few of these services that any significant group of Canadians would be willing to give up; thus, large numbers of people are needed to administer government programs. However, we live in an age of huge institutions: big business, big unions, and big government. One could argue that, while it may constitute a danger to the public, a large government organization can also counteract other big institutions in society on behalf of the public. Whatever the merit of that argument, we have a big government, and while it may have been trimmed considerably, it is not likely to become small. Its size is bound to create some dead weight within it, and it is likely by its very nature to be an agent of conformity simply because it must deal with the average citizen's needs and desires. Creativity and imagination are not normally associated with large bureaucracies, but these qualities are at times sorely needed. This is not to say that they are completely lacking in the Canadian public service, but they usually take second place to rational, administratively oriented policies that meet the needs of the greatest number of Canadians. It is not our point to argue here that the public service has intervened too deeply in the private lives of Canadians. On the contrary, that intervention has been necessary, because other institutions in society have not created a community in which there has been equal economic and social opportunity. Our purpose is to point out the dangers of building a society based solely on bureaucratic norms without regard to the diversity of norms and values in the wider Canadian community.

RECOMMENDED READING

Atkinson, Michael M., ed. *Governing Canada: Institutions and Public Policy.* Toronto: Harcourt Brace & Company, 1993.

Brooks, Stephen. *Public Policy in Canada: An Introduction*, 2nd ed. Toronto: McClelland and Stewart, 1993.

Canada. *Public Service 2000: The Renewal of the Public Service of Canada.* Ottawa: Minister of Supply and Services, 1990.

Kernaghan, K., ed. *Public Administration in Canada: Selected Readings*, 5th ed. Toronto: Methuen, 1985.

Kernaghan, Kenneth, and David Siegal. *Public Administration in Canada: A Text*, 3rd ed. Scarborough: Nelson Canada, 1995.

Osbaldeston, G.F. *Keeping Deputy Ministers Accountable.* Toronto: McGraw-Hill Ryerson, 1989.

Sutherland, S.L., and G.B. Doern. *Bureaucracy in Canada: Control and Reform.* Toronto: University of Toronto Press, 1985.

CHAPTER 10

The Legislature

THE PARLIAMENT

The early history of parliamentary democracy was largely concerned with the struggle of legislative bodies to curb the scope of executive power. Having achieved this, the next stage of the struggle had to do with widening the representative nature of legislative organs so that they could be truly said to be speaking for the entire body politic. In Canada we inherited the British system, but from the beginning there were important differences. Foremost among these was the fact that Canada, being a rural frontier community with a high proportion of enfranchised property owners, enjoyed a greater degree of mass participation than did Britain. The struggle in Canada was, therefore, directed at making the governor and the executive council responsible to the elected assembly.[1] Thus, from the inception of Canada as a political entity in 1867, we have had a representative legislative branch of government, which has been the major safeguard for democracy.

As a symbol of political authority in Canada, the Parliament buildings dominate the capital. It is here that legislators and the Cabinet ministers responsible to the legislature carry out their daily tasks; it is to this complex that Canadians look for direction in their public affairs. This symbolic and actual fusion of legislative and executive authority stands in contrast to the system in the United States, where the White House and the Capitol buildings are two separate symbols of distinct branches of government in which the former has come to supersede the latter as the symbolic focal point of government authority. Even in England, where there is a system similar to Canada's, the House of Commons must share the stage with Buckingham Palace and Number 10 Downing Street as objects of public respect. How many people in Canada know the significance of 24 Sussex Drive or Rideau Hall? We leave it to the readers to find out what these addresses signify, if they do not already know. Although the Parliament buildings symbolize the authority of the state and house the legislative branch of government, it would be wrong to give that branch primacy in the Canadian governmental process. The fulcrum of that process is in the east block of the Parliament buildings, where Cabinet ministers direct public policy. Despite the theory that Cabinet is responsible to the House of Commons, the strong party discipline previously discussed ensures that in fact the Cabinet can normally effectively control a majority of the Members of Parliament. It is rare indeed that the Commons becomes aroused enough to bring a government to its knees.[2]

Some political scientists characterize the House of Commons as having very little importance in the government of Canada.[3] However, while it is indisputably true that the House of Commons cannot occupy the role envisioned by eighteenth- and nineteenth-century theorists, it is still an institution of major importance. One need only ask the question whether government would be the same if the House of Commons did not exist in its present form to realize that it does indeed have a considerable impact on the behaviour of Canadian decision makers and the expectations of the Canadian public. While governments are in a position to initiate the only legislation that stands a chance of passing in the House of Commons, the opposition parties have considerable impact on the amount of legislation that can be passed and may affect its final form. Thus, for instance, the debate on the changes in the Crow's Nest Pass freight rate, which represented a major policy of the Trudeau government, resulted in stormy debate, and changes were made to the initial proposals of the government. And the Senate, although its supporters in its unreformed guise have been few, was able during both the Mulroney and Chrétien years to stall and even defeat legislation. These examples, and other functions of Parliament, make it difficult to accept the idea that Parliament is of no consequence in the governing of Canada.

What should Canadians expect Parliament to do? The first thing that comes to mind is the passing of laws, but there is much more than that to the role of Parliament. The French derivation of the word is "place to talk." It is, or should be, the grand arena for national debate. Its deliberations focus the attention of Canadians on the issues that their representatives consider to be most pressing. Some are national in scope, others are regional, and a few are even local in nature. Whatever the content of the debate, it is likely to merit some coverage by the news media. The Canadian public is, therefore, fed a steady diet of news based on the exchanges in the House of Commons when it is in session. Indeed, those who wish can watch the debates on the parliamentary television channel. The House of Commons dramatizes the choices that are available to parliamentarians—an important factor in reducing abstract principles and technical complexities to a level that average citizens can understand. The adversarial nature of the House allows members to hurl invectives at each other and to engage in heated debates without necessarily making the exchange a personal encounter, although this may occasionally happen. The system works because the divisions within our society are not so great that every political issue becomes a life-and-death struggle between opposing sides. The adversarial nature of Canadian politics is therefore to some degree a contrivance, albeit not a conscious one, to pump some life into issues that would not always hold the interest of a large number of Canadians. Of course, this does not hold in extremely crucial issues in which basic values and interests are genuinely divided. A concrete manifestation of its adversarial role is seen in the seating arrangement in the House of Commons that puts the government on the speaker's right hand and the opposition on his left, facing each other across a broad centre aisle.

The Canadian legislature is composed of two houses, the House of Commons and the Senate, and thus belongs to that type of legislature known as a *bicameral system*. Although the Senate is constitutionally vested with authority almost equal to the House of Commons, and although it possesses the outward symbols of power in its ornate red chambers in the centre block of the Parliament buildings, it is in reality much less important than the House of Commons in the legislative process. We will return to its role later in this chapter.

THE HOUSE OF COMMONS

The House of Commons is a popularly elected representative body composed of 301 members (as of 1997) distributed throughout the provinces according to the constitutional provisions described in Chapter 6. This is where the real legislative authority lies; indeed, when Canadians refer to Parliament they are almost always referring to the House of Commons. It is here that all important legislation is introduced by the Cabinet, great debates on contemporary issues take place, ministers are supposed to defend their policies before the probing questions of the opposition, and the media, ever present in the *press gallery*, keep Canadians informed of the daily proceedings. The introduction of television into the proceedings of the House has given a further opportunity to the public to be informed of its deliberations.[4]

What motivates someone to seek office as a member of the House of Commons (MP)? As we explained earlier, some people are politically socialized in a particular way and early in their lives acquire a fascination with politics, which leads to an ambition to pursue a political career. Others come into politics at a later age, because successful careers and some community-service involvement enhance their reputation locally and bring them to the attention of local-constituency party organizations as good potential candidates. What motivates a person to seek public office is a complex psychological question that has generated only limited research in Canada. However, although we know little of motivation, we do have a good deal of information about what kind of people successfully attain office.[5] The student of politics can readily learn something of the education, occupation, and other biographical details of those men and women who have represented the Canadian people.

In terms of experience, studies show that most Members of Parliament have held no previous elected office but were more likely to have held a position in their party's organization. One soon becomes aware that the House of Commons does not mirror the Canadian public. If it did, there would be at least 151 female members, half the members would be under 35, only about 13% would have university degrees, and the largest single group in the House of Commons would be unskilled working people and homemakers. This, of course, is not the case. In fact, there are very few female MPs, although the increasing number of female candidates is likely to lead to a larger number in the future; most are over 35 years old; a large majority of them are university educated; and only a few of them could be classed as unskilled workers or homemakers. A typical MP is likely to be a man of above-average income (he cannot avoid expenditure of some of his own money, first to win a nomination and then to get elected) who has a professional—often legal—or business background. Law seems to be a profession particularly suited to a Member of Parliament. It is an occupation that allows a partner in a firm to withdraw temporarily and serve in Parliament without losing his or her standing in the profession. On the contrary, standing and usefulness to the firm may improve when the partner returns. Canadians in other walks of life find it more difficult to drop everything to enter the House of Commons and then pick up the strands after political defeat. Thus, Members of Parliament are hardly typical Canadians. Representation in Canada, therefore, means a *geographic representation* rather than representation on the basis of income, occupation, education, sex, age, or other variables. Since ethnicity and religion have some geographic basis in Canada, the House of Commons reflects these characteristics reasonably well. The party constituency organizations try to nominate and elect a representative who may, by his or her experience, relate to all the variables in the constituency. Given the values of Canadian society, it is not surprising that the electorate opts for those who have been successful in achieving a status to which most Canadians aspire. For the most part, Members of Parliament live and have been raised in or near the constituency they represent, and it is only rarely that a party *parachutes* (brings in from outside) a well-known national figure into the riding, as was the case with Jean Chrétien in Beauséjour, New Brunswick, in 1990.[6] In the large metropolitan centres of the country, it may be somewhat less important for a candidate to have ties to the particular constituency, as long as there is some relationship to the area as a whole.

Once elected, a member of the House of Commons very quickly becomes aware of the conflicting demands of the office. On the one hand, the MP is charged with the responsibility of adequately representing perhaps 100 000 people; on the other hand, he or she must maintain professional or business and personal interests. Failure to separate these concerns from public duties can result in *conflicts of interest* that undermine respect for elected representatives. Life as an MP can hardly help but upset family life, because it at least entails separation while the member is in Ottawa. A newly elected MP soon comes to realize that he or she is a small fish in a big pond, and although the member's influence may be high in the riding, it is low as a fledgling member of the House. The MP also becomes aware very soon of the ambiguities in public issues. The party may support legislation that is not in the best interest of the riding, in which case—in order to maintain unity and to get ahead in the party—the member will have to try to accept the party position even in the face of local opposition. Only on rare occasions will members vote against their parties. This is the case even for opposition parties, as well as the government party, on whose support the Cabinet depends. Once the pomp and ceremony of the opening of Parliament is over, the fledgling member will depend on the party leaders in the House for most of the activities he or she pursues as a member.

There is a wide range of activities for every Member of Parliament. When the House of Commons is in session, visitors often remark on the relatively small number of members who take part in debates or are even present in their seats. This is not necessarily a sign that members are neglecting their duties, for they are probably doing work of much greater value for their constituents. Every day, whether or not the House is in session, the members receive requests for advice or assistance from individuals or from groups of constituents. They may be asked, for instance, to intercede with postal authorities to retain a rural post office or with Via Rail to maintain certain schedules. They are often the last resort for a frustrated citizen who has been thwarted in attempts to gain satisfaction either from a government or private institutions. Because members occupy this intermediary role, they must make themselves available to their constituents. This means that on weekends during sessions and in the various recesses of the House they try to be in their ridings as much as possible, so that they may meet their constituents and learn of their problems firsthand. Attendance at a variety of local events is important, and it is a necessary duty that gives an incumbent the opportunity to continually campaign for reelection. Constituency service has become the main con-

FIGURE 10.1
SEATING PLAN OF THE HOUSE OF COMMONS

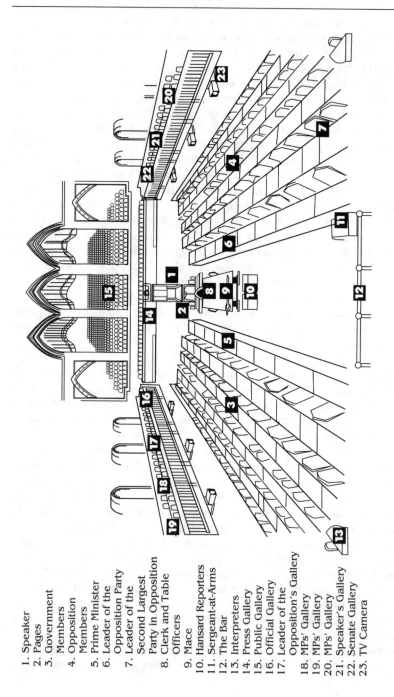

1. Speaker
2. Pages
3. Government Members
4. Opposition Members
5. Prime Minister
6. Leader of the Opposition Party
7. Leader of the Second Largest Party in Opposition
8. Clerk and Table Officers
9. Mace
10. Hansard Reporters
11. Sergeant-at-Arms
12. The Bar
13. Interpreters
14. Press Gallery
15. Public Gallery
16. Official Gallery
17. Leader of the Opposition's Gallery
18. MPs' Gallery
19. MPs' Gallery
20. MPs' Gallery
21. Speaker's Gallery
22. Senate Gallery
23. TV Camera

Source: Reproduced with the permission of the Library of Parliament Public Information Office.

cern of a majority of MPs. To facilitate this responsibility, a member can travel free on airlines and railways and has free mailing and telephone privileges. Sitting members rarely invoke political favouritism in serving the individual needs of their constituents who seek assistance. Nevertheless, when members of the governing party are able to recommend legal service for the government, appointments to minor boards and commissions in their area, and other minor rewards, they will invariably name party supporters. Good members have an elected constituency organization of party supporters in place to keep them posted on all local matters that may affect their political strength in the riding. In the 1970s funds became available for Members of Parliament to support an office in their constituencies as well as in Ottawa; this reform has enhanced the ability of MPs to perform constituency services. The quality of response forthcoming from an MP's staff both in the constituency office and in Ottawa can determine his or her reputation for good representation.

Out of the many problems that confront their constituencies, members may develop ideas for legislation. They may also have a cause they personally consider to be a major issue. For members who are not Cabinet ministers, however, the opportunity to see their ideas translated into law is rare indeed. They may get their party to support an initiative, and if their party is in power the proposal may appear in the government's legislative program at a later date. If not, a proposal may be introduced as a *private member's bill*. These have very little chance of getting through the House of Commons because, of the large number that may be submitted, only 20 are drawn in a lottery at the beginning of a session of Parliament; six will be chosen by the Committee on Procedures and House Affairs to be given enough parliamentary time to reach a vote. Other private members' bills will be discussed for just one hour and then die. The purpose, therefore, of a private member's bill is to bring to the attention of the House of Commons and the public a particular concern of the member. The member can hardly hope to have the proposal enacted, but it might influence the government to consider a change in public policy. For instance, the proposal to abolish capital punishment was first put forward in a private member's bill.

It is clear that the legislative role of individual *backbenchers* (so called because they sit behind the Cabinet ministers on the government side and behind the leaders and chief critics on the opposition side) in the House of Commons depends upon their party affiliation. In the extreme this may mean that their role is merely to vote as the party instructs them. However, in recent years there has been a groundswell from restive members of the House who think they should play a more important part in the legislative process. Periods of minority government in the 1960s and 1970s encouraged this development, because the vote of every backbencher was crucial to the government. One result of this was that the *party caucus*, which is the organization of all members of a party (including its leadership) within the House of Commons, became a more dynamic institution. This development was most important for the government party, since it is the party responsible for introducing a legislative program into the House. Under these conditions the leaders were impelled to defend their policies before the caucus to ensure that once the government introduced a legislative program into the House it would receive the full support of the party. It is probable that the more influential role of the caucus has continued even with majority government. Because backbenchers in all parties have an opportunity within their respective caucuses to criticize, maverick members who choose to criticize their party's position in the House itself have been rare and unpopular. The concept of *strict party discipline* demands that, once a party has adopted a publicly stated position, all its members must toe the line. To fail to do so on too many occasions may result in expulsion from the caucus and perhaps from the party.[7] The election of 52 Reform Party MPs in 1993 posed some interesting questions. They were committed to putting their constituencies ahead of their party and were committed to the concept of *free votes*, where party discipline does not apply. Whether this affects their ability to be a cohesive opposition party, let alone a government, is still an unanswered question, because between 1993 and 1997 the members of the Reform Party all voted the same way, with only rare exceptions.

Some changes in the procedures in the House were meant to enhance the role of backbenchers. Most important were changes in the committee system that sought to strengthen the role of committees in the legislative process. Formerly, detailed discussion was mainly carried on in some form of the *Committee of the Whole*, which is a committee consisting of all 301 members. The disadvantage of this kind of forum for debate was that important details of legislation could not be fruitfully discussed because the real advantage of a committee—that is, of a smaller, more expert body—was foregone. Various types of smaller committees did exist, but they tended to be used sparingly. Because the Committee of the Whole consists of all members of the House, it is not surprising that the leaders on all sides dominated the debate. Changes that began experimentally in 1965 and attained more permanent status in 1968 and 1969 afforded the opportunity for backbenchers to have a greater say in the determination of details of bills as they progress through the House. In addition, committees now study issues (foreign ownership, taxation, the Constitution, and auto safety) before legislation is introduced in the House and thus have an opportunity to influence the government's decision about the final form of the legislative proposal. The Joint Committee on Regulations and Other Statutory Instruments gives the House a potential vehicle to check on the executive use of legislative authority.

The most important of the changes referred to above was the establishment of *standing committees*. They were rather large, and reforms in 1983 reduced their size. As of 1997 there are 19 standing committees whose size varies from a minimum of seven to a maximum of 15. The committees have responsibilities in specialized areas such as agriculture, health, welfare, and social affairs, foreign affairs and international trade, fisheries and forestry, justice and legal affairs, finance, and economic affairs. From their titles one can see that the intention was to delegate much of the work that was formerly undertaken by the Committee of the Whole. Among their duties is the review of the estimates of the departments that fall within their area of concern. These reforms have allowed MPs to serve on the committees that were of the greatest interest to them — from constituency and personal points of view. Theoretically, they would have more opportunity to become expert legislators in a particular area, rather than being rubber stamps for most of the legislation presented in the House, and to study legislation in a more open and somewhat less partisan atmosphere.

The McGrath Committee on procedural reform reported in June 1985. Among its recommendations was a further enhancement of the power of the standing committees, to study issues and make recommendations, and the introduction of *legislative committees*, to which bills would be referred instead of to standing committees. The chairperson of these legislative committees would be appointed by the speaker from a panel of MPs designated for this role. By the mid-1990s legislative committees ceased to be the norm for clause-by-clause investigation of bills; standing committees were assuming this role once more. In addition, after 1994 committees were sometimes able to get legislation after first reading and thus have more influence over it. Moreover, there are a number of *joint committees* of the House of Commons and the Senate, and there is provision for special committees to be set up on either a joint basis or from the House alone. There also may be subcommittees of the standing committees, usually with five members.

From the procedures outlined above, one notes that the initiative for legislation rests with the government, and the role of backbenchers is to support the stand their party takes on issues in the House of Commons. In committee, however, members are able to question the details of legislation during its intensive investigation. It may happen that a bill they support in general may contain specific sections that are detrimental to the riding they represent. They may therefore wish to take issue with their own party and are more likely to give vent to disagreement in a small committee than in the House itself, with the press gallery looking on. Members may even join forces with opposition members from the same region because they have a community of interest. Committees can be more efficient than the House itself, which has to fulfil the more dramatic role of publicizing issues and so tends to adopt a more flamboyant approach. Both government and opposition parties are able to allow their members greater freedom of action in committees than they can in the more public forum of the House. Having said this, one must be reminded that an MP's role is largely dependent on party membership, and clashing with party leaders even in committee is not an easy route to follow, especially for members of the governing party.

Committee members are appointed by the Committee on Procedure and House Affairs (formerly known as the *Striking Committee*), which is chaired by the whip (or more recently, the parliamentary secretary to the government House leader) of the majority party and usually has as its members the whips or House leaders of the opposition parties. Whips are members of Parliament chosen by each party's leadership to ensure cohesive organization in the House, to help facilitate members' roles, and to make sure that members are present and voting with their party when required. The membership of committees is proportionate to the strength of the various parties in the House. The government party, therefore, if it has a majority in the House of Commons, will have a majority on all committees, and all committees will be chaired by government supporters, except for the *Committee on Public Accounts*.

Some committee appointments are looked upon as more prestigious than others because they deal with important national issues. Thus, committees such as Finance, Foreign Affairs, and International Trade, or Human Resources Development will attract the attention of more MPs, but appointments to these committees will more often than not be given to the more senior members or those with special qualifications. Each party's representatives on the Striking Committee will determine their party's choice for appointments to the various committees. Until 1983 parties could also remove or substitute members of the various committees; thus, the governing party retained an instrument for replacing any of its own members who might be troublesome. Frequent changes were also detrimental to the building up of long-term service, which might lead to the expertise that is often cited as an advantage of the committee system. Consequently, the 1983 changes strictly limited the substitution of committee members to a list of alternates equal to each party's committee representation. Changes in membership would require 24-hour notice. The McGrath recommendations were even more restrictive on changes in Committee membership. It was hoped that these changes would encourage continuity and the meaningful participation of MPs.

When reforms were first introduced in the 1960s, there was some concern that the traditional role of the House of Commons was being diminished. The opposition parties were especially concerned about this, as the dramatic function of full-scale debates in the Commons was the chief weapon they had against the government. Any limitation of this role could give the government even greater control of public policy than it previously had. As we will see later, a number of procedural changes were introduced that gave the opposition ample opportunity to publicize their objections to government policy. To assess whether the power of the House is being usurped, one has to have a proper perspective on the legitimate role of the House. Government and opposition have and will have different conceptions: the government will stress that the House is a place where Canadians expect to see legislation passed in an efficient manner; the opposition will emphasize the function of calling the government to account, publicizing its failures, making the executive responsible to the legislature, and debating the public issues of the day. These sometimes contradictory views are both nevertheless indispensable and must be reconciled. The greater use of committees for detailed examination of legislation is a step in this direction.

The reforms of 1983 regularized the parliamentary calendar into three semesters. The fall semester began one week after Labour Day, broke for a week at Remembrance Day, and recessed the Friday before Christmas. It resumed for the winter semester four weeks after the Christmas recess and continued until the Easter break. The spring semester began 12 days after the Easter break and continued to June 30. This schedule produced approximately 175 days during which Parliament would sit. In 1991 the Mulroney government used its majority to make further changes, and any future government could do the same to alter the rules. The 1991 changes reduced the number of sitting days to 134 by introducing more midterm breaks and lengthening the recesses. The argument for this hinged on the need for MPs to spend more time in their constituencies. The opposition parties did not see it that way and accused the government of trying to keep its critics out of Ottawa for longer periods. One hour was added to each sitting day to make up some of the lost time. During the summer recess, the government plans its legislative program for the new session and, as we mentioned above, outlines its intentions in the Throne Speech. The debate that follows was reduced to six days in 1991 from the eight days of former times. The opposition will challenge both the priorities and the governmental methods adopted to deal with problems. Because major issues are dealt with in expansive terms, this provides a lively start to the legislative session. During the debate the major opposition party will invariably move a motion of lack of confidence, to which the other opposition parties will attach amendments reflecting their points of view. These motions charge that the government's plans are inadequate to meet the problems of the country. Should the government lose a lack of confidence vote, it has to resign; any majority government will easily win the vote, and any minority government will have sought the support of one of the minor parties to ensure that it can govern.

In the days, weeks, and months that follow the debate on the Speech from the Throne, various government bills—which reflect the priorities that the government has set in the speech itself—are introduced. Some problems will be pressing and high on the list of government priorities, while others may be considered less vital and quite possibly may not even be dealt with during the session. By February the *estimates* of expenditures of all departments and agencies are tabled in the House and immediately referred to the various standing committees for specialized study. These committees then scrutinize all estimates for three months or more, after which their reports are made to the House. Normally in April, although economic and political considerations can frequently alter the date, the minister of finance submits the *budget* that describes the sources of government revenue and deals with any changes in taxation policy. The budget debate was reduced to four (from six) days and gives an opportunity for a wide range of comments on government policy. The remainder of the session is spent passing tax legislation based on the budget, enacting appropriation bills based on the estimates reported by the standing committees, and completing government legislation. During the session, 20 days are allotted as "opposition days"—days when the opposition can determine the subject matter for debate. Five of those days come in the fall, seven before the end of the fiscal year (March 31), and eight before the end of June. At the conclusion of each group of allotted days, the House appropriates money for the government to meet its expenses; this is called interim supply. In their present form, opposition days serve two purposes. First, they provide an outlet for the opposition to discuss issues of their own choosing rather than merely reacting to the government's initiatives. Second, they provide the format through which the government ultimately gets authorization for its spending plans. Before 1991 there were 25 opposition days. Thus, the opposition has lost five opposition days, two days off the Throne Speech debate and two off the budget debate. This gives the government nine more days to pass laws, albeit in a shorter legislative calendar.

In order for this yearly routine to be carried out efficiently, the House has adopted a complex set of procedures and appointed certain officers to ensure their effectiveness. Chief among these officers is the *speaker of the House*. The speaker, a member of the House of Commons, ensures that the rules and procedures of the Commons are applied fairly and that the rights and privileges of the individual members and of the House as a whole are upheld. The speaker is now chosen in the House of Commons by a vote that can be a real contest, rather than by confirmation of the prime minister's nominee, as in the past. The traditional method occasionally put the speaker in a difficult position, as the appointment came from the government party and on occasion the speaker acted in a partisan manner.[8] In the late 1960s, a trend seemed to be developing toward appointing a permanent speaker, acceptable to all parties. This was instigated by the incumbent speaker running unopposed by the other political parties.[9] In 1985 John Fraser won the first contested speakership under the new rules, and he was reelected in 1988.

In addition to duties during sittings of the House of Commons, the speaker oversees the Parliament Hill bureaucracy that provides the necessary support for members. This bureaucracy includes the *clerk of the*

House (who is in effect the deputy minister in charge of the House of Commons "department"), and a staff of law clerks who advise both members and the speaker on the application of the rules of the House and help draft legislation for both the government and private members. They also present to the House of Commons those petitions that they receive from the public, usually through a member. Also included in the House of Commons staff are translators who provide instantaneous translation in the two official languages and transcribers who provide a daily verbatim report of the House of Commons debates, often referred to as *Hansard*. There is also the library of Parliament, which has, in addition to a normal library staff, a small research staff available to members. Finally, there are the security, secretarial, and maintenance staffs. The auditor general reports directly to Parliament, as do the chief electoral officer, the commissioner for official languages, and the public service commission.

The procedures in the House are set down in the *standing orders*, which regulate the manner in which the day-to-day activities are carried out. There are specific times established when the House meets and, as we noted earlier, set periods during the year that are allocated to the Speech from the Throne, the budget, and opposition days. Perhaps the best way to illustrate the daily activity of the House is to outline what happened on a typical day, Monday, February 3, 1997,[10] the first sitting in the new year. The House met at 11:00 A.M. After the opening prayer, the speaker informed the House that a vacancy had occurred in the representation through the resignation of Stephen Harper (Calgary West, Reform) and that a writ would be issued for an election of a member to fill the vacancy. The session began with *private members' business*. The House resumed consideration, from November 25, 1996, of the motion that Bill C-300, an act respecting the establishment and award of a Canadian volunteer service medal and clasp to Canadians serving with a UN peacekeeping force, be read the second time and referred to a committee. The first speaker, Deborah Grey (Beaver River, Reform), paid tribute to Canadian peacekeepers and gave reasons for the award, such as the fear of the task and the uncertainty and loneliness of that kind of duty. She noted that, at a time when the military has been undergoing such difficulty, it would be appropriate to declare that the country appreciates what has been done on its behalf. John Richardson (parliamentary secretary to minister of national defence and minister of veterans affairs, Liberal) endorsed the bill and suggested minor amendments. For instance, there should be a basic medal and a clasp designating the theatre of operations. Art Hanger (Calgary Northeast, Reform) praised the initiative of his colleague Jack Fraser (Saanich–Gulf Islands, Reform) in this matter and said that the award should be inclusive, recognizing members of the RCMP and other Canadian citizens who have served in places such as Bosnia and Haiti. He mentioned a precedent for the award, a medal for service in the Korean War. George Proud (parliamentary secretary to minister of labour, Liberal) referred to several negative incidents concerning the military, but he did not think that the entire Canadian Armed Forces should be marred by it. At the same time, he did not want the Canadian forces to become more like the American forces, "flexing our muscles." He also wanted the award to be comprehensive, including those serving under NATO in Implementation Force Bosnia. Bill Blaikie (Winnipeg–Transcona, NDP) didn't want the bill buried in committee. The acting speaker (Peter Milliken) then noted that if Jack Fraser spoke next he would close the debate, under the rule that the proposer has the last word. After Fraser's remarks the question was called, the motion carried, and the bill read for the second time and referred to a committee. The sitting was suspended until noon.

When the House resumed, *government orders* were taken up. Consideration of Bill C-60 was resumed at report stage, an act to establish the Canadian Food Inspection Agency. Jean-Guy Chrétien (Frontenac, BQ) called this a parapublic agency, consolidating the services of three departments, "being readied" by the Liberals "as a patronage haven" (one of several accusations of patronage uttered on this occasion). More substantively, he wanted the agency to report to the Standing Committee on Agriculture and Agri-Food rather than directly to the minister. He asserted that the minister of agriculture was often out of touch with the problems of farming communities across Canada. Jack Williams (St. Albert, Reform) supported the proposals of the Bloc Québécois and said that the government was not really cutting back on government jobs. Much of what Williams said sounded like the rehearsing of themes for an electoral campaign, it being generally assumed that an election was in the offing. Paul Crête (Kamouraska-Rivière-Loup, BQ) observed that "the agency will play an important role in the competitive aspect of the agri-food industry in Canada" but that the bill required considerable improvement.

The response to the remarks of the official opposition was given by Jerry Pickard (parliamentary secretary to minister of agriculture and agri-food, Liberal). Pickard emphasized that the standing committee would be approving government operations for which it was not responsible, and hence he stated the necessary role of the minister whom he defended against criticisms. Pickard, consequently, could not support the motion originating with the official opposition. Antoine Dubé (Lévis, BQ) was concerned about a lack of transparency (or openness) in the proposed operation of the agency, a theme echoed by Jean Landry (Lotbinière, BQ). At this stage in the debate, the focus was on reporting or subordination, either to the minister or to the standing committee. Landry brought up the issue of provincial weight, arguing that 25% of the positions on the advisory committee should belong to Quebec. He expressed a standard separatist sentiment as well: "For as long as we are part of Canada, I will defend the interests of my fellow citizens of Quebec." Debate then proceeded to another section of the bill.

Jean-Guy Chrétien, the Bloc' s agriculture critic, addressed the fixing of fees—that is, the costs of inspecting facilities and procedures. This offered an opportunity for him to allude to "the finance minister's obsession with eliminating the deficit." Several other members of the Bloc Québécois wanted the costs deferred until the year 2000, wanted more consultation with the provinces, and reaffirmed their opposition to the bill as it stood. Pickard again responded to objections, stating that the minister must retain the responsibility of setting fees. However, he did promise consultation. The acting speaker asked if the House was ready for the question on this section of the bill. The recorded divisions (votes) were deemed, demanded, and deferred. The bill was being debated section by section, and at the end of the process a vote would be taken on the whole bill. Jay Hill (Prince George-Peace River, Reform) announced that Reform members opposed the bill. While the goal was admirable, they did not approve of umbrella-type legislation in which details and regulations would only come later. Following this intervention the speaker said that since it was about 2:00 P.M. the House would proceed to *statements by members.*

Among the statements were messages of condolence to the family of Father Guy Pinard, who was assassinated in Rwanda, as well as a tribute to the late MP André Caron and the musician Hagood Hardy. Bill Blaikie (Winnipeg-Transcona, NDP) commented on the World Trade Organization ruling that culture is not exempt from free trade, thus showing that the assurances given by the Progressive Conservatives and the Liberals in this regard were empty. The speaker had to admonish one member for his language (members are sometimes brought up for unparliamentary behaviour). Preston Manning (Calgary Southwest, Reform), critical of government failure, launched a kind of preview of an electoral attack, maintaining that the government has "broken its GST promises, mocked the unemployed, botched the AirBus investigation, gagged the Somalia Inquiry, and stonewalled the tainted-blood investigation." The government should be held accountable for these failures. Manning went on to enumerate items in Reform's populist agenda: free votes in the House, unfettered committees, citizens' initiatives, referenda, and the power to recall elected officials. The last intervention in this part of parliamentary business praised the latest Team Canada trade mission.

The time had now arrived for *oral question period.* In some instances the prime minister responded to questions, though in most the ministers concerned did so. In defending the government's decision to cut short the Somalia Inquiry on March 31, Jean Chrétien answered that the minister of defence had clearly explained why he did not consider it appropriate to give the commission any more time, in order that what must be done at the Department of National Defence may be done as soon as possible. Doug Young (minister of national defence) then responded to a question by Michel Gauthier (leader of the opposition, BQ) that the mandate of the inquiry had already been extended, which meant that it would have been in operation for more than two years. In reply to other remarks, Young said that, when the commission was first set up, its deadline was the end of December 1995. There was an exchange between Preston Manning and the prime minister, the former asking, "Given this record of abuse, why should Canadians trust either him or his government any longer?" The prime minister replied that "This government has offered the people a good government, a competent government, and in all circumstances we have done our best." Manning then asked about all those jobs that were promised by the Liberals. In answer to a further remark about the Somalia Inquiry, the prime minister said that the main objective was to restore confidence in the Armed Forces. Allan Rock (minister of justice, Liberal), responding to a question from a member of the Bloc Québécois, said that there was no political interference in the AirBus affair. David Dingwall (minister of health, Liberal) replied to a question by Pauline Picard (Drummond, BQ) about the tainted-blood inquiry (the Krever Commission). There were also questions about the cancellation of the contract at Pearson International Airport by the Liberals, war crimes, and taxation. In response to an attack on the government's policies by a member of the Bloc Québécois concerning the poor, social programs, health and welfare, the deficit, and promised reforms, Paul Martin (minister of finance, Liberal) announced that the budget would be tabled on Tuesday, February 18.

The House next took up several *points of order*. Then time was allowed for tributes to the late André Caron (Jonquière, BQ). The leader of the official opposition, Michel Gauthier, characterized Caron as "a staunch sovereigntist." This was followed by tributes by Marcel Massé on behalf of the government and by members of the Reform Party and the NDP on behalf of their contingents.

Routine Proceedings were next. Perhaps the most interesting was from the Committee of the House, a report on Bill C-70, which harmonized the GST with the provincial sales taxes in three Atlantic provinces and contained about 100 amendments.

At this point the House resumed consideration of Bill C-60, an act to establish the Canadian Food Inspection Agency. Continuing the earlier debates on sections of the bill, the House examined the transfer of authority and funding from the agencies then carrying out the functions to the new agency. The government stated that there was no new money being disbursed. However, the speaker announced that the final vote would be deferred until the next day, the bells having rung.

The House then proceeded to the consideration of Bill C-57, an act to amend the Bell Canada Act. A motion was made by the government that the bill be read the third time and passed. The intent of the bill was to stimulate an innovation in advanced technology and to promote new services on the information highway. It was seen as another step closer to the realization of a truly Canadian information highway. Bell would be permitted to hold a broadcasting licence, enabling it to compete with cable television companies. There were two very long interventions, one from a member of the Bloc Québécois, the other from a member of the Reform Party. Pierre de Savoye (Portneuf, BQ) was concerned about Quebec interests, notably that of Quebec Telephone. The report, he went on, denies the existence of Quebec culture by making it an element of the multicultural diversity of Canada. In spite of its shortcomings, the bill was supported by the Bloc. Werner Schmidt (Okanagan Centre, Reform) declared that the Reform Party was in favour of the bill. He then entered into a technical examination of the legislation with reference to data bytes, digital economy, fibre optic cables, and gigabytes. He then looked at the international ramifications of the policy. The acting speaker subsequently asked if the House was ready for the question. The question was called, the motion agreed to, and the bill read the third time and passed.

The House resumed consideration, from November 5, 1996, of the motion that Bill C-49—an act to authorize remedial and disciplinary measures in relation to members of certain administrative tribunals—be passed. Sarkis Assadourian (Don Valley North, Liberal) explained that, as part of the agency review, the legislation would eliminate several hundred positions. The reduction of duplication, he thought, should find favour with both the Bloc Québécois and the Reform Party. Paul Crête (Kamouraska–Rivière-du-Loup, BQ) proposed an amendment to delay second reading. Art Hanger (Calgary Northeast, Reform) raised the patronage issue and proposed scrapping the Immigration and Refugee Board and the National Parole Board. Jean-Guy Chrétien (Frontenac, BQ) condemned the intentions of the Liberal Party, accusing it of interfering with the notion of judicial independence, and then digressed to criticize a number of government actions, such as the appointment of the lieutenant governor of Quebec, not germane to the issue at hand. Others raised questions about appointments to administrative tribunals and the problem of openness, and one member—Ted White (North Vancouver, Reform)—said that, if the government was really concerned with eliminating patronage positions, why not begin with the appointed (nonelected) Senate. The acting speaker admonished the member not to speak disrespectfully. White was positive about the role of Senator Anne Cools in opposition to the child-support legislation, apparently to indicate that he had something positive to say about the Senate. He ended by exhorting members to vote against the legislation.

The acting speaker then broke in, noting that the time had come to adjourn. The House adjourned at 6:00 P.M.

FIGURE 10.2
HOW LAWS ARE PASSED

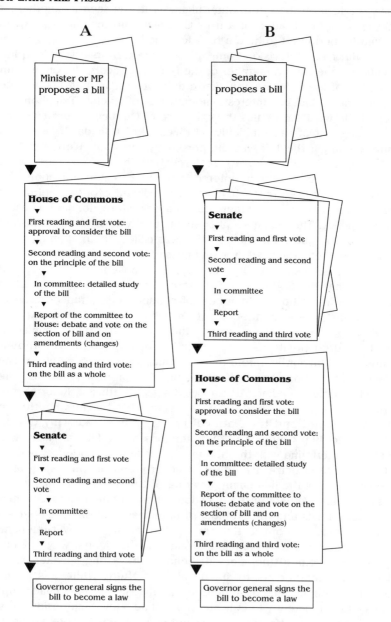

Source: Reproduced from the publication *The Canadian Citizen*, 1994, published by Citizenship and Immigration Canada. Reproduced with the permission of the Minister of Supply and Services Canada, 1997.

PASSAGE OF LEGISLATION

At this point we should describe the process necessary to translate an idea into an act of Parliament. As explained previously each session of the House begins with the *Speech from the Throne*, a general statement of the government's intentions. The six days of general debate that follow allow an opportunity for the opposition to put forward *motions of nonconfidence*. As the session proceeds, the government brings forward legislation anticipated by the Throne Speech. Once discussions in Cabinet committees and the Cabinet itself have settled on a firm policy on a particular issue, a draft bill is prepared by the Department of Justice. After 48 hours' notice has been given, it is then presented to the House of Commons by the minister responsible. On its introduction the minister simply outlines the purpose of the bill and asks that it be given a *first reading*, which is invariably granted. The bill is then printed and distributed to all members for their consideration. *Second reading* follows some time later, after members have had time to study the bill; at this stage there may be lengthy debate on the principles that the bill contains. The details are not discussed at this stage, but the House decides whether or not it will accept the need for such a bill. If second reading is successfully passed, the bill is sent to a committee (either standing or legislative) for study in detail, clause by clause. The government's draft bill is obviously what the government wants and, having won the House's approval on a second reading, is not subject to major change, but committees may exercise some power to amend the details of the government's proposal. One must keep in mind that the members are organized according to strict party discipline, and there is a limit to the amount of disagreement within party policy that a backbencher may express. On the rare occasions when a committee gets a bill after first reading, there is much greater latitude for committee initiative. When the committee concludes its study, it reports its findings to the House. This report stage allows debate and further amendments may be put forward and dealt with. When all committee proposals and further amendments have been voted upon, a vote is taken that the House concurs in the report. Finally, *third reading* provides the opportunity for the opposition to make its final attempt to defeat the bill. The purpose of this multistage procedure is to allow the government to enact legislation and to provide the opposition with ample opportunity first to debate the principle of the bill, second to investigate the details, and third, if necessary, to make a last-ditch attempt to block passage. Finally, the bill goes to the Senate, where the process is repeated.

To facilitate maintenance of party discipline in the House of Commons so that the procedures described above can work, each party has its own organization. The *House leader* of each party, appointed by the leader of the party, is responsible for the day-to-day party strategy within the House of Commons and is the tactician who attempts to influence the House of Commons in the direction the party has decided to follow. Assisting the House leaders of the parties are the *whips*, who are the agents of communication and discipline within the parties. They make certain that party policies are understood by the members and that members are present when votes on issues that are important to the party are taken within the House of Commons. This is extremely important in the government party, and the whip's job is to make certain that there are always enough members of the governing party present to win any vote in the House of Commons. Since the jobs of members entail duties that take them away from the House, the whips of the various parties are responsible for the arranging of *pairs*; according to this custom, a member of one party does not vote when paired with a member of another party who is absent.

The Members of Parliament from each party constitute the party's *caucus*. Wednesday morning caucus meetings provide a forum for leaders and followers to discuss, debate, and generally think out their party's policies. This is particularly important to the opposition parties, because they generally find themselves reacting to the government initiative in most matters, especially if the government has a majority. However, because they have the initiative, the prime minister and Cabinet present to their party's caucus legislation and policies on which considerable planning has already taken place. This means that, although there may be opposition at times, the members of the government party caucus find it difficult to alter their leader's well-laid plans. Since the meeting of the caucus takes place in secret, it allows backbenchers to be highly critical of some government policies, especially when the policies are not likely to be popular in a particular member's constituency. On such occasions the national policy of the governing party may be detrimental to the careers of particular members, and these members will not hesitate to oppose bitterly the party's policy. Regional caucuses (especially those of the two traditional major parties from Quebec), if they are united in a concern, may be able to influence the government to delay or modify—but rarely abandon—an initiative.

From what we have said, it should be evident that the operation of the House of Commons is highly structured. The prime minister and the Cabinet are the dominant forces within that structure, since they are responsible for introducing legislation and have the power as the leadership of the majority party to ensure the passage of that legislation. The role of the backbenchers in both the governing and opposition parties is restricted by the dominance of the Cabinet. However, through committees of the House and in their party's caucus, backbenchers do have some limited opportunity to influence policy, and the trend in the last few years has been toward attempting to enlarge their influence. However, the major impediment of strict party discipline remains, and voting against one's own party is not encouraged. Thus, the average backbencher of the governing party, let alone those in opposition parties, does not have a great deal of influence in the framing of the laws that pass through the legislative mill.

THE SENATE

Although constitutionally the Senate possesses almost equal power with the House of Commons, its actual role in both the political and government process has been without major significance, except on rare occasions. It lacks legitimacy for most Canadians. Because it is appointed, it runs counter to the Canadian belief that democratic government should be conducted by elected officials and not by an appointed body. Moreover, the appointments have almost always been made to reward loyal supporters of the party in power rather than to ensure that the best-qualified people become senators. Until 1965, when an age limit of 75 was imposed on newly appointed senators, all appointments to the Senate were for life. This resulted in a chamber whose members were for the most part over the age when others were expected to retire. There was, therefore, undue responsibility placed on those members of the Senate who desired and were able to play an effective role in the legislative process. All these factors have contributed to the Senate's reluctance to use the constitutional powers provided in the Constitution Act, 1867. The Canadian public no longer expects, if it ever did, the Senate to exercise any kind of control over the House of Commons.

The Senate was meant to protect the interests of wealthy and conservative Canadians, but the rest of the community could hardly be expected to support such an institutionalization of minority power. In any case the wealthy and conservative in Canada have had more effective means of protecting their interests, through positions of power in the economic, social, and political spheres. While many senators have traditionally been well connected to major corporate interests, regional representation was a more important basis for the establishment of the Senate. Ontario, Quebec, the Maritimes, and the western provinces have 24 seats each; Newfoundland's six and one each for the Yukon and the Northwest Territories bring the current total of senators to 104. However, the Senate has failed as an effective regional forum, and regions and provinces must look to the Cabinet and their own provincial governments for a strong voice on behalf of their interests. Since the Senate has failed to live up to its representative responsibilities, it has become a silent legislative partner of the House of Commons in the Parliament of Canada. Many people are concerned that the lack of influential regional representation in the institutions of the central government is a serious flaw in the Canadian federal system. Thus, either Senate reform or replacement by another body constructed to perform this role has been suggested. In 1987 the Alberta Legislative Assembly adopted a proposal that became the most widely discussed plan for Senate reform.

The reform became known as the Triple E Senate, based on its call for an elected, equal, and effective Upper House, a plan also espoused by the Canada West Foundation. Albertans invested a great deal of energy in selling the idea as a solution to what they considered to be a lack of regional input into national legislative policy. Thus, the Charlottetown Accord had Senate reform as a central concern and called for an elected Senate with six senators from each province. This Senate was to have significant powers. The rejection of the Accord by Canadians means that Senate reform must await another day.

The Senate will therefore continue in its limited actual role in Canadian government and politics. Although it usually acquiesces with the legislation passed in the House of Commons, it does scrutinize carefully and sometimes refines the details and language of legislation. Since legislation is generally introduced in the House of Commons (money bills must originate there), and this legislation is introduced by Cabinet ministers who are almost always members of the House of Commons, the Senate is presented with legislation that has already undergone major debate in the elective body. Its deliberations, therefore, take place after the issue has already been decided in the House of Commons and on the wider front of public opinion. To interfere drastically at this point would not only raise serious objections in the House of Commons but would also raise questions among the general public about the proper role of the Senate. On minor matters, such as private bills to incorporate federally chartered companies, and on government matters of a noncontroversial nature, the Senate performs a useful role in reducing the workload of the House of Commons. In performing this role, the Senate operates in relative obscurity because the issues are of little political importance to the majority of the community. But Senate committee discussions on security legislation in 1983, for example, were influential in redrafting the legislation.

In 1988 the Liberal-dominated Senate was uncharacteristically reluctant to follow the Progressive Conservative–controlled House of Commons on major issues. Drug-patent legislation was studied, amended, and sent back to the House. After a protracted period of hostility, the Progressive Conservative government eventually got its way. On the question of the Free Trade Agreement, however, the Senate Liberal majority announced flatly that it would not agree to the legislation unless the question was put before Canadians in an election. That, in fact, is what transpired. During the discussions generated by these Senate actions, the Mulroney government made many declarations about the undemocratic nature of Senate interference and suggested that reform would be undertaken. But to ensure the passage of the Goods and Services Tax (GST), Mulroney used a little-known constitutional provision that allowed him to appoint eight new senators. He thus gained a Conservative majority in the Senate, but the passage of the GST by this means diminished the Senate's reputation with the public even more. The Liberals entered office in 1993 facing a Conservative majority in the Senate, and they too found that the Senate was not always willing to rubber-stamp legislation passed by the Liberal-controlled House of Commons.

Senate committees have had a useful role in the legislative process in the conduct of investigations. Most importantly, the Senate Standing Committee on Finance and Banking has had some influence on legislation in those areas. Many members of that committee have had close ties with the financial and banking community, and this has raised questions about its objectivity.[11] Other special Senate committees have studied land use, poverty, the media, and (ironically) the problems of the aged in Canada. There is less pressure on the senators' time than on members of the House of Commons, and thus they are able to carry out extensive studies that may in future influence legislation on the matters studied. Some proponents of Senate reform consider this to be the most valuable contribution of the Senate. They therefore consider that appointments should be made more on the basis of mature expertise in various problem areas of Canadian life.

The description of both the House of Commons and the Senate shows that legislative power obviously resides almost entirely with the House. This is as it should be, as the House is the only elected body in the entire structure of government at the federal level. Even more important is the fact that the prime minister and Cabinet are drawn almost entirely from the ranks of the House, and it is this group that is responsible not only for the conduct of executive government but also for the initiation and passage of a legislative program through the House. Therefore, procedures in the House have been developed to enable the government to govern, while at the same time protecting the rights of the opposition to oppose and present its alternatives to the public. While this is the ideal, in practice both government and opposition abuse the theory at times. The politicians who control the legislative process suffer from the same human foibles as the rest of us, and one may only judge their performance by how closely they adhere to the norms of parliamentary government.

Critics of an entrenched Charter of Rights and Freedoms cited the possibility that parliamentary supremacy would be undermined by its introduction. They felt that the democratic principle of ultimate decision making residing in an elected legislative body would be eroded by this change, for it would apparently give to judges the final decision-making authority. Two factors militate against this view. One is the "notwithstanding clause" that allows circumventions of some Charter provisions should the House of Commons or provincial legislative bodies consider it necessary. This was done by the Bourassa government of Quebec in 1988 to enforce its language legislation regarding signs. Second, the courts of Canada will continue for some time to be dominated by jurists imbued with the concept of parliamentary supremacy. They are not likely to undermine it without a great deal of consideration. Thus, while the House of Commons' pride of place in the institutions of government may be somewhat less secure than it was before the entrenchment of the Charter, its fundamental role continues to a large degree.

RECOMMENDED READING

Aucoin, P., ed. *Institutional Reforms for Representative Government*. Toronto: University of Toronto Press, 1985. Studies for the Royal Commission on the Economic Union and Development Prospects for Canada, vol. 38.

Canada, House of Commons. *Report of the Special Committee on Reform of the House of Commons* (the McGrath Committee). June 1985.

Courtney, J.C., ed. *The Canadian House of Commons: Essays in Honour of Norman Ward*. Calgary: University of Calgary Press, 1985.

Franks, C.E.S. *The Parliament of Canada*. Toronto: University of Toronto Press, 1987.

Jackson, R.J., and M.M. Atkinson. *The Canadian Legislative System: Politicians and Policymaking*. Toronto: Macmillan, 1980.

CHAPTER 11

The Judiciary and the Administration of Justice

THE DEVELOPING ROLE OF THE SUPREME COURT

Parliamentary democracy seeks to guarantee the prevention of arbitrary government by providing for an independent judiciary. This means that the officials who interpret the laws of Canada are not the same as those who pass the laws (legislators) and those who administer them (the executive). However, this third branch of government, the judiciary, is more remote from most Canadians than the other two branches. Many citizens have regular dealings with the executive branch of government, by paying income taxes or collecting unemployment benefits, family allowances, and pensions. Issues of the day are debated in the legislature, which gets intensive coverage from the news media. On the other hand, average citizens do not have regular dealings with the judicial system, and except for reports on celebrated criminal cases, news media provide them with little analysis of the business of that system. Therefore, the integral role of the judiciary as a vital component of the governmental process has been little appreciated. It is our purpose in this chapter, therefore, to discuss first the part played by the judiciary in the constitutional process, and second—and even more important—the manner in which the courts are structured to perform their function of dispensing justice.

Although there have been many landmark decisions, traditionally the courts have remained in the background of the constitutional process. The main reason that the role of the judiciary has been overshadowed is the concept of *parliamentary supremacy*. This concept holds that Parliaments, either federal or provincial, may pass any legislation that falls within their respective jurisdictions; the judiciary's role in relation to this is to judge whether or not such legislation is within or outside the powers of these Parliaments as outlined in the Constitution Act, 1867. Moreover, the Supreme Court of Canada was not the final court of appeal until 1949; before then appeals on constitutional cases could be made to the Judicial Committee of the Privy Council (JCPC) in the United Kingdom. This denied the Canadian Supreme Court the opportunity to create for itself as important a role in the constitutional process as, for example, the United States Supreme Court.[1] Lacking the legitimate role of final arbiter in constitutional matters, the Supreme Court remained for the most part on the sidelines; fundamental issues in federal-provincial relations were settled by political compromise rather than judicial decisions. This is not to say that in the earlier years of Confederation the JCPC did not make important constitutional decisions that considerably altered the balance of legislative powers assigned to the federal and provincial governments. These interpretations strengthened the legislative authority of the provinces and weakened that of the federal government. However, it could be argued that, given the nature of Canadian political development, this would have happened even without the interpretation of the JCPC. It is unlikely that the provinces would have passively accepted the quasi-federal nature of the Constitution with the highly centralist bias given it by the Fathers of Confederation. Had the courts not granted the provinces more extensive legislative authority, it is probable that the provinces would have secured wider powers by political means.[2]

During the 1970s, however, and especially under the leadership of the late Chief Justice Bora Laskin, the Supreme Court became more activist and began to be considered a more important component of the overall system of public decision making. This enhanced role was seen in its most developed form in 1981, when the Supreme Court was asked to rule on the constitutional reform package and, more particularly, on the federal government's stated intention to act unilaterally if provincial agreement was not forthcoming. Thus, the Supreme Court was raised to a prominence that had been denied to it in previous decades. The adoption of an entrenched Charter of Rights and Freedoms in the Constitution Act, 1982 has provided the basis for expectations that the Supreme Court will play an even greater part in the determination of the rules that govern Canada's constitutional practice. While it is still premature to argue that ultimate decision making will in fact shift considerably from the elected House of Commons to the Supreme Court, there can be little doubt that even a cautious and conservative Supreme Court will wield more influence than was the case in the era before entrenchment. Such expectations accompanied the appointment of Chief Justice Brian Dickson in 1984. In the last half of the 1980s, the Supreme Court did achieve a larger prominence as it handed down important decisions based on provisions of the Charter of Rights and Freedoms. Of these the striking down of the federal government's abortion section in the Criminal Code and the nullifying of the prohibition of the display of English commercial signs under Quebec's Official Language Act (later reinstituted by the Quebec National Assembly using the notwithstanding clause) were most widely debated.

Although we have argued both here and in previous chapters that political pressures have been preeminent in shaping constitutional development, there is no doubt that decisions of the JCPC were important, both as a reflection of and a stimulant to attitudes opposed to the original intent of the Constitution Act, 1867. The politicians who devised the original Constitution sought to forge a strong central government capable of building a viable new nation out of a union of weak and dispersed colonies. As the leaders of the new federated colony, they proceeded to implement their intentions. In the first 20 years, neither the provinces, which lacked political strength, nor the courts, which accepted the original centralist interpretation of the Constitution, challenged this design. However, by the 1880s two factors stimulated the developments that ultimately subverted the original centralist policy. The provinces became centres of opposition to the increasing powers of the federal government, and they successfully argued their case for wider recognition of provincial authority to a sympathetic JCPC. In two cases, *Hodge v. The Queen* in 1883 and *The Maritime Bank v. The Receiver General of New Brunswick* in 1890, the JCPC ruled that, within the limits of the classes of subjects in Section 92 of the Constitution, the provincial legislature was supreme and that it was not the intention of the Constitution Act, 1867 to make the provinces subordinate to the federal government.[3] What followed was a series of cases over the years, including the *Local Prohibition Case of 1896*, and *The Toronto Electric Commissioners v. Snyder* in 1925, that had the effect of reducing the power of the federal Parliament to make laws for "Peace, Order, and Good Government," and making it the business of the courts to concentrate instead on the powers enumerated in Sections 91 and 92. Clearly, the intention of the Fathers of Confederation was to make the general powers of the federal government very wide, and the enumerated powers in Section 91 were to be only specific examples of those wide-ranging powers. The JCPC in effect limited the federal powers to the specific examples, except in times of extreme emergency such as war or apprehended insurrection. Even the Depression of the 1930s was not considered by the JCPC the type of emergency in which the federal Parliament could exercise its general power to make laws under the Peace, Order, and Good Government clause to alleviate the economic crisis. Consequently, federal statutes were ruled unconstitutional since they invaded provincial jurisdiction. Over the next 30 years, the courts made no decisions that seriously altered the constitutional balance of federal-provincial relations; rather, there was a move toward the use of federal-provincial conferences to settle federal-provincial differences. In 1976 the Supreme Court ruled that the Anti-Inflation Act could be justified under the Peace, Order, and Good Government clause as a response to what Parliament decided was an emergency. The Supreme Court defined extensive, if not unlimited, claims to federal government control in economic matters, while stating what it considered to be the implications of Section 91.

Although the modern role of the courts has been limited in the area of federal-provincial relationships, in the constitutional process it has tended to expand its role in recent years, especially in those areas affecting the rights of citizens. The 1960 Federal Bill of Rights, and similar legislation in most provinces, provided the courts with an opportunity to subject legislation to the standards guaranteed by such human rights legislation. A landmark in this trend was the case of *Regina v. Joseph Drybones*[4] in November 1969, when the Supreme Court of Canada applied the Canadian Bill of Rights in reaching its decision and invalidated a section of the Indian Act that was discriminatory. The decision was not unanimous, as three of the nine justices were concerned that the supremacy of Parliament was being undermined. The Bill of Rights was not used aggressively by the Supreme Court to overturn federal or provincial legislation. It was not until the Charter of Rights and Freedoms was available in 1982 that the Court was really in a position to take an activist role in expanding the interpretation of rights. By 1994 the Supreme Court had rendered a number of decisions that defined various rights in a way that pleased many Canadians but concerned others.[5]

THE SYSTEM OF COURTS

The Supreme Court of Canada, at the apex of the judicial system, is most obviously related to the political process as it renders the final judgement on contentious points of law. Less obvious, however, is the role of the whole system of courts that daily render judgements on the relationships between individual Canadians and between Canadians and their governments.

The provinces are mainly responsible for the administration of justice in Canada. Although *criminal law* is the responsibility of the federal government and is embodied in a Criminal Code that is uniform across the country, the provinces are responsible for prosecuting those who are charged under the Criminal Code. The Criminal Code proscribes offences against public order, disorderly conduct, offences against the person and reputation, offences against the rights of property, fraudulent transactions relating to contracts and trade, and wilful and forbidden acts in respect to certain kinds of property. This list is not exhaustive, but it does suggest the wide range of criminal offences that Canadian society considers an affront to law and order. Other federal statutes may also define other criminal offences, as, for example, does the Narcotics Control Act. As well as defining the various offences, the Criminal Code explicitly designates the procedures to be followed in criminal proceedings. Offences are either *indictable* or subject to *summary conviction*. In general terms procedure by indictment involves preliminary proceedings in which it has to be established whether a trial should indeed take place. Summary proceedings, on the other hand, do not involve pretrial procedures and deal with less serious crimes where the maximum penalty, unless explicitly stated to the contrary by law, is $2000 or six months of imprisonment or both.

FIGURE 11.1
CANADA'S COURT SYSTEM

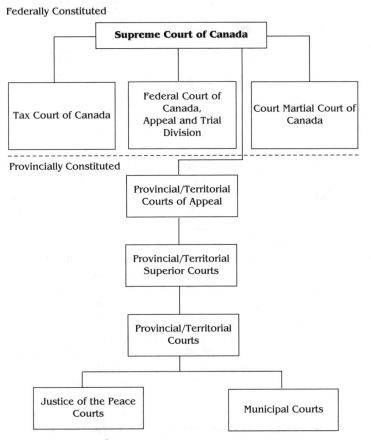

Source: Statistics Canada, *Canada Yearbook 1997*, Catalogue No. 11–402, p. 484. Reproduced by authority of the Minister of Industry, 1997.

FIGURE 11.2
CANADA'S LEGAL SYSTEM

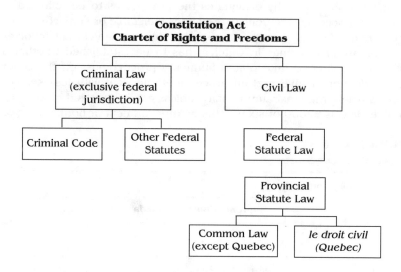

Source: Statistics Canada, *Canada Yearbook 1997*, Catalogue No. 11–402, p. 484. Reproduced by authority of the Minister of Industry, 1997.

In matters of civil law, the province defines and administers the law. This type of law deals with contracts, settling of estates, property settlements arising out of divorce cases, assigning liability in automobile accidents, and so on. That is, it generally relates to the settlement of private disputes rather than the prosecution of a suspected offender.

Although the federal government appoints and pays all judges except provincial judges and magistrates, the establishment and administration of court systems in the provinces are the responsibility of the provincial governments. Various court systems have been established in the different provinces, but they share many common characteristics.

At the apex of provincial court systems is a final court of appeal, which hears appeals on cases that have been tried in lower courts. Each province also has a superior court that hears serious indictable offences (those listed in Section 469 of the Criminal Code, such as treason, murder, and assault) and civil actions exceeding an amount defined by the province. County or district courts continue to exist only in Nova Scotia; elsewhere they have been merged with the superior court. These courts also act as surrogate or probate courts, which deal with the settlement of estates. There are about 930 provincial and territorial appeals and superior courts, judges appointed by the federal government, which also pays their salaries. Every court will not necessarily have its own roster of judges, but the same judge acting in a different capacity can preside over courts with different designations, so long as the courts are at the same level.

By far the greatest number of cases that come before courts in any province are in the provincial courts. The judges (about 1000 in number) of these courts are appointed and paid by the provinces. These judicial officials bear the brunt of hearing not only the cases on summary conviction under the Criminal Code but also some indictable offences where a jury trial is not chosen. Infractions of the provincial laws that deal with highways, traffic, liquor offences, and a host of other matters create a busy docket for these courts. In addition to this, they are responsible for the preliminary proceedings in offences that are indictable before those cases proceed to higher courts. Provincial governments may also establish at this level courts to deal with civil cases involving relatively small sums of money, with family law, and with juveniles.

There are three courts, established by Parliament, whose jurisdiction is national in scope: the Supreme Court of Canada, established in 1875; the Federal Court of Canada, organized in 1970; and the Tax Court, which replaced the Tax Appeal Board in 1985. It is especially the Supreme Court of Canada that sets the pattern for lower court decisions. Definitive judgements concerning constitutional, criminal, and civil law are ultimately made in the Supreme Court. This court consists of a chief justice and eight other judges called puisne, or lower-rank, judges, three of whom must be from Quebec. This provision is in recognition that Quebec has a different form of civil law from that of the other provinces. The makeup of this court, and especially the inclusion of some provincial role in the appointment of the judges, has been the subject of proposals for reform in recent decades. While the Constitution Act, 1982 did not change the composition of the Supreme Court, it did guarantee that no changes could be made without the unanimous consent of the provinces.

Both the Meech Lake Accord and the Charlottetown Accord called for the entrenchment of the Supreme Court in the Constitution, along with its guarantee of three Quebec judges, and further provided that the federal government would fill Supreme Court vacancies from lists provided by the provinces. Historically, a system of regional representation has evolved. One important development with regard to the membership of the Supreme Court was the appointment of Madame Justice Bertha Wilson in 1982, the first woman on the highest court and the first to head it. She was joined by Mme. Justice Claire L'Heureux-Dubé in 1987 and Madame Justice Beverley McLachlin in 1989. In 1989 Mr. Justice John Sopinka became the first person of Ukrainian descent to sit on the Supreme Court, and he was only the second (Bora Laskin was the first) justice who was neither of French nor English descent.

The Supreme Court hears appeals as provided for in the Supreme Court Act. All nine members of the court do not have to participate in every case, but a panel must consist of at least five justices. Some appeals must be heard as a matter of right (that is, the Court is obliged to consider them), but in more recent years the Court has determined which cases it wants to hear by granting hearings to those judgements of the appeals courts of the provinces where significant constitutional issues are raised. Finally, the Cabinet may refer constitutional matters to the Supreme Court for an opinion before enacting legislation. These are called *reference cases*. For example, the federal government asked the Court to give an opinion on whether the federal or provincial governments had jurisdiction over offshore mineral rights. This particular reference case reflects the Court's traditional limited role in the political process. The provinces, rather than accepting the Court's decision as the final word, immediately made it clear that they would continue to bargain with the federal government over these rights. For its part the federal government did not maintain that, since the Court had spoken, this was the end of the matter; instead, it took the Court's decision as the basis for a negotiated settlement. This could be contrasted with a similar dispute in the United States over offshore mineral rights, where the Supreme Court ruled that these rights came under the jurisdiction of the individual states. Once this decision was made, no further bargaining was necessary or possible. Newfoundland had claimed that its position was unique with respect to offshore resources and that the argument that applied to other provinces did not apply to it. Thus, ultimately the Supreme Court was called upon in 1984 to render its opinion, and it did so in favour of the position of the federal government. The response of Premier Peckford, however, was to seek a constitutional change that would render the Supreme Court's decision inoperative, and ultimately he signed the Atlantic Accord with the Mulroney government, which gave him much of what he wanted.

The other major court at the federal level is the Federal Court of Canada. This court consists of two divisions: an *appeal* division and a *trial* division. It has a chief justice and an associate chief justice, the chief justice being president of the Court of Appeal and the associate chief justice being president of the trial division. Fourteen other judges are appointed in the trial division and 10 others in the appeals division. Four of the judges must come from Quebec, and the court may meet in any part of Canada where the volume of work or other circumstances demand its services. This introduces into the Canadian judicial system a means of taking the court to the people. This is strengthened by the authority that the court has to appoint deputy judges from among those in an area with judicial experience to act in the name of the court. Any single judge of the trial division constitutes the court, whereas at least three judges must sit as the Court of Appeal.

The jurisdiction of the trial division of the Federal Court includes cases in which citizens have a claim against the Crown, usually involving contracts and other legal arrangements between the citizen and the government. In such cases the court grants relief. It is also the court of original jurisdiction for members of the Armed Forces. In addition to these duties is the authority to hear and grant relief on decisions made by federal boards, commissions, and other agencies. The trial division also acts as a referee between the federal government and a provincial government, and between provincial governments—as long as the provinces concerned have accepted the court's jurisdiction. Finally, it settles disputes on patents, copyrights, and inventions and acts on citizenship appeals, Canadian maritime law, and income and estate tax appeals. The appeal division of the Federal Court may hear appeals on decisions of the trial division. Appeals from the Tax Court go to the Federal Court, as do appeals from federal agencies whose decisions are challenged on the grounds of not adhering to accepted legal procedures and principles. It may also give advisory opinions to any of these agencies that seek its guidance. Because of the growth in the number and activities of these kinds of agencies at both the federal and provincial levels (for example, the Canadian Transport Commission and the CRTC), it is important that a higher judicial body is in place to ensure conformity to the rules of justice. It should be kept in mind that decisions by the appeal division may still be taken to the Supreme Court. However, the intention of the Federal Court Act was, among other things, to relieve the workload of cases reaching the Supreme Court.

THE ADMINISTRATION OF JUSTICE

Having sketched the broad outlines of the judicial system of courts in Canada, we will now turn to a discussion of how the state administers this system. The most important aspect of the administration of criminal justice is bringing the accused before the courts and ensuring that he or she gets a fair trial. The bulk of the day-to-day responsibility for the administration of justice lies with the provinces. However, at the federal level, the Department of Justice and the Department of the Solicitor General assume broad responsibilities for recommending changes both in the law itself and in the way it is administered. The minister of justice, who is also attorney general for Canada, is the official legal advisor to Cabinet and is empowered to advise all departments of government on matters of law; he or she is also in charge of all litigation for or against the Crown. This department, like others, has been reorganized and now has its responsibilities divided into several sectors, which are shown in Figure 11.3. The minister of justice has broad responsibilities not only to administer present laws but also to recommend improvements in the system. In this regard the Law Reform Commission of Canada reports the results of its research periodically, as it did in February 1989 on the question of abortion legislation.

FIGURE 11.3

JUSTICE CANADA: THE NEW FACE OF GOVERNMENT

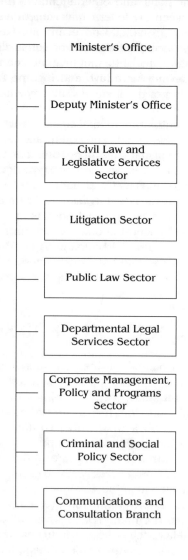

Source: *The New Face of Government 1994: A Guide to the New Federal Structure*, p. 61. Reproduced with permission.

The duties of the solicitor general for Canada also have to do with the administration of justice. This department has three major responsibilities. First, the solicitor general is responsible for the Royal Canadian Mounted Police, which enforces federal law. This federal force also acts as the provincial police in all provinces except Ontario and Quebec. During the 1980s a number of serious questions arose with regard to the operations of this national police force. The allegations of law breaking in the name of national security caused concern over the security service of the RCMP. The result was the appointment of the MacDonald Royal Commission, which conducted extensive hearings and led to the introduction of legislation that provided for a Civilian Security Intelligence Service separate from the RCMP. Second, this minister is in charge of the Canadian Penitentiary Service, which carries out the penal and correctional duties of the federal government. And third, the National Parole Board comes under the solicitor general's jurisdiction and assumes responsibility for the rehabilitation of prisoners released from federal prisons. All of these functions have been the subject of public controversy during the 1990s.

As noted the primary responsibility for directing prosecution and servicing the court system rests with the provinces. The attorneys general direct these functions in their respective provinces. Provincial attorneys general are members of the Cabinet who oversee a department that has a variety of responsibilities. They serve the legislature and government by drafting both public and private bills and acting as official legal advisors to the government and legislature. In addition, they are responsible for recommending improvements in the law and maintaining a system of courts to service all areas of their respective provinces in the civil and criminal jurisdictions. In Ontario in 1990, for instance, this entailed a reform that created the Ontario Courts of Justice, comprised of a general division that includes all federally appointed judges and a provincial division that includes all provincially appointed judges. In addition, there is a separate Ontario Court of Appeal. Justices of the peace hear less serious cases in the judicial system, especially with regard to provincial offences and violations of municipal by-laws, and Small Claims Courts hear minor civil matters. For the purposes of criminal prosecution, the director of public prosecutions is responsible for supervising the activities of 49 Crown attorneys. These are the people who represent the Crown against the accused. The administration of each of the 49 counties, districts, and judicial districts is the responsibility of a court services manager, rather than a sheriff as in the past. Sheriffs still exist, but with modified duties. All these officials are members of the Department of the Attorney General. Probationary services also come under the authority of the attorney general's department, as do the coroners who carry out investigations into the causes of death and conduct inquests when circumstances surrounding the death demand more than a cursory investigation. Finally, the law-enforcement agencies within the province of Ontario come under the supervision of the solicitor general's department.

The administration of justice often raises questions that cannot be solved within the regular structure of agencies and courts. Thus, judicial commissions of inquiry have been set up at both the federal and provincial levels. There was, for instance, the Cliche Commission in Quebec on labour racketeering in the 1970s; in Ontario widespread alarm at the death of 36 babies at Toronto's Sick Children's Hospital led to the appointment of the Grange Commission in 1983. The Marshall Inquiry in 1987–88 in Nova Scotia into the wrongful conviction of a Micmac Indian for murder delved into allegations of racism and incompetence in the law-enforcement and judicial system of that province. In 1988–89 the Code Commission in Alberta investigated the causes of the failure of the Principal Group of financial companies and in so doing raised questions about the adequacy of a provincial overview of financial institutions. At the federal level, the Krever Commission on the question of HIV-infected blood and the Somalia Inquiry into murders committed by Canadian soldiers have been the most notable of the 1990s. The reports of commissions such as these often place upon governments the need to reform legislation or administrative practices. They also lead, at times, to action in the regular court system.

FAIR AND EQUITABLE JUSTICE

Fundamental to the role of the courts is the provision of a fair trial and, if necessary, appeals to higher courts for individuals who have been apprehended and charged with breaking the law. The courts also attempt to arbitrate fairly in civil cases involving disputes among citizens, corporations, or public agencies. In this situation there is tension between those who seek the most efficient and stringent means of ensuring public safety and those whose chief concern is fair treatment for the accused and rehabilitation for the guilty, when possible. Canada's record in both law enforcement and protection of the legal rights of the accused compares favourably with that of most developed countries, but in this area there is never room for complacency. This is not to say, however, that there are not glaring imperfections in our system. Any civil libertarian may point to specific instances of injustice involving, for example, the unreasonable imposition of exorbitant bail, overzealous prosecution, and "hanging judges." In the 1980s, with the growing awareness of Native rights and the larger number of aboriginals imprisoned, the question of racism in law enforcement became an issue for the Native community—and indeed for visible minorities in urban centres. On the other hand, victims' support groups and staunch supporters of law and order will counter with as many examples of obviously guilty defendants who have "beaten the rap" by a legal technicality or have been given light sentences. They will also refer to growing crime rates. Both of these types of claims point up certain inadequacies in the law and the human weaknesses of those who judge and administer the law. Provisions of the Charter of Rights and Freedoms have strengthened the hand of those who want to introduce more stringent approaches to the question of fair and equal treatment before the courts.

The present system of appointing judges is not without its critics. It is beyond doubt that leaving judicial appointments to the federal and provincial Cabinets (with attorneys general playing the key role) in their respective spheres has resulted in partisan appointments, although flagrant partisanship has declined for federal appointments. On too many occasions, partisan appointees may have brought disrespect to the bench, but they are the exceptions rather than the rule. It is not necessarily true that this has resulted in incompetent appointees, but feminists would argue that the overwhelming number of male judges has denied the bench a sufficient understanding of women's circumstances, especially in sexual assault cases. Within the ranks of all major parties, nonetheless, one should expect that there will be a large number of deserving male and female candidates for the bench. To make partisanship a disqualifying factor would deny appointments to the most politically active people in the country, since most political activity takes place within the party structure. In terms of bias, the doctrinal differences between the major parties are not so neatly delineated that an appointee's membership in one party or another is the key factor in his or her judicial philosophy. All of this having been said, the number of judicial (and other) appointments made by the Liberal government in 1984 just before the election campaign raised the issue to public prominence. Recent federal governments, with the exception of the 1984 incident, have, however, been less overtly partisan in political appointments than were their predecessors. The most widely recommended alternative to appointment by the Cabinet usually involves the establishment of a commission of learned legalists who would submit names to the Cabinet. That this procedure would necessarily lead to better appointments is questionable. The legal profession also has its bias in the direction of the status quo rather than radical change. Since the early 1970s, the attorney general has had an advisor on judicial appointments, and he or she has normally consulted with provincial counterparts as well as with members of the provincial bar associations. The present system does not ensure that bad choices will not sometimes be made, but while any alternative may lessen the risk, it is not likely that the judiciary would be radically different in composition.

Perhaps a more serious problem is the lack of monetary incentive for highly regarded lawyers to accept appointments to judgeships during their most productive years. In most professions the higher one ascends the ladder of achievement, the more money one normally receives. Thus, if one assumes that judges should be the most able people in the legal profession, it follows that they should be among the highest paid in that profession. Such is certainly not the case, and provincial court judges can often expect to make less than the most successful lawyers in their province. In recent years, however, Supreme Court and superior court judges have come to be more adequately paid. This having been said, most Canadians would view judges' salaries as excellent in comparison to their own, and large increases are not likely to be popular. In addition, the Crown attorneys and their assistants, on whose shoulders rests the prosecution of criminals, while reasonably rewarded, cannot aspire to the income levels of the more successful criminal lawyers. Prosecutions are often conducted by inexperienced young assistant Crown attorneys who use the position to gain courtroom experience and as a stepping stone to private practice. It seems reasonable that the state should ensure that all prosecutions are conducted by experienced lawyers.

Perhaps more important is that judges and prosecuting officials are too few in number. This results in a backlog of cases that denies to an accused the right to a speedy trial or, in a civil suit, the prompt settling of a contentious issue. The inadequate number of prosecutors often means they are unable to prepare carefully the kind of case that would stand up against an expert defence lawyer. This is particularly true if the accused is a wealthy person or a corporation, so that the charge that there is one law for the rich and another for the poor is all too often correct. Perhaps the worst effect of the lack of public attention to the courts has been the continuance of inadequate standards, not only of pay and staff but also of physical facilities. Too many courtrooms across Canada are old, ill-heated, perhaps even unsafe structures.

The cost of litigation is often another factor that may prevent a citizen from getting justice. Legal-aid plans in many of the provinces ensure that in criminal proceedings a defendant can be adequately represented and appeal the case to the highest courts. However, this is not so frequently the case in civil actions, and the prohibitive costs of seeking a lawyer and paying a variety of court fees may discourage a citizen from seeking redress. Even if the case is brought before a local court, a citizen may not be able to afford the added costs of appeals, while the corporation or person that he or she is suing may be capable and willing to take the matter to a higher court.

Another problem in ensuring equal justice to all Canadians is the differing standards that apply in different provinces. It is obvious from a review of the crime statistics published annually in the Canada Year Book that the likelihood of conviction is higher in some provinces than in others and that the sentencing attitudes may vary as well.

If a necessary aspect of the "Rule of Law" in Canada is that all Canadians are accorded equal treatment in the courts, the foregoing problems tend to thwart that objective. Although it may be impossible ever to attain that objective completely, there is considerable room for improvement in the Canadian system. Expenditures of comparatively small sums of money by the federal and provincial governments could go a long way to improve the situation, but beyond that there must also be a public awareness of the role of the courts in Canadian society. An enlightened public opinion is the best guarantee that acceptable standards of justice will be dispensed by our courts. The judiciary is not totally isolated from the political process, and this means that an aroused public can ultimately ensure that they will get the standards of justice they consider necessary. If the public continues to disregard the need to improve the judicial system, they will have to accept the continuance of the present inadequacies in the administration of justice.

CONCLUSIONS

At the beginning of the text, we spoke of the democratic character of Canadian society. We have now completed an examination of the judiciary, which—at least in its origin—is not democratic, for its members are appointed, not elected. The increased power of the federal judiciary resulting from the adoption of the Charter of Rights and Freedoms in the Constitution Act, 1982 and its capability of overturning legislative acts leads us to some reflections about the relation between the democratic principle and the enhanced power of the judiciary. A noted political observer has gone so far as to speak of a revolutionary change in Canada brought on by the entrenchment of the Charter. Seymour Martin Lipset says that "Canada now has a constitution that both empowers the judiciary to overrule parliament by ruling that legislation is inconsistent with the Charter and allows the legislative bodies to limit the authority of the courts to do so."[6] The latter limitation does not exist in the United States. So potentially, at least, there are grounds for serious conflict between these two powers.

There were two sources of opposition to royal absolutism in the seventeenth century in England. On the one hand, there was the political demand that Parliament and not the monarch alone should be supreme. It was argued that this had indeed been so before royal usurpation took place. On the other hand, there was the legal attack on absolute power identified with Sir Edward Coke, the defender of common law and judicial independence. An independent judiciary is one in which the judges were not subject to political intervention once cases were under judicial consideration (*sub judice*). The successful revolution established parliamentary supremacy and recognized judicial independence. Of course, in the English case the House of Lords, the upper house of Parliament, is the highest court of appeal, the counterpart of a Supreme Court. It was believed, no doubt, that once the remnants of absolutism had been eliminated and common law recognized as basic law, after the Constitution, the conflicts endemic to the system of royal absolutism would also disappear, particularly the conflict between royal administrators and the exponents of the common law. The liberal politi-cal system eventually evolved into the liberal democratic system in which parliamentary supremacy also means democratic supremacy. Since the Canadian model is that of subordination of the executive to the legislative power—traditionally known as responsible government—the judiciary had no separate standing, as in the United States, where the separation and balance-of-powers model of governance was adopted. However, in both instances the members of the judiciary came to assert their power to review legislation. This occurred fairly early in the American case and later in the Canadian case, as we have noted above.

What precisely are the judges, particularly the judges on the Supreme Court, expected to do? Or what are the limits under which they should operate? One time-honoured distinction still invoked is that the task of the judiciary is not to make the law but simply to interpret it. Strictly understood, this means *judicial restraint*; it generally means judicial deference to democratic legislation. It means that judges do not take initiatives, do not make rules, but only rulings. The opposite conception of the judiciary is called *judicial activism*, which permits judges to take initiatives and indeed to participate to some extent in the legislative process.

It may be premature to try to detect trends in the decisions of the Supreme Court since the adoption of the Constitution Act, 1982. Even two decades seem too brief a period to do so. Some have detected an initial spurt of activism, followed by an attitude more inclined to defer to the legislatures. But the political situation has undoubtedly been altered because it allows for end-runs around the legislatures by appeals to the Court. This may seem a very attractive tactic for certain groups that are unlikely to have their way in the legislature or after their views have not prevailed in a democratic body. Frequently, appeals to the courts are based on ostensive "rights," and recently one has seen a process by which demands are transformed into needs and needs into rights. This has been described as an inflation of rights talk. There is an assumption in certain legal theories that matters of rights and freedoms are specifically the province of judges and lawyers, that the defence of fundamental rights is or should be the prerogative of the judiciary. Whether this is indeed the case cannot be decided by mere assertion but must be put to the test of experience. This means that the issue is whether the judiciary or the democratic legislative body is a better safe-guard of rights, both individual and collective, over a period of time.

Since the Supreme Court now has a firm constitutional basis for intervening to protect individual rights and civil liberties, appeals to it must be made in terms of those values and not merely in terms of interests or simple demands. Hence the reformulation of demands and interests as rights.

The Canadian Supreme Court has the option either to override legislative acts or to defer to legislative decision making. The former action requires a specific constitutional justification; the latter course need only invoke the clause stipulating "subject only to such reasonable limits prescribed by law as can be demonstrably justified in a free and democratic society." The important decision by the Supreme Court to strike down certain sections of the Quebec language law (*Ford v. Attorney-General of Quebec, 1988*) is an illustration of the first; the decision of the Supreme Court to support mandatory retirement (*McKinney v. University of Guelph, 1990*), even though age discrimination was involved, is a significant example of the second. Of course, in the first instance there may subsequently be a new legislative act or the employment of the notwithstanding clause by government. When the section of the Criminal Code dealing with abortion was declared unconstitutional on fairly narrow grounds (*Morgenthaler, Smoling and Scott v. The Queen, 1988*), there was an attempt by the government to produce new legislation on the matter, but it failed in the Senate. In any case, there are clearly many new opportunities for conflict between legislatures and the judiciary that did not exist prior to the entrenchment of the Charter of Rights and Freedoms. From a democratic point of view, the most serious encroachment by the judiciary on the powers of Parliament has been the assertion by a provincial court and the Supreme Court to "read into" legislation content that is not expressly there.[7] This appears to be a rather clear instance of a tendency to make law rather than merely to interpret it.

We suggest that there may be three different attitudes toward the increased power of the judiciary. The radical democrat, one who places great emphasis on parliamentary supremacy and who assumes that an increase in the power of one body is a decrease in the power of the other, might not have been totally opposed to a limited Charter of Rights and Freedoms but would object to much of what is contained in the Constitution Act, 1982, mainly because of the increased power it gives to unelected officials over those who are elected. A moderate democrat might not object to the Charter at all but would prefer to see judges exercise restraint. The conditional democrat is one who is relatively indifferent to who makes the decisions, as long as they produce desired outcomes. This third category would include those who systematically or habitually have recourse to judicial decision making in preference to democratic decision making or to circumventing it. As long as the decisions of Parliament are acceptable or only mildly unacceptable, there is a commitment to the process. However, the legal avenue is simply an alternative course and may indeed be considered preferable. This may be a way of being liberal without being genuinely democratic. And this attitude is best illustrated in policy matters rather than in what are explicitly rights issues. For instance, one goes to court because one doesn't like an aspect of defence policy, such as the testing of Cruise missiles, or one doesn't favour an aspect of economic policy, such as anti-inflation measures.

In any case, the increased power of judges implied in the Charter of Rights and Freedoms, as well as the claims of judges to what have been called stretching prerogatives, may require the same kind of attention now expended on the behaviour of elected officials.

RECOMMENDED READING

Bernier, I., and A. Lajoie, eds. *The Supreme Court as an Instrument of Political Change.* Toronto: University of Toronto Press, 1985.

Fitzgerald, P., and K. McShane. *Looking at Law: Canada's Legal System,* 3rd ed. Ottawa: By Books, 1985.

McCormick, Peter, and Ian Greene. *Judges and Judging.* Toronto: James Lorimer and Company, 1991.

Millar, P.S., and C. Baar. *Judicial Administration in Canada.* Montreal: McGill-Queen's University Press, 1981.

Morton, F.L. *Law, Politics and the Judicial System in Canada.* Calgary: University of Calgary Press, 1984.

Russell, P.H. *The Third Branch of Government: A Political Science Study of the Canadian Judiciary.* Toronto: McGraw-Hill Ryerson, 1987.

NOTES

CHAPTER 1

1. The proposition that the United States had a mission to expand from the Atlantic to the Pacific, termed "manifest destiny," was believed by some people also to give the Americans the mandate to expand northward into Canada. At present, this threat seems more economic than military.

2. Jean-Charles Bonenfant, "Quebec," *Canadian Annual Review of Politics and Public Affairs, 1974* (Toronto: University of Toronto Press, 1975), p. 188.

3. *Quebec Policy on the French Language* (Québec: l'Editeur Officiel du Québec, 1977), p. 73.

4. René Durocher, "Quebec," *Canadian Annual Review of Politics and Public Affairs, 1977* (Toronto: University of Toronto Press, 1979), p. 151.

5. Ibid., pp. 152–53.

6. The seigneurs were responsible for dividing and settling the land, but J.C. Falardeau claims most of them failed in their obligations and had little permanent effect on the early settlers. See "Seventeenth Century Parish in French Canada," in Marcel Rioux and Yves Martin, eds., *French Canadian Society*, Carleton Library Series no. 18 (Toronto: McClelland and Stewart, 1964), pp. 19–32. This book of readings discusses the basic institutions of early French Canada and the evolution of French Canadian society.

7. In Upper and Lower Canada, groups known as the "Family Compact" and "Chateau Clique," respectively, surrounded the governors and tried to rule as wealthy oligarchies. See R.W. Langstone, *Responsible Government in Canada* (Toronto: Dent, 1931).

8. John Locke (1632–1704), in *Two Treatises of Government*, laid the foundations of a liberal political philosophy based on the natural rights possessed by man anterior to political society. Man's right to "life, liberty, and estates" is the end for which civil government is established, and it is only established by the consent of the governed. There is also provision made for rebellion in

Locke's theory if the majority consents to it. He is sometimes seen as one of the first proponents of individualistic political theory.

9. "Possessive individualism" refers to those aspects of the political philosophy of liberalism that tend to reduce man morally and socially to the status of a "proprietor" and to define the state and society in terms of the ease of exchange between these "proprietors." See C.B. Macpherson, *The Political Theory of Possessive Individualism: Hobbes to Locke* (Oxford: Clarendon Press, 1964).

10. Edmund Burke (1729–97) thought of political organization as a social organism evolving through time, the task of which is to promote such goals as social stability, cohesion, and integration. Attacking the natural rights theory, he maintained the preeminence of prescriptive right: "Our constitution is a prescriptive constitution; it is a constitution whose sole authority is that it has existed time out of mind" (*Reform of Representation in the House of Commons* (1782)). Because of the values he supported, Burke is generally considered to be an archetypal conservative, but liberals such as Laurier paid tribute to his influence.

11. See Chapter 4, pp. 89–93.

12. An English utilitarian and leader of the Philosophic Radicals, Jeremy Bentham (1748–1832) maintained that the aim of social striving should be the greatest good for the greatest number— good being equated with pleasure or the absence of pain. In his voluminous writings, we find an attempt to erect a system of jurisprudence that would codify and reform civil, penal, and constitutional law. In his *Constitutional Code*, he decided that rule by a democratic majority was most likely to produce the greatest good for the greatest number. Bentham was a strong critic of the great jurist Blackstone and a scathing critic of the natural rights theory. J.S. Mill said, "Bentham has been in this age and country the great questioner of things established" (*Mill on Bentham and Coleridge* (London: Chatto and Windus, 1950), p. 41).

13. Nineteenth-century reform in Britain was closely associated with extension of the franchise. Three reform acts were passed: in 1832, 1867, and 1884. See George Macaulay Trevelyan, *British History in the Nineteenth Century* (London: Longmans Green, 1924).

14. A possible exception to this might be seen in the attention that Quebec separatists and nationalists give to the patriots of the 1837 rebellion in Quebec led by Louis Joseph Papineau.

15. The "Quiet Revolution" refers to Quebec's political and social transformation in the early 1960s that coincided with the end of the Duplessis provincial regime. Under Lesage's Liberal government, industrialization was encouraged by attracting private investment and creating a vigorous public sector. Accompanying the processes of industrialization and bureaucratization was a new

positive Quebec nationalism. Thus, Quebec emphasized the ideas of "special status" and called for the decentralization of the federal political system through resistance to federal social-economic programs and constitutional reform. See Dale Posgate and Kenneth McRoberts, *Québec: Social Change and Political Crisis*, 3rd ed. (Toronto: McClelland and Stewart, 1988), Ch. 6.

16. It was for this reason that the Canadian Broadcasting Corporation was created and the Canadian Radio-Television and Telecommunications Commission has adopted rules on Canadian content in broadcasting. As well, the federal government took steps to remove the "Canadian" status of *Time* and *Reader's Digest* on the grounds that they are essentially American publications. Among other reasons, this move was taken to encourage the growth of Canadian news magazines.

17. Max Weber (1864–1920), a German sociologist, developed a treatment of authority that has been extremely fruitful in discussions concerning the relationship between political power and legitimacy. Claims are made to legitimacy, says Weber, on a legal/rational basis, a traditional basis, and on the basis of charisma. The third type of authority has become common currency among social scientists to such an extent that the term "charismatic" has been emptied of meaning, or at least has been given a meaning different from that assigned it by Weber. See also his notion of the routinization of charisma. See N.H. Gerth and C. Wright Mills, *From Max Weber: Essays in Sociology* (London: Oxford University Press, 1953). "Protestant ethic" is a term also derived from Max Weber, from his famous book *The Protestant Ethic and the Spirit of Capitalism*. Weber's thesis was that capitalism could not be accounted for in purely economic and technological terms, as Karl Marx and Auguste Comte believed, but was in large part the result of an ascetic secular morality associated with the stress of Calvinist theology on predestination and salvation. Weber's thesis is ideational, while Marx's is primarily materialistic. Like "charisma," "Protestant ethic" has entered into the ordinary vocabulary of social scientists.

18. See Gerald M. Craig, ed., *Lord Durham's Report*, Carleton Library Series no. 1 (Toronto: McClelland and Stewart, 1963).

CHAPTER 2

1. For example, regional representation in the federal Cabinet is required for any prime minister in forming the Cabinet. Speakers in the House of Commons in Canada have alternated between English speaking and French speaking, and that convention seems now to apply to the governors general as well.

2. Although the Act is divided into 11 parts containing 147 sections, the last two are of only historical interest. Part X deals with the intercolonial railway and consists of just one section, and Part XI consists of only two sections that deal with the admission of other colonies. Part X was repealed by the Statute Law Pension Act of 1893 and no longer appears in the document. See Section 145 in Appendix A.

3. Each colony had its valued history and traditions and wished to preserve them. See P.B. Waite, *Confederation Debates in the Province of Canada 1865*, Carleton Library Series no. 2 (Toronto: McClelland and Stewart, 1963).

4. The Quebec Act of 1774 protected the French-speaking settlers' language and religious rights; the Constitutional Act of 1791 separated Quebec into Upper Canada (Ontario) and Lower Canada (Quebec) and provided, among other things, for elected assemblies that met the demands of English-speaking settlers.

5. Although there was one legislature, important laws could not be passed unless both a majority of the French-speaking legislators and a majority of the English-speaking legislators approved. This was the dual-majority system.

6. As will be discussed later, the federal government has the power to disallow provincial legislation, but this has lapsed with disuse, and now each jurisdiction must take into account the activities of the other.

7. After World War I, Canada became a member of the League of Nations; in 1923 it signed the Halibut Fishing Treaty with the United States without any British involvement. In 1926 the Balfour Declaration stated that Canada and the other dominions were autonomous nations within the British Commonwealth of Nations; in 1931 Canada's autonomy was confirmed by the Statute of Westminster.

8. The popular view in English-speaking Canada is that the granting of separate school rights was a concession to the French Catholic minority. What has been conveniently forgotten is that the original constitutional guarantee was made to protect the English-speaking Protestant minority in Quebec. There have been several initiatives to curtail denominational control over education in two provinces. A successful referendum was held in Newfoundland to eliminate total denominational control over the educational system. The provincial government then petitioned the federal government to amend the Constitution. This amendment passed the House but was blocked by the Senate. However, the change will come into effect in 1997 if repassed by the House. Meanwhile, the government of Quebec has been considering changing denominational boards in the province's educational system to linguistically based bodies; this change would also require an amendment to Section 93 of the Canadian Constitution.

9. A possible example of this is the action of the governor general in Rhodesia in 1965, after the government made a unilateral declaration of independence that was clearly unconstitutional. The governor general's refusal to accept this had little effect as he had no political power to substantiate his position. While prerogative powers may theoretically exist to defend the Constitution, they have little practical application. In Australia in 1975, in a system similar to that of Canada, the governor general exercised his judgement about the ability to govern of the incumbent prime minister and Cabinet. In 1926 this issue was supposedly settled for Canada, but at some point in the future it is not inconceivable that a governor general could cite the 1975 Australian experience as a relevant precedent for the parliamentary system in Canada. In the Grenada situation of 1983, the governor general was the only legitimate political authority after a military coup.

10. See R.I. Cheffins, *The Constitutional Process in Canada*, 2nd ed. (Toronto: McGraw-Hill, 1976), p. 27. Professor Cheffins's book is a clear and concise exposition of the constitutional process. See also R.I. Cheffins and P.A. Johnson, *The Revised Canadian Constitution: Politics as Law* (Toronto: McGraw-Hill Ryerson, 1986), Ch. 3.

11. For instance, the War Measures Act, which was applied during the two world wars, empowered the Cabinet of the day to have control over practically every aspect of citizens' lives—for example, rationing, price controls, and the establishment of the necessary bureaucracy. When the Act was imposed during the FLQ crisis in Quebec in October 1970, many Canadians were concerned that the government had overreacted in giving itself extraordinary powers without sufficient justification. A new Emergencies Act, 1988 replaced the War Measures Act.

12. The Royal Commission on Government Organization (Ottawa: Queen's Printer, 1963), commonly known as the Glassco Commission, did an exhaustive study of the executive branch and made hundreds of recommendations to improve the efficiency of the public service. During the 1960s a Special Committee of the House of Commons recommended streamlining the rules of the House, which had not undergone any fundamental changes since Confederation. In 1984 the McGrath Committee was formed, and by June 1985 it had submitted three reports. Many of its recommendations were adopted and are in operation in the 1990s. See C.E.S. Franks, *The Parliament of Canada* (Toronto: University of Toronto Press, 1987), Ch. 6.

13. The history of constitutional change in the United States provides a useful comparison. Despite the existence of an amendment procedure, formal amendments are relatively rare, and constitutional change depends heavily on constitutional interpretations of the Supreme Court.

14. Cheffins, *Constitutional Process*, p. 126.
15. For a chronology of events, see David Milne, *The New Canadian Constitution* (Toronto: James Lorimer and Company, 1982), pp. 9–11.
16. The sovereigntist approach is embodied in *Québec-Canada, A New Deal* (Québec: l'Editeur Officiel du Québec, 1979). A belief that the federal system could be effective if there was a proper regard for respective jurisdictions was expressed by Jean-Luc Pepin in "Co-operative Federalism," in Paul Fox, ed., *Politics: Canada*, 3rd ed. (Toronto: McGraw-Hill, 1970), pp. 71–77. Later, however, Pepin, as cochairman of the Task Force on National Unity, made much broader suggestions for a restructured federalism in *A Future Together* (Ottawa: Minister of Supply and Services, 1979). Under Trudeau's guidance the federal government produced *A Time for Action: Toward the Renewal of the Canadian Federation* (Ottawa: Minister of Supply and Services, 1978). Finally, in 1980 the Constitutional Commission of the Quebec Liberal Party, under Claude Ryan, issued *A New Canadian Federation* (Montreal: The Liberal Party of Quebec, 1980).

CHAPTER 3

1. In order to describe the Canadian Constitution with its unitary state modifications, K.C. Wheare, in his classical study, called it quasi-federal. See *Federal Government*, 4th ed. (New York: Oxford University Press, 1964), p. 19.
2. In defiance of the Manitoba Act of 1870, by which Manitoba came into Confederation, the Manitoba legislature in 1890 enacted laws denying French-speaking Catholics public support for separate schools. Since Section 93(1) of the Constitution Act, 1867 forbade such legislation and Section 93(4) provided for remedial legislation by the federal government, the issue became a national one that strained English-French relations. The federal Conservative Party ultimately decided to enact remedial legislation, but it was turned out of office in 1896 before it could do so. The Laurier government, which took office in 1896, decided not to act, believing that the maintenance of provincial rights overrode the need to protect minority educational rights in this instance.
3. The landmark case was *Hodge v. The Queen* (1883). See R.I. Cheffins, *The Constitutional Process in Canada*, 2nd ed. (Toronto: McGraw-Hill, 1976), pp. 31–32.
4. When the federal government was challenged before the Supreme Court on the constitutionality of the Anti-Inflation Act, it defended its position on two grounds. First, it argued that curbing inflation

was a matter of concern to the nation as a whole, hence within the jurisdiction of the federal Parliament. Second, it argued that the legislation was necessary because there was an emergency. When the Supreme Court ruled in favour of the federal government by a vote of seven to two on July 12, 1976, it did not accept, however, both of these arguments. The Court refused Ottawa's claim to what could be far-reaching centralization of power—the national concern argument—but did uphold the right of Parliament to legislate in order to cope with what is seen as an economic crisis of national dimensions. Furthermore, the majority decision stated that it would not pass on the factual question of whether such a crisis existed; that is something for Parliament to decide. Even one of the dissenting opinions, that of Justice Beetz, agreed that the legislation would be valid if it were crisis legislation. He simply argued that the terms of the Act did not support this rationale.

5. For general reference, consult John Strick, *Canadian Public Finance*, 2nd ed. (Toronto: Holt, Rinehart and Winston, 1978).

6. Mitchell Hepburn was an onion farmer who, after attaining the leadership of the Liberal Party in Ontario, led them to victory in 1934. A demagogue of the first order, his one-man rule was soon at loggerheads with the federal government—even though after 1935 it was led by Mackenzie King, a fellow Liberal. William Aberhart was a high-school principal and radio evangelist who turned politician after embracing the Social Credit theory of the English engineer Major Douglas. He founded the Social Credit Party of Alberta and won a resounding victory in 1935. The party remained in power until 1971. Maurice Duplessis was a disenchanted Conservative in Quebec who founded the Union Nationale Party and led it to victory in 1936. Except for a period out of office from 1940 to 1944, he governed Quebec until his death in 1959. He allied himself with the Roman Catholic hierarchy and business leaders in Quebec to forestall social change that could make inroads into Quebec's traditional society. He stressed nationalism, and his regime was noteworthy for its political corruption.

7. Legislation included the nationalization of the Bank of Canada, the Prairie Farm Rehabilitation Act, and the Prairie Farm Assistance Act; the federal government also obtained agreement for an amendment to the Constitution Act, 1867 in 1940 that allowed the federal government to institute an unemployment insurance program.

8. A popular bumper sticker gives some flavour of their sentiments: "Let those eastern bastards freeze in the dark."

9. A good example of this would be the Atlantic Development Board, which was established in 1962 to foster economic growth and development in the Atlantic provinces. Since then a variety of policies and structures have been established, the latest being the Atlantic Canada Opportunities Agency (ACOA).

10. See the *Report on Intergovernmental Liaison on Fiscal and Economic Matters,* Institute of Intergovernmental Relations, Queen's University (Ottawa: Queen's Printer, 1968), Burns Report. The tables at the conclusion of this report show that officers of the provinces and the federal government form as many as 150 committees, and perhaps 50 of them meet annually or more often.

11. Donald V. Smiley, "Executive Federalism," *Canada in Question: Federalism in the Eighties,* 3rd ed. (Toronto: McGraw-Hill Ryerson, 1980), Ch. 4.

12. During the heated discussion on the federal government's White Paper on Taxation published in 1970, the Ontario Treasury Department forecast that the new taxation rates would yield much higher returns than the federal finance experts had estimated. On this basis, the Ontario government accused the federal authorities of introducing a tax increase under the guise of tax reform.

CHAPTER 4

1. For a book that deals with the role of ideology in Canadian party politics, see W. Christian and C. Campbell, *Political Parties and Ideologies in Canada,* 3rd ed. (Toronto: McGraw-Hill Ryerson, 1990). The authors argue for the importance of ideological diversity in Canadian politics against those who stress consensus politics. They maintain that "most liberals are in the Liberal Party, most conservatives in the Conservative Party, and most socialists in the NDP" (p. ix). Where we speak of four ideologies (conservatism, liberalism, socialism, and populism), they speak of nationalism instead of populism.

2. It is ordinary usage to denote the political party by employing a capital letter (Liberal, Conservative), while the philosophy or ideology is denoted by a small letter (liberal, conservative, liberals, conservatives). Thus, in one instance we refer to Liberal policies, meaning the policies of a party; in many instances we refer to the perception and ideology of liberals, meaning ideologues. Were this distinction not clearly understood, it might seem ridiculous to say that not all liberals are to be found in the Liberal Party.

3. For an examination of the influence of revolutionary socialism in Canada, see Norman Penner, *The Canadian Left* (Scarborough: Prentice-Hall Canada, 1977). Revolutionary socialism is a marginal phenomenon in Canada. Genuinely Canadian political ideologies are not revolutionary.

4. Of course, following Michael Oakeshott, one can distinguish between conservatism as an ideology (doctrine) and as a disposition. "My theme is not a creed or a doctrine, but a disposition. To be

conservative is to be disposed to think and behave in certain manners . . ." *Rationalism in Politics* (London: Methuen, 1962), p. 168. Oakeshott is often taken as the very model of the contemporary conservative. However, his essay "The Political Economy of Freedom" (ibid., pp. 37–58) is a sympathetic reflection on the neoliberalism of the Chicago school. We will see later that what was formerly called neoliberalism has now become known as neoconservatism. Thus, Hannah F. Pitkin's excellent study of Oakeshott's political philosophy figures in a recent book, edited by Lewis A. Coser and Irving Howe, *The New Conservatives, a Critique from the Left* (New York: New American Library, 1977), pp. 243–88.

5. See George Macauley Trevelyan, *British History in the Nineteenth Century* (London: Longmans Green, 1924), especially pp. 195–201.

6. Louis Hartz, *The Founding of New Societies* (New York: Harcourt Brace, 1964). Included is an article by Kenneth D. McRae entitled "The Structure of Canadian History." For a further discussion of the issues brought up by Hartz and his followers, note also the well-known article by Gad Horowitz, "Conservatism, Liberalism, and Socialism in Canada: An Interpretation," *Canadian Journal of Economics and Political Science* 32 (May 1966), pp. 143–71. George Grant compares Canadian and American political values in *Lament for a Nation*, Carleton Library Series no. 50 (Toronto: McClelland and Stewart, 1965), *Philosophy in the Mass Age* (Vancouver: Copp Clark, 1966), and *Technology and Empire: Perspectives on North America* (Toronto: House of Anansi, 1969).

7. See W.C. Soderlund, R.C. Nelson, and R.H. Wagenberg, "A Critique of the Hartz Theory of Political Development as Applied to Canada," *Comparative Politics* 12.1 (October 1979).

8. Alexander Brady, *Democracy in the Dominions* (Toronto: University of Toronto Press, 1958), p. 99.

9. *Ibid.*, p. 522.

10. André Siegfried, *The Race Question in Canada*, Carleton Library Series no. 29 (Toronto: McClelland and Stewart, 1966), p. 15.

11. Robert Kelley, *The Transatlantic Persuasion: The Liberal Democratic Mind in the Age of Gladstone* (New York: Alfred A. Knopf, 1969), p. 52.

12. Wilfrid Laurier, "Political Liberalism," *The Speeches of Wilfrid Laurier* (Montreal: Librairie Beauchemin, 1920), p. 52.

13. The Jesuits' Estates were properties in Quebec over whose disposition there was considerable controversy. In addition to the relatively simple matter of the disposition of property, there was also the issue of provincial-federal relationships and, as was often the case in the past in Quebec, a religious issue. The settlement of the Jesuits' Estates controversy is covered in Donald Creighton's *John A. Macdonald: The Old Chieftain* (Toronto: Macmillan, 1955), pp. 514–20.

14. Laurier, "Political Liberalism," p. 73.
15. *Ibid.*, p. 76.
16. Wilfrid Laurier, "The Jesuits' Estates," *The Speeches of Wilfrid Laurier*, p. 521. It is interesting to note that Henri Bourassa, one-time wayfarer with Laurier in the Liberal Party, felt called upon to make a similar declaration in 1900: "I am a Liberal of the English school. I am a disciple of Burke, of Fox, of Bright, of Gladstone, and of all those Little Englanders who have made England and the Empire what they are today" (in Brady, *Democracy in the Dominions*, p. 527).
17. See Brady, *Democracy in the Dominions*, p. 109.
18. Laurier, "The Jesuits' Estates," *The Speeches of Wilfrid Laurier*, p. 522.
19. C.B. Macpherson, *The Political Theory of Possessive Individualism* (London: Oxford University Press, 1962).
20. Theodore Lowi, *The End of Liberalism* (New York: Norton, 1969). Hugh Thorburn discusses Lowi's concept of interest-group liberalism or pluralism as it ties into the workings of elite accommodation in Canada, not only between political elites but also in the interplay between political leaders and business leaders, particularly foreign business leaders ("Canadian Pluralist Democracy in Crisis," *Canadian Journal of Political Science* 11.4 (December 1978), pp. 723–38).
21. We refer to the fine collection of essays edited by Paul Pross, *Pressure Group Behaviour in Canadian Politics* (Toronto: McGraw-Hill Ryerson, 1975).
22. Brady, *Democracy in the Dominions*, p. 90.
23. J.A. Corry, *Democratic Government and Politics* (Toronto: University of Toronto Press, 1946). See especially Ch. 10, "Pressure Groups."
24. Brady, *Democracy in the Dominions*, particularly p. 12.
25. Not so long ago, the ideology now termed neoconservatism was more widely known as neoliberalism, in that it was considered to be a renewal of the original individualist liberalism, with particular emphasis on economic freedom, the market economy, and the minimal state. The term "neoliberalism" was somewhat misleading, as it was the opposite of the new liberalism expressed, for example, in Leonard Hobhouse's *Liberalism* (New York: Oxford University Press, 1964). It is significant that F.A. Hayek, one of the foremost exponents of the ideology we are about to examine, insists on calling himself a neoliberal. See the chapter entitled "Why I Am Not a Conservative" in *The Constitution of Liberty* (Chicago: University of Chicago Press, 1960), pp. 395–411. We bow to custom, then, in speaking of this ideology as neoconservatism; it appears after the section on liberalism because it arises as a reaction against it.

26. See Michael Freeden, *The New Liberalism* (Oxford: The Clarendon Press, 1978).

27. F.A. Hayek, *The Political Order of a Free People*, Vol. 3 of *Law, Legislation, and Liberty* (London: Routledge and Kegan Paul, 1979). Hayek refers to the "playball of group interests" and a "bargaining democracy" (p. 99).

28. *The Globe and Mail* devoted several pages to the neoconservative phenomenon on August 27, 1979. The Fraser Institute in Vancouver is a kind of neoconservative "think tank" in Canada.

29. Milton and Rose Friedman, *Free to Choose* (New York: Harcourt Brace Jovanovich, 1980). For a more academic formulation of Milton Friedman's position, consult *Capitalism and Freedom* (Chicago: University of Chicago Press, 1962).

30. C.B. Macpherson, *Democracy in Alberta* (Toronto: University of Toronto Press, 1953), p. 241.

31. Charles Taylor, *The Pattern of Politics* (Toronto: McClelland and Stewart, 1970).

32. A good example of the combination of socialism and nationalism can be found in James and Robert Laxer, *The Liberal Idea of Canada: Pierre Trudeau and the Question of Canada's Survival* (Toronto: James Lorimer and Company, 1977). The book reflects current democratic-socialist sentiment in Canada that supports a "planned economy" (p. 129).

33. Richard Hofstadter, "North America," in Ghita Ionescu and Ernest Gellner, eds., *Populism: Its Meanings and National Characteristics* (London: Weidenfeld and Nicolson, 1969).

34. Macpherson, *Democracy in Alberta*. See also J.A. Irving, *The Social Credit Movement in Alberta* (Toronto: University of Toronto Press, 1959).

35. Andrew Heywood, *Political Ideologies: An Introduction* (London: Macmillan, 1992), pp. 229–39.

CHAPTER 5

1. For a discussion of this notion of politics, see Bernard Crick, *In Defence of Politics* (London: Pelican Books, 1964), p. 21.

2. The nature of power and influence is discussed by Robert A. Dahl, *Modern Political Analysis*, 5th ed. (Englewood Cliffs: Prentice-Hall, 1991), Chs. 3 and 4.

3. In their book *Canadian Political Parties: Origin, Character, Impact* (Scarborough: Prentice-Hall of Canada, 1975), pp. 18–19, F.C. Engelmann and Mildred A. Schwartz talk in terms of cadre parties that are success oriented and nonideological and of mass parties that are ideologically oriented and less able to construct coalitions of voters.

4. An account of the Waffle movement can be found in W. Christian and C. Campbell, *Political Parties and Ideologies in Canada*, 3rd ed. (Toronto: McGraw-Hill Ryerson, 1990), pp. 31, 209–13, 215-16, 222, 262, 267–68, and in Conrad Winn and John McMenemy, *Political Parties in Canada* (Toronto: McGraw-Hill Ryerson, 1976), p. 40.

5. See Lawrence LeDuc, "Citizens' Revenge: The Canadian Voter and the 1993 Federal Election," in Paul W. Fox and Graham White, eds. *Politics Canada*, 8th ed. (Toronto: McGraw-Hill, 1995), pp. 140–54.

6. Our use of the term "class" is based on a classification of groups with similar characteristics. These characteristics include income, occupation, and education. See John Porter, *The Vertical Mosaic* (Toronto: University of Toronto Press, 1965), Ch. 1. For a more specific comparison of the effect of social class and voting, see Robert R. Alford, *Party and Society: The Anglo-American Democracies* (Chicago: Rand McNally, 1963).

7. This form of party politics is consistent with a theory of society known as consociational democracy (in which decision making is largely a matter of agreement between leaders of various social groupings) or, as it is usually referred to, elite accommodation. See Arend Lijphart, "Consociational Democracy," K.D. McRae, "Consociationalism and the Canadian Political System," and S.J.R. Noel, "Consociational Democracy and Canadian Federalism," in Kenneth D. McRae, ed., *Consociational Democracy: Political Accommodation in Segmented Societies*, Carleton Library Series no. 79 (Toronto: McClelland and Stewart, 1974).

8. See Elections Canada, *Canada's Electoral System* (Ottawa, 1988).

9. The term "riding" is used interchangeably with constituency.

10. Both the Liberals and Progressive Conservatives have had policy discussions that involved not only intellectuals and senior party officials but also constituency delegates. Two such conferences were the Progressive Conservative Priorities for Canada Conference held in Niagara Falls, October 9–13, 1969, and the Liberals at Harrison Hot Springs, BC, November 21-23, 1970.

11. While most Canadians are not politically active, a large majority of them do identify with particular parties to varying degrees of consistency and intensity.

    Party Identification (based on data from the 1979 National Election Study conducted by Jon Pammett, Lawrence LeDuc, Jane Jenson, and Harold Clarke)

    (a) *Direction of Party Identification*

None at any level	5.1%
Identified only at federal level	4.2%
Identified only at provincial level	5.9%
Different identification at each level	23.0%
Identification stronger at federal level	9.7%
Identification stronger at provincial level	11.0%
Consistent party identification at both levels	41.1%

(b) *Intensity of Party Identification*

	Fed.	Prov.	Both
Very strong	20.7%	34.4%	20.5%
Fairly strong	48.9%	47.7%	31.5%
Weak	30.4%	17.9%	8.5%
Federal stronger than provincial			18.0%
Provincial stronger than federal			21.6%

See also H. Clarke et al., *Political Choice in Canada* (Toronto: McGraw-Hill Ryerson, 1979), Ch. 6, and Allan Kornberg et al., *Citizen Politicians, Canada* (Durham: Carolina Academic Press, 1979). Even more recently, the subject is discussed in William Mishler, *Political Participation in Canada* (Toronto: Macmillan of Canada, 1979), pp. 42–51, and in Allan Kornberg, William Mishler, and Harold C. Clarke, *Representative Democracy in the Canadian Provinces* (Scarborough: Prentice-Hall Canada, 1982), pp. 99–104.

12. The capital punishment debate in 1976 was almost a classic confrontation between the two points of view, with abolitionists arguing that Members of Parliament should look to their own consciences in deciding the issue, while retentionists urged MPs to follow public opinion, which was clearly in favour of capital punishment.

13. Sylvia B. Bashavkin, *Toeing the Lines: Women and Party Politics in English Canada* (Toronto: University of Toronto Press, 1985), and Janine Brodie, *Women and Politics in Canada* (Toronto: McGraw-Hill Ryerson, 1985).

CHAPTER 6

1. John C. Courtney, "Parliament and Representation: The Unfinished Agenda of Electoral Redistributions," *Canadian Journal of Political Science* (December 1988), pp. 675–90.

2. *Report of the Electoral Boundaries Commission for the Province of Ontario, 1983*, and *Revision of Federal Electoral Boundaries. Federal Election Boundaries Commission for Ontario*, 1994.

3. Bill C-63, an act to amend the Canada Elections Act, the Parliament of Canada Act, and the Referendum Act, Royal Assent, December 18, 1996.

4. The Canada Mortgage and Housing Corporation, in granting mortgages, requires the services of lawyers in the areas where the mortgages apply. Those lawyers who support the party in power will

receive the legal fees that the corporation is required to pay. Public-relations firms in the larger Canadian centres may also be in line for substantial contracts when various types of advertising programs must be undertaken by the government. Both major parties maintain "patronage lists" naming those people and firms to whom they may direct business.

5. *Elections Canada Thirty-Fifth General Election 1993 Contributions and Expenses of Registered Political Parties and Candidates* (Ottawa: Chief Electoral Officer, 1995), pp. xvii–xxi.

6. In the past those candidates who were not particularly wealthy found it much more difficult to undertake a successful campaign. Often a candidate had to borrow substantial amounts of money to contest an election. Many excellent candidates backed away from seeking a nomination because of their lack of financial resources. The Election Expenses Act mitigated, but did not eliminate, this situation. See K.Z. Paltiel, *Political Party Financing in Canada* (Toronto: McGraw-Hill, 1970), and F. Leslie Seidle and Khayyam Zev Paltiel, "Party Finance, the Election Expenses Act, and Campaign Spending in 1979 and 1980," in Howard R. Penniman, ed., *Canada at the Polls, 1979 and 1980* (Washington and London: American Enterprise Institute for Public Policy Research, 1981), pp. 226–79.

7. H. Clarke et al., "Voting Behaviour and the Outcome of the 1979 Federal Election: The Impact of Leaders and Issues," *Canadian Journal of Political Science* 15 (September 1982), pp. 517–52.

8. Walter C. Soderlund et al., *Media and Elections in Canada* (Toronto: Holt, Rinehart and Winston of Canada, 1984).

9. See Jon Pammett et al., "The 1974 Federal Election: A Preliminary Report," Carleton Occasional Papers no. 4, (Ottawa: Department of Political Science, Carleton University), pp. 9–12 and the subsequent book by these authors, *Political Choice in Canada* (Toronto: McGraw-Hill Ryerson, 1979).

10. *Politics and the Media: An Examination of the Issues Raised by the Quebec Referendum and the May 1979 and 1980 Federal Elections* (Toronto: Reader's Digest Foundation, 1981).

11. The contending arguments regarding the electoral system appear in the *Canadian Journal of Political Science*. Alan C. Cairns, "The Electoral System and the Party System in Canada 1921–1965," *CJPS* 1.1 (March 1968), pp. 55–80; and J.A.A. Lovink, "On Analysing the Impact of the Electoral System on the Party System in Canada," *CJPS* 3.4 (December 1970), pp. 497–516. We are indebted to the National Election Study of 1974 for our data.

12. See Lawrence LeDuc, "Citizens' Revenge: The Canadian Voter and the 1993 Federal Election," in Paul Fox and Graham White, eds. *Politics Canada*, 8th ed. (Toronto: McGraw-Hill, 1995), pp. 140–54.

13. See Harold Clarke et al., *Political Choice in Canada,* for the most comprehensive work available on Canadian voting behaviour. See also Allan Frizzell et al., eds., *The Canadian General Election of 1993* (Ottawa: Carleton University Press, 1994).

14. The data used in this comparison are taken from *The Gallup Report* published by The Canadian Institute of Public Opinion, released on July 20, 1968.

CHAPTER 7

1. Our terminology is taken from F.C. Englemann and Mildred A. Schwartz, *Canadian Political Parties: Origin, Character, Impact* (Scarborough: Prentice-Hall, 1975), Ch. 7. For works that are mainly concerned with interest- and pressure-group behaviour, see Robert Presthus, *Elite Accommodation in Canadian Politics* (Toronto: Macmillan, 1973), Paul Pross, *Group Politics and Public Policy,* 2nd ed. (Toronto: Oxford University Press, 1992), and W.D. Coleman and Grace Scogstad, *Policy Communities and Public Policy in Canada* (Toronto: Copp Clark Pitman, 1990).

2. See Linda Trimble, "Becoming Full Citizens: Women and Politics in Canada," in R. Krause and R. Wagenberg, eds., *Introductory Readings in Canadian Government and Politics,* 2nd ed. (Toronto: Copp Clark, 1995), pp. 261–86.

3. The doctors' strike is discussed by Janet Walker Gouldner in an addendum to S.M. Lipset's book *Agrarian Socialism* (New York: Anchor Books, Doubleday, 1968), pp. 391–404.

4. This particular case was documented by Geoffrey Stevens in a two-part article in *The Globe and Mail* of December 5 and 6, 1969. Stevens's source was an MA thesis by Ronald W. Lang at the University of Waterloo.

5. See Robert M. Campbell and Leslie A. Pal, *The Real Worlds of Canadian Politics: Cases in Process and Policy,* 3rd ed. (Peterborough: Broadview Press, 1994), pp. 27–82.

6. Colin Campbell, *The Canadian Senate: A Lobby from Within* (Toronto: Macmillan, 1978). The fall from grace of Walter Gordon, minister of finance for the Pearson government, after presenting his budget on June 13, 1963, was at least in part attributable to his unpopularity among business interests. On June 19, 1963, he withdrew his proposal for a 30% takeover tax on foreign interests. This was especially ironic considering the later concern regarding foreign economic control in Canada that resulted in the Foreign Investment Review Act. Gordon appears to be having the last laugh. For a well-written account of these events, see Peter C. Newman, *Distemper of Our Times* (Toronto: McClelland and Stewart, 1968).

7. While Presthus, speaking of the Canadian political situation, treats interest-group activity in the context of the theory of elite accommodation (*Elite Accommodation in Canadian Politics*, Ch. 1), Theodore Lowi refers to the American political system as "interest-group liberalism" (*The End of Liberalism* [New York: Norton, 1969], p. 46). Our own position places the emphasis on interest-group conflict.

8. Frederick J. Fletcher and Robert J. Drummond, *Attitude Trends, 1960–1978* (Montreal: Institute for Research on Public Policy, 1979).

9. Among those who strongly favoured conscription for overseas service during the two world wars, there is often a convenient disregard for the fact that many people outside Quebec objected to having young men conscripted for service overseas.

10. R.H. Wagenberg et al., "Campaigns, Images and Polls: Mass Media Coverage of the 1984 Canadian Election," *Canadian Journal of Political Science* 21 (March 1988), pp. 117–29.

11. This is a three-volume report of the Special Senate Committee on Mass Media (generally known as the Davey Report after its chairman, Senator Keith Davey). Volume 1, *The Uncertain Mirror*, gives a graphic description of the present lamentable state of the Canadian mass media. The report was published by Information Canada in 1970.

12. Arthur Siegel, *Politics and the Media in Canada* (Toronto: McGraw-Hill Ryerson, 1983), pp. 110–11. See also W.I. Romanow and W.C. Soderlund, *Media Canada: An Introductory Analysis*, 2nd ed. (Toronto: Copp Clark Pitman, 1996), especially Part 3.

13. Advertising in American magazines that are distributed in Canada may not be claimed as a business expense for tax purposes. However, the Canadian editions of *Time* and *Reader's Digest* were given Canadian status, and thus advertisers were not deterred from buying space in those magazines.

14. Another problem in the area of the media involves a question of federalism, in that Quebec insists that it control the regulation of cable television within its borders as an instrument for propagating Québécois culture.

15. See John Porter, *The Vertical Mosaic*, Part 2. An attempt to update Porter's research has been made by Wallace Clement, *The Canadian Corporate Elite*, Carleton Library Series no. 89 (Toronto: McClelland and Stewart, 1975). At the same time, Peter C. Newman, in a journalistic and more personalized approach to the question, came out with *The Canadian Establishment* (Toronto: McClelland and Stewart, 1975), Vol. 1, followed by *The Canadian Establishment: The Acquisitors* (Toronto: McClelland and Stewart, 1990), Vol. 2.

16. The concept of power and influence and the mistakes that can be made in analyzing them are effectively discussed in Robert A. Dahl, *Modern Political Analysis*, 5th ed. (Englewood Cliffs: Prentice-Hall, 1991), Ch. 3, pp. 12–34.

17. Allan Kornberg et al., *Representative Democracy in the Canadian Provinces* (Scarborough: Prentice-Hall Canada, 1982), pp. 70–73.

18. See Porter, *The Vertical Mosaic*, p. 369, and Gad Horowitz's contribution in Trevor Lloyd and Jack McLeod, eds., *Agenda 1970: Proposals for a Creative Politics* (Toronto: University of Toronto Press, 1968).

19. See the anthology edited by Elia Zureik and Robert M. Pike, *Socialization and Values in Canadian Society*, 2 vols. (Toronto: McClelland and Stewart, 1975), and Jon H. Pammett and Michael S. Whittington, *Foundations of Political Culture: Political Socialization in Canada* (Toronto: Macmillan, 1976).

20. Peter C. Newman, in a journalist's assessment, argues that, in a relatively short period of time, Canadians have undergone what might be called a revolutionary change in attitudes (*The Canadian Revolution 1985–1995: From Deference to Defiance* (Toronto: Viking, 1995)). Neil Nevitte, a political scientist, also finds a decline in deference based on survey research (*The Decline of Deference: Canadian Value Change in Cross-National Perspective* (Peterborough: Broadview Press, 1996)). Another book, based on interviews with 2600 Canadians regarding social values, finds growing rejection of institutions and traditional elites. While religion, for instance, continues to play a major role in American politics, according to the author it is not a significant factor in Canadian politics, and he believes that its declining role will continue (Michael Adams, *Sex in the Snow: Canadian Social Values at the End of the Millennium* (Toronto: Viking/Penguin, 1997)).

21. See John C. Johnstone's *Young People's Images of Canadian Society: An Opinion Survey of Canadian Youth 13 to 20 Years of Age*, Studies of the Royal Commission on Bilingualism and Biculturalism, Vol. 11 (Ottawa: Queen's Printer, 1969), Information Canada. On the socialization process in Canada, see R. Pike and E. Zureik, *Socialization and Values in Contemporary Canada*, Vol. 1, *Political Socialization*; Vol. 2, *Socialization, Social Stratification and Ethnicity*, Carleton Library Series nos. 84 and 85 (Toronto: McClelland and Stewart, 1975). See as well Mildred A. Schwartz, *Politics and Territory: The Sociology of Regional Persistence in Canada* (Montreal: McGill-Queen's University Press, 1974); Harold Clarke et al., *Political Choice in Canada* (Toronto: McGraw-Hill Ryerson, 1979); and D.J. Elkins and R. Simeon, *Small Worlds: Parties and Provinces in Canadian Political Life* (Toronto: Methuen, 1980).

CHAPTER 8

1. See Chapter 2, note 11.
2. Much of the French-speaking population of Quebec has historically been unenthusiastic about the symbolism of such a British institution, even after 1952, when Canadians, rather than British noblemen, began to be appointed, with anglophones and francophones alternating in office. Among younger Canadians of all ethnic backgrounds, there is massive indifference to the Crown. Nonetheless, the removal of the monarchy has not become a major issue in Canada, as it has in Australia, at the end of the twentieth century.
3. See Peter Aucoin, "Prime Ministerial Leadership, Position, Power and Politics," in Maureen Mancuso et al., eds., *Leaders and Leadership in Canada* (Toronto: Oxford University Press, 1994), pp. 99–117.
4. This was in the election of 1874. In 1917 the Union Government, which combined the Conservative Party and the proconscription Liberals, received 57% of the vote. One of the factors that helped the Unionists was the Military Voters Act and the War Time Elections Act. These measures made the election atypical. Thus, this election was neither a straight party contest nor was it conducted on the basis of a fair franchise. See J. Murray Beck, *Pendulum of Power: Canada's Federal Elections* (Scarborough: Prentice-Hall, 1968), Ch. 13.
5. In 1970 Prime Minister Trudeau took the new step of terminating appointments of parliamentary secretaries after two years and appointing new ones. This had the effect of giving more MPs a chance to assist ministers in their work. Under the Reorganization of Government Act in 1971, no ceiling is placed on the number of parliamentary secretaries who may be appointed. All these secretaries receive extra remuneration above their salaries as MPs.
6. For a somewhat gossipy journalistic account of the role of Eddy Goldenberg, Chrétien's right-hand man in the PMO, who bears the title senior policy advisor, see Jennifer Curtis, "Good as Goldenberg," *Saturday Night*, February 1997, pp. 42–48.
7. The view that Canada is evolving toward a presidential system was argued by Denis Smith in "President and Parliament: The Transformation of Parliamentary Government in Canada," in O. Kruhlak, R. Schultz, and S. Pobihushchy, eds., *Canadian Political Process* (Toronto: Holt, Rinehart and Winston, 1970), pp. 367–82. See also Thomas A. Hockin, *The Apex of Power: The Prime Minister and Political Leadership in Canada*, 2nd ed. (Scarborough: Prentice-Hall, 1977) for a number of essays that deal with various aspects of the prime minister's role, and Leslie Pal and David Taras, eds., *Prime Ministers and Premiers: Political Leadership and Public Policy in Canada* (Toronto: Prentice-Hall, 1988).

8. Machiavelli advised that "violence should be inflicted once for all; people will then forget what it tastes like and so be less resentful. Benefits should be conferred gradually; and in that way they will taste better" (*The Prince*, George Bull, trans. [Harmondsworth, UK: Penguin Books, 1961]).

9. This was underlined in the James Coyne affair of 1961. The then-minister of finance, Donald Fleming, clashed with Coyne, who was governor of the Bank of Canada, as to the proper monetary and fiscal policy the government should pursue. Fleming introduced a bill into the House that in effect dismissed Coyne from office as governor of the Bank. Although this passed the House of Commons, the Senate, after hearings in committee, defeated the bill and allowed Coyne to resign. The case is documented in Peter C. Newman, *Renegade in Power* (Toronto: McClelland and Stewart, 1963), pp. 295–321.

CHAPTER 9

1. See Chapter 2.

2. See W.L. White and J.C. Strick, *Policy, Politics and the Treasury Board in Canadian Government* (Toronto: Survey Research Associates, 1970), pp. 17–18. For a detailed history of the early period, see R.M. Dawson, *The Civil Service of Canada* (London: Oxford University Press, 1929).

3. The Financial Administration Act of 1952 as amended in 1967 lists 26 government departments, 13 departmental corporations, 15 agency corporations, 14 proprietary corporations, and 46 diverse agencies designated as departments for purposes of the Act. This classification shows the nature of the budgetary control exercised by the Treasury Board and Parliament over these units. See A.M. Willms, "Crown Agencies," in A.M. Willms and W.D.K. Kernaghan, eds., *Public Administration in Canada: Selected Readings* (Toronto: Methuen, 1968), pp. 158–66. While reorganizations, additions, and deletions to all of the categories established by the Act have taken place, the essential definitions still pertain in the 1990s.

4. Royal Commission on Government Organization, 5 (Ottawa: Queen's Printer, 1963), p. 102.

5. See White and Strick, *Policy*, pp. 119–22.

6. Max Weber is noted for his theory of bureaucracy. For Weber, a bureaucracy is an organization that has legal authority. In its ideal form, it is a highly centralized hierarchical system in which there are well-defined functions, a system of appeal from the lower echelons to the higher, as well as a technique for discipline. Members

are recruited on the basis of examinations or other forms of competition, are given sufficient, though differential, remuneration,
are protected by civil service status or tenure, and no functionary
is proprietor of his post. The bureaucrat is an anonymous execu-
tor of policy. This impersonality is one of the basic traits of a
bureaucracy. See *Max Weber on Law in Economy and Society*, Max
Rheinstein, ed., Max Rheinstein and Edward Shils, trans.
(Cambridge: Harvard University Press, 1954), Part 3, Ch. 6.

7. An exception to this was introduced in Saskatchewan by the CCF:
   a civil servant may take a leave of absence to run for elective
   office in that province. If the individual wins, he or she resigns the
   position, but if he or she loses, the position is regained.

8. Deputy minister is the normal title for the top person. However,
   there are other designations that hold equivalent rank—for example, clerk of the Privy Council, secretary of the Treasury Board,
   and undersecretary of state for external affairs. Because of the
   central nature of the position, clerk of the Privy Council is often
   regarded as the top public servant.

9. See Donald C. Rowat, ed., *The Ombudsman: Citizen's Defender*,
   2nd ed. (Toronto: University of Toronto Press, 1968).

CHAPTER 10

1. The first elected assemblies in what is now Canada met in 1758 in
   Halifax, Nova Scotia; in 1773 in Prince Edward Island; and in 1784
   in New Brunswick. Upper and Lower Canada first established
   elected assemblies in 1791. See R.M. Dawson, *The Government of
   Canada*, 4th rev. ed. (Toronto: University of Toronto Press, 1963),
   Ch. 1. The Dawson text was the definitive book on Canadian government for a generation after its publication in 1947.

2. This has happened only four times since 1867. The first instance
   was in 1926, when Arthur Meighen's short-lived government was
   defeated on a vote of confidence; the second time was in 1963,
   when the Diefenbaker government suffered a similar fate; more
   recently, in 1974 and 1979, the minority Trudeau and Clark governments failed to win the confidence of the House on their
   respective budget proposals. On one other occasion, the Pearson
   government, in February 1968, lost a vote in the third reading of a
   bill on taxation. Taxation legislation has always been considered to
   be a matter of confidence. However, in this instance the government refused to resign on the basis that the bill had reached third
   reading and had therefore received acceptance in principle on second reading. Consequently, Pearson asked for a vote of confidence, which was won.

3. Two of the better-known exponents of this view are Denis Smith, "President and Parliament: The Transformation of Parliamentary Government in Canada," in Thomas A. Hockin, ed., *Apex of Power: The Prime Minister and Political Leadership in Canada* (Scarborough: Prentice-Hall, 1971), pp. 224–41, and Roman R. March, *The Myth of Parliament* (Scarborough: Prentice-Hall, 1974). An excellent study of the Parliament in Canada is found in R.J. Jackson and M.M. Atkinson, *The Canadian Legislative System*, 2nd ed. (Toronto: Macmillan, 1980). More recent is C.E.S. Franks, *The Parliament of Canada* (Toronto: University of Toronto Press, 1987).

4. For an analysis of the impact of this innovation, see R.G. Price and Harold D. Clarke, "Television and the House of Commons," in Clarke et al., eds., *Parliament, Policy and Representation* (Toronto: Methuen, 1980), pp. 58–83.

5. Ibid. See Allan Kornberg, *Canadian Legislative Behaviour* (New York: Holt, Rinehart and Winston, 1967). Another study that examines the motives of provincial legislators for initiating their legislative careers is Harold D. Clarke, Richard G. Price, and Robert Krause, "Backbenchers," in David J. Bellamy, Jon H. Pammett, and Donald C. Rowat, eds., *The Provincial Political Systems: Comparative Essays* (Toronto: Methuen, 1976), pp. 220–21. See also Ch. 12 in Allan Kornberg and William Mischler, *Influence in Parliament* (Durham, NC: Duke University Press, 1976), and R.G. Price et al., "The Socialization of Freshman Legislators: The Case of Canadian MPs," in J. Pammett and M. Wittington, eds., *Foundations of Political Culture* (Toronto: Macmillan, 1976).

6. Sometimes, when important party figures are not elected in a constituency, an elected member from a safe constituency for his or her party may resign to create a vacancy. Usually, the constituency will accept this since it gets prestigious representation. This happened in the case of Mackenzie King in 1925, who lost his seat in the constituency of York, Ontario, and was subsequently elected in Prince Albert, Saskatchewan. More recently, Tommy Douglas, leader of the NDP from 1961 to 1971, lost in Regina in 1962, but a vacancy was made by a resignation of a member in British Columbia that provided Douglas with a seat. When Douglas lost again in 1968, he refused to accept a seat through the resignation of any sitting NDP member, but he returned after the death of Colin Cameron from Vancouver Island.

7. In April 1967 the Liberal Party in effect invited Ralph Cowan, MP for York Humber, to leave its caucus. This was after a long series of statements by Cowan that were critical of his party's policy with regard to French-English relations in Canada. Although not expelled from the caucus, his constituency organization refused him the nomination in the 1968 election. He ran as an independent Liberal and lost. David Kilgour and Alex Kindy voted against the Goods and

Services Tax in 1990 and were expelled by the Progressive Conservative caucus. In 1996 John Nunziata was expelled by the Liberal caucus for failing to support the Liberal government's budget, especially the retaining of the Goods and Services Tax.

8. This was evident in the behaviour of the then-speaker, René Beaudoin, during the Pipeline Debate of 1956. See H.G. Thorburn, "Parliament and Policy Making: The Case of the Trans-Canada Gas Pipeline," *Canadian Journal of Economics and Political Science* 23.4 (November 1957), pp. 516–31.

9. The NDP did contest the election in the constituency of Stormont, where Lucien Lamoureux, speaker in the previous House when he had sat as a Liberal, ran as an independent. The local NDP organization felt that the constituency should not be denied partisan representation. There have been suggestions that the speaker should be elected from a constituency called "Parliament Hill," whose electors would be the 301 Members of Parliament.

10. House of Commons, Debates, 134, no. 121, 2nd Session, 35th Parliament, Monday, February 3, 1997 (Ottawa: Queen's Printer).

11. See Colin Campbell, *The Canadian Senate: A Lobby from Within* (Toronto: Macmillan, 1978).

CHAPTER 11

1. The constitutional development of Canada has been almost the inverse of that in the United States. While the latter went from confederation to a federal system and has weakened federalism by depriving states and municipalities of funds, Canada has moved from the centralism of 1867 toward classic federalism as defined by K.C. Wheare, *Federal Government*, 4th ed. (London: Oxford University Press, 1964).

2. When Alberta and Saskatchewan attained provincial status in 1905, they were denied control over their natural resources. However, they were eventually able (in 1930) to assume control, because the federal government could not deny them what had been granted to the other provinces. This shows that the federal government, no matter how strong its constitutional position, is unable to ignore provincial demands, especially when these demands are supported by the people of the province.

3. See R.I. Cheffins, *The Constitutional Process in Canada*, 2nd ed. (Toronto: McGraw-Hill Ryerson, 1976), pp. 39, 108.

4. See Walter Tarnopolsky, *The Canadian Bill of Rights*, Carleton Library Series no. 83 (Toronto: McClelland and Stewart, 1975), and his article "The Supreme Court and the Canadian Bill of Rights," *Canadian Bar Review* 53.14 (December 1975), pp. 649–74.

5. For an assessment of the Charter of Rights and its application, see Ian Greene, *The Charter of Rights* (Toronto: James Lorimer and Company, 1989).
6. Seymour Martin Lipset, *Continental Divide: The Values and Institutions of the United States and Canada* (New York: Routledge, Chapman and Hall, 1990), p. 104.
7. Jeffrey Simpson discusses this tendency in his column in *The Globe and Mail*, August 12, 1992. In a recent book, the Supreme Court is again discussed by Simpson, *The Anxious Years: Politics in the Age of Mulroney and Chrétien* (Toronto: Lester Publications, 1996), pp. 66, 88, 92–93, and 197. The decisions of the Supreme Court are to be found in *Supreme Court Reports*.

The Constitution Act, 1867

30 & 31 Victoria, c. 3.
(Consolidated with amendments)

An Act for the Union of Canada, Nova Scotia, and New Brunswick, and the Government thereof; and for Purposes connected therewith.

(*29th March, 1867.*)

Whereas the Provinces of Canada, Nova Scotia and New Brunswick have expressed their Desire to be federally united into One Dominion under the Crown of the United Kingdom of Great Britain and Ireland, with a Constitution similar in Principle to that of the United Kingdom:

And whereas such a Union would conduce to the Welfare of the Provinces and promote the Interests of the British Empire:

And whereas on the Establishment of the Union by Authority of Parliament it is expedient, not only that the Constitution of the Legislative Authority in the Dominion be provided for, but also that the Nature of the Executive Government therein be declared:

And whereas it is expedient that Provision be made for the eventual Admission into the Union of other Parts of British North America:

I. PRELIMINARY

1.   This Act may be cited as the *Constitution Act, 1867*.

2.   Repealed.

II. UNION

3.   It shall be lawful for the Queen, by and with the Advice of Her Majesty's Most Honourable Privy Council, to declare by Proclamation that, on and after a Day therein appointed, not being more than Six Months after the passing of this Act, the Provinces of Canada, Nova

Source: Justice Canada

Scotia, and New Brunswick shall form and be One Dominion under the Name of Canada; and on and after that Day those Three Provinces shall form and be One Dominion under that Name accordingly.

4. Unless it is otherwise expressed or implied, the Name Canada shall be taken to mean Canada as constituted under this Act.

5. Canada shall be divided into Four Provinces, named Ontario, Quebec, Nova Scotia, and New Brunswick.

6. The Parts of the Province of Canada (as it exists at the passing of this Act) which formerly constituted respectively the Provinces of Upper Canada and Lower Canada shall be deemed to be severed, and shall form Two separate Provinces. The Part which formerly constituted the Province of Upper Canada shall constitute the Province of Ontario; and the Part which formerly constituted the Province of Lower Canada shall constitute the Province of Quebec.

7. The Provinces of Nova Scotia and New Brunswick shall have the same Limits as at the passing of this Act.

8. In the general Census of the Population of Canada which is hereby required to be taken in the Year One thousand eight hundred and seventy-one, and in every Tenth Year thereafter, the respective Populations of the Four Provinces shall be distinguished.

III. EXECUTIVE POWER

9. The Executive Government and Authority of and over Canada is hereby declared to continue and be vested in the Queen.

10. The Provisions of this Act referring to the Governor General extend and apply to the Governor General for the Time being of Canada, or other the Chief Executive Officer or Administrator for the Time being carrying on the Government of Canada on behalf and in the Name of the Queen, by whatever Title he is designated.

11. There shall be a Council to aid and advise in the Government of Canada, to be styled the Queen's Privy Council for Canada; and the Persons who are to be Members of that Council shall be from Time to Time chosen and summoned by the Governor General and sworn in as Privy Councillors, and Members thereof may be from Time to Time removed by the Governor General.

12. All Powers, Authorities, and Functions, which under any Act of the Parliament of Great Britain, or of the Parliament of the United Kingdom of Great Britain and Ireland, or of the Legislature of Upper Canada, Lower Canada, Canada, Nova Scotia, or New Brunswick, are at the Union vested in or exerciseable by the respective Governors or Lieutenant Governors of those Provinces, with the Advice, or with the Advice and Consent, of the respective Executive Councils thereof, or in conjunction with those Councils, or with any Number of Members thereof, or by those Governors or Lieutenant Governors individually, shall, as far as the same continue in existence and capable of being exercised after the Union in relation to the Government of Canada, be vested in and exerciseable by the Governor General, with the Advice or with the Advice and Consent of or in conjunction with the Queen's Privy Council for Canada, or any Member thereof, or by the Governor General individually, as the Case requires, subject nevertheless (except with respect to such as exist under Acts of the Parliament of Great Britain or of the Parliament of the United Kingdom of Great Britain and Ireland) to be abolished or altered by the Parliament of Canada.

13. The Provisions of this Act referring to the Governor General in Council shall be construed as referring to the Governor General acting by and with the Advice of the Queen's Privy Council for Canada.

14. It shall be lawful for the Queen, if Her Majesty thinks fit, to authorize the Governor General from Time to Time to appoint any Person or any Persons jointly or severally to be his Deputy or Deputies within any Part or Parts of Canada, and in that Capacity to exercise during the Pleasure of the Governor General such of the Powers, Authorities, and Functions of the Governor General as the Governor General deems it necessary or expedient to assign to him or them, subject to any Limitations or Directions expressed or given by the Queen; but the Appointment of such a Deputy or Deputies shall not affect the Exercise by the Governor General himself of any Power, Authority or Function.

15. The Command-in-Chief of the Land and Naval Militia, and of all Naval and Military Forces, of and in Canada, is hereby declared to continue and be vested in the Queen.

16. Until the Queen otherwise directs, the Seat of Government of Canada shall be Ottawa.

IV. LEGISLATIVE POWER

17. There shall be One Parliament for Canada, consisting of the Queen, an Upper House styled the Senate, and the House of Commons.

18. The privileges, immunities, and powers to be held, enjoyed, and exercised by the Senate and by the House of Commons, and by the Members thereof respectively, shall be such as are from time to time defined by Act of the Parliament of Canada, but so that any Act of the Parliament of Canada defining such privileges, immunities, and powers shall not confer any privileges, immunities, or powers exceeding those at the passing of such Act held, enjoyed, and exercised by the Commons House of Parliament of the United Kingdom of Great Britain and Ireland, and by the Members thereof.

19. The Parliament of Canada shall be called together not later than Six Months after the Union.

20. Repealed.

The Senate

21.   The Senate shall, subject to the Provisions of this Act, consist of One Hundred and four Members, who shall be styled Senators.

22.   In relation to the Constitution of the Senate Canada shall be deemed to consist of Four Divisions:

    1.   Ontario;

    2.   Quebec;

    3.   The Maritime Provinces, Nova Scotia and New Brunswick, and Prince Edward Island;

    4.   The Western Provinces of Manitoba, British Columbia, Saskatchewan, and Alberta;

which Four Divisions shall (subject to the Provisions of this Act) be equally represented in the Senate as follows: Ontario by twenty-four senators; Quebec by twenty-four senators; the Maritime Provinces and Prince Edward Island by twenty-four senators, ten thereof representing Nova Scotia, ten thereof representing New Brunswick, and four thereof representing Prince Edward Island; the Western Provinces by twenty-four senators, six thereof representing Manitoba, six thereof representing British Columbia, six thereof representing Saskatchewan, and six thereof representing Alberta; Newfoundland shall be entitled to be represented in the Senate by six members; the Yukon Territory and the Northwest Territories shall be entitled to be represented in the Senate by one member each.

In the Case of Quebec each of the Twenty-four Senators representing that Province shall be appointed for One of the Twenty-four Electoral Divisions of Lower Canada specified in Schedule A, to Chapter One of the Consolidated statutes of Canada.

23.   The Qualification of a Senator shall be as follows:

    (1)   He shall be of the full age of Thirty Years:

    (2)   He shall be either a natural-born Subject of the Queen, or a Subject of the Queen naturalized by an Act of the Parliament of Great Britain, or of the Parliament of the United Kingdom of Great Britain and Ireland, or of the Legislature of One of the Provinces of Upper Canada, Lower Canada, Canada, Nova Scotia, or New Brunswick, before the Union, or of the Parliament of Canada, after the Union:

    (3)   He shall be legally or equitably seised as of Freehold for his own Use and Benefit of Lands or Tenements held in Free and Common Socage, or seised or possessed for his own Use and Benefit of Lands or Tenements held in Francalleu or in Roture, within the Province for which he is appointed, of the Value of Four thousand Dollars, over and above all Rents, Dues, Debts, Charges, Mortgages, and Incumbrances due or payable out of or charged on or affecting the same:

(4) His Real and Personal Property shall be together worth Four thousand Dollars over and above his Debts and Liabilities:

(5) He shall be resident in the Province for which he is appointed:

(6) In the Case of Quebec he shall have his Real Property Qualification in the Electoral Division for which he is appointed, or shall be resident in that Division.

24. The Governor General shall from Time to Time, in the Queen's Name, by Instrument under the Great Seal of Canada, summon qualified Persons to the Senate; and, subject to the Provisions of this Act, every Person so summoned shall become and be a Member of the Senate and a Senator.

25. Repealed.

26. If at any Time on the Recommendation of the Governor General the Queen thinks fit to direct that Four or Eight Members be added to the Senate, the Governor General may by Summons to Four or Eight qualified Persons (as the Case may be), representing equally the Four Divisions of Canada, add to the Senate accordingly.

27. In case of such Addition being at any Time made, the Governor General shall not summon any Person to the Senate, except upon a further like Direction by the Queen on the like Recommendation, to represent one of the Four Divisions until such Division is represented by Twenty-four Senators and no more.

28. The Number of Senators shall not at any Time exceed One Hundred and twelve.

29. (1) Subject to subsection (2), a Senator shall, subject to the provisions of this Act, hold his place in the Senate for life.

(2) A Senator who is summoned to the Senate after the coming into force of this subsection shall, subject to this Act, hold his place in the Senate until he attains the age of seventy-five years.

30. A Senator may by Writing under his Hand addressed to the Governor General resign his Place in the Senate, and thereupon the same shall be vacant.

31. The Place of a Senator shall become vacant in any of the following Cases:

(1) If for Two consecutive Sessions of the Parliament he fails to give his Attendance in the Senate:

(2) If he takes an Oath or makes a Declaration or Acknowledgement of Allegiance, Obedience, or Adherence to a Foreign Power, or does an Act whereby he becomes a Subject or Citizen, or entitled to the Rights or Privileges of a Subject or Citizen, of a Foreign Power.

(3) If he is adjudged Bankrupt or Insolvent, or applies for the Benefit of any Law relating to Insolvent Debtors, or becomes a public Defaulter:

(4) If he is attainted of Treason or convicted of Felony or of any infamous Crime:

(5) If he ceases to be qualified in respect of Property or of Residence; provided, that a Senator shall not be deemed to have ceased to be qualified in respect of Residence by reason only of his residing at the Seat of the Government of Canada while holding an Office under that Government requiring his Presence there.

32. When a Vacancy happens in the Senate by Resignation, Death or otherwise, the Governor General shall by Summons to a fit and qualified Person fill the Vacancy.

33. If any Question arises respecting the Qualification of a Senator or a Vacancy in the Senate the same shall be heard and determined by the Senate.

34. The Governor General may from Time to Time, by Instrument under the Great Seal of Canada, appoint a Senator to be Speaker of the Senate, and may remove him and appoint another in his Stead.

35. Until the Parliament of Canada otherwise provides, the Presence of at least Fifteen Senators, including the Speaker, shall be necessary to constitute a Meeting of the Senate for the Exercise of its Powers.

36. Questions arising in the Senate shall be decided by a Majority of Voices, and the Speaker shall in all Cases have a Vote, and when the Voices are equal the Decision shall be deemed to be in the Negative.

The House of Commons

37. The House of Commons shall, subject to the Provisions of this Act, consist of two hundred and eighty-two members of whom ninety-five shall be elected for Ontario, seventy-five for Quebec, eleven for Nova Scotia, ten for New Brunswick, fourteen for Manitoba, twenty-eight for British Columbia, four for Prince Edward Island, twenty-one for Alberta, fourteen for Saskatchewan, seven for Newfoundland, one for the Yukon Territory and two for the Northwest Territories.

38. The Governor General shall from Time to Time, in the Queen's Name, by Instrument under the Great Seal of Canada, summon and call together the House of Commons.

39. A Senator shall not be capable of being elected or of sitting or voting as a Member of the House of Commons.

40. Until the Parliament of Canada otherwise provides, Ontario, Quebec, Nova Scotia and New Brunswick shall, for the Purposes of the Election of Members to serve in the House of Commons, be divided into Electoral districts as follows:

1.—Ontario

Ontario shall be divided into the Counties, Ridings of Counties, Cities, Parts of Cities, and Towns enumerated in the First Schedule to this Act, each whereof shall be an Electoral District, each such District as numbered in that Schedule being entitled to return One Member.

2.—Quebec

Quebec shall be divided into Sixty-five Electoral Districts, composed of the Sixty-five Electoral Divisions into which Lower Canada is at the passing of this Act divided under Chapter Two of the Consolidated Statutes of Canada, Chapter Seventy-five of the Consolidated Statutes for Lower Canada, and the Act of the Province of Canada of the Twenty-third Year of the Queen, Chapter One, or any other Act amending the same in force at the Union, so that each such Electoral Division shall be for the Purposes of this Act an Electoral District entitled to return One Member.

3.—Nova Scotia

Each of the Eighteen Counties of Nova Scotia shall be an Electoral District. The County of Halifax shall be entitled to return Two Members, and each of the other Counties One Member.

4.—New Brunswick

Each of the Fourteen Counties into which New Brunswick is divided, including the City and County of St. John, shall be an Electoral District. The City of St. John shall also be a separate Electoral District. Each of those Fifteen Electoral Districts shall be entitled to return One Member.

41. Until the Parliament of Canada otherwise provides, all Laws in force in the several Provinces at the Union relative to the following Matters or any of them, namely,—the Qualifications and Disqualifications of Persons to be elected or to sit or vote as Members of the House of Assembly or Legislative Assembly in the several Provinces, the Voters at Elections of such Members, the Oaths to be taken by Voters, the Returning Officers, their Powers and Duties, the Proceedings at Elections, the Periods during which Elections may be continued, the Trial of controverted Elections, and Proceedings incident thereto, the vacating of Seats of Members, and the Execution of new Writs in case of Seats vacated otherwise than by Dissolution,—shall respectively apply to Elections of Members to serve in the House of Commons for the same several Provinces.

Provided that, until the Parliament of Canada otherwise provides, at any Election for a Member of the House of Commons for the District of Algoma, in addition to Persons qualified by the Law of the Province of

Canada to vote, every Male British Subject, aged Twenty-one Years or upwards, being a Householder, shall have a Vote.

42. Repealed.

43. Repealed.

44. The House of Commons on its first assembling after a General Election shall proceed with all practicable Speed to elect One of its Members to be Speaker.

45. In case of a Vacancy happening in the Office of Speaker by Death, Resignation, or otherwise, the House of Commons shall with all practicable Speed proceed to elect another of its Members to be Speaker.

46. The Speaker shall preside at all Meetings of the House of Commons.

47. Until the Parliament of Canada otherwise provides, in case of the Absence for any Reason of the Speaker from the Chair of the House of Commons for a Period of Forty-eight consecutive Hours, the House may elect another of its Members to act as Speaker, and the Member so elected shall during the Continuance of such Absence of the Speaker have and execute all the Powers, Privileges, and Duties of Speaker.

48. The Presence of at least Twenty Members of the House of Commons shall be necessary to constitute a Meeting of the House for the Exercise of its Powers, and for that Purpose the Speaker shall be reckoned as a Member.

49. Questions arising in the House of Commons shall be decided by a Majority of Voices other than that of the Speaker, and when the Voices are equal, but not otherwise, the Speaker shall have a Vote.

50. Every House of Commons shall continue for Five Years from the Day of the Return of the Writs for choosing the House (subject to be sooner dissolved by the Governor General), and no longer.

51. (1) The number of members of the House of Commons and the representation of the provinces therein shall on the coming into force of this subsection and thereafter on the completion of each decennial census, be readjusted by such authority, in such manner, and from such time as the Parliament of Canada from time to time provides, subject and according to the following rules:

> 1. There shall be assigned to each of the provinces a number of members equal to the number obtained by dividing the total population of the provinces by two hundred and seventy-nine and by dividing the population of each province by the quotient so obtained, counting any remainder in excess of 0.50 as one after the said process of division.
>
> 2. If the total number of members that would be assigned to a province by the application of rule 1 is less than the total number assigned to that province on the date of coming into force of this subsection, there shall be added to the number of

members so assigned such number of members as will result in the province having the same number of members as were assigned on that date.

(2) The Yukon Territory as bounded and described in the schedule to chapter Y-2 of the Revised Statutes of Canada, 1970, shall be entitled to one member, and the Northwest Territories as bounded and described in section 2 of chapter N-22 of the Revised Statutes of Canada, 1970, shall be entitled to two members.

51A. Notwithstanding anything in this Act a province shall always be entitled to a number of members in the House of Commons not less than the number of senators representing such province.

52. The Number of Members of the House of Commons may be from Time to Time increased by the Parliament of Canada, provided the proportionate Representation of the Provinces prescribed by this Act is not thereby disturbed.

Money Votes; Royal Assent

53. Bills for appropriating any Part of the Public Revenue, or for imposing any Tax or Import, shall originate in the House of Commons.

54. It shall not be lawful for the House of Commons to adopt or pass any Vote, Resolution, Address, or Bill for the Appropriation of any Part of the Public Revenue, or of any Tax or Impost, to any Purpose that has not been first recommended to that House by Message of the Governor General in the Session in which such Vote, Resolution, Address, or Bill is proposed.

55. Where a Bill passed by the Houses of the Parliament is presented to the Governor General for the Queen's Assent, he shall declare, according to his Discretion, but subject to the Provisions of this Act and to Her Majesty's Instructions, either that he assents thereto in the Queen's Name, or that he withholds the Queen's Assent, or that he reserves the Bill for the Signification of the Queen's Pleasure.

56. Where the Governor General assents to a Bill in the Queen's Name, he shall by the first convenient Opportunity send an authentic Copy of the Act to one of Her Majesty's Principal Secretaries of State, and if the Queen in Council within Two Years after Receipt thereof by the Secretary of State thinks fit to disallow the Act, such Disallowance (with a Certificate of the Secretary of State of the Day on which the Act was received by him) being signified by the Governor General, by Speech or Message to each of the Houses of the Parliament or by Proclamation, shall annul the Act from and after the Day of such Signification.

57. A Bill reserved for the Signification of the Queen's Pleasure shall not have any Force unless and until, within Two Years from the Day on which it was presented to the Governor General for the Queen's

Assent, the Governor General signifies, by Speech or Message to each of the Houses of the Parliament or by Proclamation, that it has received the Assent of the Queen in Council.

An Entry of every such Speech, Message, or Proclamation shall ' be made in the Journal of each House, and a Duplicate thereof duly attested shall be delivered to the proper Officer to be kept among the Records of Canada.

V. PROVINCIAL CONSTITUTIONS

Executive Power

58. For each Province there shall be an Officer, styled the Lieutenant Governor, appointed by the Governor General in Council by Instrument under the Great Seal of Canada.

59. A Lieutenant Governor shall hold Office during the Pleasure of the Governor General; but any Lieutenant Governor appointed after the Commencement of the First Session of the Parliament of Canada shall not be removeable within Five Years from his Appointment, except for Cause assigned, which shall be communicated to him in Writing within One Month after the Order for his Removal is made, and shall be communicated by Message to the Senate and to the House of Commons within One Week thereafter if the Parliament is then sitting, and if not then within One Week after the Commencement of the next Session of the Parliament.

60. The Salaries of the Lieutenant Governors shall be fixed and provided by the Parliament of Canada.

61. Every Lieutenant Governor shall, before assuming the Duties of his Office, make and subscribe before the Governor General or some Person authorized by him Oaths of Allegiance and Office similar to those taken by the Governor General.

62. The Provisions of this Act referring to the Lieutenant Governor extend and apply to the Lieutenant Governor for the Time being of each Province, or other the Chief Executive Officer or Administrator for the Time being carrying on the Government of the Province, by whatever Title he is designated.

63. The Executive Council of Ontario and of Quebec shall be composed of such Persons as the Lieutenant Governor from Time to Time thinks fit, and in the first instance of the following Officers, namely,—the Attorney General, the Secretary and Registrar of the Province, the Treasurer of the Province, the Commissioner of Crown Lands, and the Commissioner of Agriculture and Public Works, with in Quebec, the Speaker of the Legislative Council and the Solicitor General.

64. The Constitution of the Executive Authority in each of the Provinces of Nova Scotia and New Brunswick shall, subject to the

Provisions of this Act, continue as it exists at the Union until altered under the Authority of this Act.

65. All Powers, Authorities, and Functions which under any Act of the Parliament of Great Britain, or of the Parliament of the United Kingdom of Great Britain and Ireland, or of the Legislature of Upper Canada, Lower Canada, or Canada, were or are before or at the Union vested in or exerciseable by the respective Governors or Lieutenant Governors of those Provinces, with the Advice or with the Advice and Consent of the respective Executive Councils thereof, or in conjunction with those Councils, or with any Number of Members thereof, or by those Governors or Lieutenant Governors individually, shall, as far as the same are capable of being exercised after the Union in relation to the Government of Ontario and Quebec respectively, be vested in and shall or may be exercised by the Lieutenant Governor of Ontario and Quebec respectively, with the Advice or with the Advice and Consent of or in conjunction with the respective Executive Councils, or any Members thereof, or by the Lieutenant Governor individually, as the Case requires, subject nevertheless (except with respect to such as exist under Acts of the Parliament of Great Britain, or of the Parliament of the United Kingdom of Great Britain and Ireland,) to be abolished or altered by the respective Legislatures of Ontario and Quebec.

66. The Provisions of this Act referring to the Lieutenant Governor in Council shall be construed as referring to the Lieutenant Governor of the Province acting by and with the Advice of the Executive Council thereof.

67. The Governor General in Council may from Time to Time appoint an Administrator to execute the office and Functions of Lieutenant Governor during his Absence, Illness, or other Inability.

68. Unless and until the Executive Government of any Province otherwise directs with respect to that Province, the Seats of Government of the Provinces shall be as follows, namely,—of Ontario, the City of Toronto; of Quebec, the City of Quebec; of Nova Scotia, the City of Halifax; and of New Brunswick, the City of Fredericton.

Legislative Power

1.—Ontario

69. There shall be a Legislature for Ontario consisting of the Lieutenant Governor and of One House, styled the Legislative Assembly of Ontario.

70. The Legislative Assembly of Ontario shall be composed of Eighty-two Members, to be elected to represent the Eighty-two Electoral Districts set forth in the First Schedule to this Act.

2.—Quebec

71. There shall be a Legislature for Quebec consisting of the Lieutenant Governor and of Two Houses, styled the Legislative Council of Quebec and the Legislative Assembly of Quebec.

72. The Legislative Council of Quebec shall be composed of Twenty-four Members, to be appointed by the Lieutenant Governor, in the Queen's Name, by Instrument under the Great Seal of Quebec, One being appointed to represent each of the Twenty-four Electoral Divisions of Lower Canada in this Act referred to, and each holding Office for the Term of his Life, unless the Legislature of Quebec otherwise provides under the Provisions of this Act.

73. The Qualifications of the Legislative Councillors of Quebec shall be the same as those of the Senators for Quebec.

74. The Place of a Legislative Councillor of Quebec shall become vacant in the Cases, *mutatis mutandis*, in which the Place of Senator becomes vacant.

75. When a Vacancy happens in the Legislative Council of Quebec by Resignation, Death, or otherwise, the Lieutenant Governor, in the Queen's Name, by Instrument under the Great Seal of Quebec, shall appoint a fit and qualified Person to fill the Vacancy.

76. If any Question arises respecting the Qualification of a Legislative Councillor of Quebec, or a Vacancy in the Legislative Council of Quebec, the same shall be heard and determined by the Legislative Council.

77. The Lieutenant Governor may from Time to Time, by Instrument under the Great Seal of Quebec, appoint a Member of the Legislative Council of Quebec to be Speaker thereof, and may remove him and appoint another in his Stead.

78. Until the Legislature of Quebec otherwise provides, the Presence of at least Ten Members of the Legislative Council, including the Speaker, shall be necessary to constitute a Meeting for the Exercise of its Powers.

79. Questions arising in the Legislative Council of Quebec shall be decided by a Majority of Voices, and the Speaker shall in all Cases have a Vote, and when the Voices are equal the Decision shall be deemed to be in the Negative.

80. The Legislative Assembly of Quebec shall be composed of Sixty-five Members, to be elected to represent the Sixty-five Electoral Divisions or Districts of Lower Canada in this Act referred to, subject to Alteration thereof by the Legislature of Quebec: Provided that it shall not be lawful to present to the Lieutenant Governor of Quebec for Assent any Bill for altering the Limits of any of the Electoral Divisions or Districts mentioned in the Second Schedule to this Act, unless the Second and Third Readings of such Bill have been passed in the Legislative Assembly with the Concurrence of the Majority of the

Members representing all those Electoral Divisions or Districts, and the Assent shall not be given to such Bill unless an Address has been presented by the Legislative Assembly to the Lieutenant Governor stating that it has been so passed.

3.—Ontario and Quebec

81. Repealed.

82. The Lieutenant Governor of Ontario and of Quebec shall from Time to Time, in the Queen's Name, by Instrument under the Great Seal of the Province, summon and call together the Legislative Assembly of the Province.

83. Until the Legislature of Ontario or of Quebec otherwise provides, a Person accepting or holding in Ontario or in Quebec any Office, Commission, or Employment, permanent or temporary, at the Nomination of the Lieutenant Governor, to which an annual Salary, or any Fee, Allowance, Emolument, or Profit of any Kind or Amount whatever from the Province is attached, shall not be eligible as a Member of the Legislative Assembly of the respective Province, nor shall he sit or vote as such; but nothing in this Section shall make ineligible any Person being a member of the Executive Council of the respective Province, or holding any of the following Offices, that is to say, the Offices of Attorney General, Secretary and Registrar of the Province, Treasurer of the Province, Commissioner of Crown Lands, and Commissioner of Agriculture and Public Works, and in Quebec Solicitor General, or shall disqualify him to sit or vote in the House for which he is elected, provided he is elected while holding such Office.

84. Until the legislatures of Ontario and Quebec respectively otherwise provide, all Laws which at the Union are in force in those Provinces respectively, relative to the following Matters, or any of them, namely,— the Qualifications and Disqualifications of Persons to be elected or to sit or vote as Members of the Assembly of Canada, the Qualifications or Disqualifications of Voters, the Oaths to be taken by Voters, the Returning Officers, their Powers and Duties, the Proceedings at Elections, the Periods during which such Elections may be continued, and the Trial of controverted Elections and the Proceedings incident thereto, the vacating of the Seats of Members and the issuing and execution of new Writs, in case of Seats vacated otherwise than by Dissolution,—shall respectively apply to Elections of Members to serve in the respective Legislative Assemblies of Ontario and Quebec.

Provided that, until the Legislature of Ontario otherwise provides, at any Election for a Member of the Legislative Assembly of Ontario for the District of Algoma, in addition to Persons qualified by the Law of the Province of Canada to vote, every male British Subject, aged Twenty-one Years or upwards, being a Householder, shall have a vote.

85. Every Legislative Assembly of Ontario and every Legislative Assembly of Quebec shall continue for Four Years from the Day of the Return of the Writs for choosing the same (subject nevertheless to either the Legislative Assembly of Ontario or the Legislative Assembly of Quebec being sooner dissolved by the Lieutenant Governor of the Province), and no longer.

86. There shall be a Session of the Legislature of Ontario and of that of Quebec once at least in every Year, so that Twelve Months shall not intervene between the last Sitting of the Legislature in each Province in one Session and its first Sitting in the next Session.

87. The following Provisions of this Act respecting the House of Commons of Canada shall extend and apply to the Legislative Assemblies of Ontario and Quebec, that is to say,—the Provisions relating to the Election of a Speaker originally and on Vacancies, the Duties of the Speaker, the Absence of the Speaker, the Quorum, and the Mode of voting, as if those Provisions were here re-enacted and made applicable in Terms to each such Legislative Assembly.

4.—Nova Scotia and New Brunswick

88. The Constitution of the Legislature of each of the Provinces of Nova Scotia and New Brunswick shall, subject to the Provisions of this Act, continue as it exists at the Union until altered under the Authority of this Act.

89. Repealed.

6.—The Four Provinces.

90. The following Provisions of this Act respecting the Parliament of Canada, namely,—the Provisions relating to Appropriation and Tax Bills, the Recommendation of Money Votes, the Assent to Bills, the Disallowance of Acts, and the Signification of Pleasure on Bills reserved,—shall extend and apply to the Legislatures of the several Provinces as if those Provisions were here re-enacted and made applicable in Terms to the respective Provinces and the Legislatures thereof, with the Substitution of the Lieutenant Governor of the Province for the Governor General, of the Governor General for the Queen and for a Secretary of State, of One Year for Two Years, and of the Province for Canada.

VI. DISTRIBUTION OF LEGISLATIVE POWERS

Powers of the Parliament

91. It shall be lawful for the Queen, by and with the Advice and Consent of the Senate and House of Commons, to make Laws for the

Peace, Order, and good Government of Canada, in relation to all Matters not coming within the Classes of Subjects by this Act assigned exclusively to the Legislatures of the Provinces; and for greater Certainty, but not so as to restrict the Generality of the foregoing Terms of this Section, it is hereby declared that (notwithstanding anything in this Act) the exclusive Legislative Authority of the Parliament of Canada extends to all Matters coming within the Classes of Subjects next hereinafter enumerated; that is to say,—

1. Repealed.
1A. The Public Debt and Property.
2. The Regulation of Trade and Commerce.
2A. Unemployment insurance.
3. The raising of Money by any Mode or System of Taxation.
4. The borrowing of Money on the Public Credit.
5. Postal Service.
6. The Census and Statistics.
7. Militia, Military and Naval Service, and Defence.
8. The fixing of and providing for the Salaries and Allowances of civil and other Officers of the Government of Canada.
9. Beacons, Buoys, Lighthouses, and Sable Island.
10. Navigation and Shipping.
11. Quarantine and the Establishment and Maintenance of Marine Hospitals.
12. Sea Coast and Inland Fisheries.
13. Ferries between a Province and any British or Foreign Country or between Two Provinces.
14. Currency and Coinage.
15. Banking, Incorporation of Banks, and the Issue of Paper Money.
16. Savings Banks.
17. Weights and Measures.
18. Bills of Exchange and Promissory Notes.
19. Interest.
20. Legal Tender.
21. Bankruptcy and Insolvency.
22. Patents of Invention and Discovery.
23. Copyrights.
24. Indians, and Lands reserved for the Indians.
25. Naturalization and Aliens.
26. Marriage and Divorce.
27. The Criminal Law, except the Constitution of Courts of Criminal Jurisdiction, but including the Procedure in Criminal Matters.
28. The Establishment, Maintenance, and Management of Penitentiaries.
29. Such Classes of Subjects as are expressly excepted in the Enumeration of the Classes of Subjects by this Act assigned exclusively to the Legislatures of the Provinces.

And any Matter coming within any of the Classes of Subjects enumerated in this Section shall not be deemed to come within the Class of Matters of a local or private Nature comprised in the Enumeration of the Classes of Subjects by this Act assigned exclusively to the Legislatures of the Provinces.

Exclusive Powers of Provincial Legislatures

92. In each Province the Legislature may exclusively make Laws in relation to Matters coming within the Classes of Subject next hereinafter enumerated; that is to say,—

1. Repealed.
2. Direct Taxation within the Province in order to the raising of a Revenue for Provincial Purposes.
3. The borrowing of Money on the sole Credit of the Province.
4. The Establishment and Tenure of Provincial Offices and the Appointment and Payment of Provincial Officers.
5. The Management and Sale of the Public Lands belonging to the Province and of the Timber and Wood thereon.
6. The Establishment, Maintenance, and Management of Public and Reformatory Prisons in and for the Province.
7. The Establishment, Maintenance, and Management of Hospitals, Asylums, Charities, and Eleemosynary Institutions in and for the Province, other than Marine Hospitals.
8. Municipal Institutions in the Province.
9. Shop, Saloon, Tavern, Auctioneer, and other Licences in order to the raising of a Revenue for Provincial, Local, or Municipal Purposes.
10. Local Works and Undertakings other than such as are of the following Classes:—

(a) Lines of Steam or other Ships, Railways, Canals, Telegraphs, and other Works and Undertakings connecting the Province with any other or others of the Provinces, or extending beyond the Limits of the Province;

(b) Lines of Steam Ships between the Province and any British or Foreign Country;

(c) Such Works as, although wholly situate within the Province, are before or after their Execution declared by the Parliament of Canada to be for the general Advantage of Canada or for the Advantage of Two or more of the Provinces.

11. The Incorporation of Companies with Provincial Objects.
12. The Solemnization of Marriage in the Province.
13. Property and Civil Rights in the Province.
14. The Administration of Justice in the Province, including the Constitution, Maintenance, and Organization of Provincial Courts, both of Civil and of Criminal Jurisdiction, and including

Procedure in Civil Matters in those Courts.

15. The Imposition of Punishment by Fine, Penalty, or Imprisonment for enforcing any Law of the Province made in relation to any Matter coming within any of the Classes of Subjects enumerated in this Section.

16. Generally all Matters of a merely local or private Nature in the Province.

Non-Renewable Natural Resources, Forestry Resources and Electrical Energy

92A. (1) In each province, the legislature may exclusively make laws in relation to

(a) exploration for non-renewable natural resources in the province;

(b) development, conservation and management of non-renewable natural resources and forestry resources in the province, including laws in relation to the rate of primary production therefrom; and

(c) development, conservation and management of sites and facilities in the province for the generation and production of electrical energy.

(2) In each province, the legislature may make laws in relation to the export from the province to another part of Canada of the primary production from non-renewable natural resources and forestry resources in the province and the production from facilities in the province for the generation of electrical energy, but such laws may not authorize or provide for discrimination in prices or in supplies exported to another part of Canada.

(3) Nothing in subsection (2) derogates from the authority of Parliament to enact laws in relation to the matters referred to in that subsection and, where such a law of Parliament and a law of a province conflict, the law of Parliament prevails to the extent of the conflict.

(4) In each province, the legislature may make laws in relation to the raising of money by any mode or system of taxation in respect of

(a) non-renewable natural resources and forestry resources in the province and the primary production therefrom, and

(b) sites and facilities in the province for the generation of electrical energy and the production therefrom,whether or not such production is exported in whole or in part from the province, but such laws may not authorize or provide for taxation that differentiates between production exported to another part of Canada and production not exported from the province.

(5)   The expression "primary production" has the meaning assigned by the Sixth Schedule.

(6)   Nothing in subsections (1) to (5) derogates from any powers or rights that a legislature or government of a province had immediately before the coming into force of this section.

Education

93.   In and for each Province the Legislature may exclusively make Laws in relation to Education, subject and according to the following Provisions:—

(1)   Nothing in any such Law shall prejudicially affect any Right or Privilege with respect to Denominational Schools which any Class of Persons have by Law in the Province at the Union:

(2)   All the Powers, Privileges, and Duties at the Union by Law conferred and imposed in Upper Canada on the Separate Schools and School Trustees of the Queen's Roman Catholic Subjects shall be and the same are hereby extended to the Dissentient Schools of the Queen's Protestant and Roman Catholic Subjects in Quebec:

(3)   Where in any Province a System of Separate or Dissentient Schools exists by Law at the Union or is thereafter established by the Legislature of the Province, an Appeal shall lie to the Governor General in Council from any Act or Decision of any Provincial Authority affecting any Right or Privilege of the Protestant or Roman Catholic Minority of the Queen's Subjects in relation to Education:

(4)   In case any such Provincial Law as from Time to Time seems to the Governor General in Council requisite for the due Execution of the Provisions of this Section is not made, or in case any Decision of the Governor General in Council on any Appeal under this Section is not duly executed by the proper Provincial Authority in that Behalf, then and in every such Case, and as far only as the Circumstances of each Case require, the Parliament of Canada may make remedial Laws for the due Execution of the Provisions of this Section and of any Decision of the Governor General in Council under this Section.

Uniformity of Laws in Ontario, Nova Scotia and New Brunswick

94.   Notwithstanding anything in this Act, the Parliament of Canada may make Provision for the Uniformity of all or any of the Laws relative to Property and Civil Rights in Ontario, Nova Scotia, and New Brunswick, and of the Procedure of all or any of the Courts in Those

Three Provinces, and from and after the passing of any Act in that Behalf the Power of the Parliament of Canada to make Laws in relation to any Matter comprised in any such Act shall, notwithstanding anything in this Act, be unrestricted; but any Act of the Parliament of Canada making Provision for such Uniformity shall not have effect in any Province unless and until it is adopted and enacted as Law by the Legislature thereof.

Old Age Pensions

94A. The Parliament of Canada may make laws in relation to old age pensions and supplementary benefits, including survivors, and disability benefits irrespective of age, but no such law shall affect the operation of any law present or future of a provincial legislature in relation to any such matter.

Agriculture and Immigration

95.   In each Province the Legislature may make Laws in relation to Agriculture in the Province, and to Immigration into the Province; and it is hereby declared that the Parliament of Canada may from Time to Time make Laws in relation to Agriculture in all or any of the Provinces, and to Immigration into all or any of the Provinces; and any Law of the Legislature of a Province relative to Agriculture or to Immigration shall have effect in and for the Province as long and as far only as it is not repugnant to any Act of the Parliament of Canada.

VII. JUDICATURE

96.   The Governor General shall appoint the Judges of the Superior, District, and County Courts in each Province, except those of the Courts of Probate in Nova Scotia and New Brunswick.

97.   Until the laws relative to Property and Civil Rights in Ontario, Nova Scotia, and New Brunswick, and the Procedure of the Courts in those Provinces, are made uniform, the Judges of the Courts of those Provinces appointed by the Governor General shall be selected from the respective Bars of those Provinces.

98.   The Judges of the Courts of Quebec shall be selected from the Bar of that Province.

99.   (1) Subject to subsection two of this section, the Judges of the Superior Courts shall hold office during good behaviour, but shall be removable by the Governor General on Address of the Senate and House of Commons.

(2)   A Judge of a Superior Court, whether appointed before or after the coming into force of this section, shall cease to hold office upon attaining the age of seventy-five years, or upon the coming into force of this section if at that time he has already attained that age.

100. The Salaries, Allowances, and Pensions of the Judges of the Superior, District, and County Courts (except the Courts of Probate in Nova Scotia and New Brunswick), and of the Admiralty Courts in Cases where the Judges thereof are for the Time being paid by Salary, shall be fixed and provided by the Parliament of Canada.

101. The Parliament of Canada may, notwithstanding anything in this Act, from Time to Time provide for the Constitution, Maintenance, and Organization of a General Court of Appeal for Canada, and for the Establishment of any additional Courts for the better Administration of the Laws of Canada.

VIII. REVENUES;
DEBTS; ASSETS; TAXATION

102. All Duties and Revenues over which the respective Legislatures of Canada, Nova Scotia, and New Brunswick before and at the Union had and have Power of Appropriation, except such Portions thereof as are by this Act reserved to the respective Legislatures of the Provinces, or are raised by them in accordance with the special Powers conferred on them by this Act, shall form One Consolidated Revenue Fund, to be appropriated for the Public Service of Canada in the Manner and subject to the Charges of this Act provided.

103. The Consolidated Revenue Fund of Canada shall be permanently charged with the Costs, Charges, and Expenses incident to the Collection, Management, and Receipt thereof, and the same shall form the First Charge thereon, subject to be reviewed and audited in such Manner as shall be ordered by the Governor General in Council until the Parliament otherwise provides.

104. The annual Interest of the Public Debts of the several Provinces of Canada, Nova Scotia, and New Brunswick at the Union shall form the Second Charge on the Consolidated Revenue Fund of Canada.

105. Unless altered by the Parliament of Canada, the Salary of the Governor General shall be Ten thousand Pounds Sterling Money of the United Kingdom of Great Britain and Ireland, payable out of the Consolidated Revenue Fund of Canada, and the same shall form the Third Charge thereon.

106. Subject to the several Payments by this Act charged on the Consolidated Revenue Fund of Canada, the same shall be appropriated by the Parliament of Canada for the Public Service.

107. All Stocks, Cash, Banker's Balances, and Securities for Money belonging to each Province at the Time of the Union, except as in this Act mentioned, shall be the Property of Canada, and shall be taken in Reduction of the Amount of the respective Debts of the Provinces at the Union.

108. The Public Works and Property of each Province, enumerated in the Third Schedule to this Act, shall be the Property of Canada.

109. All Lands, Mines, Minerals, and Royalties belonging to the several Provinces of Canada, Nova Scotia, and New Brunswick at the Union, and all Sums then due or payable for such Lands, Mines, Minerals, or Royalties, shall belong to the several Provinces of Ontario, Quebec, Nova Scotia, and New Brunswick in which the same are situate or arise, subject to any Trusts existing in respect thereof, and to any Interest other than that of the Province in the same.

110. All Assets connected with such Portions of the Public Debt of each Province as are assumed by that Province shall belong to that Province.

111. Canada shall be liable for the Debts and Liabilities of each Province existing at the Union.

112. Ontario and Quebec conjointly shall be liable to Canada for the Amount (if any) by which the Debt of the Province of Canada exceeds at the Union Sixty-two million five hundred thousand Dollars, and shall be charged with Interest at the Rate of Five Per Centum per Annum thereon.

113. The Assets enumerated in the Fourth Schedule to this Act belonging at the Union to the Province of Canada shall be the Property of Ontario and Quebec conjointly.

114. Nova Scotia shall be liable to Canada for the Amount (if any) by which its Public Debt exceeds at the Union Eight million Dollars, and shall be charged with Interest at the Rate of Five per Centum per Annum thereon.

115. New Brunswick shall be liable to Canada for the Amount (if any) by which its Public Debt exceeds at the Union Seven million Dollars, and shall be charged with Interest at the Rate of Five Per Centum per Annum thereon.

116. In case the Public Debts of Nova Scotia and New Brunswick do not at the Union amount to Eight million and Seven million Dollars respectively, they shall respectively receive by half-yearly Payments in advance from the Government of Canada Interest at Five per Centum per Annum on the Difference between the actual Amounts of their respective Debts and such stipulated Amounts.

117. The several Provinces shall retain all their respective Public Property not otherwise disposed of in this Act, subject to the Right of Canada to assume any Lands or Public Property required for Fortifications or for the Defence of the Country.

118. Repealed.

119. New Brunswick shall receive by half-yearly Payments in advance from Canada for the period of Ten years from the Union an additional Allowance of Sixty-three thousand Dollars per Annum; but as long as the Public Debt of that Province remains under Seven million Dollars, a Deduction equal to the Interest at Five per Centum per Annum on such Deficiency shall be made from that Allowance of Sixty-three thousand Dollars.

120. All Payments to be made under this Act, or in discharge of Liabilities created under any Act of the Provinces of Canada, Nova Scotia, and New Brunswick respectively, and assumed by Canada, shall, until the Parliament of Canada otherwise directs, be made in such Form and Manner as may from Time to Time be ordered by the Governor General in Council.

121. All Articles of the Growth, Produce, or Manufacture of any one of the Provinces shall, from and after the Union, be admitted free into each of the other Provinces.

122. The Customs and Excise Laws of each Province shall, subject to the Provisions of this Act, continue in force until altered by the Parliament of Canada.

123. Where Customs Duties are, at the Union, leviable on any Goods, Wares, or Merchandises in any Two Provinces, those Goods, Wares, and Merchandises may, from and after the Union, be imported from one of those Provinces into the other of them on Proof of Payment of the Customs Duty leviable thereon in the Province of Exportation, and on Payment of such further Amount (if any) of Customs Duty as is leviable thereon in the Province of Importation.

124. Nothing in this Act shall affect the Right of New Brunswick to levy the Lumber Dues provided in Chapter Fifteen of Title Three of the Revised Statutes of New Brunswick, or in any Act amending that Act before or after the Union, and not increasing the Amount of such Dues; but the Lumber of any of the Provinces other than New Brunswick shall not be subject to such Dues.

125. No Lands or Property belonging to Canada or any Province shall be liable to Taxation.

126. Such Portions of the Duties and Revenues over which the respective Legislatures of Canada, Nova Scotia, and New Brunswick had before the Union Power of Appropriation as are by this Act reserved to the respective Governments or Legislatures of the Provinces, and all Duties and Revenues raised by them in accordance with the special Powers conferred upon them by this Act, shall in each Province form One Consolidated Revenue Fund to be appropriated for the Public Service of the Province.

IX. MISCELLANEOUS PROVISIONS

General

127. Repealed.

128. Every Member of the Senate or House of Commons of Canada shall before taking his Seat therein take and subscribe before the Governor General or some Person authorized by him, and every Member of a Legislative Council or Legislative Assembly of any

Province shall before taking his Seat therein take and subscribe before the Lieutenant Governor of the Province or some Person authorized by him, the Oath of Allegiance contained in the Fifth Schedule to this Act; and every Member of the Senate of Canada and every Member of the Legislative Council of Quebec shall also, before taking his Seat therein, take and subscribe before the Governor General, or some Person authorized by him, the Declaration of Qualification contained in the same Schedule.

129. Except as otherwise provided by this Act, all Laws in force in Canada, Nova Scotia, or New Brunswick at the Union, and all Courts of Civil and Criminal Jurisdiction, and all legal Commissions, Powers, and Authorities, and all Officers, Judicial, Administrative, and Ministerial, existing therein at the Union, shall continue in Ontario, Quebec, Nova Scotia, and New Brunswick respectively, as if the Union had not been made; subject nevertheless (except with respect to such as are enacted by or exist under Acts of the Parliament of Great Britain or of the Parliament of the United Kingdom of Great Britain and Ireland), to be repealed, abolished, or altered by the Parliament of Canada, or by the Legislature of the respective Province, according to the Authority of the Parliament or of that Legislature under this Act.

130. Until the Parliament of Canada otherwise provides, all Officers of the several Provinces having Duties to discharge in relation to Matters other than those coming within the Classes of Subjects by this Act assigned exclusively to the Legislatures of the Provinces shall be Officers of Canada, and shall continue to discharge the Duties of their respective Offices under the same Liabilities, Responsibilities, and Penalties as if the Union had not been made.

131. Until the Parliament of Canada otherwise provides, the Governor General in Council may from Time to Time appoint such Officers as the Governor General in Council deems necessary or proper for the effectual Execution of this Act.

132. The Parliament and Government of Canada shall have all Powers necessary or proper for performing the Obligations of Canada or of any Province thereof, as Part of the British Empire, towards Foreign Countries, arising under Treaties between the Empire and such Foreign Countries.

133. Either the English or the French Language may be used by any Person in the Debates of the Houses of the Parliament of Canada and of the Houses of the Legislature of Quebec; and both those Languages shall be used in the respective Records and Journals of those Houses; and either of those Languages may be used by any Person or in any Pleading or Process in or issuing from any Court of Canada established under this Act, and in or from all or any of the Courts of Quebec.

The Acts of the Parliament of Canada and of the Legislature of Quebec shall be printed and published in both those Languages.

Ontario and Quebec

134. Until the Legislature of Ontario or of Quebec otherwise provides, the Lieutenant Governors of Ontario and Quebec may each appoint under the Great Seal of the Province the following Officers, to hold Office during Pleasure, that is to say,—the Attorney General, the Secretary and Registrar of the Province, the Treasurer of the Province, the Commissioner of Crown Lands, and the Commissioner of Agriculture and Public Works, and in the Case of Quebec the Solicitor General, and may, by Order of the Lieutenant Governor in Council, from Time to Time prescribe the Duties of those Officers, and of the several Departments over which they shall preside or to which they shall belong, and of the Officers and Clerks thereof, and may also appoint other and additional Officers to hold Office during Pleasure, and may from Time to Time prescribe the Duties of those Officers, and of the several Departments over which they shall preside or to which they shall belong, and of the Officers and Clerks thereof.

135. Until the Legislature of Ontario or Quebec otherwise provides, all Rights, Powers, Duties, Functions, Responsibilities, or Authorities at the passing of this Act vested in or imposed on the Attorney General, Solicitor General, Secretary and Registrar of the Province of Canada, Minister of Finance, Commissioner of Crown Lands, Commissioner of Public Works, and Minister of Agriculture and Receiver General, by any Law, Statute, or Ordinance of Upper Canada, Lower Canada, or Canada, and not repugnant to this Act, shall be vested in or imposed on any Officer to be appointed by the Lieutenant Governor for the discharge of the same or any of them; and the Commissioner of Agriculture and Public Works shall perform the Duties and Functions of the Office of Minister of Agriculture at the passing of this Act imposed by the Law of the Province of Canada, as well as those of the Commissioner of Public Works.

136. Until altered by the Lieutenant Governor in Council, the Great Seals of Ontario and Quebec respectively shall be the same, or of the same Design, as those used in the Provinces of Upper Canada and Lower Canada respectively before their Union as the Province of Canada.

137. The words "and from thence to the End of the then next ensuing Session of the Legislature," or Words to the same Effect, used in any temporary Act of the Province of Canada not expired before the Union, shall be construed to extend and apply to the next Session of the Parliament of Canada if the Subject Matter of the Act is within the Powers of the same as defined by this Act, or to the next Sessions of the Legislatures of Ontario and Quebec respectively if the Subject Matter of the Act is within the Powers of the same as defined by this Act.

138. From and after the Union the Use of the Words "Upper Canada," instead of "Ontario," or "Lower Canada" instead of "Quebec," in any

Deed, Writ, Process, Pleading, Document, Matter, or Thing shall not invalidate the same.

139. Any Proclamation under the Great Seal of the Province of Canada issued before the Union to take effect at a Time which is subsequent to the Union, whether relating to that Province, or to Upper Canada, or to Lower Canada, and the several Matters and Things therein proclaimed, shall be and continue of like Force and Effect as if the Union had not been made.

140. Any Proclamation which is authorized by any Act of the Legislature of the Province of Canada to be issued under the Great Seal of the Province of Canada, whether relating to that Province, or to Upper Canada, or to Lower Canada, and which is not issued before the Union, may be issued by the Lieutenant Governor of Ontario or Quebec, as its Subject Matter requires, under the Great Seal thereof; and from and after the Issue of such Proclamation the same and the several Matters and Things therein proclaimed shall be and continue of the like Force and Effect in Ontario or Quebec as if the Union had not been made.

141. The Penitentiary of the Province of Canada shall, until the Parliament of Canada otherwise provides, be and continue the Penitentiary of Ontario and of Quebec.

142. The Division and Adjustment of the Debts, Credits, Liabilities, Properties, and Assets of Upper Canada and Lower Canada shall be referred to the Arbitrament of Three Arbitrators, One chosen by the Government of Ontario, One by the Government of Quebec, and One by the Government of Canada; and the Selection of the Arbitrators shall not be made until the Parliament of Canada and the Legislatures of Ontario and Quebec have met; and the Arbitrator chosen by the Government of Canada shall not be a Resident either in Ontario or in Quebec.

143. The Governor General in Council may from Time to Time order that such and so many of the Records, Books, and Documents of the Province of Canada as he thinks fit shall be appropriated and delivered either to Ontario or to Quebec, and the same shall thenceforth be the Property of that Province; and any Copy thereof or Extract therefrom, duly certified by the Officer having charge of the Original thereof, shall be admitted as Evidence.

144. The Lieutenant Governor of Quebec may from Time to Time, by Proclamation under the Great Seal of the Province, to take effect from a Day to be appointed therein, constitute Townships in those Parts of the Province of Quebec in which Townships are not then already constituted, and fix the Metes and Bounds thereof.

X. INTERCOLONIAL RAILWAY

145. Repealed.

XI. ADMISSION OF OTHER COLONIES

146. It shall be lawful for the Queen, by and with the Advice of Her Majesty's Most Honourable Privy Council, on Addresses from the Houses of the Parliament of Canada, and from the Houses of the respective Legislatures of the Colonies or Provinces of Newfoundland, Prince Edward Island, and British Columbia, to admit those Colonies or Provinces, or any of them, into the Union, and on Address from the Houses of the Parliament of Canada to admit Rupert's Land and the North-western Territory, or either of them, into the Union, on such Terms and Conditions in each Case as are in the Addresses expressed and as the Queen thinks fit to approve, subject to the Provisions of this Act; and the Provisions of any Order in Council in that Behalf shall have effect as if they had been enacted by the Parliament of the United Kingdom of Great Britain and Ireland.

147. In case of the Admission of Newfoundland and Prince Edward Island, or either of them, each shall be entitled to a Representation in the Senate of Canada of Four Members, and (notwithstanding anything in this Act) in case of the Admission of Newfoundland the normal Number of Senators shall be Seventy-six and their maximum Number shall be Eighty-two; but Prince Edward Island when admitted shall be deemed to be comprised in the Third of Three Divisions into which Canada is, in relation to the Constitution of the Senate, divided by this Act, and accordingly, after the Admission of Prince Edward Island, whether Newfoundland is admitted or not, the Representation of Nova Scotia and New Brunswick in the Senate shall, as Vacancies occur, be reduced from Twelve to Ten Members respectively, and the Representation of each of those Provinces shall not be increased at any Time beyond Ten, except under the Provisions of this Act for the Appointment of Three or Six additional Senators under the Direction of the Queen.

The Constitution Act, 1982(79)

SCHEDULE B

CONSTITUTION ACT, 1982

Part I

CANADIAN CHARTER OF RIGHTS AND FREEDOMS

Whereas Canada is founded upon principles that recognize the supremacy of God and the rule of law:

Guarantee of Rights and Freedoms

1. *The Canadian Charter of Rights and Freedoms* guarantees the rights and freedoms set out in it subject only to such reasonable limits prescribed by law as can be demonstrably justified in a free and democratic society.

Fundamental Freedoms

2. Everyone has the following fundamental freedoms:
(a) freedom of conscience and religion;
(b) freedom of thought, belief, opinion and expression, including freedom of the press and other media of communication;
(c) freedom of peaceful assembly; and
(d) freedom of association.

Democratic Rights

3. Every citizen of Canada has the right to vote in an election of members of the House of Commons or of a legislative assembly and to be qualified for membership therein.

Source: Justice Canada

4.   (1) No House of Commons and no legislative assembly shall continue for longer than five years from the date fixed for the return of the writs of a general election of its members.

(2)   In time of real or apprehended war, invasion or insurrection, a House of Commons may be continued by Parliament and a legislative assembly may be continued by the legislature beyond five years if such continuation is not opposed by the votes of more than one-third of the members of the House of Commons or the legislative assembly, as the case may be.

5.   There shall be a sitting of Parliament and of each legislature at least once every twelve months.

Mobility Rights

6.   (1) Every citizen of Canada has the right to enter, remain in and leave Canada.

(2)   Every citizen of Canada and every person who has the status of a permanent resident of Canada has the right

> (a)   to move to and take up residence in any province; and
>
> (b)   to pursue the gaining of a livelihood in any province.

(3)   The rights specified in subsection (2) are subject to

> (a)   any laws or practices of general application in force in a province other than those that discriminate among persons primarily on the basis of province of present or previous residence; and
>
> (b)   any laws providing for reasonable residency requirements as a qualification for the receipt of publicly provided social services.

(4)   Subsections (2) and (3) do not preclude any law, program or activity that has as its object the amelioration in a province of conditions of individuals in that province who are socially or economically disadvantaged if the rate of employment in that province is below the rate of employment in Canada.

Legal Rights

7.   Everyone has the right to life, liberty and security of the person and the right not to be deprived thereof except in accordance with the principles of fundamental justice.

8.   Everyone has the right to be secure against unreasonable search or seizure.

9.   Everyone has the right not to be arbitrarily detained or imprisoned.

10.   Everyone has the right on arrest or detention

> (a)   to be informed promptly of the reasons therefor;
>
> (b)   to retain and instruct counsel without delay and to be informed of that right; and

(c) to have the validity of the detention determined by way of *habeas corpus* and to be released if the detention is not lawful.

11. Any person charged with an offence has the right

(a) to be informed without unreasonable delay of the specific offence;

(b) to be tried within a reasonable time;

(c) not to be compelled to be a witness in proceedings against that person in respect of the offence;

(d) to be presumed innocent until proven guilty according to law in a fair and public hearing by an independent and impartial tribunal;

(e) not to be denied reasonable bail without just cause;

(f) except in the case of an offence under military law tried before a military tribunal, to the benefit of trial by jury where the maximum punishment for the offence is imprisonment for five years or a more severe punishment;

(g) not to be found guilty on account of any act or omission unless, at the time of the act or omission, it constituted an offence under Canadian or international law or was criminal according to the general principles of law recognized by the community of nations;

(h) if finally acquitted of the offence, not to be tried for it again and, if finally found guilty and punished for the offence, not to be tried or punished for it again; and

(i) if found guilty of the offence and if the punishment for the offence has been varied between the time of commission and the time of sentencing, to the benefit of the lesser punishment.

12. Everyone has the right not to be subjected to any cruel and unusual treatment or punishment.

13. A witness who testifies in any proceedings has the right not to have any incriminating evidence so given used to incriminate that witness in any other proceedings, except in a prosecution for perjury or for the giving of contradictory evidence.

14. A party or witness in any proceedings who does not understand or speak the language in which the proceedings are conducted or who is deaf has the right to the assistance of an interpreter.

Equality Rights

15. (1) Every individual is equal before and under the law and has the right to the equal protection and equal benefit of the law without discrimination and, in particular, without discrimination based on race, national or ethnic origin, colour, religion, sex, age or mental or physical disability.

(2) Subsection (1) does not preclude any law, program or activity that has as its object the amelioration of conditions of disadvantaged

individuals or groups including those that are disadvantaged because of race, national or ethnic origin, colour, religion, sex, age or mental or physical disability.

Official Languages of Canada

16. (1) English and French are the official languages of Canada and have equality of status and equal rights and privileges as to their use in all institutions of the Parliament and government of Canada.

(2)   English and French are the official languages of New Brunswick and have equality of status and equal rights and privileges as to their use in all institutions of the legislature and government of New Brunswick.

(3)   Nothing in this Charter limits the authority of Parliament or a legislature to advance the equality of status or use of English and French.

17. (1) Everyone has the right to use English or French in any debates and other proceedings of Parliament.

(2)   Everyone has the right to use English or French in any debates and other proceedings of the legislature of New Brunswick.

18. (1) The statutes, records and journals of Parliament shall be printed and published in English and French and both language versions are equally authoritative.

(2)   The statutes, records and journals of the legislature of New Brunswick shall be printed and published in English and French and both language versions are equally authoritative.

19. (1) Either English or French may be used by any person in, or in any pleading in or process issuing from, any court established by Parliament.

(2)   Either English or French may be used by any person in, or in any pleading in or process issuing from, any court of New Brunswick.

20. (1) Any member of the public in Canada has the right to communicate with, and to receive available services from, any head or central office of an institution of the Parliament or government of Canada in English or French, and has the same right with respect to any other office of any such institution where

    (*a*)   there is a significant demand for communications with and services from that office in such language; or

    (*b*)   due to the nature of the office, it is reasonable that communications with and services from that office be available in both English and French.

(2)   Any member of the public in New Brunswick has the right to communicate with, and to receive available services from, any office of an institution of the legislature or government of New Brunswick in English or French.

21. Nothing in sections 16 to 20 abrogates or derogates from any right, privilege or obligation with respect to the English and French languages, or either of them, that exists or is continued by virtue of any other provision of the Constitution of Canada.

22. Nothing in sections 16 to 20 abrogates or derogates from any legal or customary right or privilege acquired or enjoyed either before or after the coming into force of this Charter with respect to any language that is not English or French.

Minority Language Educational Rights

23.   (1) Citizens of Canada

(*a*)   whose first language learned and still understood is that of the English or French linguistic minority population of the province in which they reside, or

(*b*)   who have received their primary school instruction in Canada in English or French and reside in a province where the language in which they received that instruction is the language of the English or French linguistic minority population of the province,

have the right to have their children receive primary and secondary school instruction in that language in that province.

(2)   Citizens of Canada of whom any child has received or is receiving primary or secondary school instruction in English or French in Canada, have the right to have all their children receive primary and secondary school instruction in the same language.

(3)   The right of citizens of Canada under subsections (1) and (2) to have their children receive primary and secondary school instruction in the language of the English or French linguistic minority population of a province

(*a*)   applies wherever in the province the number of children of citizens who have such a right is sufficient to warrant the provision to them out of public funds of minority language instruction; and

(*b*)   includes, where the number of those children so warrants, the right to have them receive that instruction in minority language educational facilities provided out of public funds.

Enforcement

24.   (1) Anyone whose rights or freedoms, as guaranteed by this Charter, have been infringed or denied may apply to a court of competent jurisdiction to obtain such remedy as the court considers appropriate and just in the circumstances.

(2)   Where, in proceedings under subsection (1), a court concludes that evidence was obtained in a manner that infringed or denied any rights or freedoms guaranteed by this Charter, the evidence shall be excluded if it is established that, having regard to all the circumstances, the admission of it in the proceedings would bring the administration of justice into disrepute.

General

25. The guarantee in this Charter of certain rights and freedoms shall not be construed so as to abrogate or derogate from any aboriginal, treaty or other rights or freedoms that pertain to the aboriginal peoples of Canada including

(a) any rights or freedoms that have been recognized by the Royal Proclamation of October 7, 1763; and

(b) any rights or freedoms that may be acquired by the aboriginal peoples of Canada by way of land claims settlement.

26. The guarantee in this Charter of certain rights and freedoms shall not be construed as denying the existence of any other rights or freedoms that exist in Canada.

27. This Charter shall be interpreted in a manner consistent with the preservation and enhancement of the multicultural heritage of Canadians.

28. Notwithstanding anything in this Charter, the rights and freedoms referred to in it are guaranteed equally to male and female persons.

29. Nothing in this Charter abrogates or derogates from any rights or privileges guaranteed by or under the Constitution of Canada in respect of denominational, separate or dissentient schools.

30. A reference in this Charter to a Province or to the legislative assembly or legislature of a province shall be deemed to include a reference to the Yukon Territory and the Northwest Territories, or to the appropriate legislative authority thereof, as the case may be.

31. Nothing in this Charter extends the legislative powers of any body or authority.

Application of Charter

32. (1) This Charter applies

(a) to the Parliament and government of Canada in respect of all matters within the authority of Parliament including all matters relating to the Yukon Territory and Northwest Territories; and

(b) to the legislature and government of each province in respect of all matters within the authority of the legislature of each province.

(2) Notwithstanding subsection (1), section 15 shall not have effect until three years after this section comes into force.

33. (1) Parliament or the legislature of a province may expressly declare in an Act of Parliament or of the legislature, as the case may be, that the Act or a provision thereof shall operate notwithstanding a provision included in section 2 or sections 7 to 15 of this Charter.

(2)   An Act or a provision of an Act in respect of which a declaration made under this section is in effect shall have such operation as it would have but for the provision of this Charter referred to in the declaration.

(3)   A declaration made under subsection (1) shall cease to have effect five years after it comes into force or on such earlier date as may be specified in the declaration.

(4)   Parliament or the legislature of a province may re-enact a declaration made under subsection (1).

(5)   Subsection (3) applies in respect of a re-enactment made under subsection (4).

Citation

34. This Part may be cited as the *Canadian Charter of Rights and Freedoms*.

PART II

RIGHTS OF THE ABORIGINAL PEOPLES OF CANADA

35. (1) The existing aboriginal and treaty rights of the aboriginal peoples of Canada are hereby recognized and affirmed.

(2)   In this Act, "aboriginal peoples of Canada" includes the Indian, Inuit, and Métis peoples of Canada.

(3)   For greater certainty, in subsection (1) "treaty rights" includes rights that now exist by way of land claims agreements or may be so acquired.

(4)   Notwithstanding any other provision of this Act, the aboriginal and treaty rights referred to in subsection (1) are guaranteed equally to male and female persons.(94)

35.1 The government of Canada and the provincial governments are committed to the principle that, before any amendment is made to Class 24 of section 91 of the *"Constitution Act, 1867"*, to section 25 of this Act or to this Part,

> (*a*) a constitutional conference that includes in its agenda an item relating to the proposed amendment, composed of the Prime Minister of Canada and the first ministers of the provinces, will be convened by the Prime Minister of Canada; and
>
> (*b*) the Prime Minister of Canada will invite representatives of the aboriginal peoples of Canada to participate in the discussions on that item.

Part III

Equalization and Regional Disparities

36. (1) Without altering the legislative authority of Parliament or of the provincial legislatures, or the rights of any of them with respect to the exercise of their legislative authority, Parliament and the legislatures, together with the government of Canada and the provincial governments, are committed to

(*a*) promoting equal opportunities for the well-being of Canadians;

(*b*) furthering economic development to reduce disparity in opportunities; and

(*c*) providing essential public services of reasonable quality to all Canadians.

(2)   Parliament and the government of Canada are committed to the principle of making equalization payments to ensure that provincial governments have sufficient revenues to provide reasonably comparable levels of public services at reasonably comparable levels of taxation.

Part IV

Constitutional Conferences

37.

Part IV.I

Constitutional Conference

37.1

Part V

Procedure for Amending Constitution of Canada

38. (1) An amendment to the Constitution of Canada may be made by proclamation issued by the Governor General under the Great Seal of Canada where so authorized by

(*a*) resolutions of the Senate and House of Commons; and

(*b*) resolutions of the legislative assemblies of at least two-thirds of the provinces that have, in the aggregate, according to the then latest general census, at least fifty per cent of the population of all the provinces.

(2)   An amendment made under subsection (1) that derogates from the legislative powers, the proprietary rights or any other rights or privileges of the legislature or government of a province shall require a resolution supported by a majority of the members of each of the Senate, the House of Commons and the legislative assemblies required under subsection (1).

(3)   An amendment referred to in subsection (2) shall not have effect in a province the legislative assembly of which has expressed its dissent thereto by resolution supported by a majority of its members prior to the issue of the proclamation to which the amendment relates unless that legislative assembly, subsequently, by resolution supported by a majority of its members, revokes its dissent and authorizes the amendment.

(4)   A resolution of dissent made for the purposes of subsection (3) may be revoked at any time before or after the issue of the proclamation to which it relates.

39.   (1) A proclamation shall not be issued under subsection 38(1) before the expiration of one year from the adoption of the resolution initiating the amendment procedure thereunder, unless the legislative assembly of each province has previously adopted a resolution of assent or dissent.

(2)   A proclamation shall not be issued under subsection 38(1) after the expiration of three years from the adoption of the resolution initiating the amendment procedure thereunder.

40.   Where an amendment is made under subsection 38(1) that transfers provincial legislative powers relating to education or other cultural matters from provincial legislatures to Parliament, Canada shall provide reasonable compensation to any province to which the amendment does not apply.

41.   An amendment to the Constitution of Canada in relation to the following matters may be made by proclamation issued by the Governor General under the Great Seal of Canada only where authorized by resolutions of the Senate and House of Commons and of the legislative assembly of each province:

> (a)   the office of the Queen, the Governor General and the Lieutenant Governor of a province;
>
> (b)   the right of a province to a number of members in the House of Commons not less than the number of Senators by which the province is entitled to be represented at the time this Part comes into force;
>
> (c)   subject to section 43, the use of the English or the French language;
>
> (d)   the composition of the Supreme Court of Canada; and
>
> (e)   an amendment to this Part.

42.   (1) An amendment to the Constitution of Canada in relation to the following matters may be made only in accordance with subsection 38(1):

(a) the principle of proportionate representation of the provinces in the House of Commons prescribed by the Constitution of Canada;

(b) the powers of the Senate and the method of selecting Senators;

(c) the number of members by which a province is entitled to be represented in the Senate and the residence qualifications of Senators;

(d) subject to paragraph 41(d), the Supreme Court of Canada;

(e) the extension of existing provinces into the territories; and

(f) notwithstanding any other law or practice, the establishment of new provinces.

(2)   Subsections 38(2) to (4) do not apply in respect of amendments in relation to matters referred to in subsection (1).

43.   An amendment to the Constitution of Canada in relation to any provision that applies to one or more, but not all, provinces, including

(a) any alteration to boundaries between provinces, and

(b) any amendment to any provision that relates to the use of the English or the French language within a province, may be made by proclamation issued by the Governor General under the Great Seal of Canada only where so authorized by resolutions of the Senate and House of Commons and of the legislative assembly of each province to which the amendment applies.

44.   Subject to sections 41 and 42, Parliament may exclusively make laws amending the Constitution of Canada in relation to the executive government of Canada or the Senate and House of Commons.

45.   Subject to section 41, the legislature of each province may exclusively make laws amending the constitution of the province.

46.   (1) The procedures for amendment under sections 38, 41, 42 and 43 may be initiated either by the Senate or the House of Commons or by the legislative assembly of a province.

(2)   A resolution of assent made for the purposes of this Part may be revoked at any time before the issue of a proclamation authorized by it.

47.   (1) An amendment to the Constitution of Canada made by proclamation under section 38, 41, 42 or 43 may be made without a resolution of the Senate authorizing the issue of the proclamation if, within one hundred and eighty days after the adoption by the House of Commons of a resolution authorizing its issue, the Senate has not adopted such a resolution and if, at any time after the expiration of that period, the House of Commons again adopts the resolution.

(2)   Any period when Parliament is prorogued or dissolved shall not be counted in computing the one hundred and eighty day period referred to in subsection (1).

48.   The Queen's Privy Council for Canada shall advise the Governor General to issue a proclamation under this Part forthwith on the adoption of the resolutions required for an amendment made by proclamation under this Part.

49. A constitutional conference composed of the Prime Minister of Canada and the first ministers of the provinces shall be convened by the Prime Minister of Canada within fifteen years after this Part comes into force to review the provisions of this Part.

PART VI

AMENDMENT TO THE CONSTITUTION ACT, 1867

50.

51.

PART VII

GENERAL

52. (1) The Constitution of Canada is the supreme law of Canada, and any law that is inconsistent with the provisions of the Constitution is, to the extent of the inconsistency, of no force or effect.

(2)   The Constitution of Canada includes

(a)   *the Canada Act 1982*, including this Act;

(b)   the Acts and orders referred to in the schedule; and

(c)   any amendment to any Act or order referred to in paragraph (a) or (b).

(3)   Amendments to the Constitution of Canada shall be made only in accordance with the authority contained in the Constitution of Canada.

53. (1) The enactments referred to in Column I of the schedule are hereby repealed or amended to the extent indicated in Column II thereof and, unless repealed, shall continue as law in Canada under the names set out in Column III thereof.

(2)   Every enactment, except the *Canada Act 1982*, that refers to an enactment referred to in the schedule by the name in Column I thereof is hereby amended by substituting for that name the corresponding name in Column III thereof, and any British North America Act not referred to in the schedule may be cited as the *Constitution Act* followed by the year and number, if any, of its enactment.

54. Part IV is repealed on the day that is one year after this Part comes into force and this section may be repealed and this Act renumbered, consequentially upon the repeal of Part IV and this section, by proclamation issued by the Governor General under the Great Seal of Canada.

54.1

55.   A French version of the portions of the Constitution of Canada referred to in the schedule shall be prepared by the Minister of Justice of Canada as expeditiously as possible and, when any portion thereof sufficient to warrant action being taken has been so prepared, it shall be put forward for enactment by proclamation issued by the Governor General under the Great Seal of Canada pursuant to the procedure then applicable to an amendment of the same provisions of the Constitution of Canada.

56.   Where any portion of the Constitution of Canada has been or is enacted in English and French or where a French version of any portion of the Constitution is enacted pursuant to section 55, the English and French versions of that portion of the Constitution are equally authoritative.

57.   The English and French versions of this Act are equally authoritative.

58.   Subject to section 59, this Act shall come into force on a day to be fixed by proclamation issued by the Queen or the Governor General under the Great Seal of Canada.

59.   (1) Paragraph 23(1)(a) shall come into force in respect of Quebec on a day to be fixed by proclamation issued by the Queen or the Governor General under the Great Seal of Canada.

(2)   A proclamation under subsection (1) shall be issued only where authorized by the legislative assembly or government of Quebec.

(3)   This section may be repealed on the day paragraph 23(1)(a) comes into force in respect of Quebec and this Act amended and renumbered, consequentially upon the repeal of this section, by proclamation issued by the Queen or the Governor General under the Great Seal of Canada.

60.   This Act may be cited as the *Constitution Act, 1982*, and the Constitution Acts, 1867 to 1975 (No. 2) and this Act may be cited together as the *Constitution Acts, 1867 to 1982*.

61.   A reference to the "*Constitution Acts, 1867 to 1982*" shall be deemed to include a reference to the "*Constitution Amendment Proclamation, 1983*".

NAME INDEX

SUBJECT INDEX

Aboriginal peoples, *see* Native peoples
Acadians, 22
Act of Succession of 1702, 37
Act of Union of 1840, 36
Advance polls, 128
Age, and party support, 146, 150
AirBus affair, 185
Alberta, 24, 25, 51, 63, 65, 107, 127
    parties, 62
    populism, 97
    resources, 64, 274
    Senate reform proposal, 232
    taxes, 61
Anti-Inflation Board, 87
Anti-Semitism, 97
Atlantic Canada, 21–23, 231
Attorney general, 243
Auditor general, 202
Authority, attitudes toward, 29, 169,
    see also Elites

Bank of Canada, 190
Bill of Rights of 1689, 35, 37
Bill of Rights of 1960, 36, 49, 238
Bill 101, 15–16
Bills, passage of in Commons, 7–8
Blakeney-Notley Declaration, 93
Bloc Québécois, 107, 108, 111, 142
British Columbia, 63, 109, 127
    neoconservative policy in, 91
    regional history, 26
    voter behaviour, 143
British North America Act, *see*
    Constitution Act of 1867
Brokerage politics, 188, *see also*
    Interest groups
    liberalism and, 85–86
    parties, 108
Budget, 189, 222, *see also* Deficits
Bureaucracy, 47, 88, 193–209, *see*
    also Public service
    growth of provincial, 68
    and public ownership, 84
    red tape, 193–94

Business community
    campaign financing, 130ff
    interest groups representing, 156ff
Business Council on National Issues,
    156

Cabinet, 5, 124, 158, 177
    committees, 182
    increasing power of, 47, 48
    ministers, 9, 182–85
    regional representation, 255n
    role and composition, 6, 8, 181–91
    size, 182
Canada Act, 52–53
Canada Assistance Plan, 66
Canada Elections Act, 124, 128
Canada Health Act, 66
Canada Mortgage and Housing
    Corporation (CMHC), 61
Canada Pension Plan, 66
Canada–U.S. Free Trade Agreement,
    13, 24, 28, 108, 132, 187
Canadian Broadcasting Corporation
    (CBC), 164, 190, 201
Canadian content, 164
Canadian Federation of Independent
    Business, 156
Canadian Manufacturers' Association,
    156
Canadian Radio-Television and
    Telecommunications
    Commission   (CRTC),
    164, 201
Capitalism, 96
    relation to liberalism, 83–84
    socialist critique of, 92
Central administrative agencies, 188
Charlottetown Accord, 8, 39, 241
    and Native peoples, 17, 54
    rejection of, 54
    revenue sharing, 66
Charter of Rights and Freedoms, 10,
    45–47, 52, 123, 155, 236,
    303–309